Takane & Hana

5

STORY AND ART BY

Yuki Shiwasu

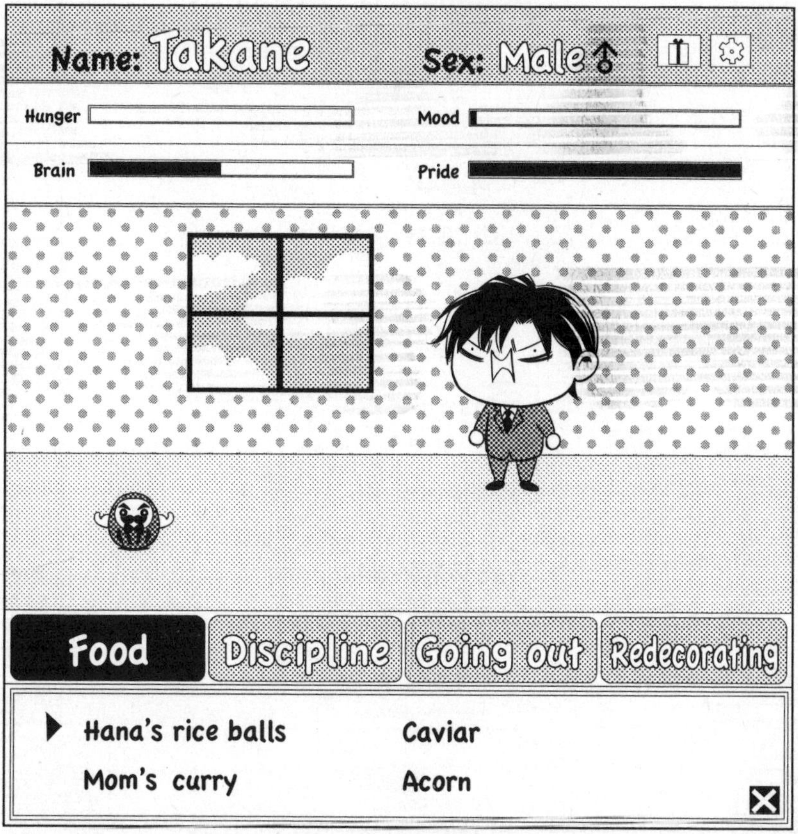
Name: Takane
Sex: Male
Hunger
Mood
Brain
Pride
Food
Discipline
Going out
Redecorating
Hana's rice balls
Caviar
Mom's curry
Acorn

Takane & Hana

5

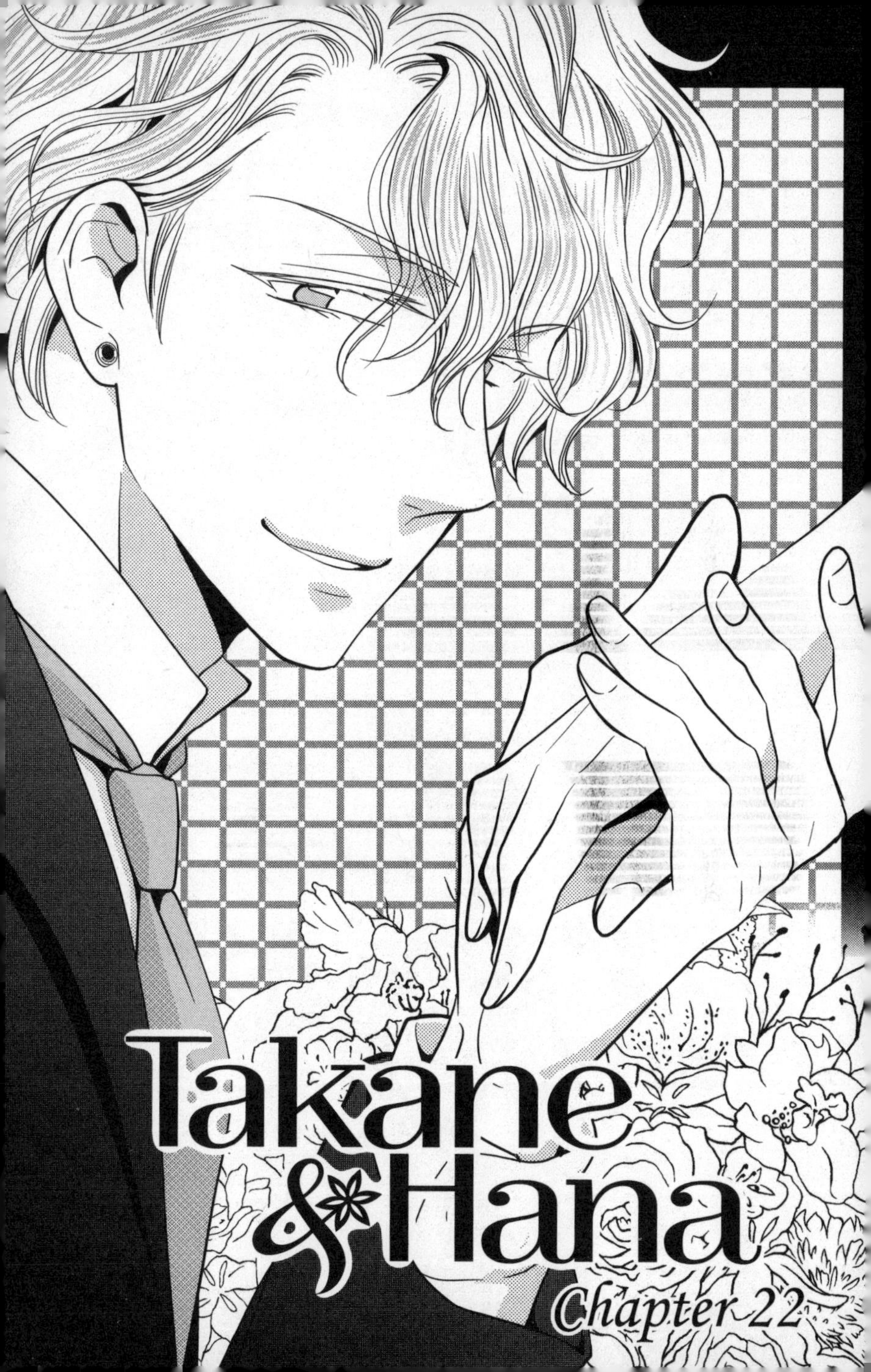
Takane & Hana
Chapter 22

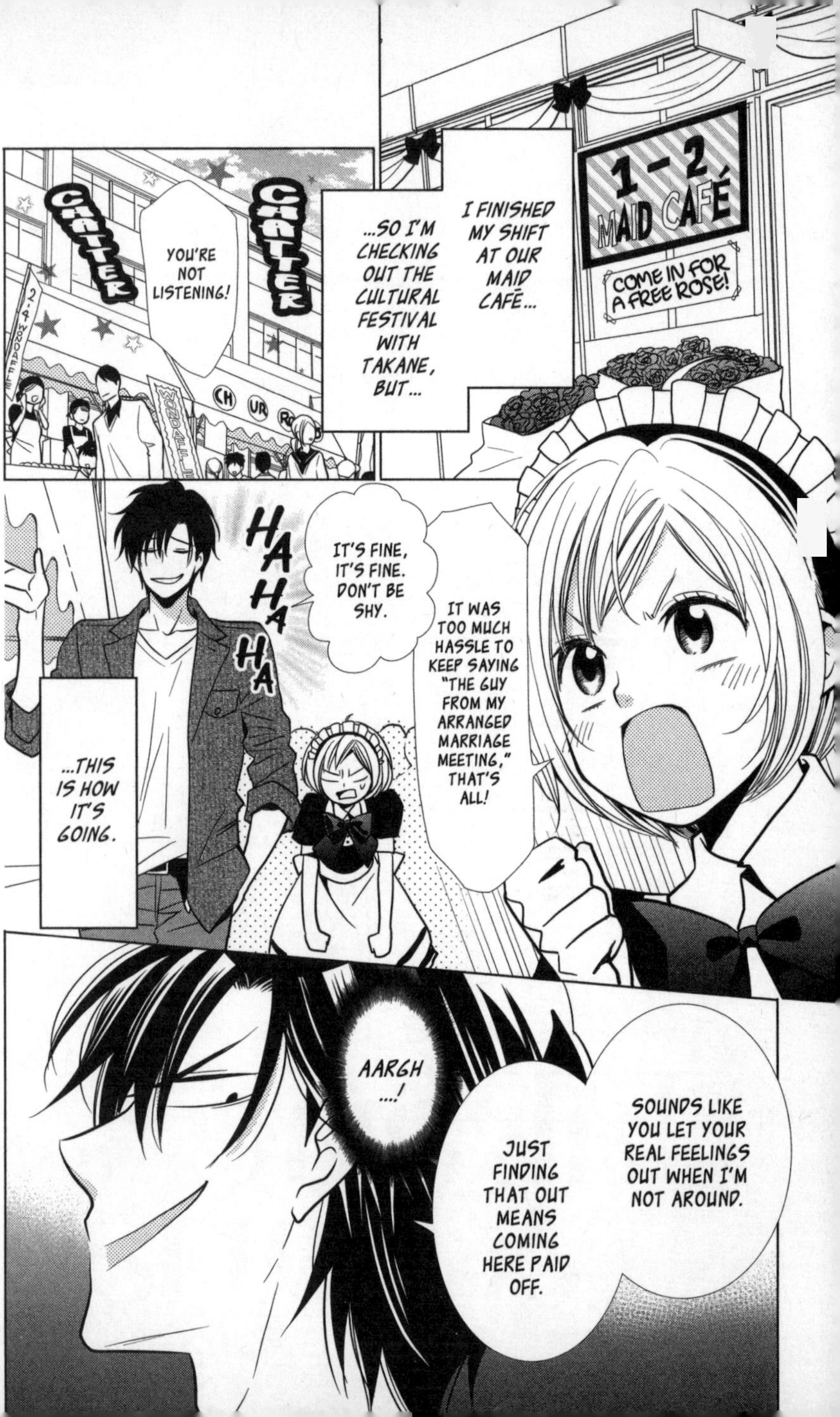
1-2 MAID CAFÉ
COME IN FOR A FREE ROSE!
I FINISHED MY SHIFT AT OUR MAID CAFÉ...
...SO I'M CHECKING OUT THE CULTURAL FESTIVAL WITH TAKANE, BUT...
CHATTER
CHATTER
YOU'RE NOT LISTENING!
2-4 WONDAFFLE
WONDAFFLE
IT WAS TOO MUCH HASSLE TO KEEP SAYING "THE GUY FROM MY ARRANGED MARRIAGE MEETING," THAT'S ALL!
IT'S FINE, IT'S FINE. DON'T BE SHY.
HA HA HA HA
...THIS IS HOW IT'S GOING.
SOUNDS LIKE YOU LET YOUR REAL FEELINGS OUT WHEN I'M NOT AROUND.
JUST FINDING THAT OUT MEANS COMING HERE PAID OFF.
AARGH ...!

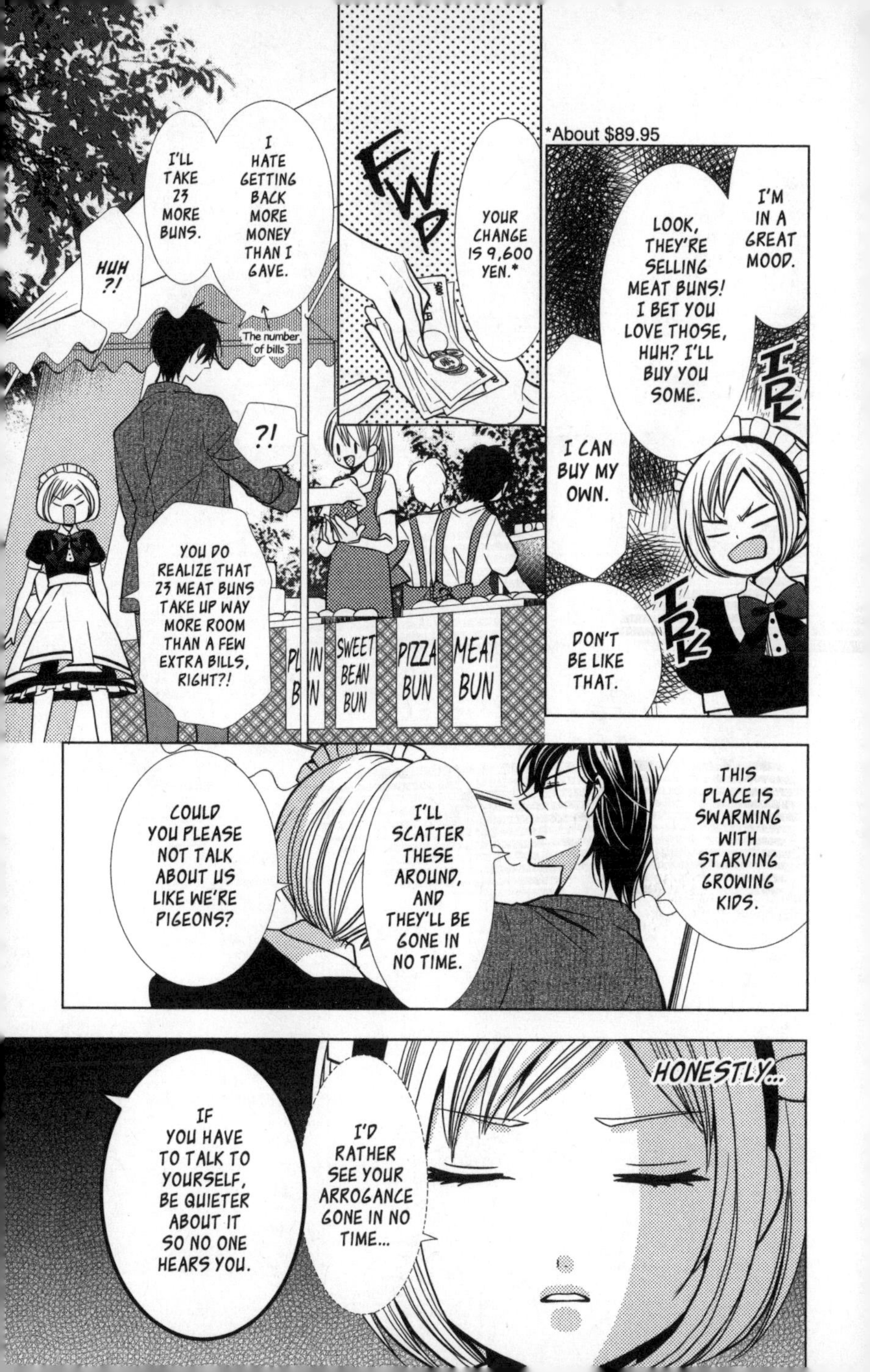
I'M IN A GREAT MOOD.
LOOK, THEY'RE SELLING MEAT BUNS! I BET YOU LOVE THOSE, HUH? I'LL BUY YOU SOME.
IRK
I CAN BUY MY OWN.
IRK
DON'T BE LIKE THAT.
*About $89.95
FWP
YOUR CHANGE IS 9,600 YEN.*
I HATE GETTING BACK MORE MONEY THAN I GAVE.
I'LL TAKE 23 MORE BUNS.
The number of bills
HUH?!
?!
MEAT BUN
PIZZA BUN
SWEET BEAN BUN
PLAIN BUN
YOU DO REALIZE THAT 23 MEAT BUNS TAKE UP WAY MORE ROOM THAN A FEW EXTRA BILLS, RIGHT?!
THIS PLACE IS SWARMING WITH STARVING GROWING KIDS.
I'LL SCATTER THESE AROUND, AND THEY'LL BE GONE IN NO TIME.
COULD YOU PLEASE NOT TALK ABOUT US LIKE WE'RE PIGEONS?
HONESTLY...
I'D RATHER SEE YOUR ARROGANCE GONE IN NO TIME...
IF YOU HAVE TO TALK TO YOURSELF, BE QUIETER ABOUT IT SO NO ONE HEARS YOU.

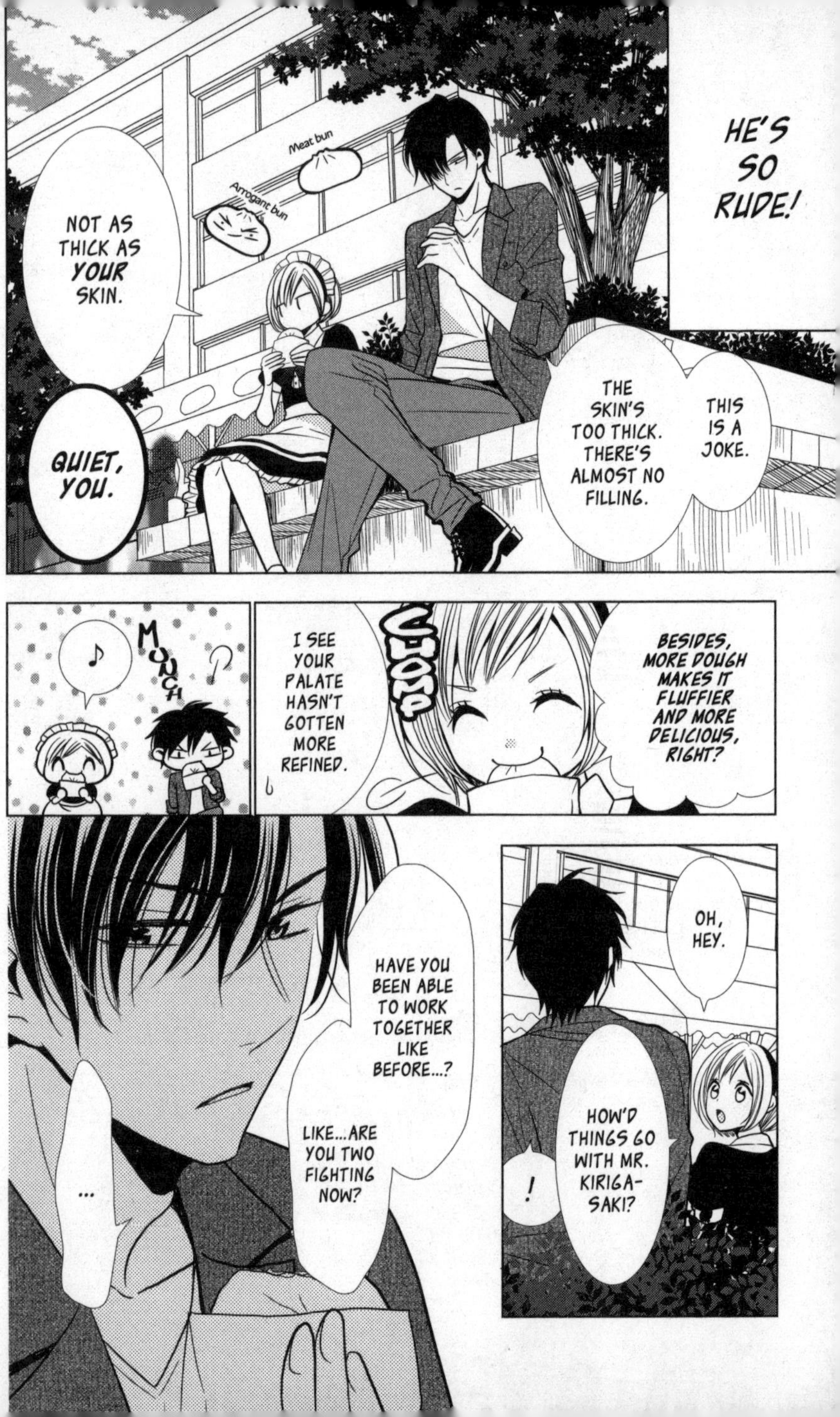
HE'S SO RUDE!
THIS IS A JOKE.
THE SKIN'S TOO THICK. THERE'S ALMOST NO FILLING.
Meat bun
Arrogant bun
NOT AS THICK AS YOUR SKIN.
QUIET, YOU.
BESIDES, MORE DOUGH MAKES IT FLUFFIER AND MORE DELICIOUS, RIGHT?
CHOMP
I SEE YOUR PALATE HASN'T GOTTEN MORE REFINED.
MUNCH
♪
OH, HEY.
HOW'D THINGS GO WITH MR. KIRIGA-SAKI?
!
HAVE YOU BEEN ABLE TO WORK TOGETHER LIKE BEFORE...?
LIKE...ARE YOU TWO FIGHTING NOW?
...

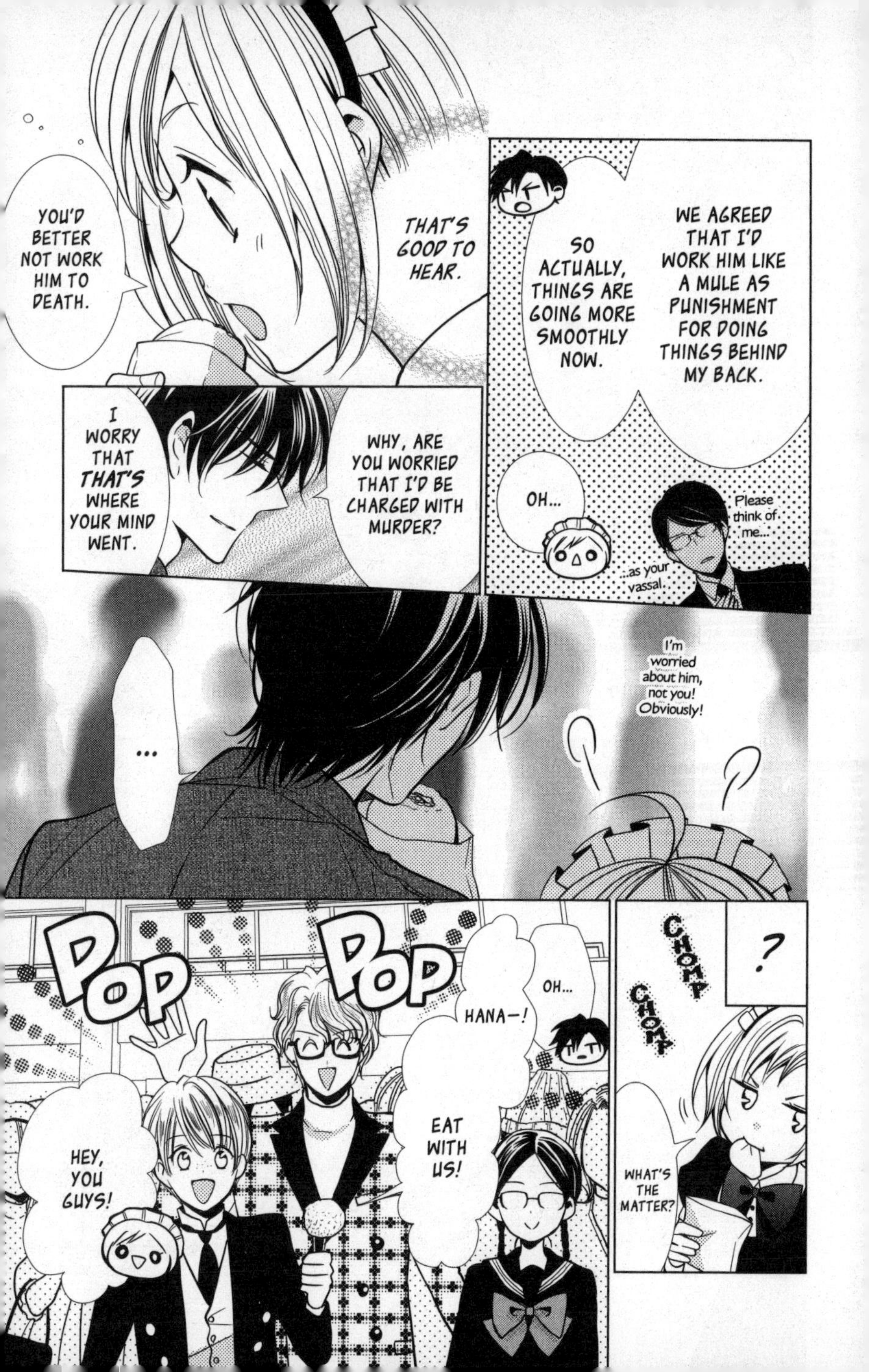

WE AGREED THAT I'D WORK HIM LIKE A MULE AS PUNISHMENT FOR DOING THINGS BEHIND MY BACK.
SO ACTUALLY, THINGS ARE GOING MORE SMOOTHLY NOW.
OH...
Please think of me...
...as your vassal.
THAT'S GOOD TO HEAR.
YOU'D BETTER NOT WORK HIM TO DEATH.
WHY, ARE YOU WORRIED THAT I'D BE CHARGED WITH MURDER?
I WORRY THAT *THAT'S* WHERE YOUR MIND WENT.
I'm worried about him, not you! Obviously!
...
?
CHOMP
CHOMP
WHAT'S THE MATTER?
OH...
HANA-!
EAT WITH US!
POP
POP
HEY, YOU GUYS!

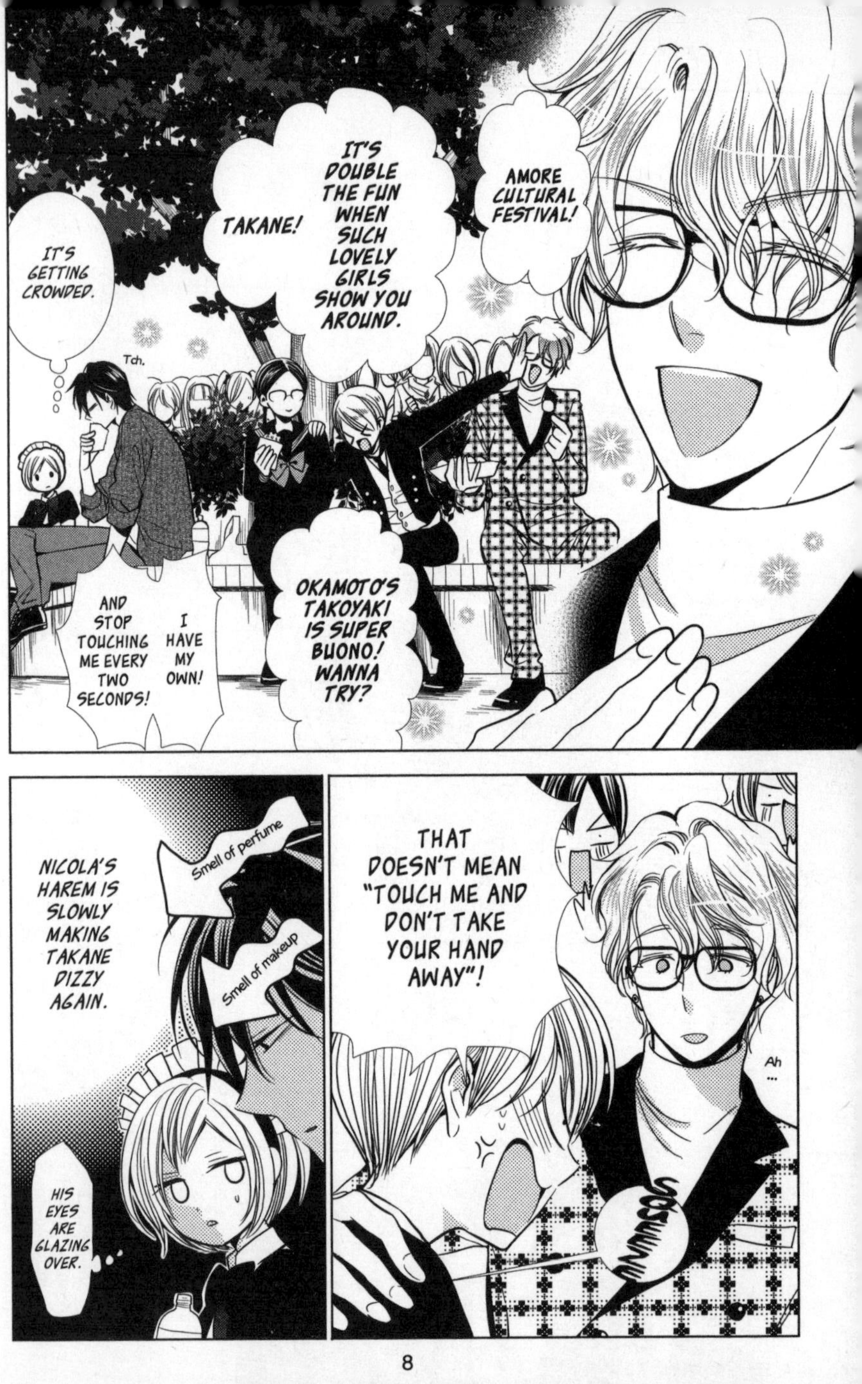
AMORE CULTURAL FESTIVAL!
IT'S DOUBLE THE FUN WHEN SUCH LOVELY GIRLS SHOW YOU AROUND.
TAKANE!
IT'S GETTING CROWDED.
Tch.
OKAMOTO'S TAKOYAKI IS SUPER BUONO! WANNA TRY?
I HAVE MY OWN!
AND STOP TOUCHING ME EVERY TWO SECONDS!
THAT DOESN'T MEAN "TOUCH ME AND DON'T TAKE YOUR HAND AWAY"!
Ah ...
Smell of perfume
Smell of makeup
NICOLA'S HAREM IS SLOWLY MAKING TAKANE DIZZY AGAIN.
HIS EYES ARE GLAZING OVER.

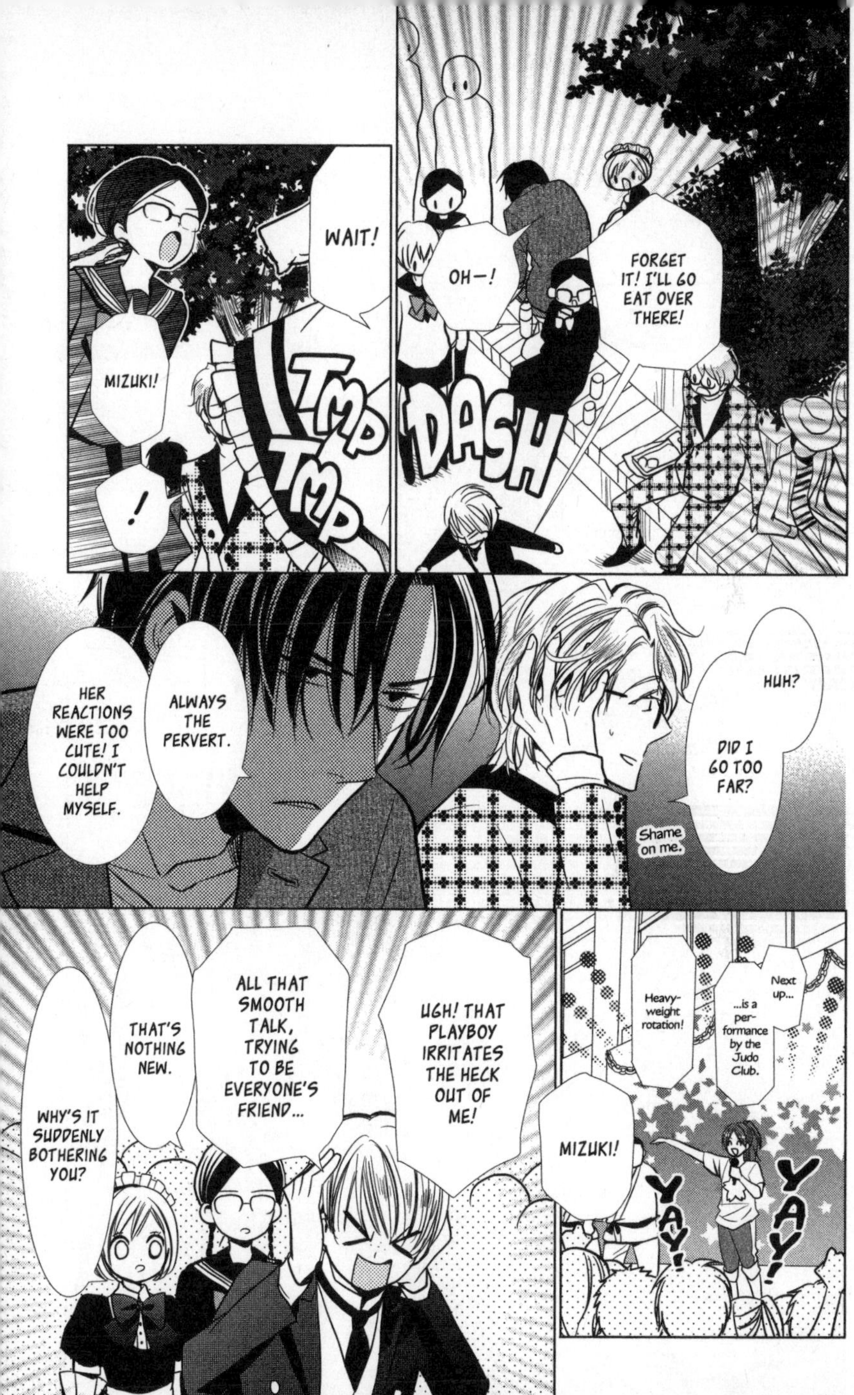
FORGET IT! I'LL GO EAT OVER THERE!
OH—!
DASH
WAIT!
TMP TMP
MIZUKI!
!
HUH?
DID I GO TOO FAR?
Shame on me.
ALWAYS THE PERVERT.
HER REACTIONS WERE TOO CUTE! I COULDN'T HELP MYSELF.
Next up...
...is a performance by the Judo Club.
Heavy-weight rotation!
MIZUKI!
YAY!
YAY!
UGH! THAT PLAYBOY IRRITATES THE HECK OUT OF ME!
ALL THAT SMOOTH TALK, TRYING TO BE EVERYONE'S FRIEND...
THAT'S NOTHING NEW.
WHY'S IT SUDDENLY BOTHERING YOU?

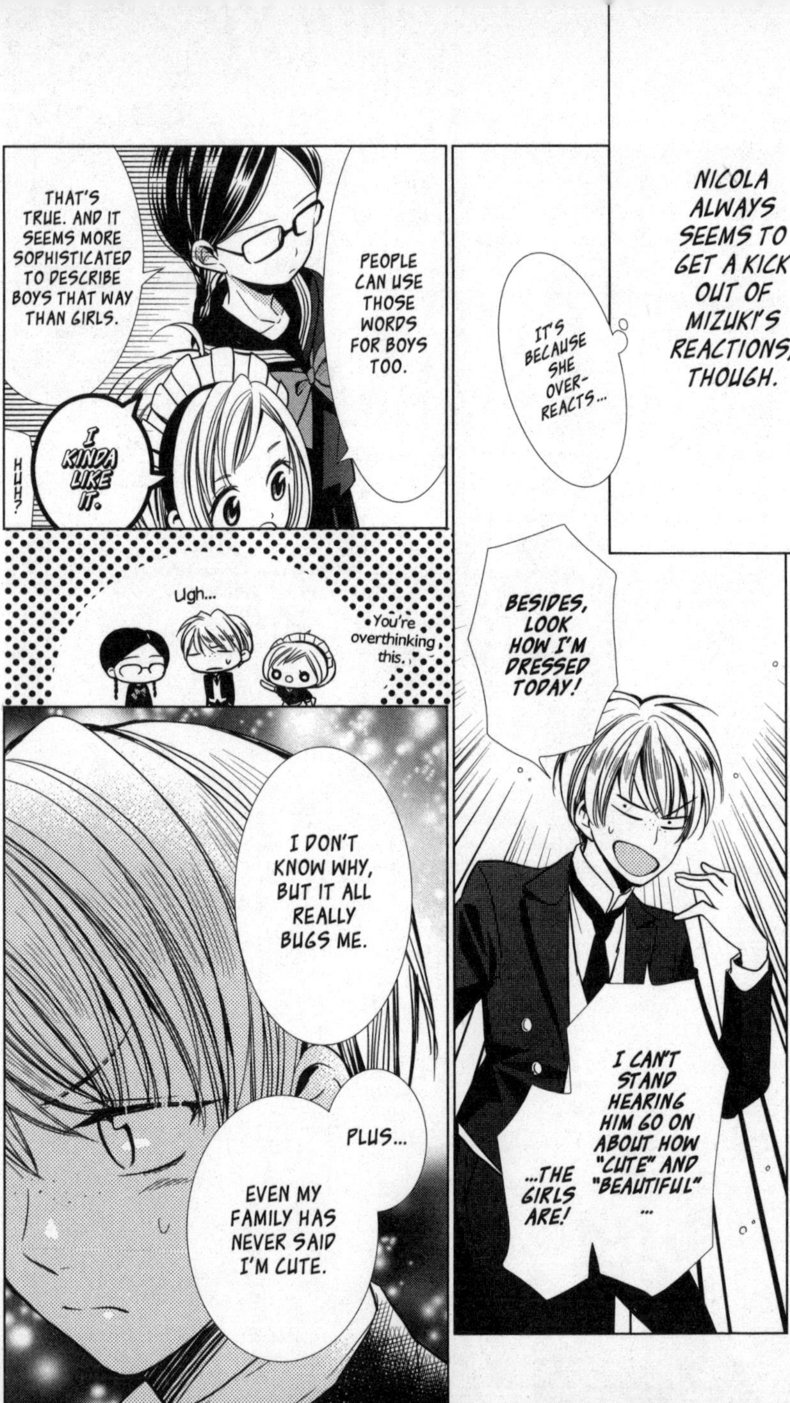
NICOLA ALWAYS SEEMS TO GET A KICK OUT OF MIZUKI'S REACTIONS, THOUGH.
IT'S BECAUSE SHE OVER-REACTS...
BESIDES, LOOK HOW I'M DRESSED TODAY!
I CAN'T STAND HEARING HIM GO ON ABOUT HOW "CUTE" AND "BEAUTIFUL" ...
...THE GIRLS ARE!
PEOPLE CAN USE THOSE WORDS FOR BOYS TOO.
THAT'S TRUE. AND IT SEEMS MORE SOPHISTICATED TO DESCRIBE BOYS THAT WAY THAN GIRLS.
I KINDA LIKE IT.
HUH?
Ugh...
You're overthinking this.
I DON'T KNOW WHY, BUT IT ALL REALLY BUGS ME.
PLUS...
EVEN MY FAMILY HAS NEVER SAID I'M CUTE.

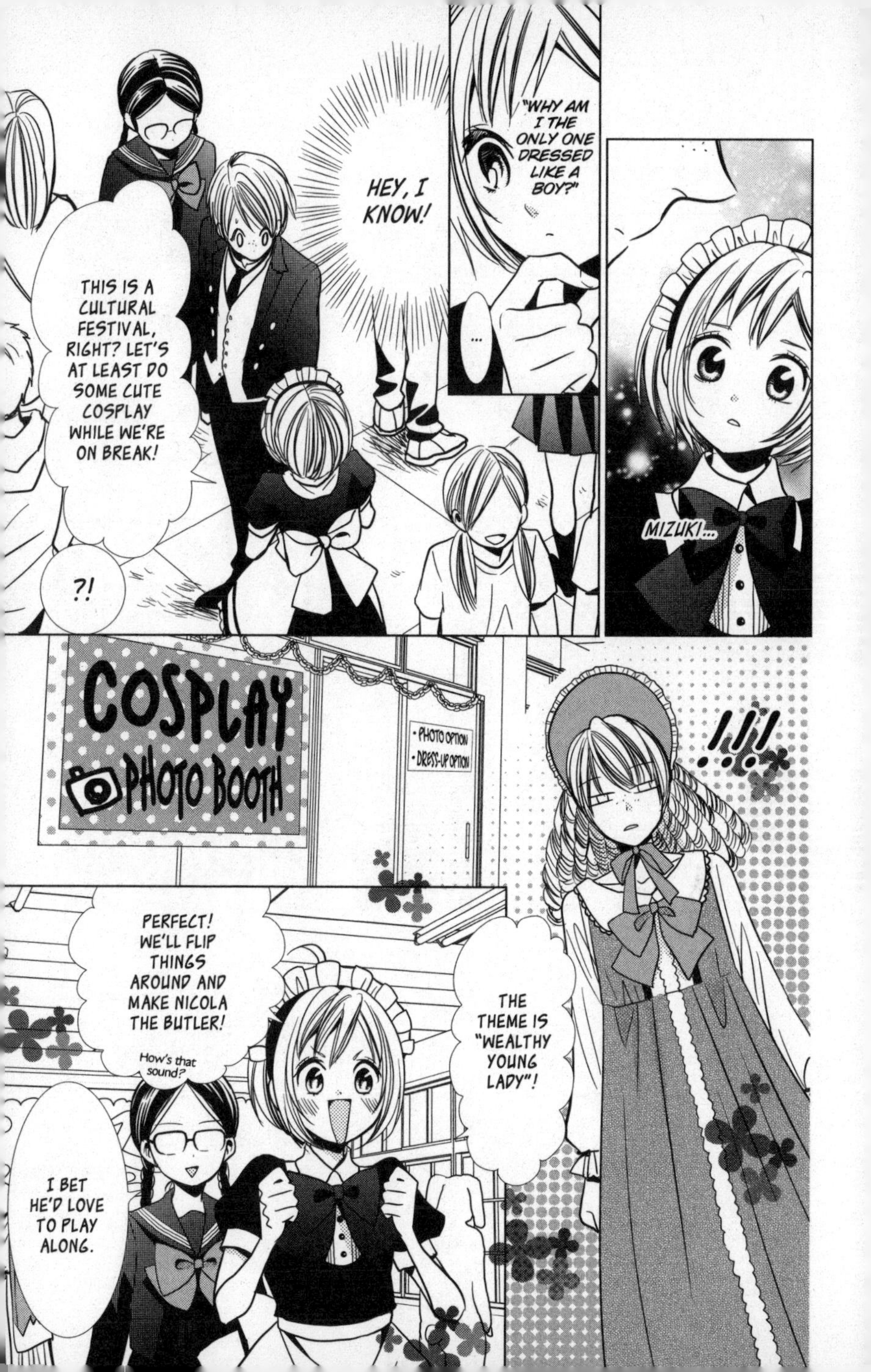
MIZUKI...
"WHY AM I THE ONLY ONE DRESSED LIKE A BOY?"
...
HEY, I KNOW!
THIS IS A CULTURAL FESTIVAL, RIGHT? LET'S AT LEAST DO SOME CUTE COSPLAY WHILE WE'RE ON BREAK!
?!
!!!!
COSPLAY PHOTO BOOTH
• PHOTO OPTION
• DRESS-UP OPTION
THE THEME IS "WEALTHY YOUNG LADY"!
PERFECT! WE'LL FLIP THINGS AROUND AND MAKE NICOLA THE BUTLER!
How's that sound?
I BET HE'D LOVE TO PLAY ALONG.

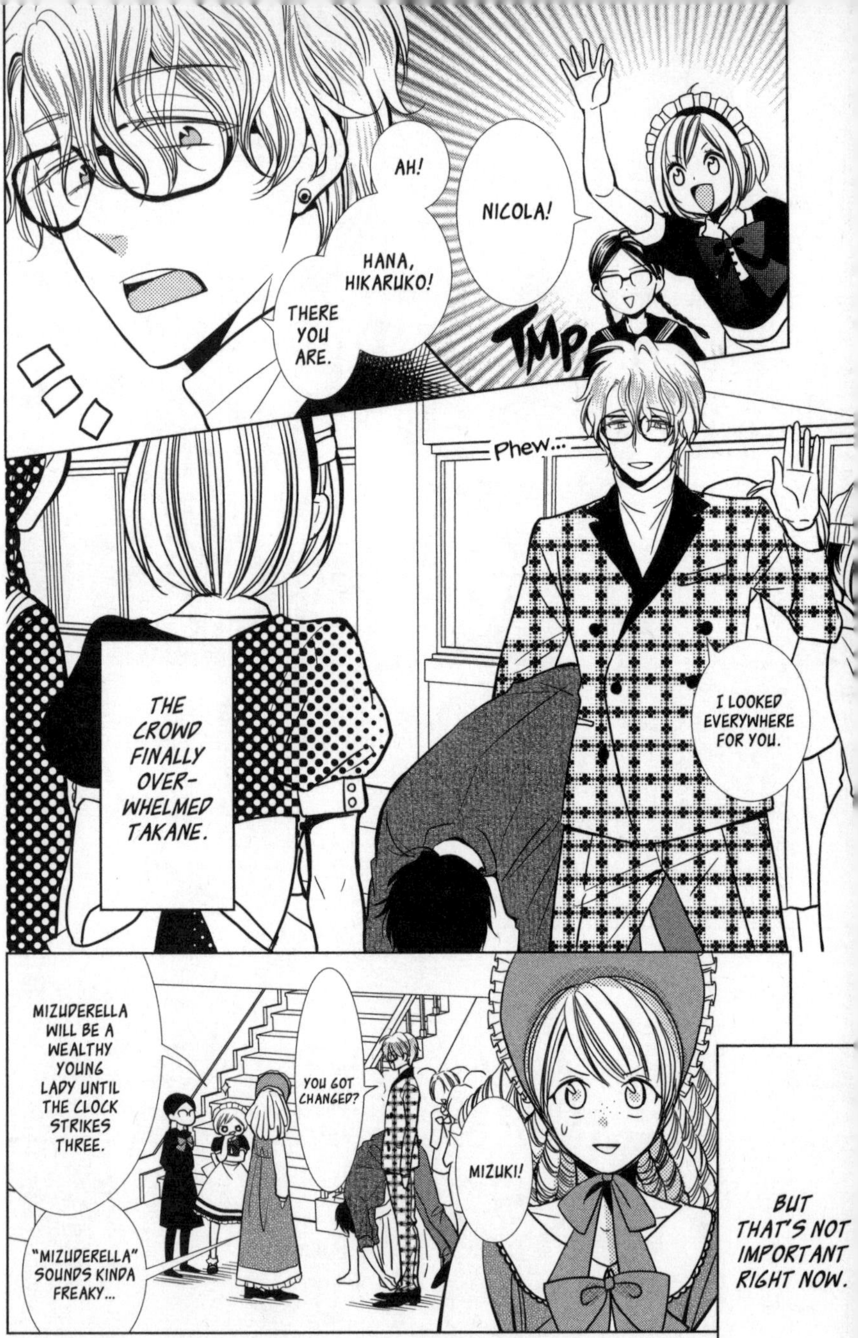
NICOLA!
AH!
HANA, HIKARUKO!
THERE YOU ARE.
TMP
Phew...
I LOOKED EVERYWHERE FOR YOU.
THE CROWD FINALLY OVER-WHELMED TAKANE.
BUT THAT'S NOT IMPORTANT RIGHT NOW.
MIZUKI!
YOU GOT CHANGED?
MIZUDERELLA WILL BE A WEALTHY YOUNG LADY UNTIL THE CLOCK STRIKES THREE.
"MIZUDERELLA" SOUNDS KINDA FREAKY...

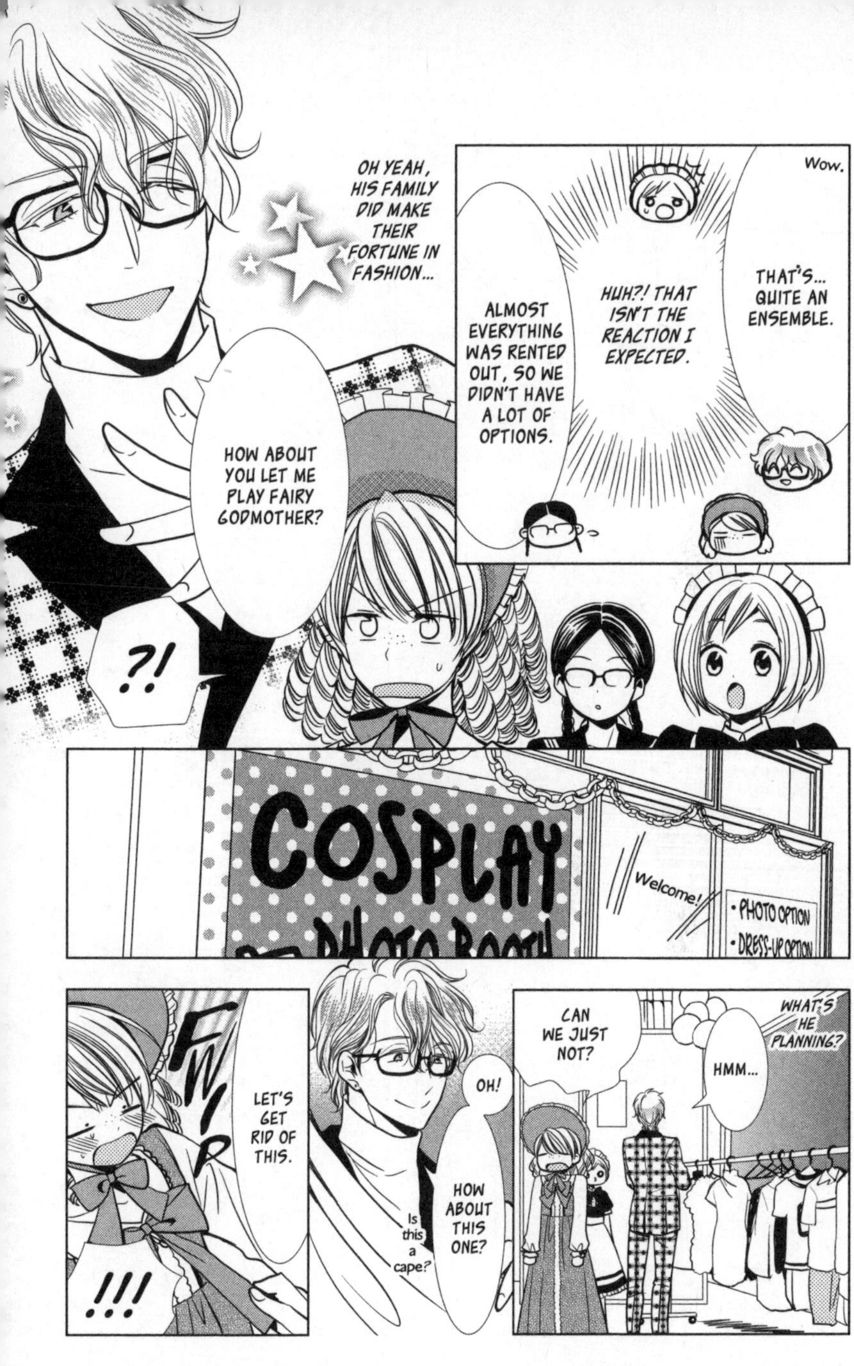
Wow.
THAT'S... QUITE AN ENSEMBLE.
HUH?! THAT ISN'T THE REACTION I EXPECTED.
ALMOST EVERYTHING WAS RENTED OUT, SO WE DIDN'T HAVE A LOT OF OPTIONS.
OH YEAH, HIS FAMILY DID MAKE THEIR FORTUNE IN FASHION...
HOW ABOUT YOU LET ME PLAY FAIRY GODMOTHER?
?!
COSPLAY
Welcome!
• PHOTO OPTION
• DRESS-UP OPTION
WHAT'S HE PLANNING?
HMM...
CAN WE JUST NOT?
OH!
HOW ABOUT THIS ONE?
Is this a cape?
LET'S GET RID OF THIS.
FWIP
!!!

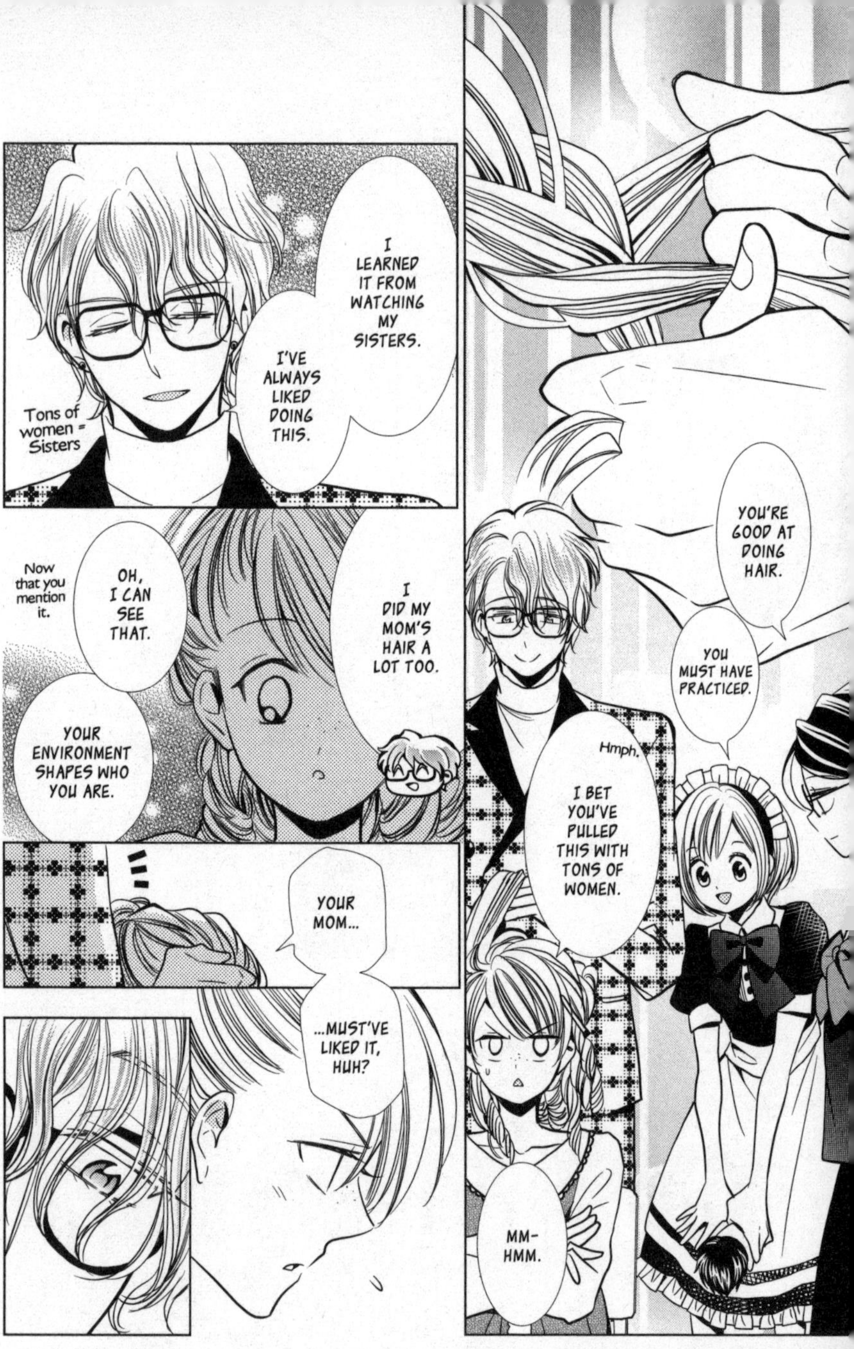
YOU'RE GOOD AT DOING HAIR.
YOU MUST HAVE PRACTICED.
Hmph.
I BET YOU'VE PULLED THIS WITH TONS OF WOMEN.
MM-HMM.
I LEARNED IT FROM WATCHING MY SISTERS.
I'VE ALWAYS LIKED DOING THIS.
Tons of women = Sisters
I DID MY MOM'S HAIR A LOT TOO.
OH, I CAN SEE THAT.
Now that you mention it.
YOUR ENVIRONMENT SHAPES WHO YOU ARE.
YOUR MOM...
...MUST'VE LIKED IT, HUH?

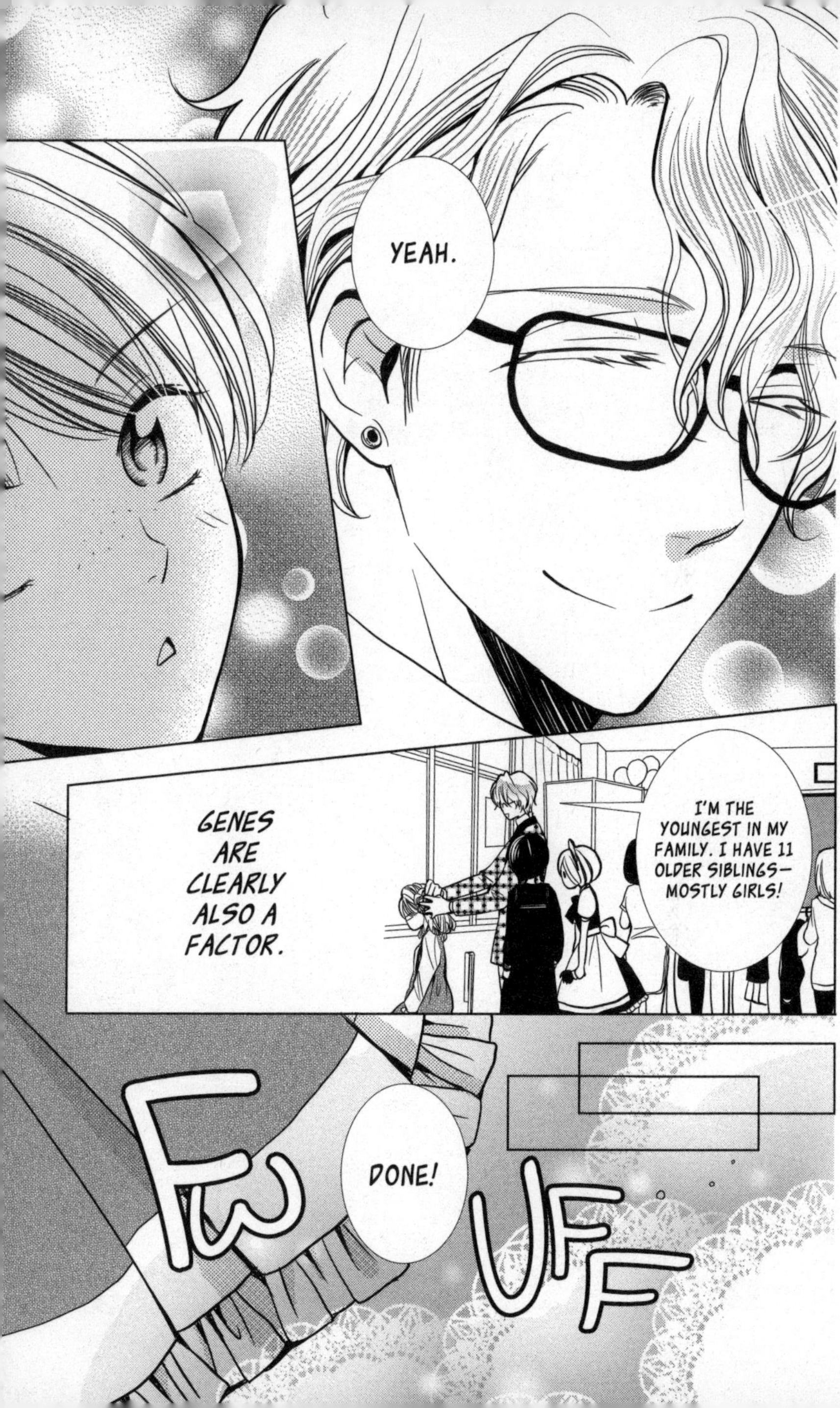
YEAH.
I'M THE YOUNGEST IN MY FAMILY. I HAVE 11 OLDER SIBLINGS—MOSTLY GIRLS!
GENES ARE CLEARLY ALSO A FACTOR.
DONE!
FWUFF

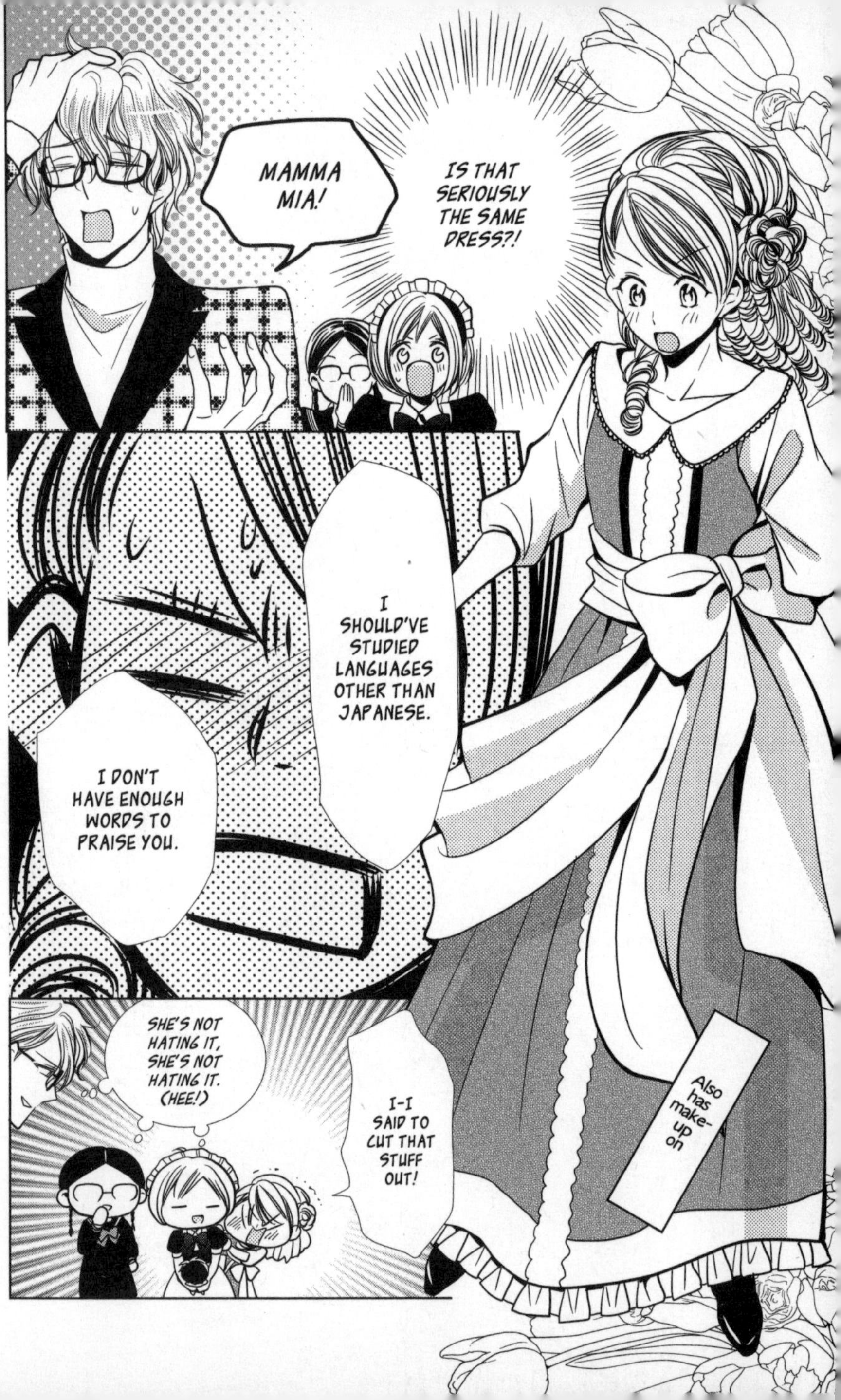
IS THAT SERIOUSLY THE SAME DRESS?!
MAMMA MIA!
I SHOULD'VE STUDIED LANGUAGES OTHER THAN JAPANESE.
I DON'T HAVE ENOUGH WORDS TO PRAISE YOU.
SHE'S NOT HATING IT, SHE'S NOT HATING IT. (HEE!)
I-I SAID TO CUT THAT STUFF OUT!
Also has make-up on

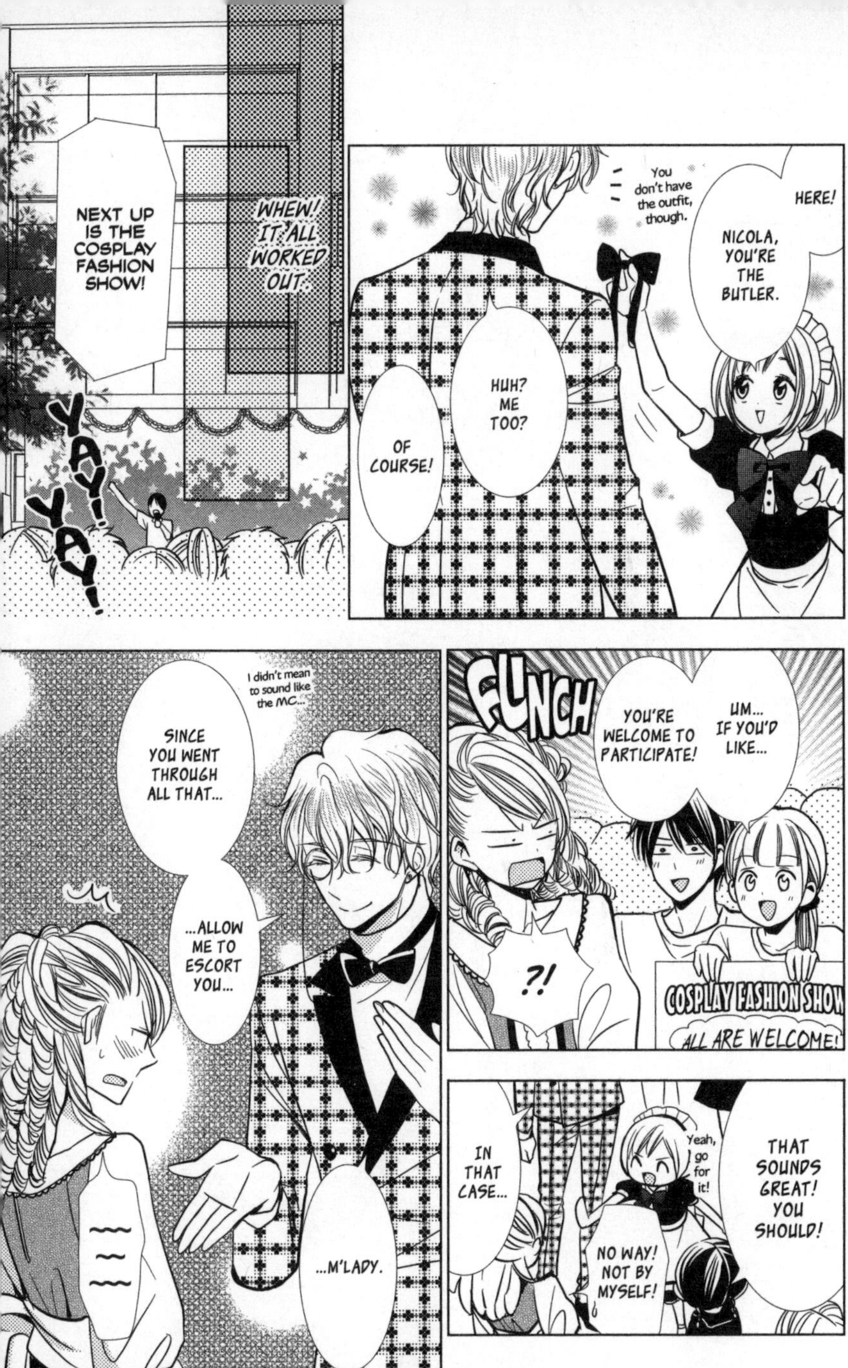
HERE!
NICOLA, YOU'RE THE BUTLER.
You don't have the outfit, though.
HUH? ME TOO?
OF COURSE!
WHEW! IT ALL WORKED OUT.
NEXT UP IS THE COSPLAY FASHION SHOW!
YAY! YAY!
UM... IF YOU'D LIKE...
YOU'RE WELCOME TO PARTICIPATE!
CLINCH
?!
COSPLAY FASHION SHOW
ALL ARE WELCOME!
THAT SOUNDS GREAT! YOU SHOULD!
Yeah, go for it!
IN THAT CASE...
NO WAY! NOT BY MYSELF!
I didn't mean to sound like the MC...
SINCE YOU WENT THROUGH ALL THAT...
...ALLOW ME TO ESCORT YOU...
...M'LADY.

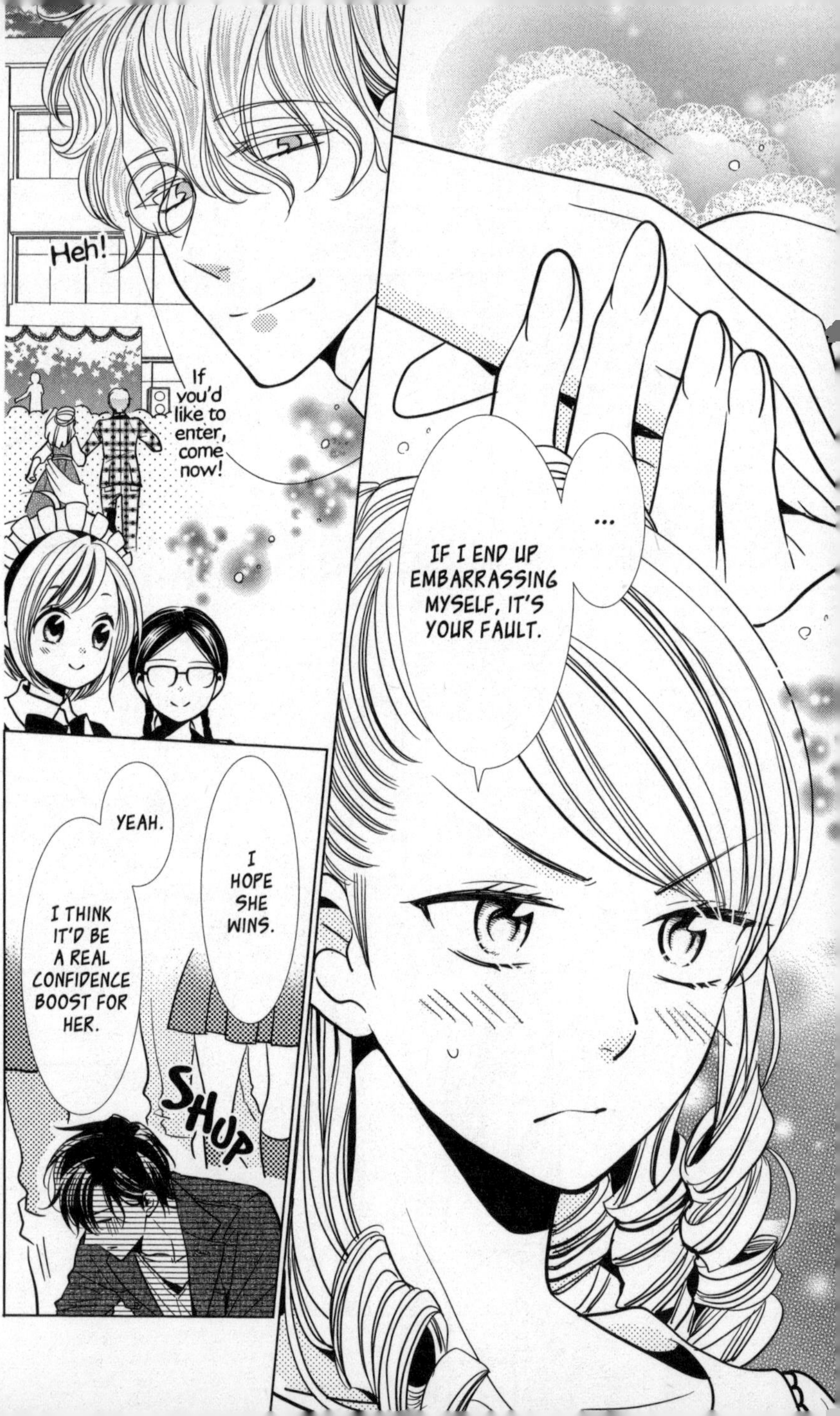
...
IF I END UP EMBARRASSING MYSELF, IT'S YOUR FAULT.
Heh!
If you'd like to enter, come now!
I HOPE SHE WINS.
YEAH.
I THINK IT'D BE A REAL CONFIDENCE BOOST FOR HER.
SHUP

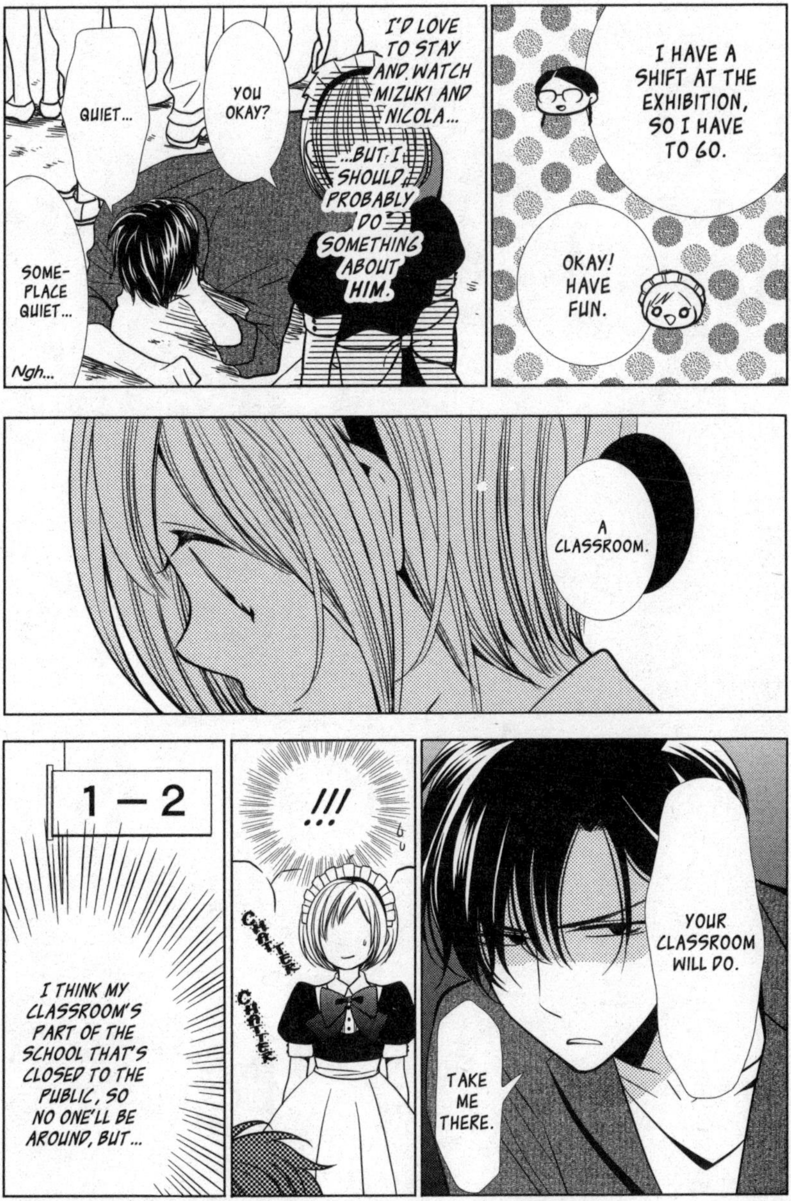
I HAVE A SHIFT AT THE EXHIBITION, SO I HAVE TO GO.
OKAY! HAVE FUN.
I'D LOVE TO STAY AND WATCH MIZUKI AND NICOLA...
...BUT I SHOULD PROBABLY DO SOMETHING ABOUT HIM.
YOU OKAY?
QUIET...
SOME-PLACE QUIET...
Ngh...
A CLASSROOM.
YOUR CLASSROOM WILL DO.
TAKE ME THERE.
!!!
1 — 2
I THINK MY CLASSROOM'S PART OF THE SCHOOL THAT'S CLOSED TO THE PUBLIC, SO NO ONE'LL BE AROUND, BUT...

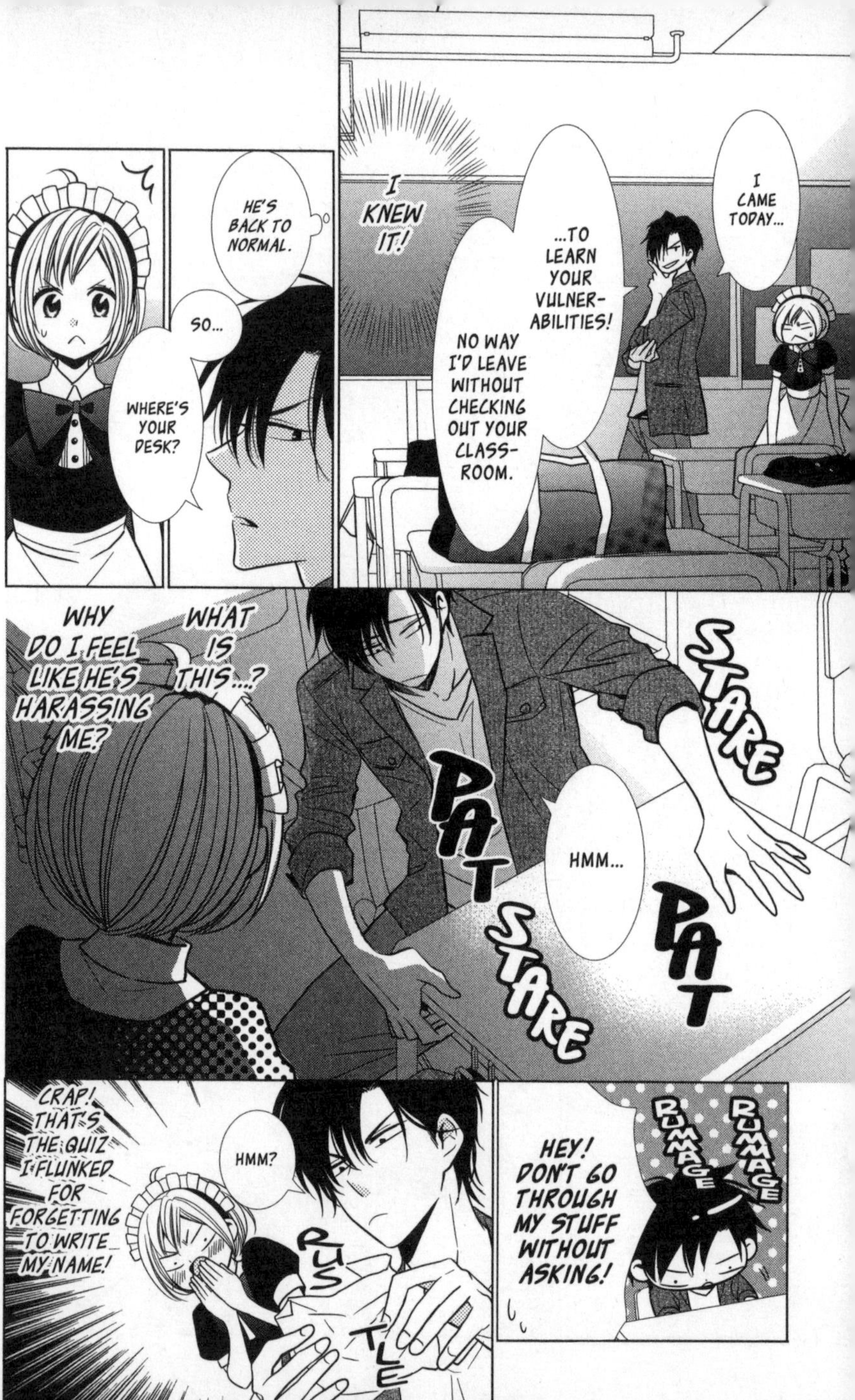
I CAME TODAY...
...TO LEARN YOUR VULNER-ABILITIES!
NO WAY I'D LEAVE WITHOUT CHECKING OUT YOUR CLASS-ROOM.
I KNEW IT!
HE'S BACK TO NORMAL.
SO...
WHERE'S YOUR DESK?
STARE
HMM...
PAT PAT
STARE
WHAT IS THIS...?
WHY DO I FEEL LIKE HE'S HARASSING ME?
RUMMAGE RUMMAGE
HEY! DON'T GO THROUGH MY STUFF WITHOUT ASKING!
HMM?
RUSTLE
CRAP! THAT'S THE QUIZ I FLUNKED FOR FORGETTING TO WRITE MY NAME!

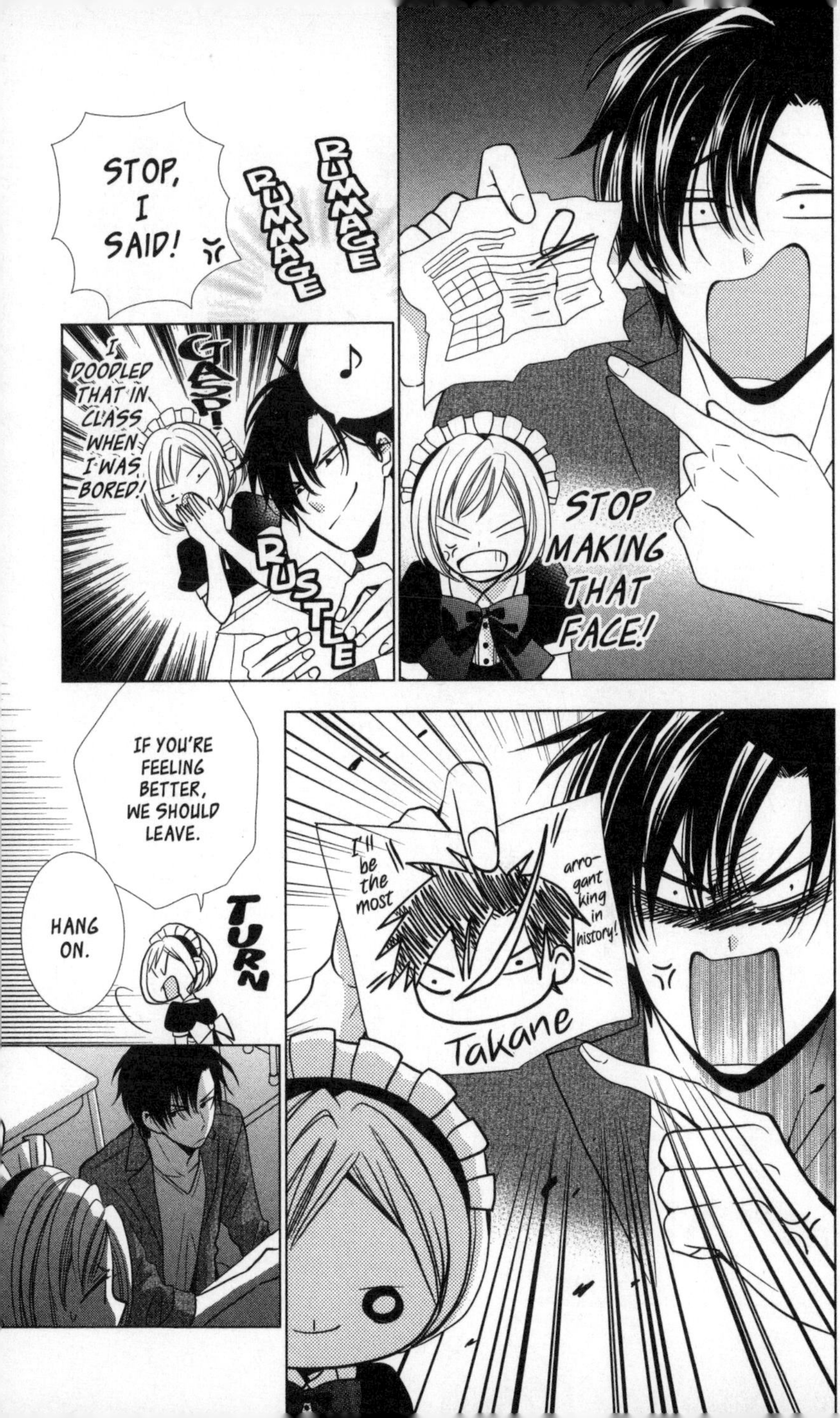
STOP MAKING THAT FACE!
RUMMAGE RUMMAGE
STOP, I SAID!
♪
GASP!
I DOODLED THAT IN CLASS WHEN I WAS BORED!
RUSTLE
I'll be the most arrogant king in history!
Takane
IF YOU'RE FEELING BETTER, WE SHOULD LEAVE.
HANG ON.
TURN

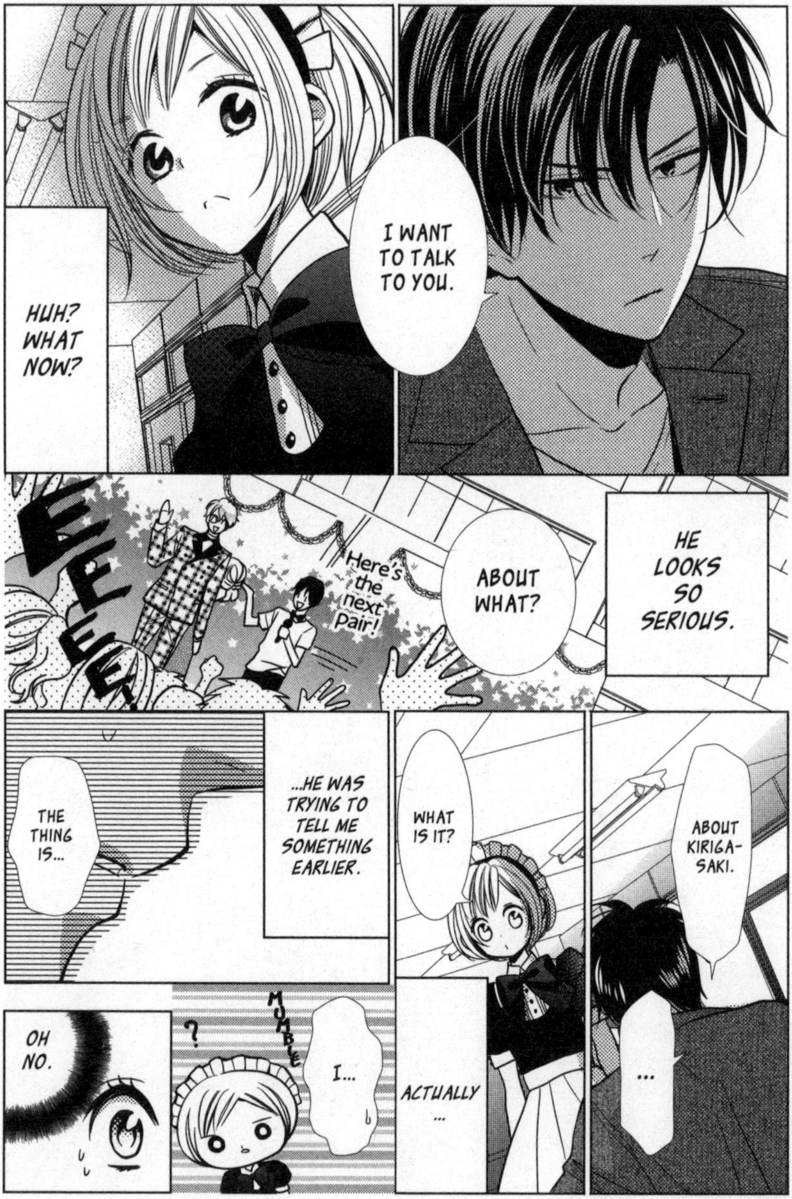
I WANT TO TALK TO YOU.
HUH? WHAT NOW?
HE LOOKS SO SERIOUS.
ABOUT WHAT?
Here's the next pair!
EEEEE!
ABOUT KIRIGA-SAKI.
...
WHAT IS IT?
ACTUALLY ...
...HE WAS TRYING TO TELL ME SOMETHING EARLIER.
THE THING IS...
MUMBLE
I...
?
OH NO.

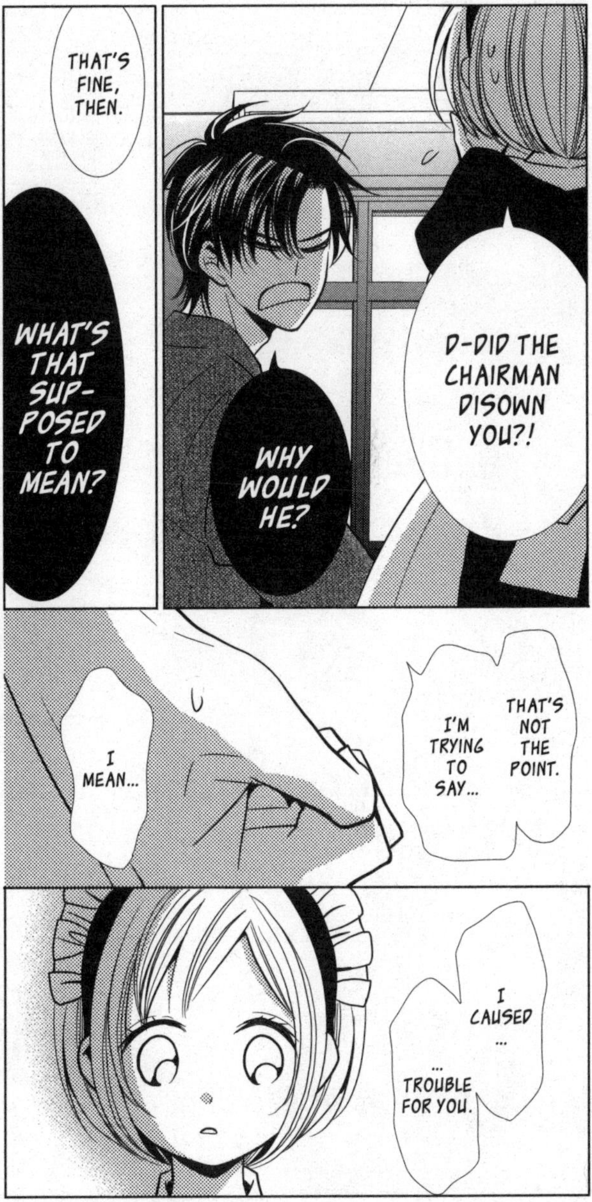
D-DID THE CHAIRMAN DISOWN YOU?!
WHY WOULD HE?
THAT'S FINE, THEN.
WHAT'S THAT SUP-POSED TO MEAN?
THAT'S NOT THE POINT.
I'M TRYING TO SAY...
I MEAN...
I CAUSED ...
... TROUBLE FOR YOU.

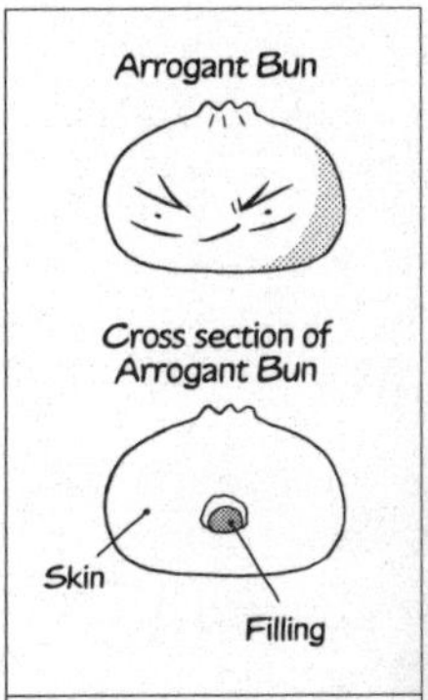
Arrogant Bun
Cross section of Arrogant Bun
Skin
Filling

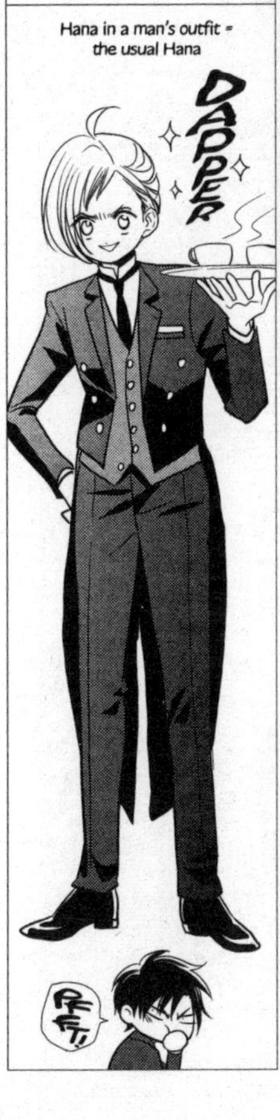
Hana in a man's outfit = the usual Hana
DAPPER
PFFT!

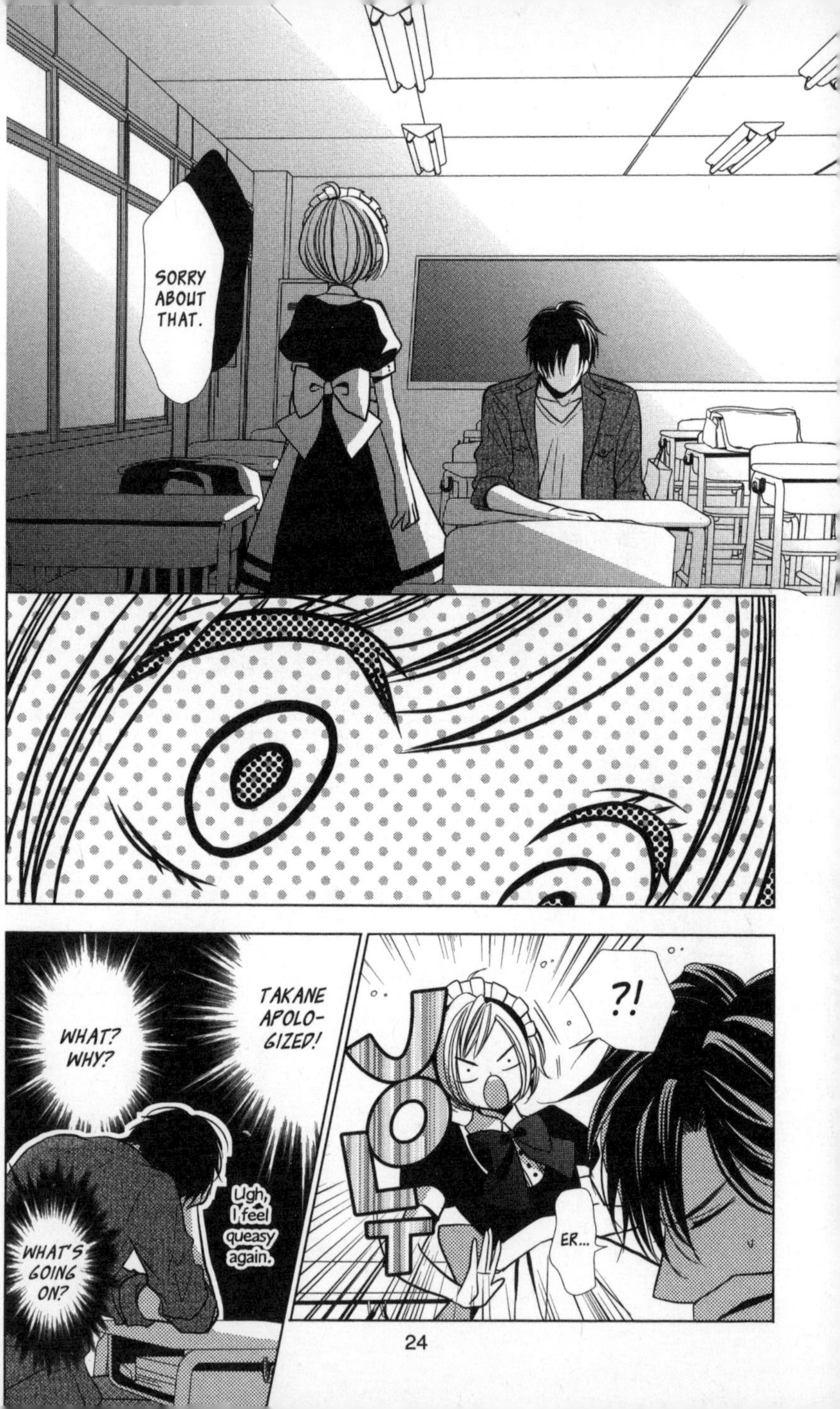
SORRY ABOUT THAT.
?!
ER...
TAKANE APOLOGIZED!
WHAT? WHY?
Ugh, I feel queasy again.
WHAT'S GOING ON?

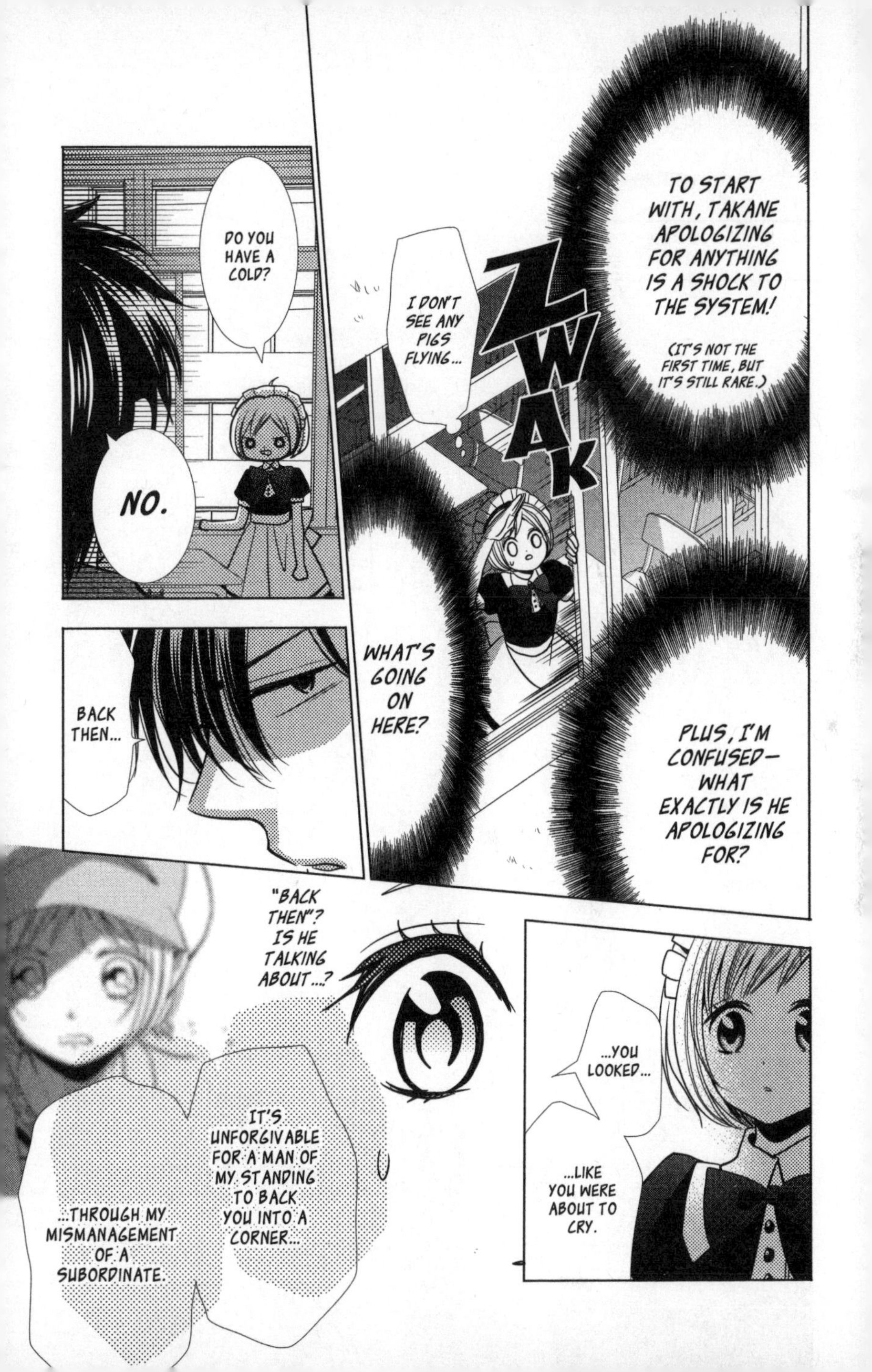
TO START WITH, TAKANE APOLOGIZING FOR ANYTHING IS A SHOCK TO THE SYSTEM!
(IT'S NOT THE FIRST TIME, BUT IT'S STILL RARE.)
ZWAK
I DON'T SEE ANY PIGS FLYING...
WHAT'S GOING ON HERE?
PLUS, I'M CONFUSED— WHAT EXACTLY IS HE APOLOGIZING FOR?
DO YOU HAVE A COLD?
NO.
BACK THEN...
...YOU LOOKED...
...LIKE YOU WERE ABOUT TO CRY.
"BACK THEN"? IS HE TALKING ABOUT...?
IT'S UNFORGIVABLE FOR A MAN OF MY STANDING TO BACK YOU INTO A CORNER...
...THROUGH MY MISMANAGEMENT OF A SUBORDINATE.

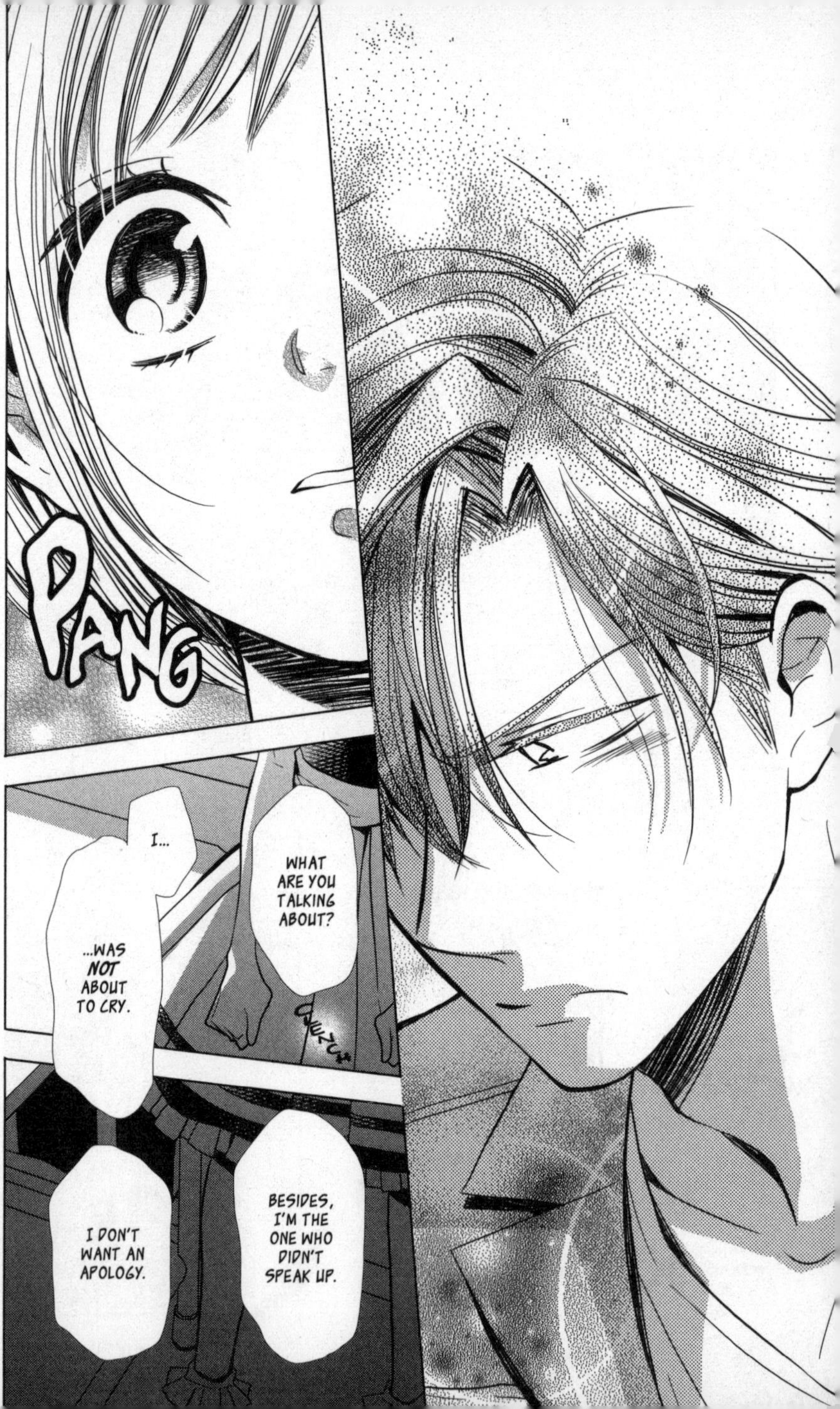
PANG
WHAT ARE YOU TALKING ABOUT?
I... ...WAS NOT ABOUT TO CRY.
CLENCH
BESIDES, I'M THE ONE WHO DIDN'T SPEAK UP.
I DON'T WANT AN APOLOGY.

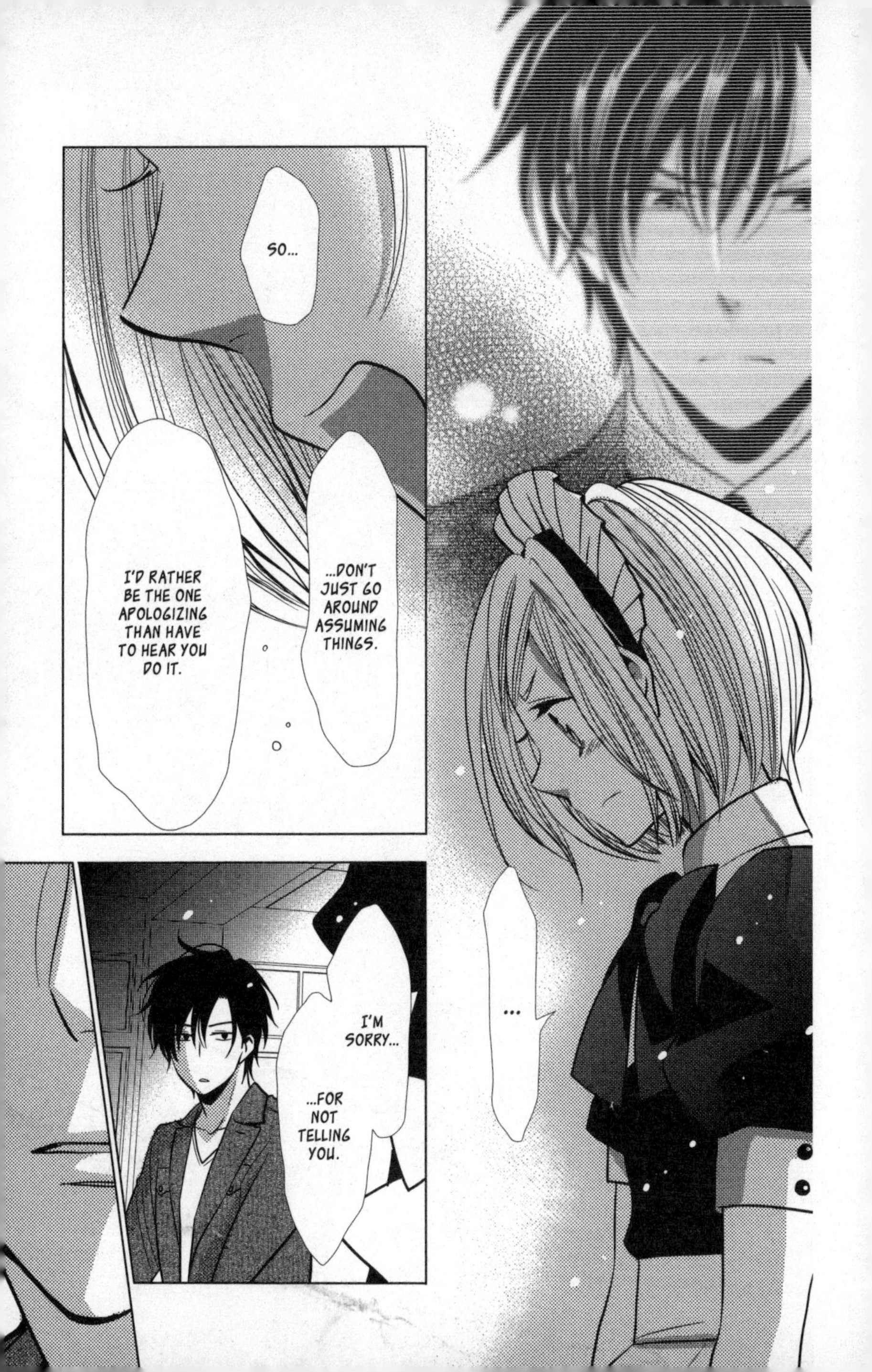
...
SO...
...DON'T JUST GO AROUND ASSUMING THINGS.
I'D RATHER BE THE ONE APOLOGIZING THAN HAVE TO HEAR YOU DO IT.
I'M SORRY...
...FOR NOT TELLING YOU.

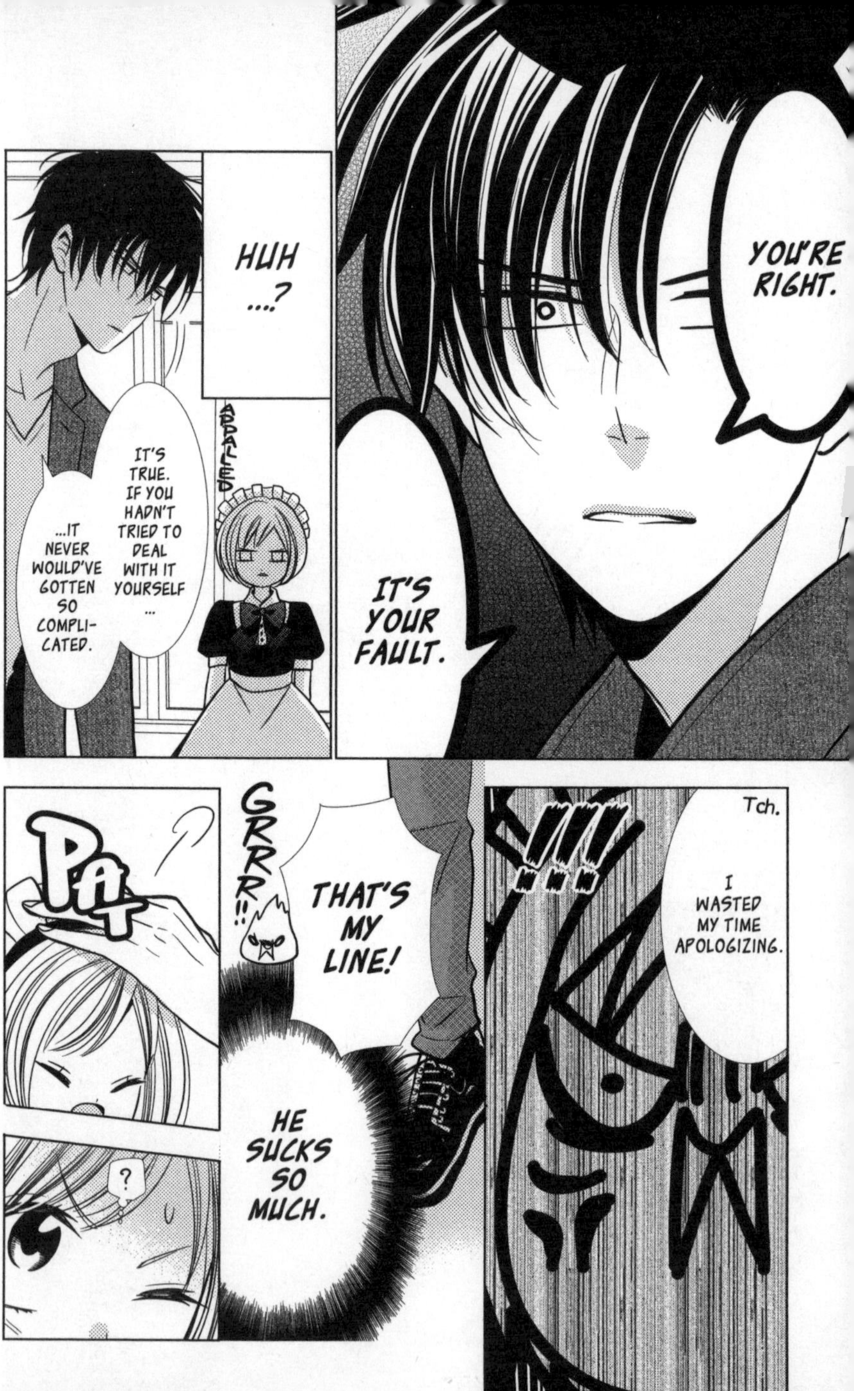
YOU'RE RIGHT.
IT'S YOUR FAULT.
HUH ...?
APPALLED
IT'S TRUE. IF YOU HADN'T TRIED TO DEAL WITH IT YOURSELF ...
...IT NEVER WOULD'VE GOTTEN SO COMPLI-CATED.
Tch.
!!!
I WASTED MY TIME APOLOGIZING.
GRRR!!
THAT'S MY LINE!
HE SUCKS SO MUCH.
PAT
?

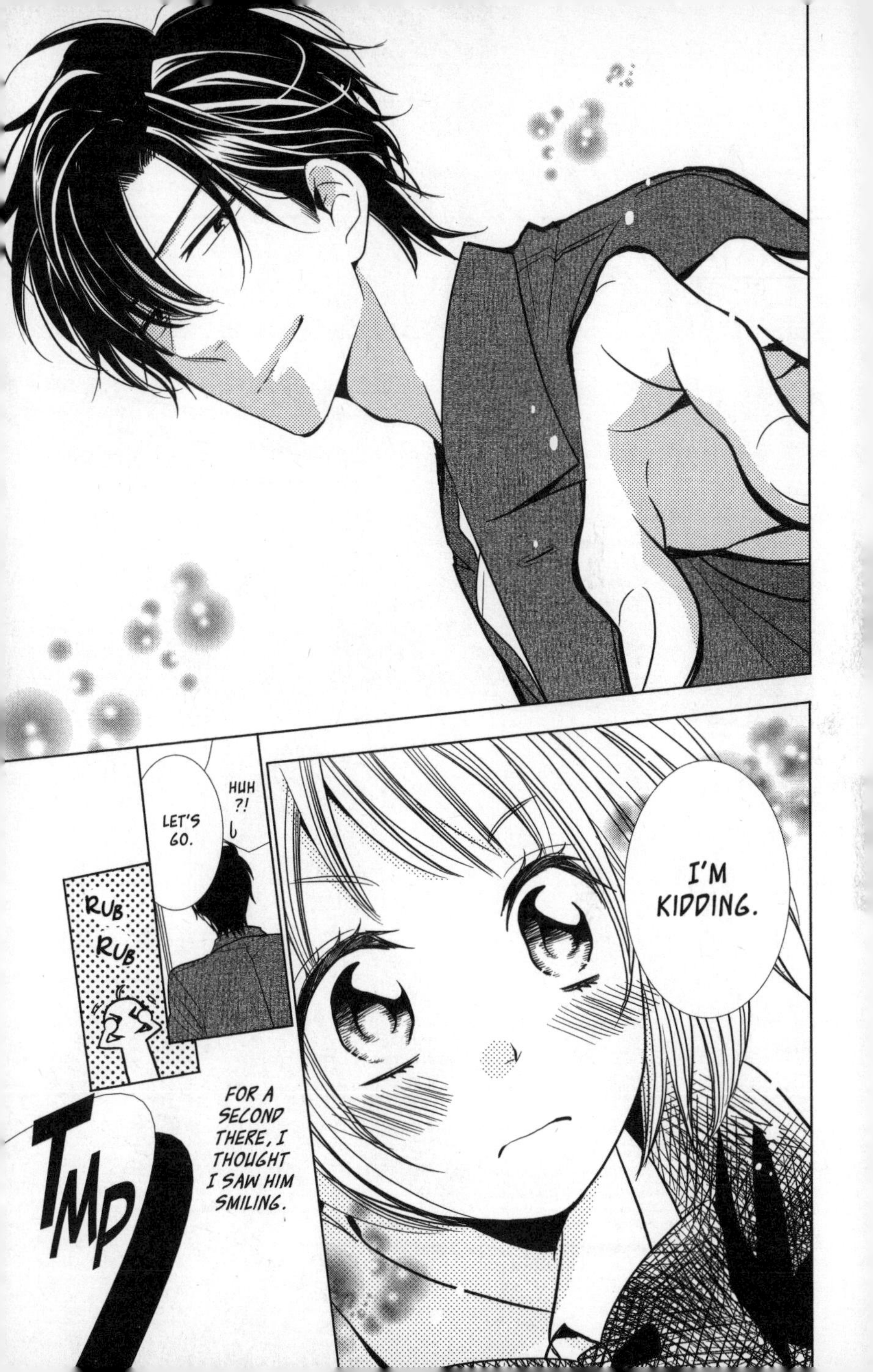
I'M KIDDING.
HUH ?!
LET'S GO.
RUB RUB
FOR A SECOND THERE, I THOUGHT I SAW HIM SMILING.
TMP

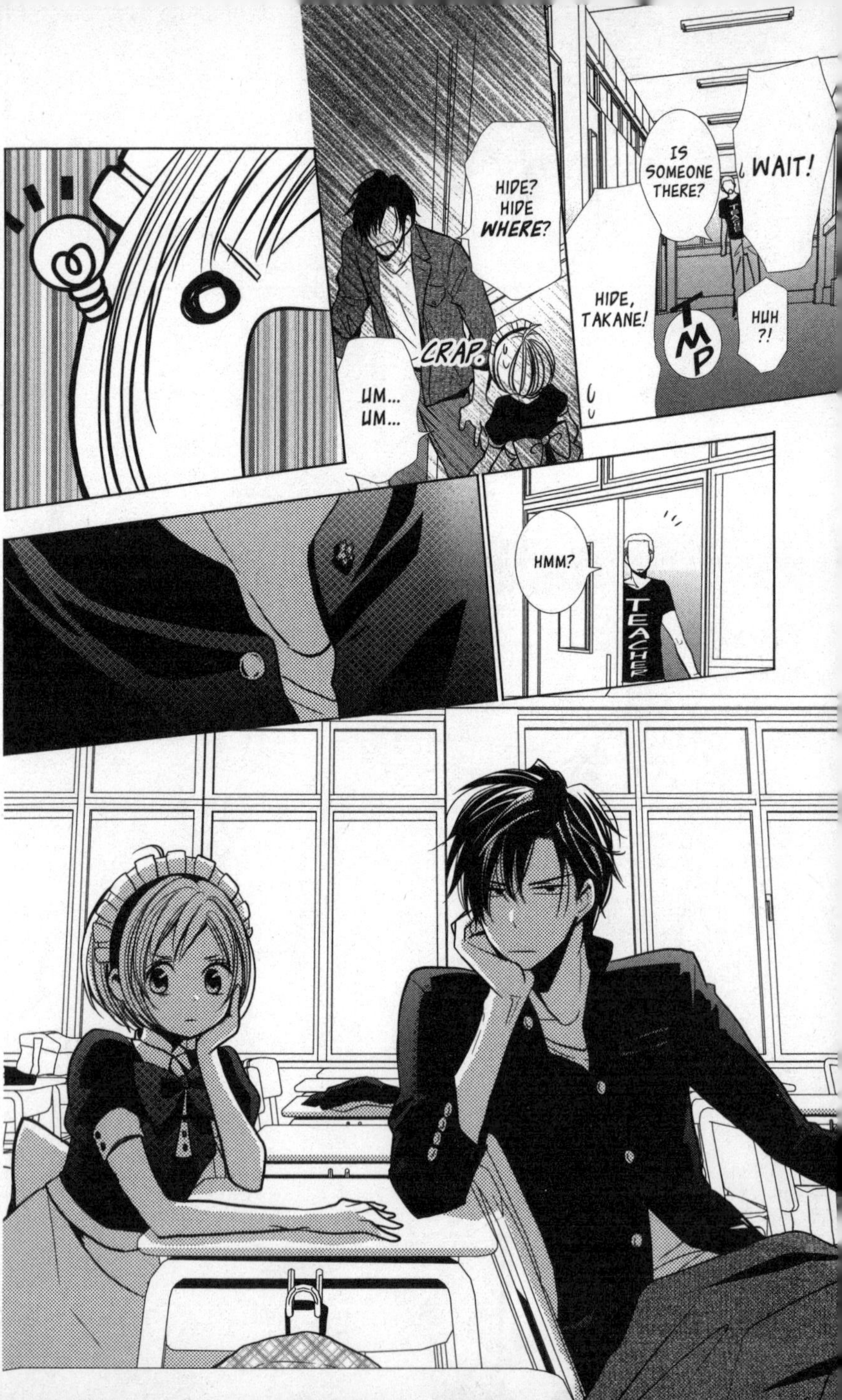

WAIT!
IS SOMEONE THERE?
HUH ?!
TMP
HIDE, TAKANE!
HIDE? HIDE WHERE?
CRAP.
UM... UM...
HMM?
TEACHER

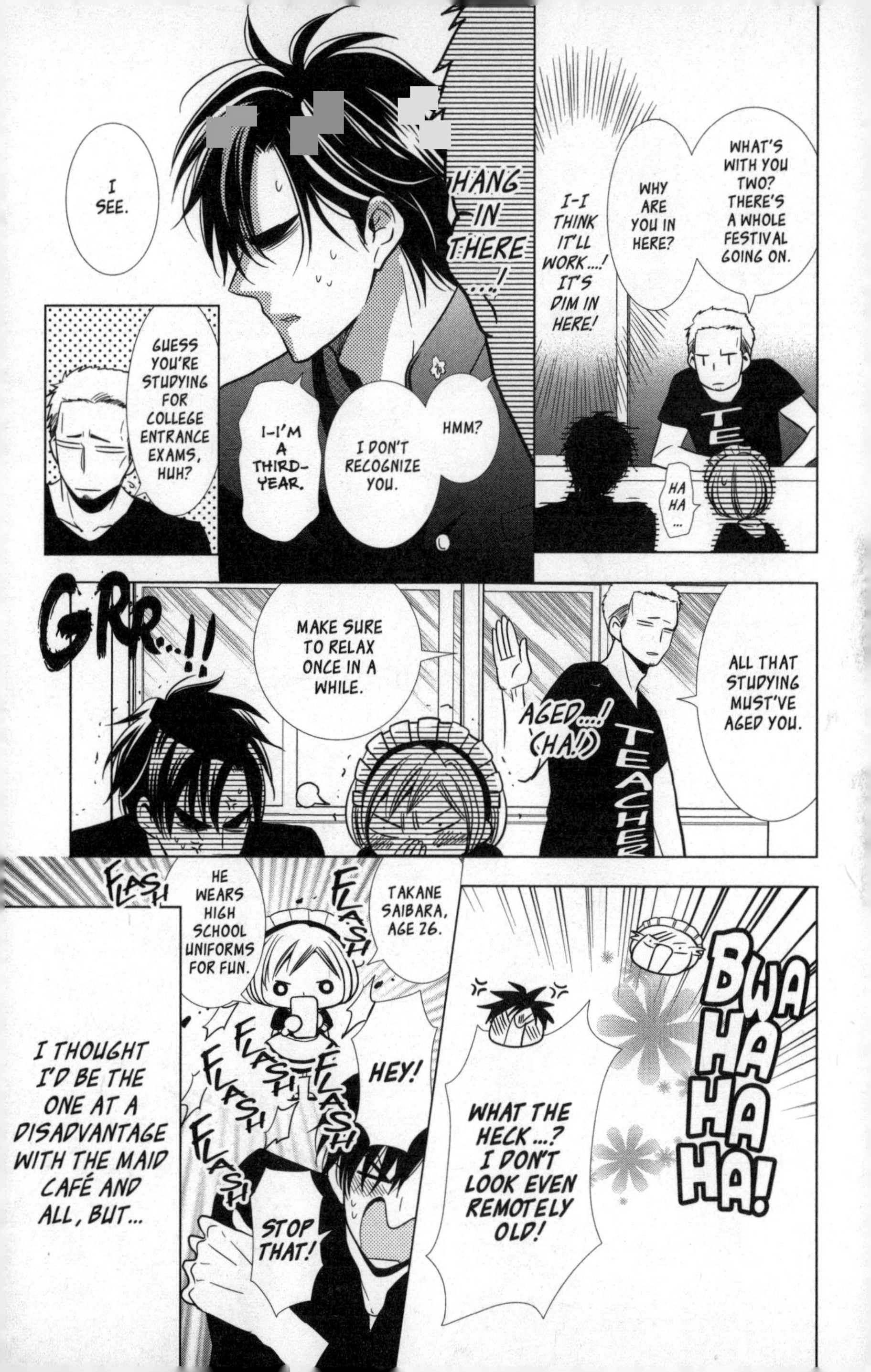
WHAT'S WITH YOU TWO? THERE'S A WHOLE FESTIVAL GOING ON.
WHY ARE YOU IN HERE?
I-I THINK IT'LL WORK...! IT'S DIM IN HERE!
HA HA ...
HANG IN THERE ...!
HMM?
I DON'T RECOGNIZE YOU.
I-I'M A THIRD-YEAR.
I SEE.
GUESS YOU'RE STUDYING FOR COLLEGE ENTRANCE EXAMS, HUH?
ALL THAT STUDYING MUST'VE AGED YOU.
AGED...! (HA!)
MAKE SURE TO RELAX ONCE IN A WHILE.
GRR...!!
BWAHAHAHAHA!
WHAT THE HECK ...? I DON'T LOOK EVEN REMOTELY OLD!
TAKANE SAIBARA, AGE 26.
HE WEARS HIGH SCHOOL UNIFORMS FOR FUN.
FLASH
FLASH
HEY!
FLASH
FLASH
FLASH
FLASH
STOP THAT!
I THOUGHT I'D BE THE ONE AT A DISADVANTAGE WITH THE MAID CAFÉ AND ALL, BUT...

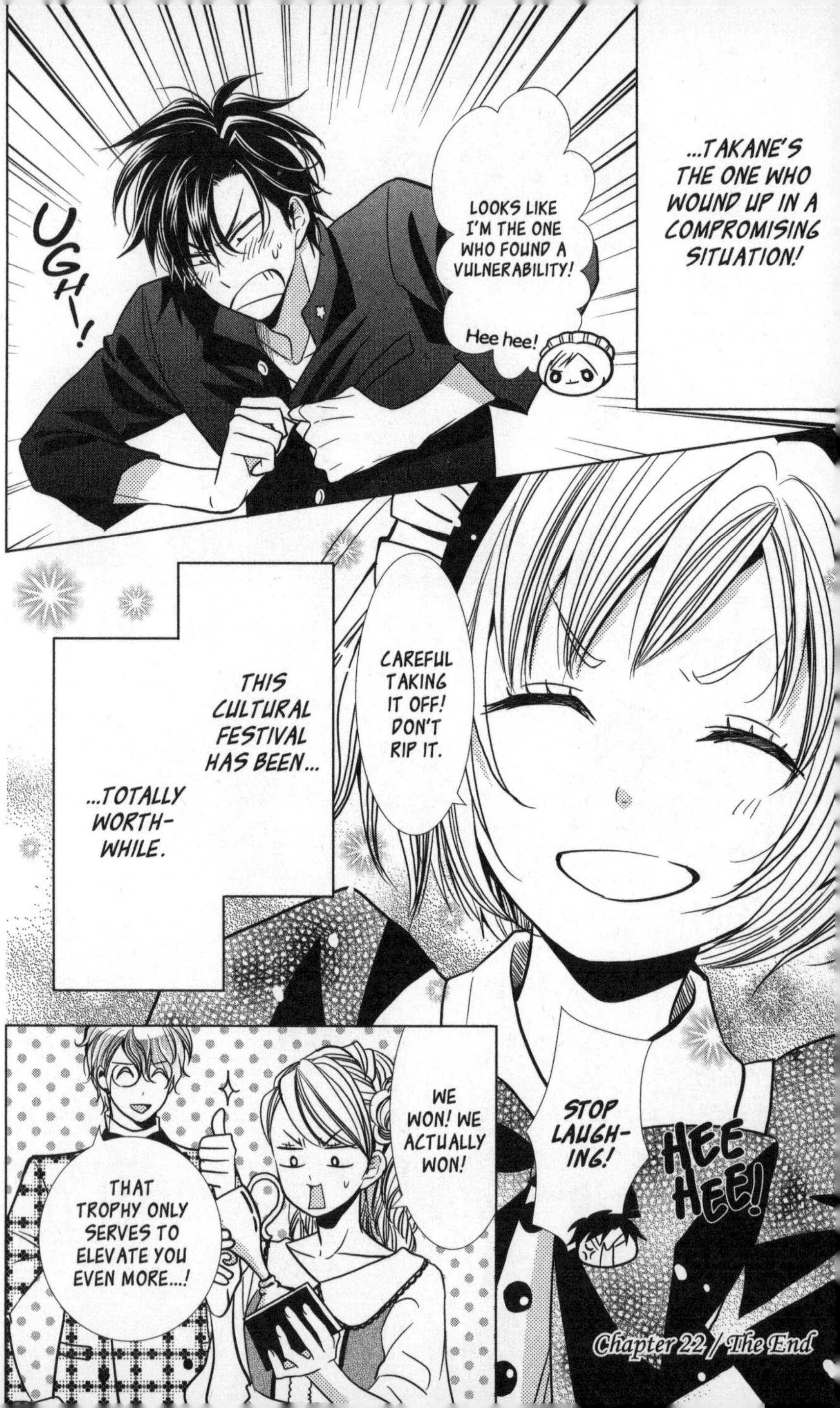
...TAKANE'S THE ONE WHO WOUND UP IN A COMPROMISING SITUATION!
LOOKS LIKE I'M THE ONE WHO FOUND A VULNERABILITY!
Hee hee!
UGH!
CAREFUL TAKING IT OFF! DON'T RIP IT.
THIS CULTURAL FESTIVAL HAS BEEN...
...TOTALLY WORTH-WHILE.
HEE HEE!
STOP LAUGH-ING!
WE WON! WE ACTUALLY WON!
THAT TROPHY ONLY SERVES TO ELEVATE YOU EVEN MORE...!
Chapter 22 / The End

Boys' School Uniform

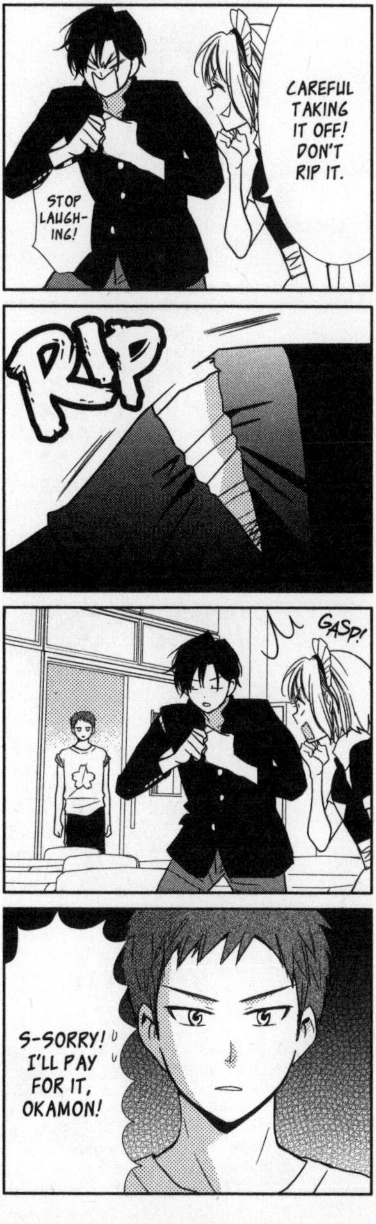
CAREFUL TAKING IT OFF! DON'T RIP IT.
STOP LAUGHING!
RIP
GASP!
S-SORRY! I'LL PAY FOR IT, OKAMON!

Tough Talk

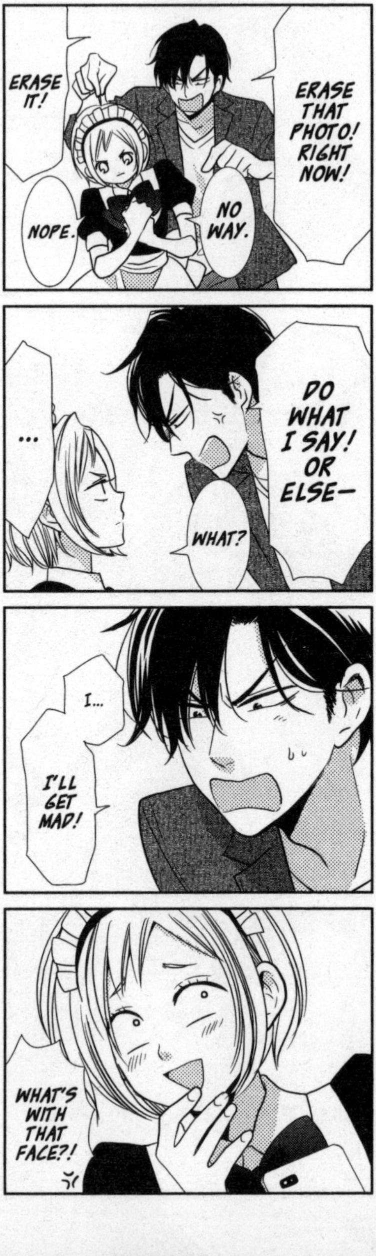
ERASE THAT PHOTO! RIGHT NOW!
ERASE IT!
NO WAY.
NOPE.
DO WHAT I SAY! OR ELSE—
...
WHAT?
I...
I'LL GET MAD!
WHAT'S WITH THAT FACE?!

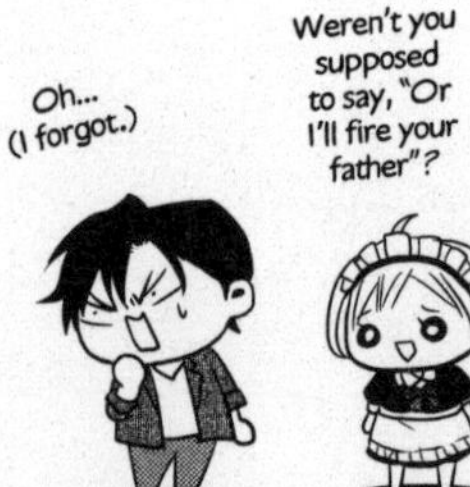
Weren't you supposed to say, "Or I'll fire your father"?
Oh... (I forgot.)

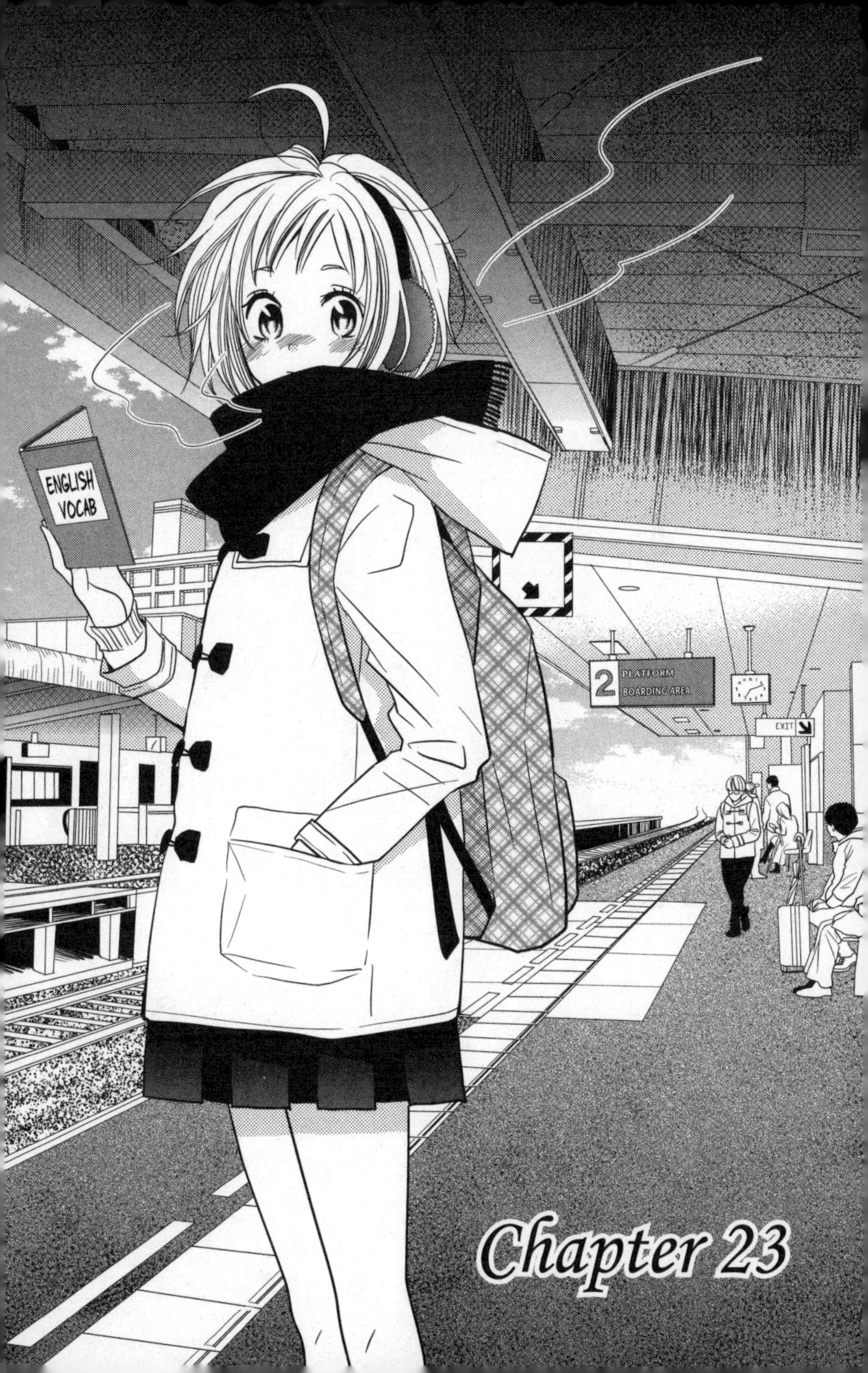
ENGLISH VOCAB
2 PLATFORM BOARDING AREA
EXIT
Chapter 23

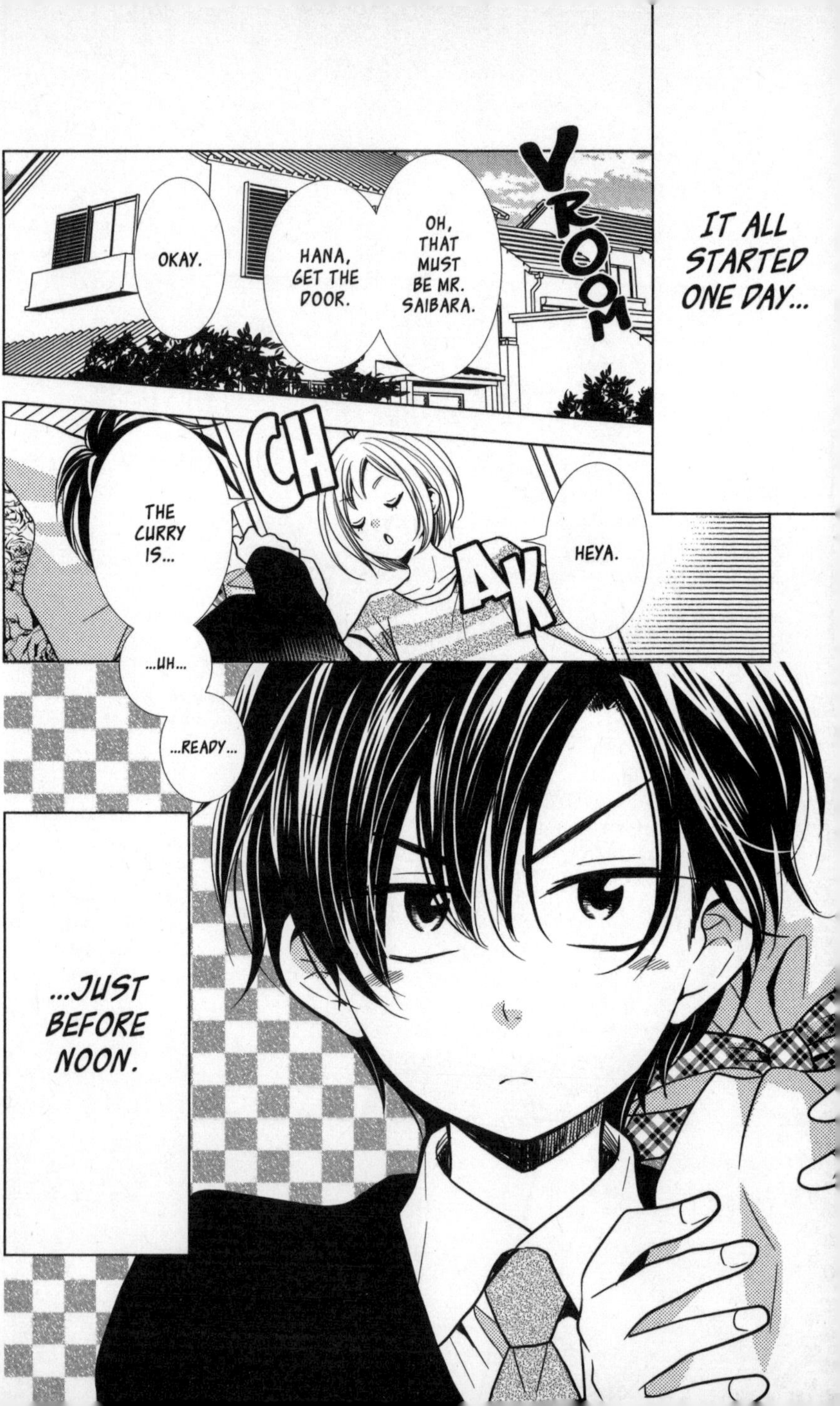
IT ALL STARTED ONE DAY...
VROOM
OH, THAT MUST BE MR. SAIBARA.
HANA, GET THE DOOR.
OKAY.
HEYA.
CH
AK
THE CURRY IS...
...UH...
...READY...
...JUST BEFORE NOON.

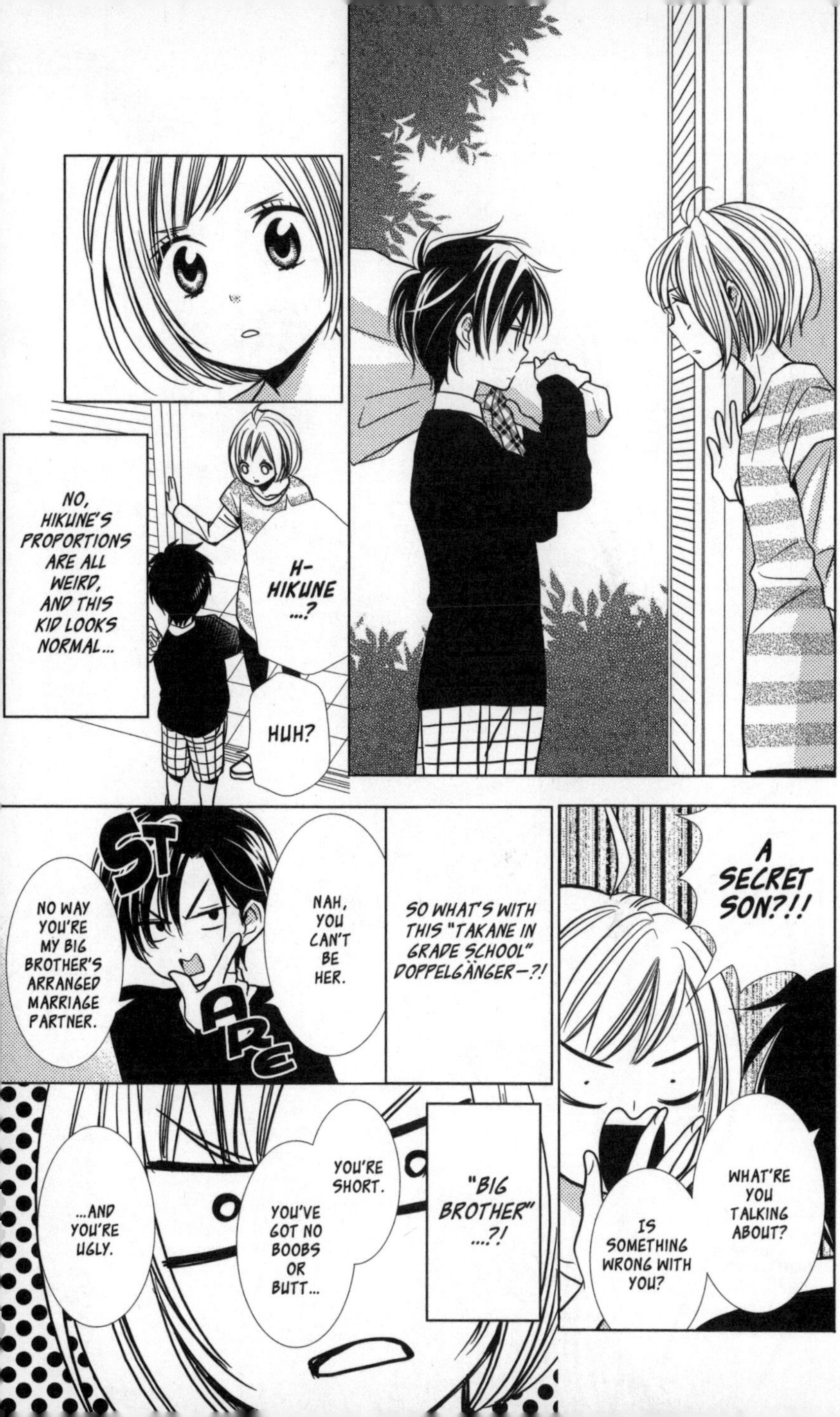
H-HIKUNE...?
HUH?
NO, HIKUNE'S PROPORTIONS ARE ALL WEIRD, AND THIS KID LOOKS NORMAL...
A SECRET SON?!!
WHAT'RE YOU TALKING ABOUT?
IS SOMETHING WRONG WITH YOU?
SO WHAT'S WITH THIS "TAKANE IN GRADE SCHOOL" DOPPELGÄNGER—?!
NAH, YOU CAN'T BE HER.
STARE
NO WAY YOU'RE MY BIG BROTHER'S ARRANGED MARRIAGE PARTNER.
"BIG BROTHER"...?!
YOU'RE SHORT.
YOU'VE GOT NO BOOBS OR BUTT...
...AND YOU'RE UGLY.

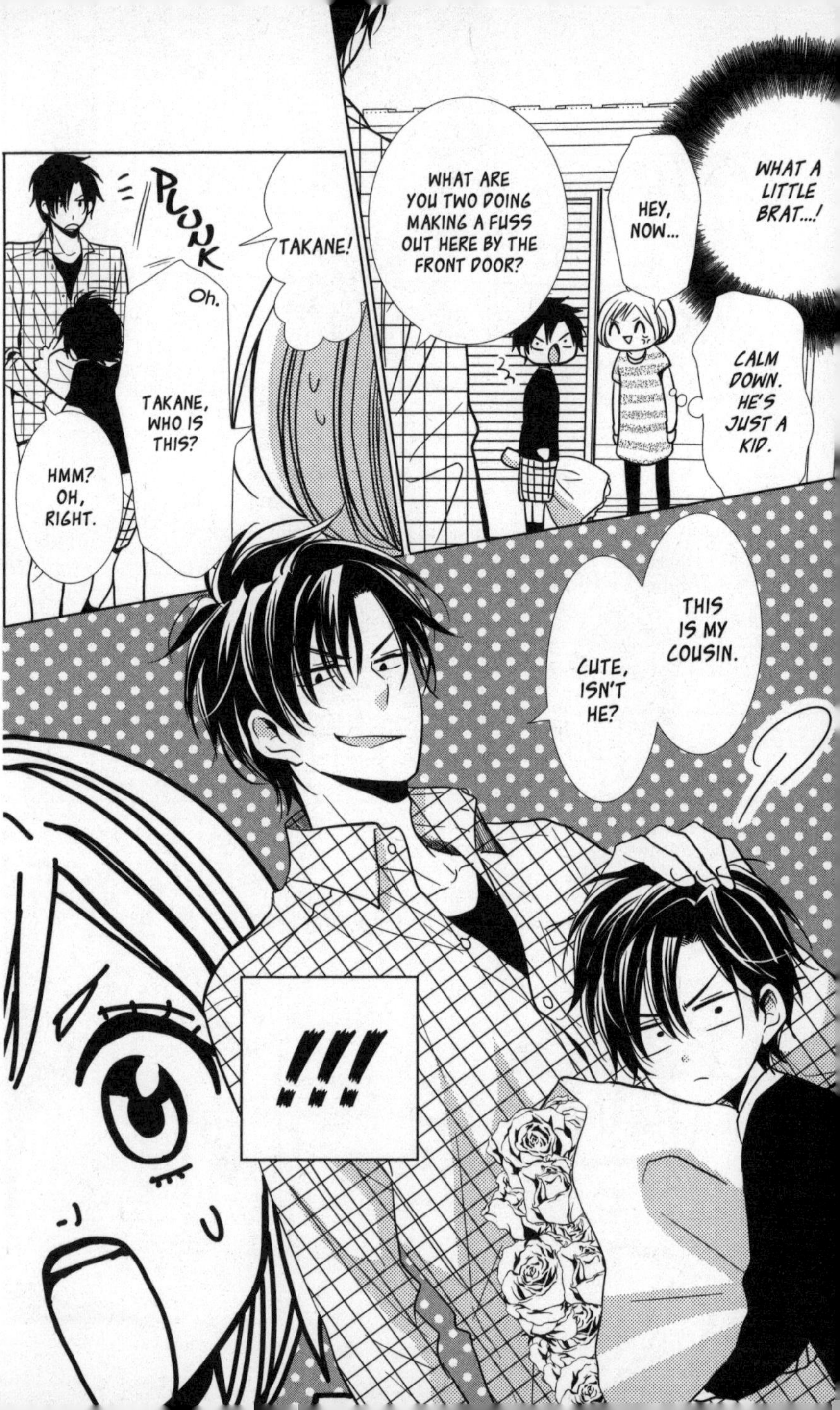
WHAT A LITTLE BRAT...!
CALM DOWN. HE'S JUST A KID.
HEY, NOW...
WHAT ARE YOU TWO DOING MAKING A FUSS OUT HERE BY THE FRONT DOOR?
TAKANE!
PLUNK
Oh.
TAKANE, WHO IS THIS?
HMM? OH, RIGHT.
THIS IS MY COUSIN.
CUTE, ISN'T HE?
!!!

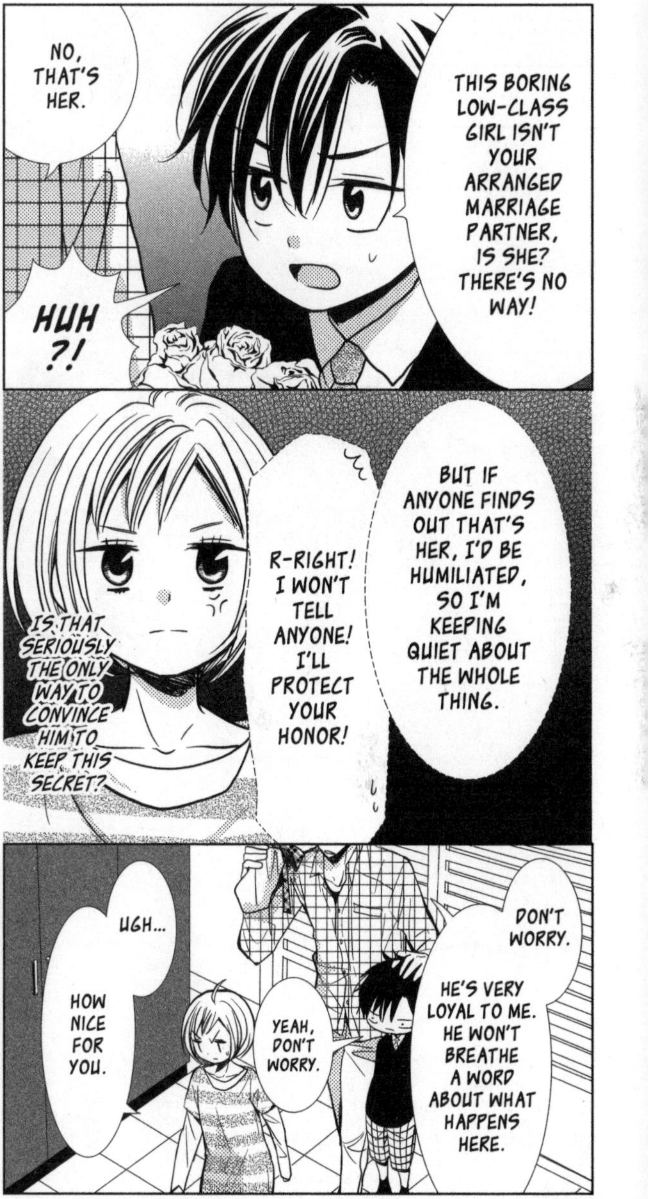
THIS BORING LOW-CLASS GIRL ISN'T YOUR ARRANGED MARRIAGE PARTNER, IS SHE? THERE'S NO WAY!
NO, THAT'S HER.
HUH ?!
BUT IF ANYONE FINDS OUT THAT'S HER, I'D BE HUMILIATED, SO I'M KEEPING QUIET ABOUT THE WHOLE THING.
R-RIGHT! I WON'T TELL ANYONE! I'LL PROTECT YOUR HONOR!
IS THAT SERIOUSLY THE ONLY WAY TO CONVINCE HIM TO KEEP THIS SECRET?
DON'T WORRY.
HE'S VERY LOYAL TO ME. HE WON'T BREATHE A WORD ABOUT WHAT HAPPENS HERE.
YEAH, DON'T WORRY.
UGH...
HOW NICE FOR YOU.

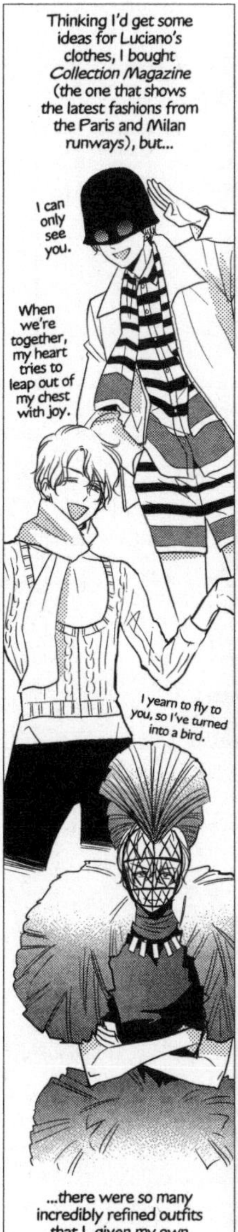
Thinking I'd get some ideas for Luciano's clothes, I bought *Collection Magazine* (the one that shows the latest fashions from the Paris and Milan runways), but...
I can only see you.
When we're together, my heart tries to leap out of my chest with joy.
I yearn to fly to you, so I've turned into a bird.
...there were so many incredibly refined outfits that I, given my own mediocre sense of style, couldn't really replicate them.

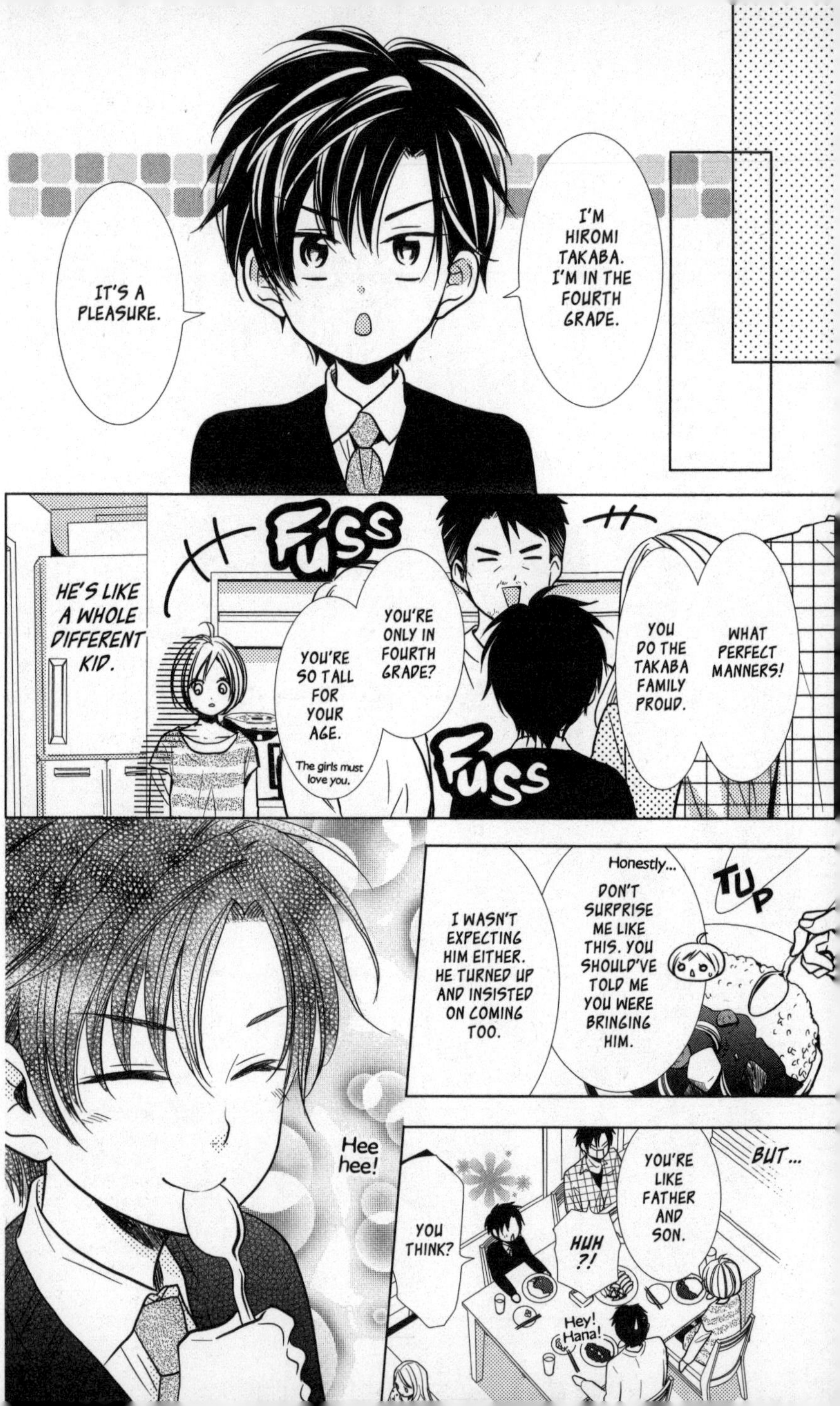
I'M HIROMI TAKABA. I'M IN THE FOURTH GRADE.
IT'S A PLEASURE.
WHAT PERFECT MANNERS!
YOU DO THE TAKABA FAMILY PROUD.
FUSS
YOU'RE ONLY IN FOURTH GRADE?
YOU'RE SO TALL FOR YOUR AGE.
The girls must love you.
FUSS
HE'S LIKE A WHOLE DIFFERENT KID.
TUP
Honestly...
DON'T SURPRISE ME LIKE THIS. YOU SHOULD'VE TOLD ME YOU WERE BRINGING HIM.
I WASN'T EXPECTING HIM EITHER. HE TURNED UP AND INSISTED ON COMING TOO.
BUT...
YOU'RE LIKE FATHER AND SON.
HUH?!
Hey! Hana!
YOU THINK?
Hee hee!

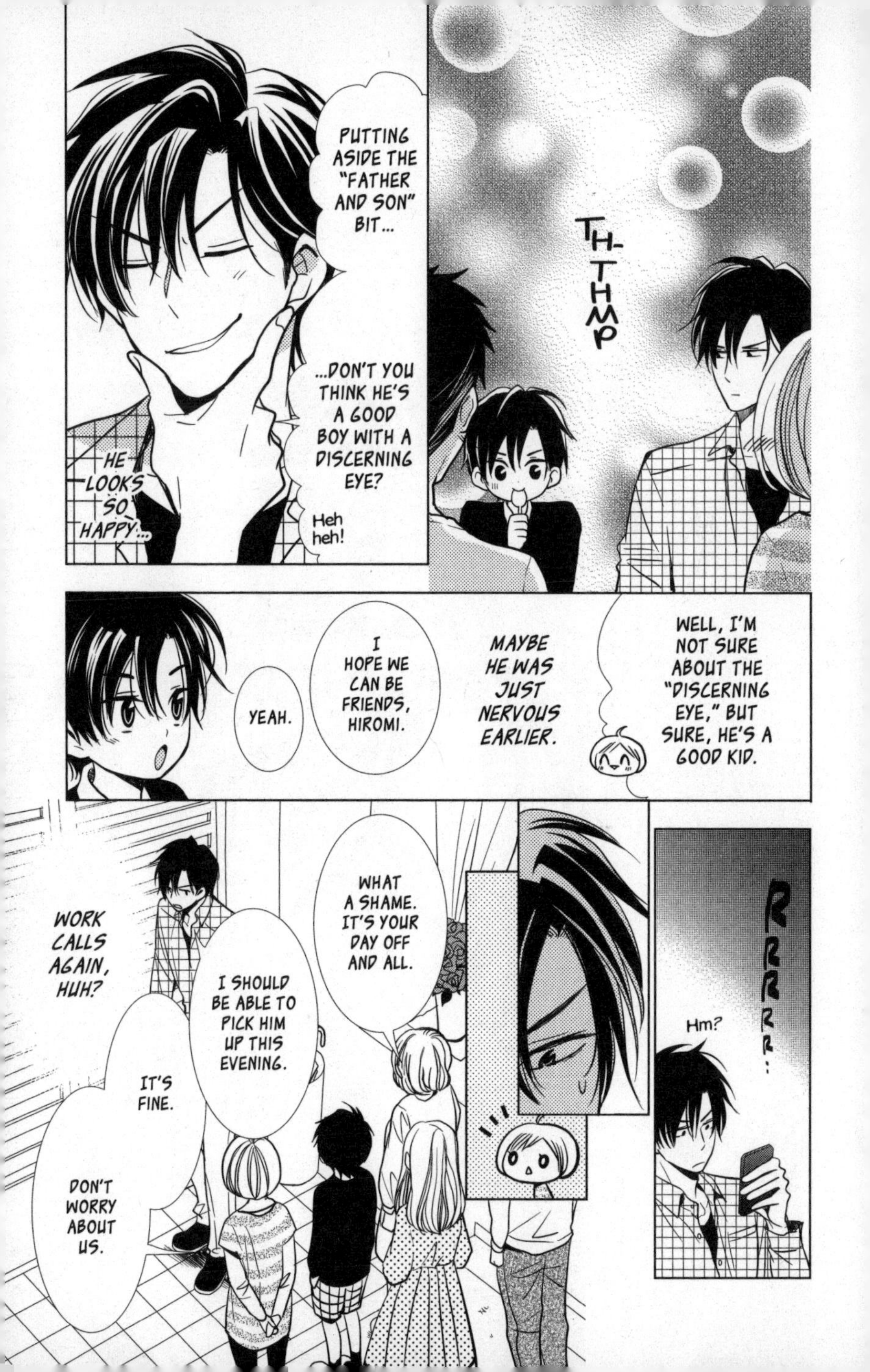
TH-THMP
PUTTING ASIDE THE "FATHER AND SON" BIT...
...DON'T YOU THINK HE'S A GOOD BOY WITH A DISCERNING EYE?
Heh heh!
HE LOOKS SO HAPPY...
WELL, I'M NOT SURE ABOUT THE "DISCERNING EYE," BUT SURE, HE'S A GOOD KID.
MAYBE HE WAS JUST NERVOUS EARLIER.
I HOPE WE CAN BE FRIENDS, HIROMI.
YEAH.
RRRRR..
Hm?
WHAT A SHAME. IT'S YOUR DAY OFF AND ALL.
WORK CALLS AGAIN, HUH?
I SHOULD BE ABLE TO PICK HIM UP THIS EVENING.
IT'S FINE.
DON'T WORRY ABOUT US.

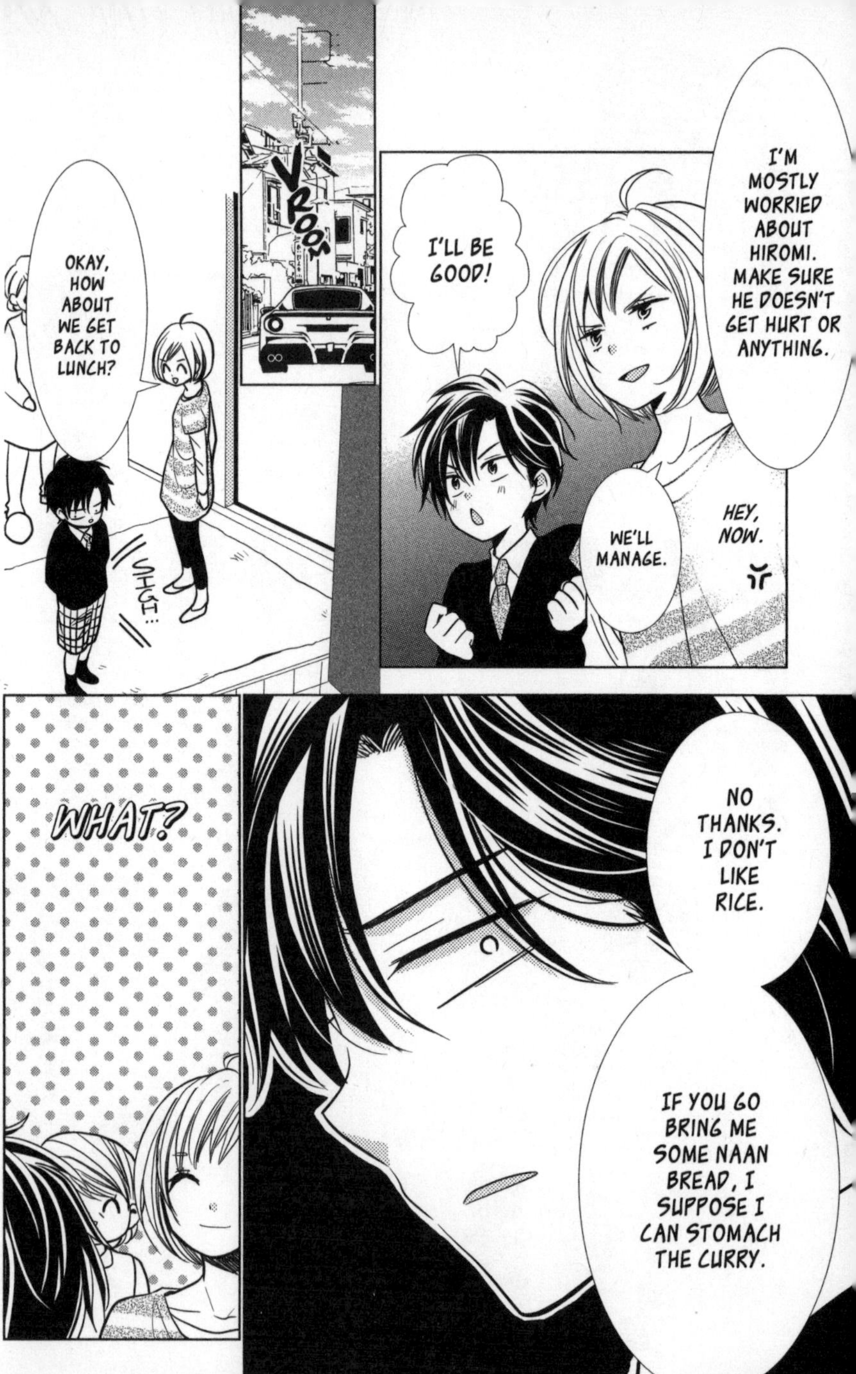
I'M MOSTLY WORRIED ABOUT HIROMI. MAKE SURE HE DOESN'T GET HURT OR ANYTHING.
I'LL BE GOOD!
HEY, NOW.
WE'LL MANAGE.
VROOM
OKAY, HOW ABOUT WE GET BACK TO LUNCH?
SIGH...
NO THANKS. I DON'T LIKE RICE.
IF YOU GO BRING ME SOME NAAN BREAD, I SUPPOSE I CAN STOMACH THE CURRY.
WHAT?

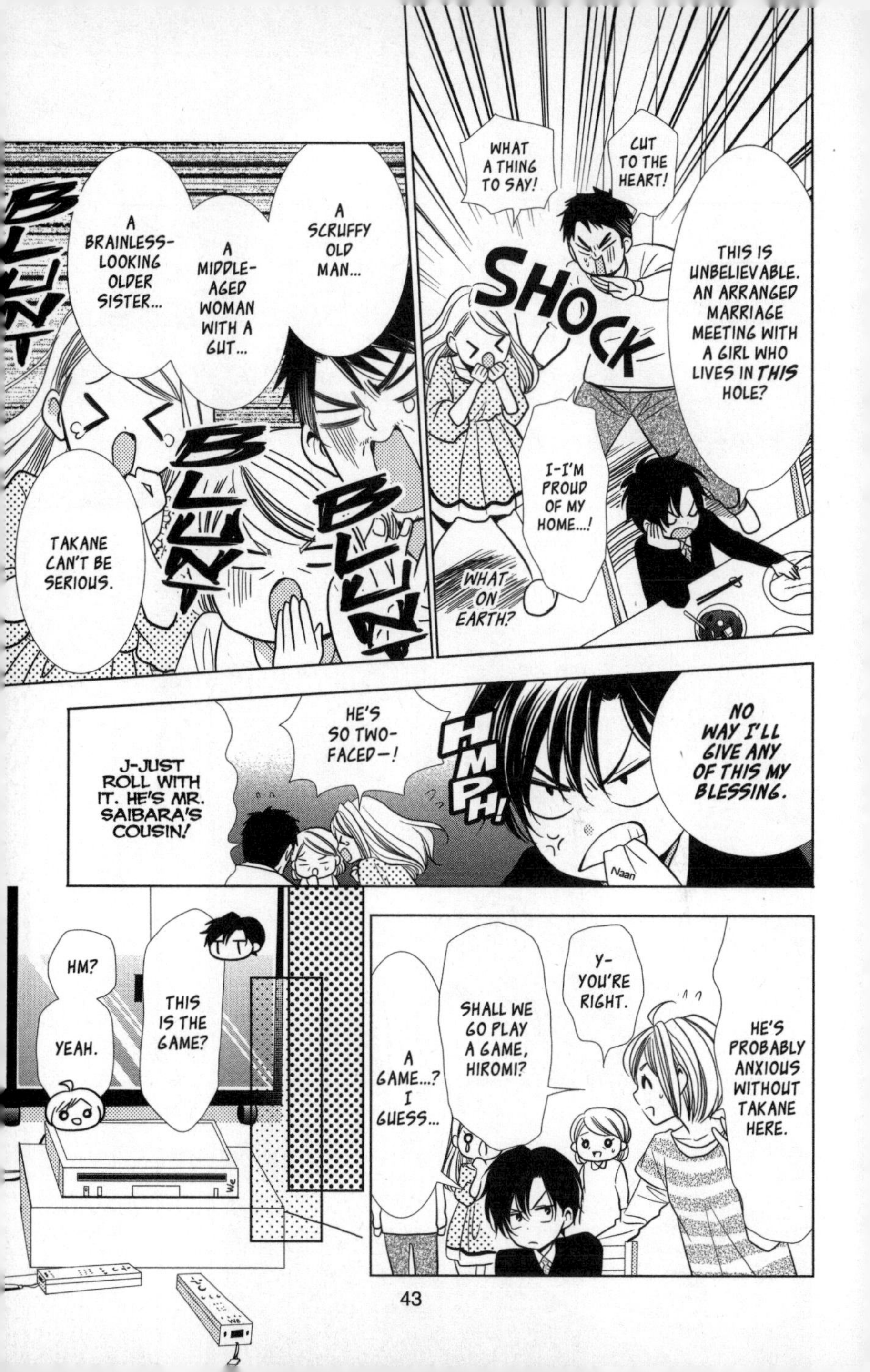
THIS IS UNBELIEVABLE. AN ARRANGED MARRIAGE MEETING WITH A GIRL WHO LIVES IN *THIS* HOLE?
SHOCK
CUT TO THE HEART!
WHAT A THING TO SAY!
I-I'M PROUD OF MY HOME...!
WHAT ON EARTH?
A SCRUFFY OLD MAN...
A MIDDLE-AGED WOMAN WITH A GUT...
A BRAINLESS-LOOKING OLDER SISTER...
BLUNT
BLUNT
BLUNT
TAKANE CAN'T BE SERIOUS.
NO WAY I'LL GIVE ANY OF THIS MY BLESSING.
HMPH!
HE'S SO TWO-FACED—!
J-JUST ROLL WITH IT. HE'S MR. SAIBARA'S COUSIN!
Naan
HE'S PROBABLY ANXIOUS WITHOUT TAKANE HERE.
Y-YOU'RE RIGHT.
SHALL WE GO PLAY A GAME, HIROMI?
A GAME...? I GUESS...
THIS IS THE GAME?
HM?
YEAH.

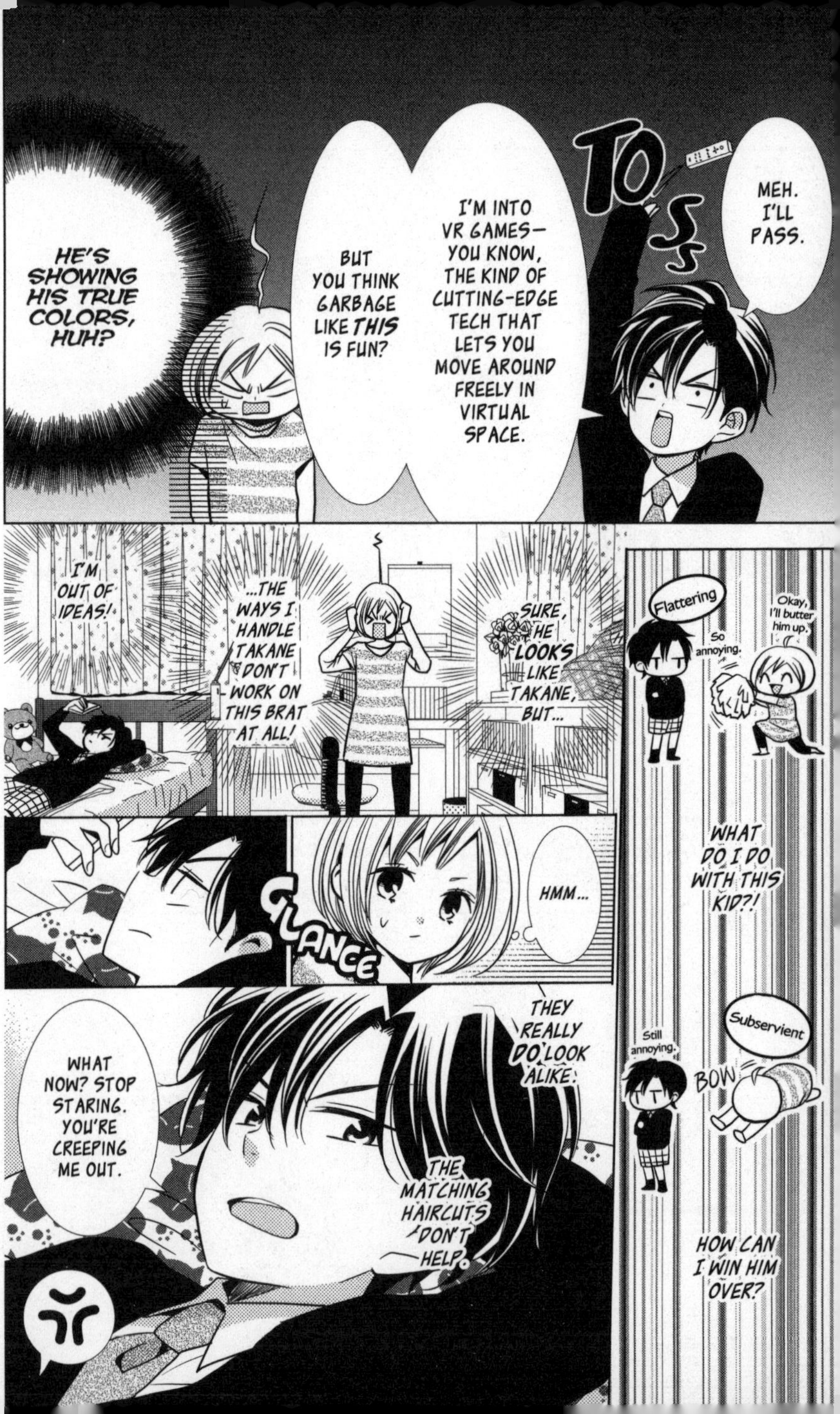
TOSS
MEH. I'LL PASS.
I'M INTO VR GAMES—YOU KNOW, THE KIND OF CUTTING-EDGE TECH THAT LETS YOU MOVE AROUND FREELY IN VIRTUAL SPACE.
BUT YOU THINK GARBAGE LIKE THIS IS FUN?
HE'S SHOWING HIS TRUE COLORS, HUH?
Flattering
Okay, I'll butter him up.
So annoying.
WHAT DO I DO WITH THIS KID?!
Subservient
Still annoying.
BOW
HOW CAN I WIN HIM OVER?
SURE, HE LOOKS LIKE TAKANE, BUT...
...THE WAYS I HANDLE TAKANE DON'T WORK ON THIS BRAT AT ALL!
I'M OUT OF IDEAS!
HMM...
GLANCE
THEY REALLY DO LOOK ALIKE.
THE MATCHING HAIRCUTS DON'T HELP.
WHAT NOW? STOP STARING. YOU'RE CREEPING ME OUT.

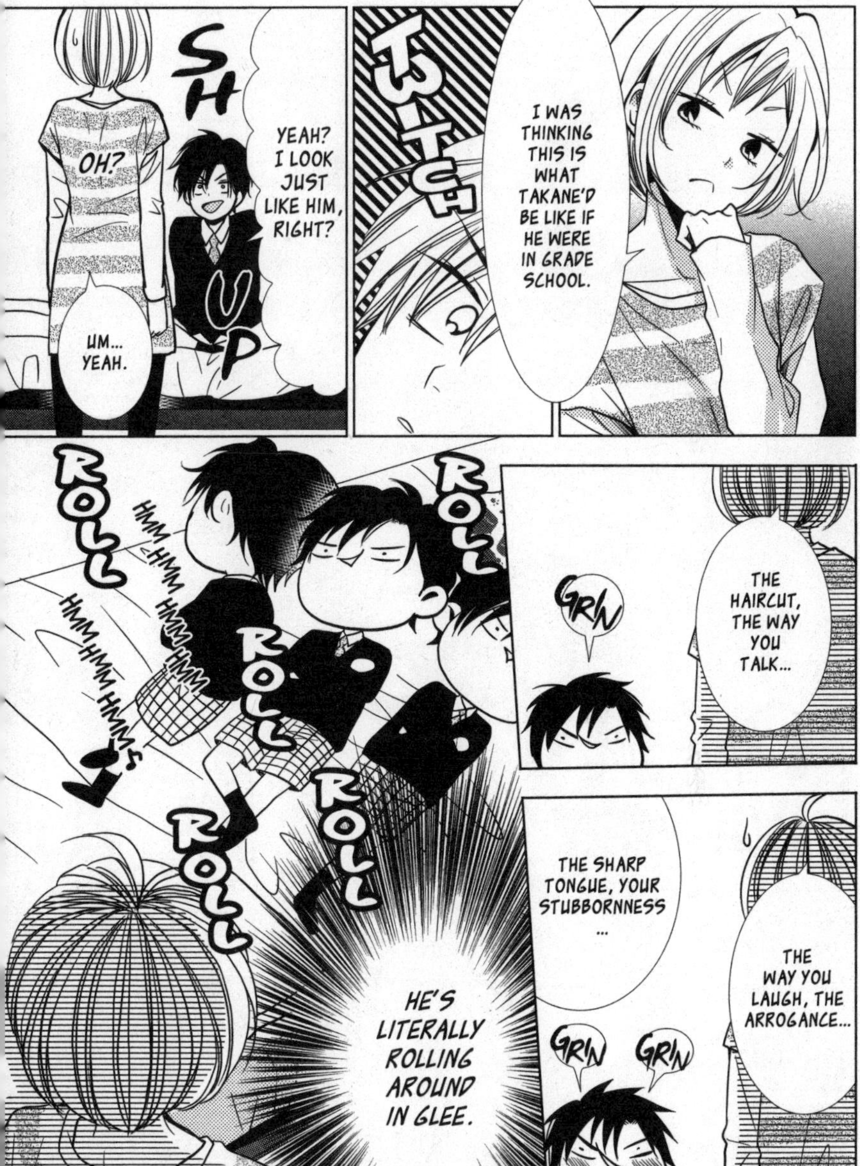
I WAS THINKING THIS IS WHAT TAKANE'D BE LIKE IF HE WERE IN GRADE SCHOOL.
TWITCH
SH
YEAH? I LOOK JUST LIKE HIM, RIGHT?
UP
OH?
UM... YEAH.
THE HAIRCUT, THE WAY YOU TALK...
GRIN
THE WAY YOU LAUGH, THE ARROGANCE...
THE SHARP TONGUE, YOUR STUBBORNNESS ...
GRIN
GRIN
ROLL
ROLL
HMM HMM HMM HMM
HMM HMM HMM HMM ♪
ROLL
ROLL
ROLL
HE'S LITERALLY ROLLING AROUND IN GLEE.

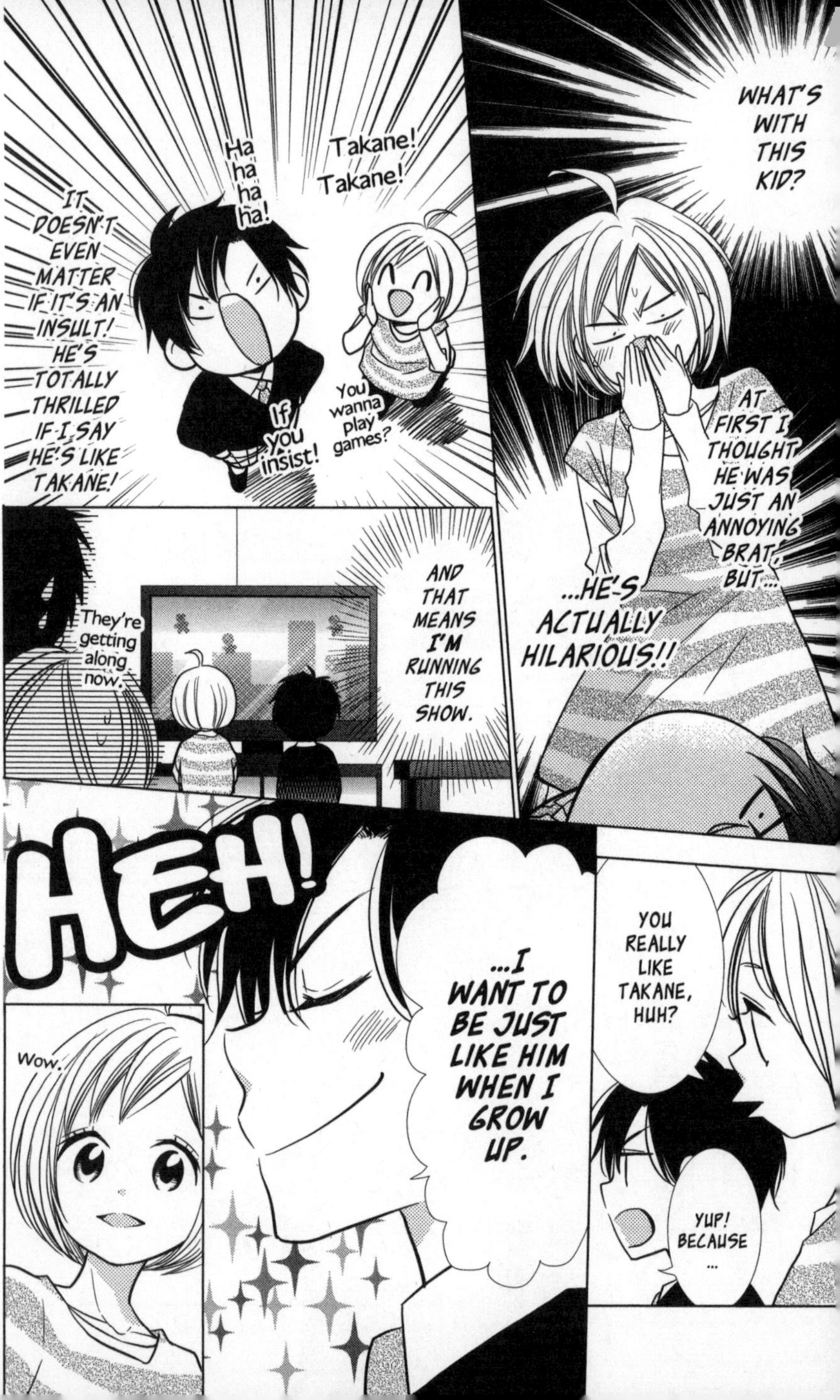
WHAT'S WITH THIS KID?
AT FIRST I THOUGHT HE WAS JUST AN ANNOYING BRAT, BUT...
...HE'S ACTUALLY HILARIOUS!!
Takane! Takane!
Ha ha ha ha!
You wanna play games?
If you insist!
IT DOESN'T EVEN MATTER IF IT'S AN INSULT! HE'S TOTALLY THRILLED IF I SAY HE'S LIKE TAKANE!
AND THAT MEANS I'M RUNNING THIS SHOW.
They're getting along now.
YOU REALLY LIKE TAKANE, HUH?
YUP! BECAUSE ...
...I WANT TO BE JUST LIKE HIM WHEN I GROW UP.
HEH!
Wow.

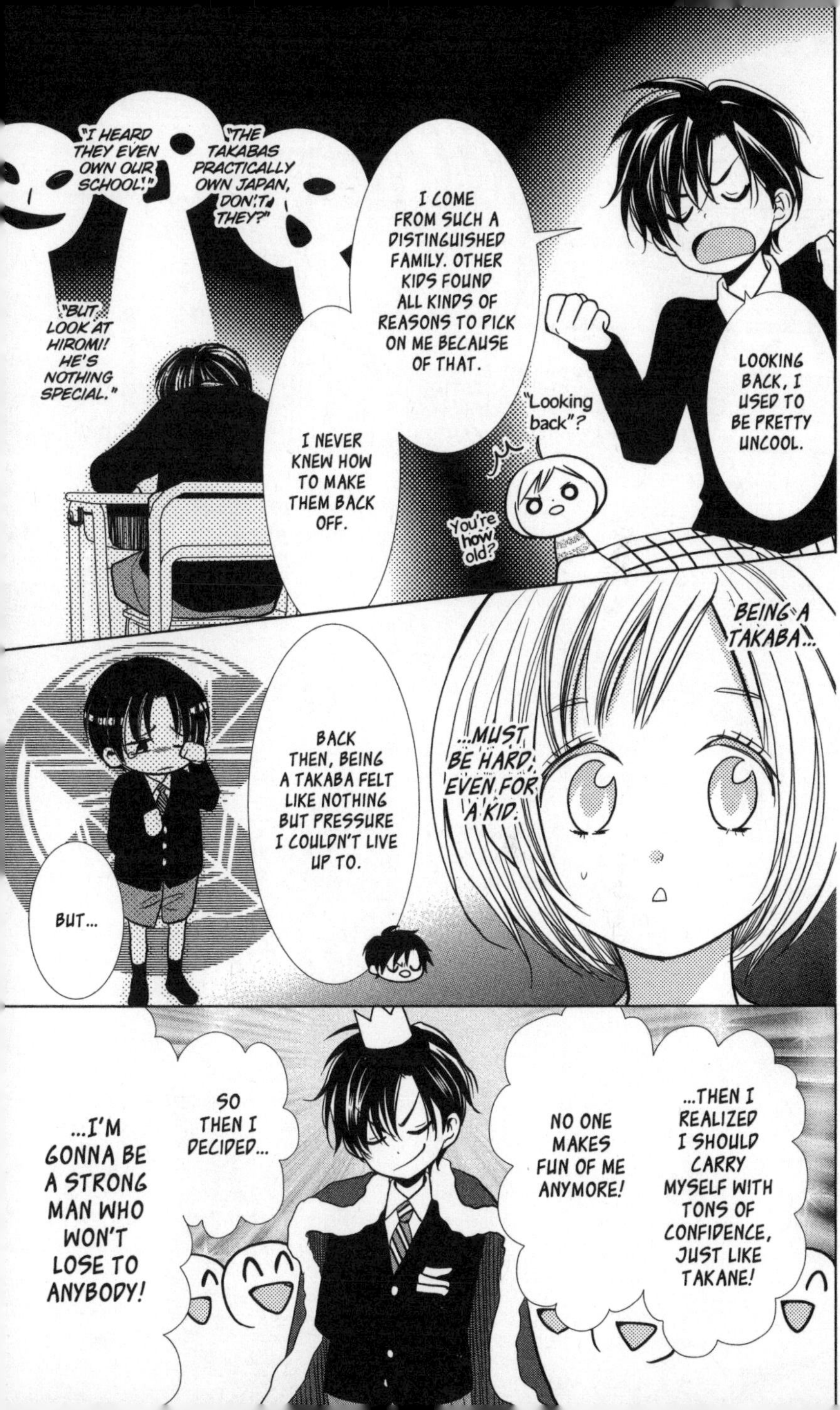
LOOKING BACK, I USED TO BE PRETTY UNCOOL.
"Looking back"?
You're how old?
I COME FROM SUCH A DISTINGUISHED FAMILY. OTHER KIDS FOUND ALL KINDS OF REASONS TO PICK ON ME BECAUSE OF THAT.
I NEVER KNEW HOW TO MAKE THEM BACK OFF.
"THE TAKABAS PRACTICALLY OWN JAPAN, DON'T THEY?"
"I HEARD THEY EVEN OWN OUR SCHOOL!"
"BUT LOOK AT HIROMI! HE'S NOTHING SPECIAL."
BEING A TAKABA...
...MUST BE HARD, EVEN FOR A KID.
BACK THEN, BEING A TAKABA FELT LIKE NOTHING BUT PRESSURE I COULDN'T LIVE UP TO.
BUT...
...THEN I REALIZED I SHOULD CARRY MYSELF WITH TONS OF CONFIDENCE, JUST LIKE TAKANE!
NO ONE MAKES FUN OF ME ANYMORE!
SO THEN I DECIDED...
...I'M GONNA BE A STRONG MAN WHO WON'T LOSE TO ANYBODY!

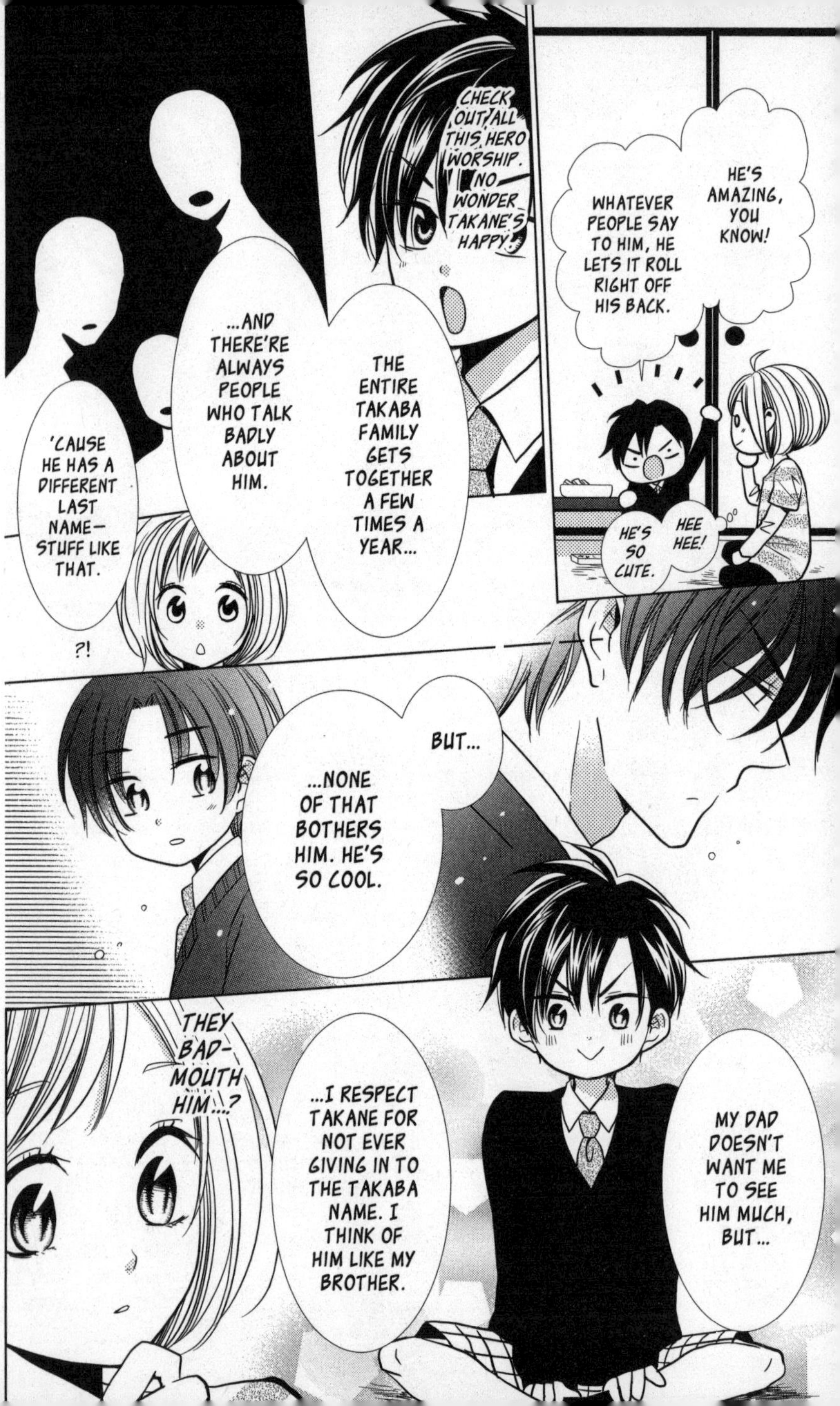
HE'S AMAZING, YOU KNOW!
WHATEVER PEOPLE SAY TO HIM, HE LETS IT ROLL RIGHT OFF HIS BACK.
HEE HEE!
HE'S SO CUTE.
CHECK OUT ALL THIS HERO WORSHIP. NO WONDER TAKANE'S HAPPY.
THE ENTIRE TAKABA FAMILY GETS TOGETHER A FEW TIMES A YEAR...
...AND THERE'RE ALWAYS PEOPLE WHO TALK BADLY ABOUT HIM.
'CAUSE HE HAS A DIFFERENT LAST NAME—STUFF LIKE THAT.
?!
BUT...
...NONE OF THAT BOTHERS HIM. HE'S SO COOL.
MY DAD DOESN'T WANT ME TO SEE HIM MUCH, BUT...
...I RESPECT TAKANE FOR NOT EVER GIVING IN TO THE TAKABA NAME. I THINK OF HIM LIKE MY BROTHER.
THEY BAD-MOUTH HIM...?

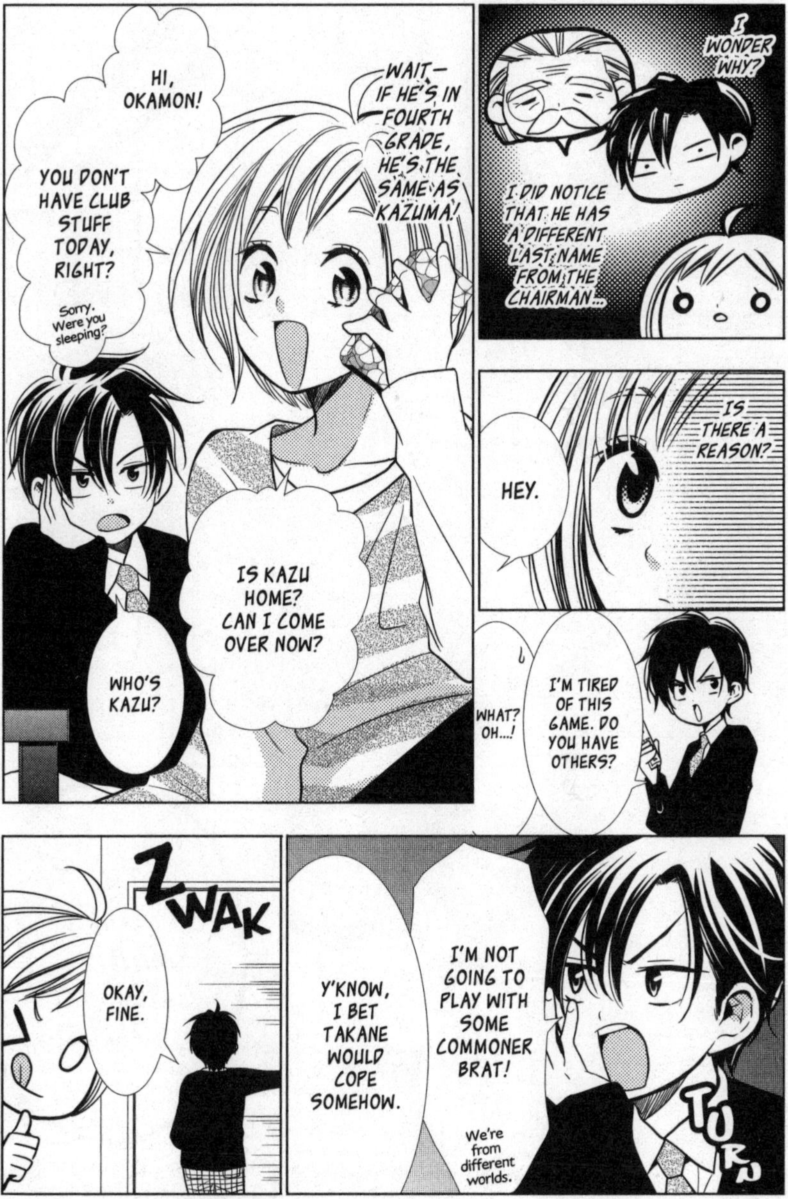
I WONDER WHY?
I DID NOTICE THAT HE HAS A DIFFERENT LAST NAME FROM THE CHAIRMAN...
IS THERE A REASON?
HEY.
I'M TIRED OF THIS GAME. DO YOU HAVE OTHERS?
WHAT? OH...!
WAIT—IF HE'S IN FOURTH GRADE, HE'S THE SAME AS KAZUMA!
HI, OKAMON!
YOU DON'T HAVE CLUB STUFF TODAY, RIGHT?
Sorry. Were you sleeping?
IS KAZU HOME? CAN I COME OVER NOW?
WHO'S KAZU?
I'M NOT GOING TO PLAY WITH SOME COMMONER BRAT!
TURN
Y'KNOW, I BET TAKANE WOULD COPE SOMEHOW.
We're from different worlds.
ZWAK
OKAY, FINE.

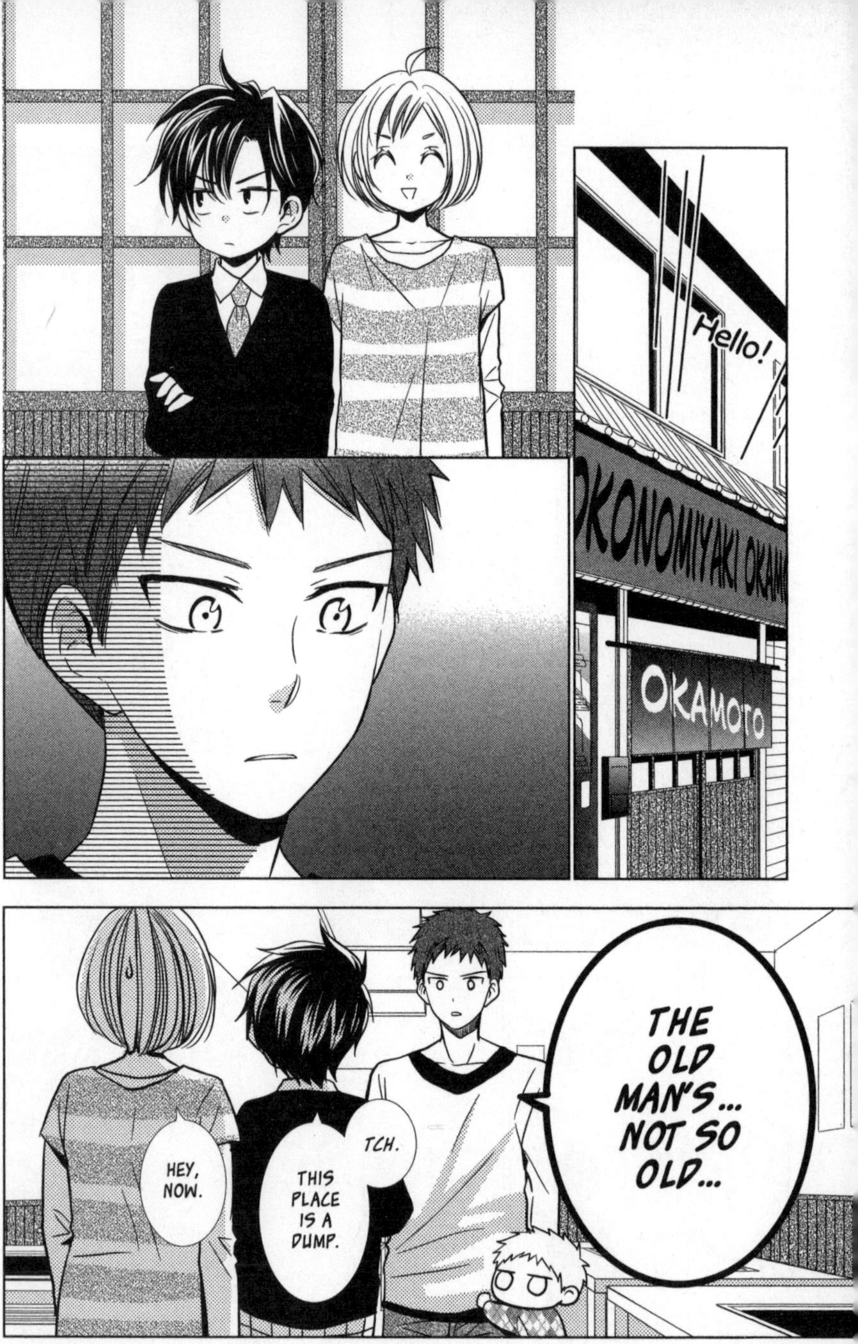
Hello!
OKONOMIYAKI
OKAMOTO
THE OLD MAN'S... NOT SO OLD...
TCH.
THIS PLACE IS A DUMP.
HEY, NOW.

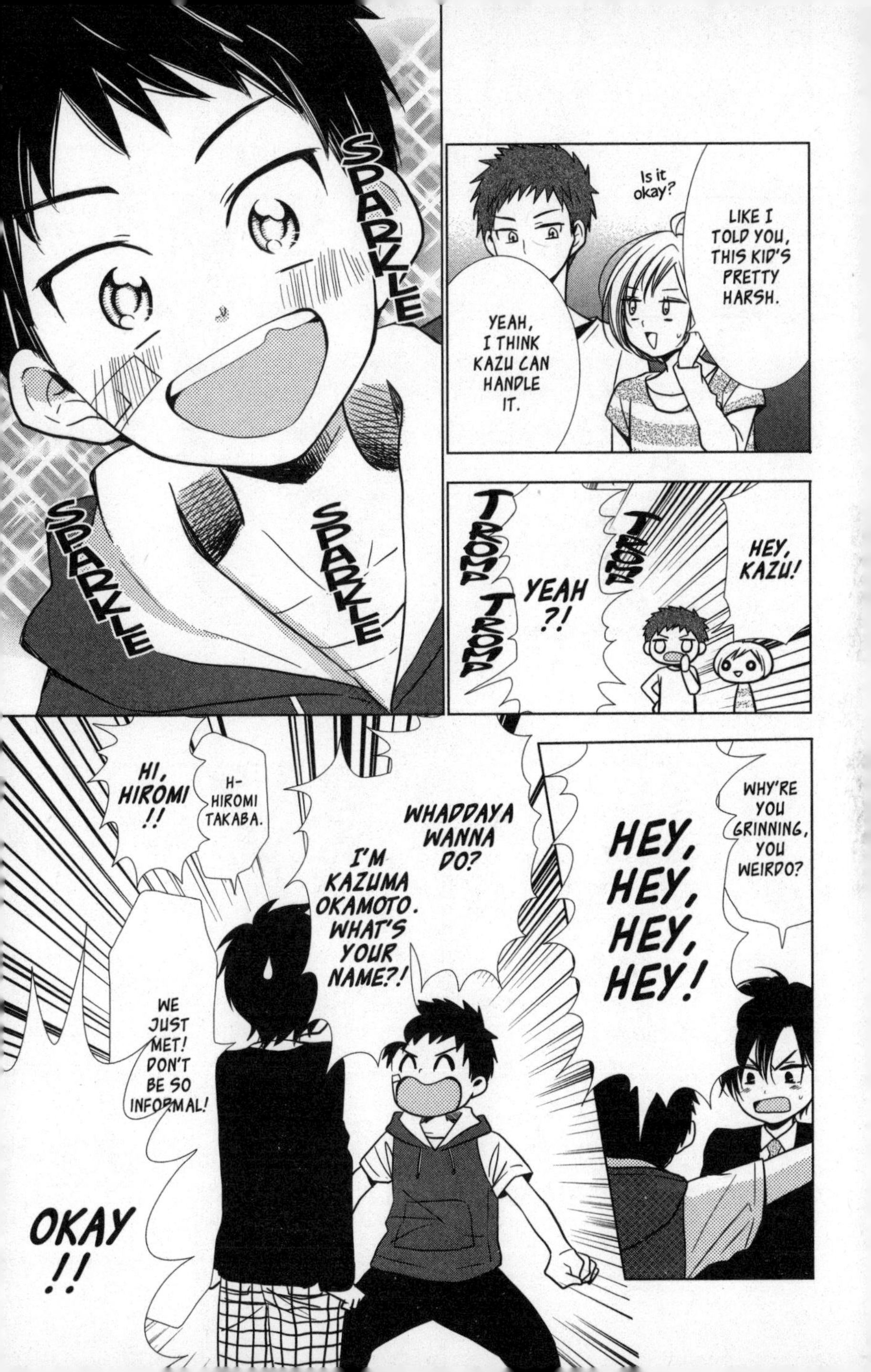

LIKE I TOLD YOU, THIS KID'S PRETTY HARSH.
Is it okay?
YEAH, I THINK KAZU CAN HANDLE IT.
HEY, KAZU!
TROMP
YEAH?!
TROMP TROMP
SPARKLE
SPARKLE
SPARKLE
WHY'RE YOU GRINNING, YOU WEIRDO?
HEY, HEY, HEY, HEY!
WHADDAYA WANNA DO?
I'M KAZUMA OKAMOTO. WHAT'S YOUR NAME?!
H-HIROMI TAKABA.
HI, HIROMI!!
WE JUST MET! DON'T BE SO INFORMAL!
OKAY!!

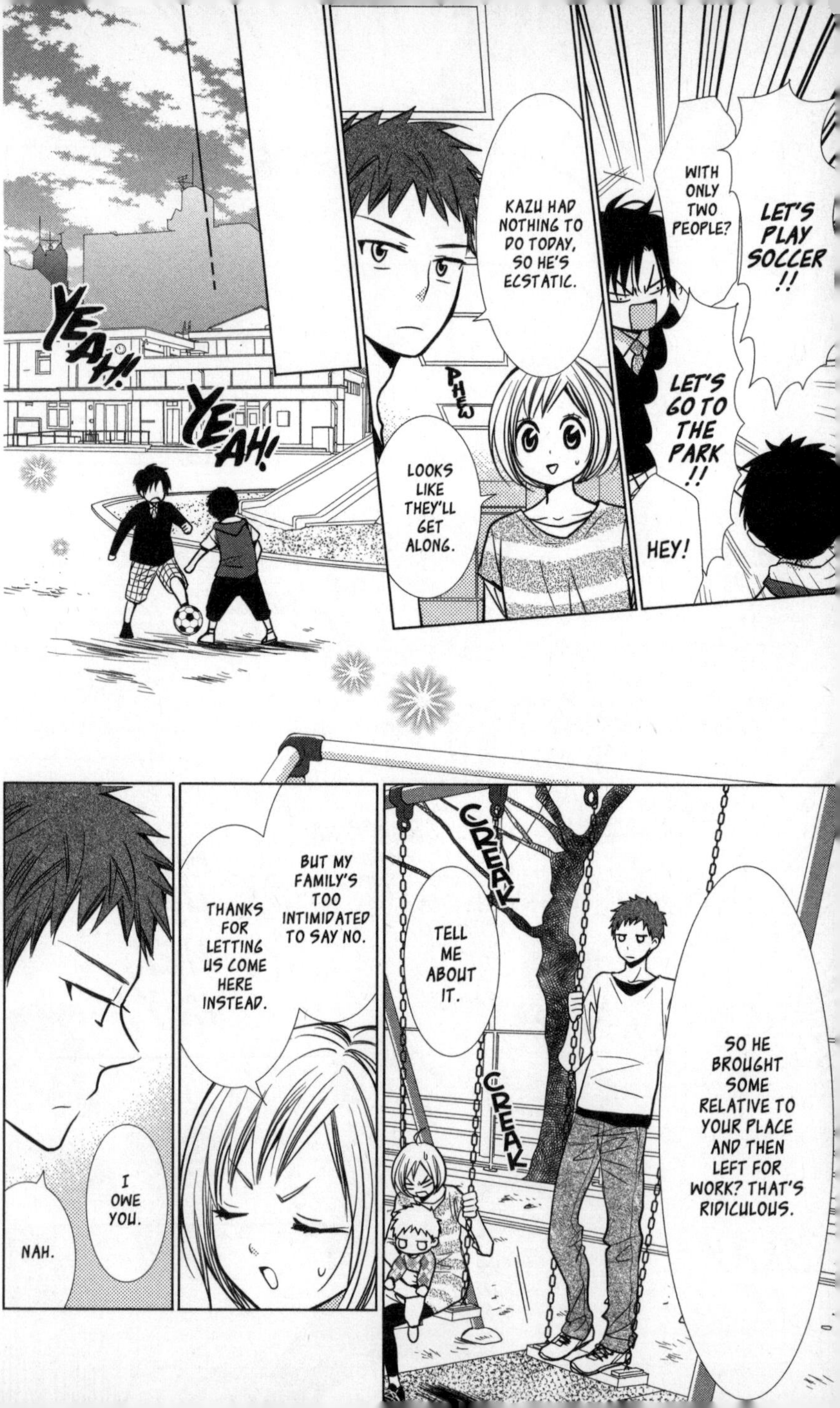
LET'S PLAY SOCCER!!
WITH ONLY TWO PEOPLE?
LET'S GO TO THE PARK!!
HEY!
KAZU HAD NOTHING TO DO TODAY, SO HE'S ECSTATIC.
PHEW
LOOKS LIKE THEY'LL GET ALONG.
YEAH!
YEAH!
SO HE BROUGHT SOME RELATIVE TO YOUR PLACE AND THEN LEFT FOR WORK? THAT'S RIDICULOUS.
CREAK
TELL ME ABOUT IT.
CREAK
BUT MY FAMILY'S TOO INTIMIDATED TO SAY NO.
THANKS FOR LETTING US COME HERE INSTEAD.
I OWE YOU.
NAH.

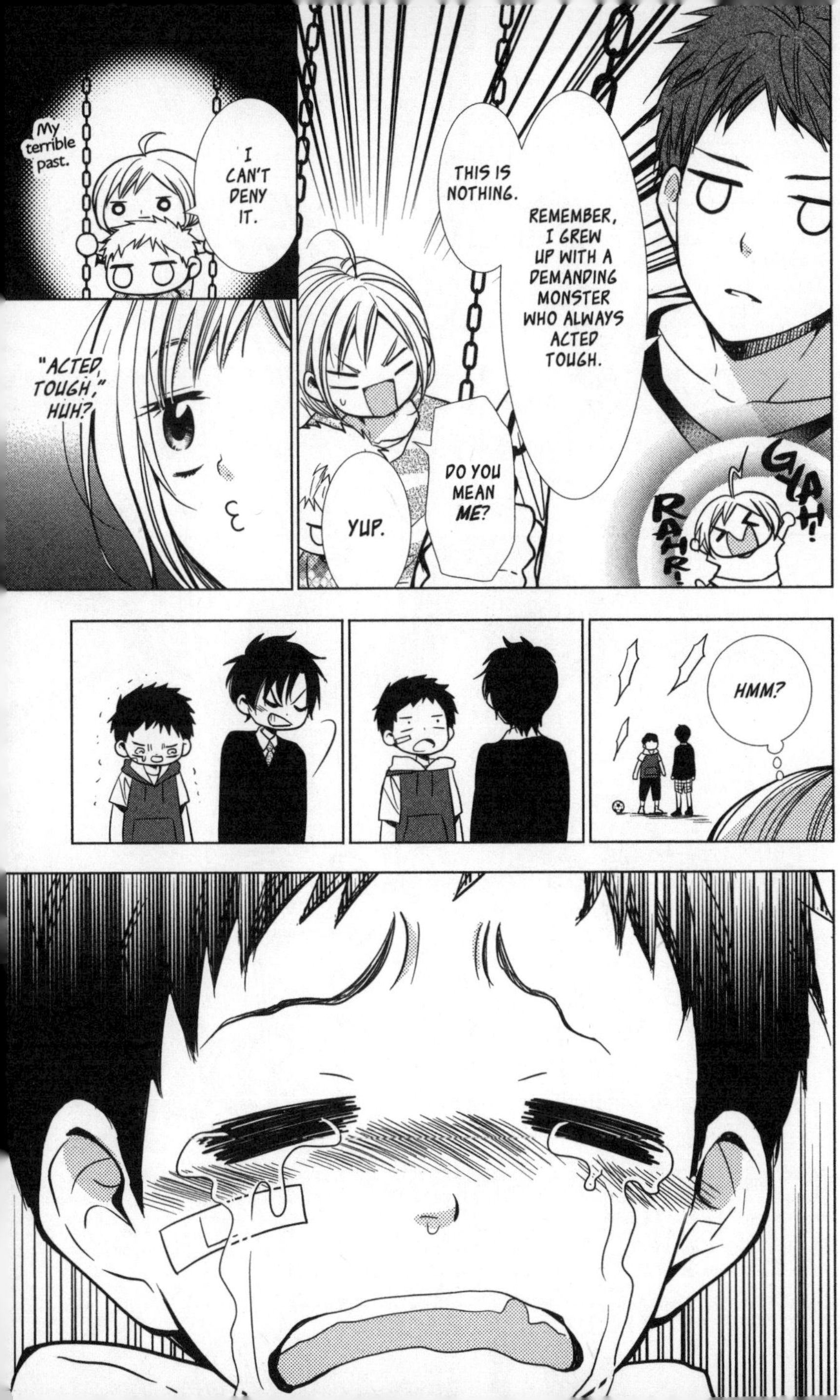
THIS IS NOTHING.
REMEMBER, I GREW UP WITH A DEMANDING MONSTER WHO ALWAYS ACTED TOUGH.
GAAH!
RAHR!
DO YOU MEAN ME?
YUP.
I CAN'T DENY IT.
My terrible past.
"ACTED TOUGH," HUH?
HMM?

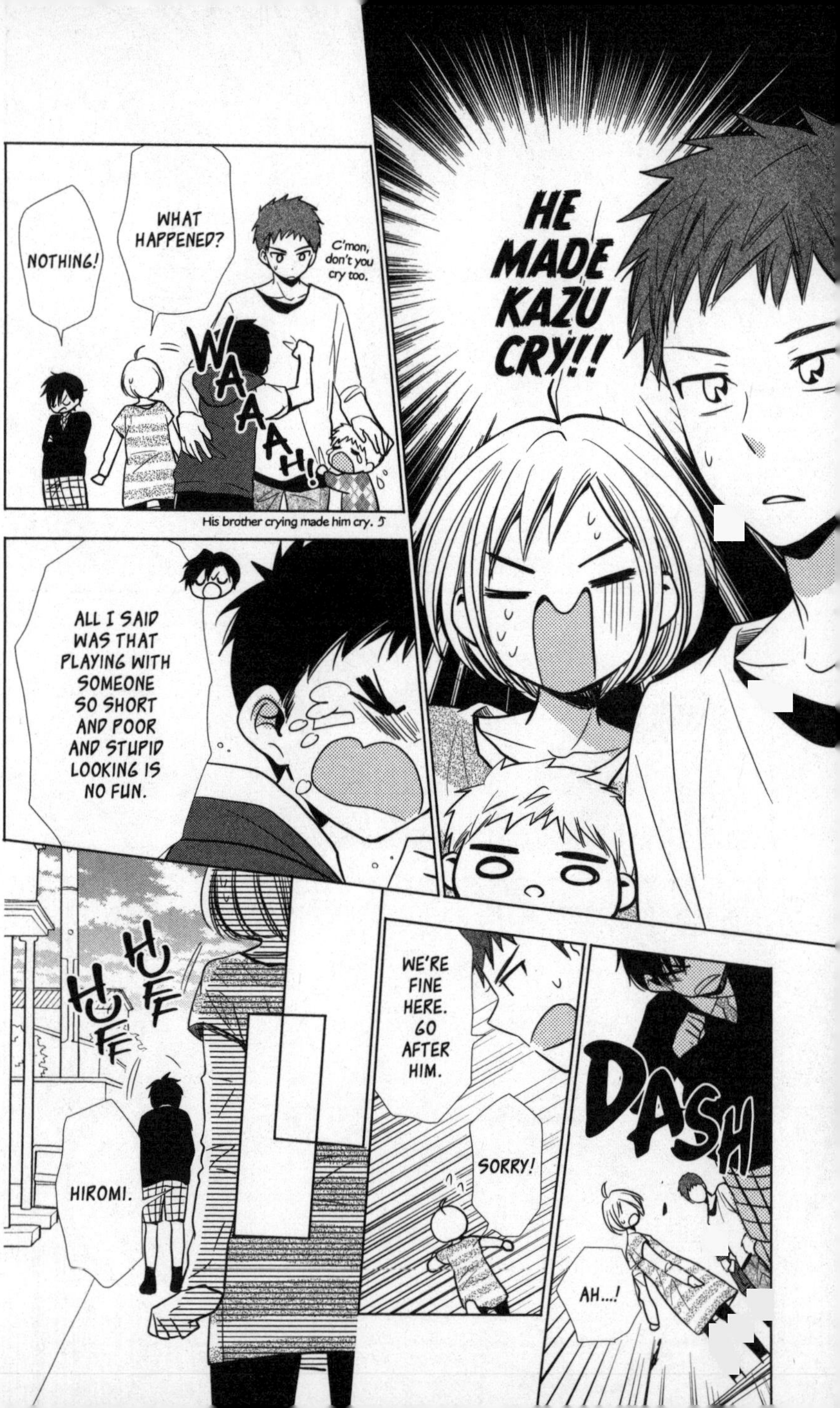
HE MADE KAZU CRY!!
C'mon, don't you cry too.
WHAT HAPPENED?
NOTHING!
WAAAAH!
His brother crying made him cry.
ALL I SAID WAS THAT PLAYING WITH SOMEONE SO SHORT AND POOR AND STUPID LOOKING IS NO FUN.
DASH
AH...!
WE'RE FINE HERE. GO AFTER HIM.
SORRY!
HUFF HUFF
HIROMI.

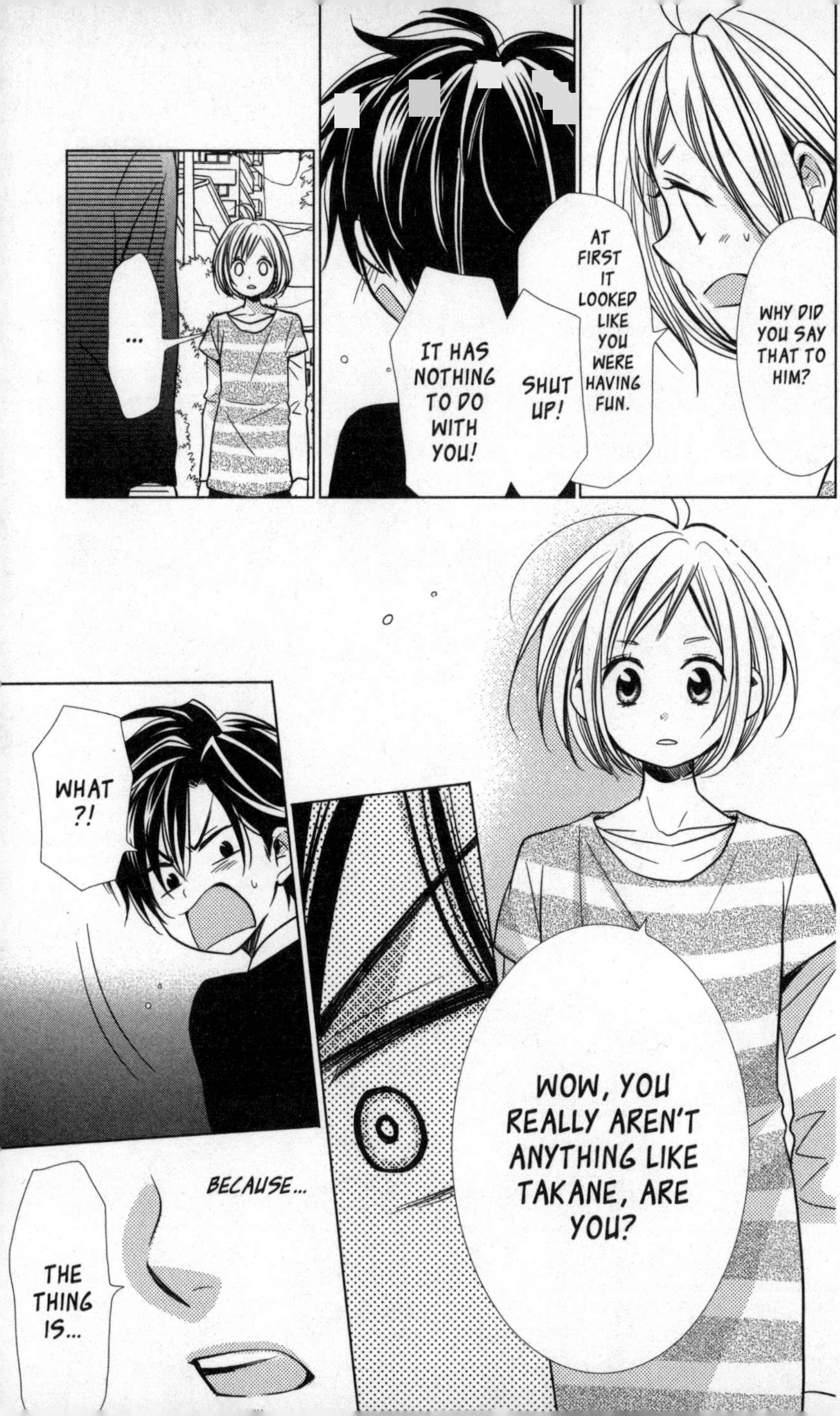
WHY DID YOU SAY THAT TO HIM?
AT FIRST IT LOOKED LIKE YOU WERE HAVING FUN.
SHUT UP!
IT HAS NOTHING TO DO WITH YOU!
...
WOW, YOU REALLY AREN'T ANYTHING LIKE TAKANE, ARE YOU?
WHAT ?!
BECAUSE...
THE THING IS...

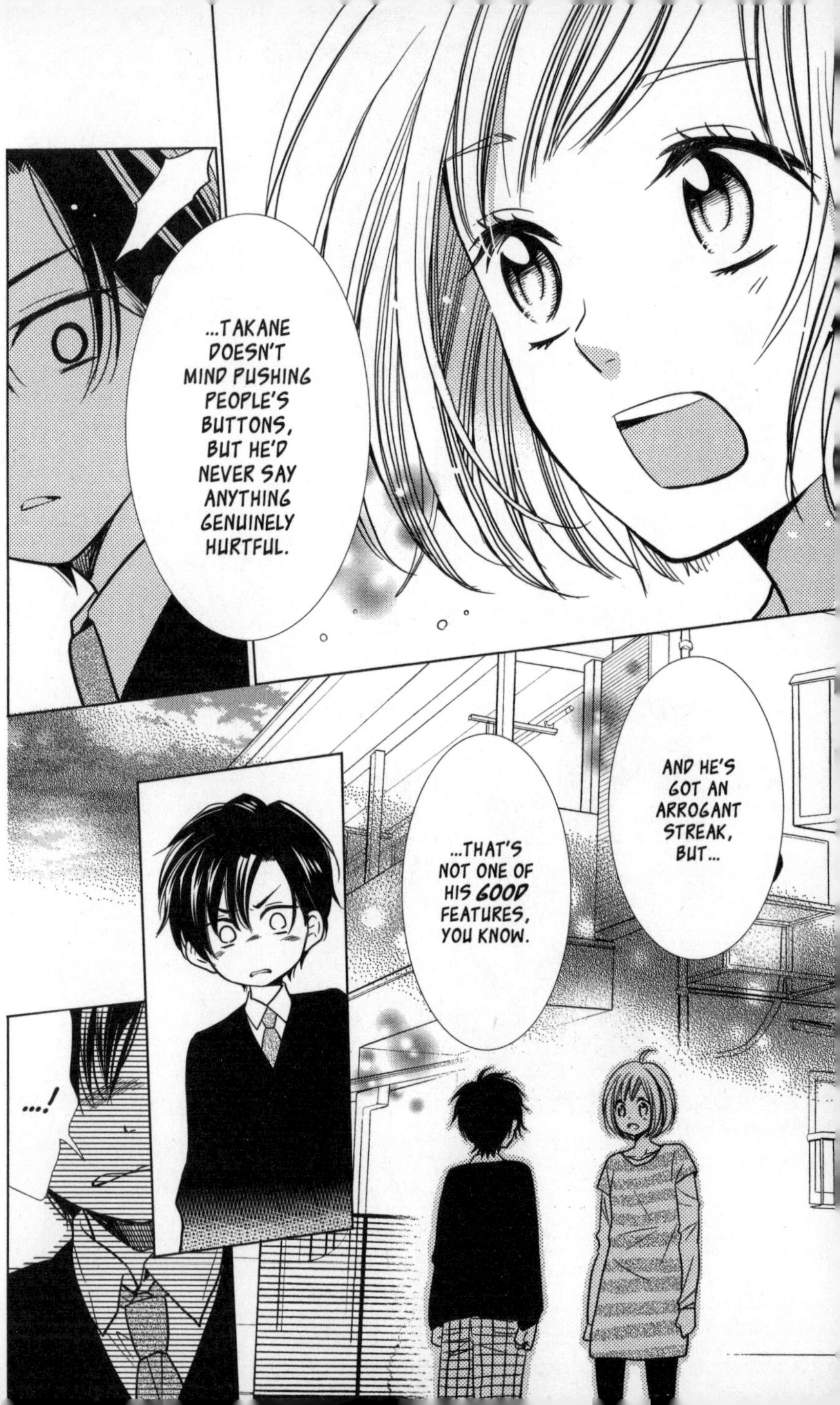
...TAKANE DOESN'T MIND PUSHING PEOPLE'S BUTTONS, BUT HE'D NEVER SAY ANYTHING GENUINELY HURTFUL.
AND HE'S GOT AN ARROGANT STREAK, BUT...
...THAT'S NOT ONE OF HIS *GOOD* FEATURES, YOU KNOW.
...!

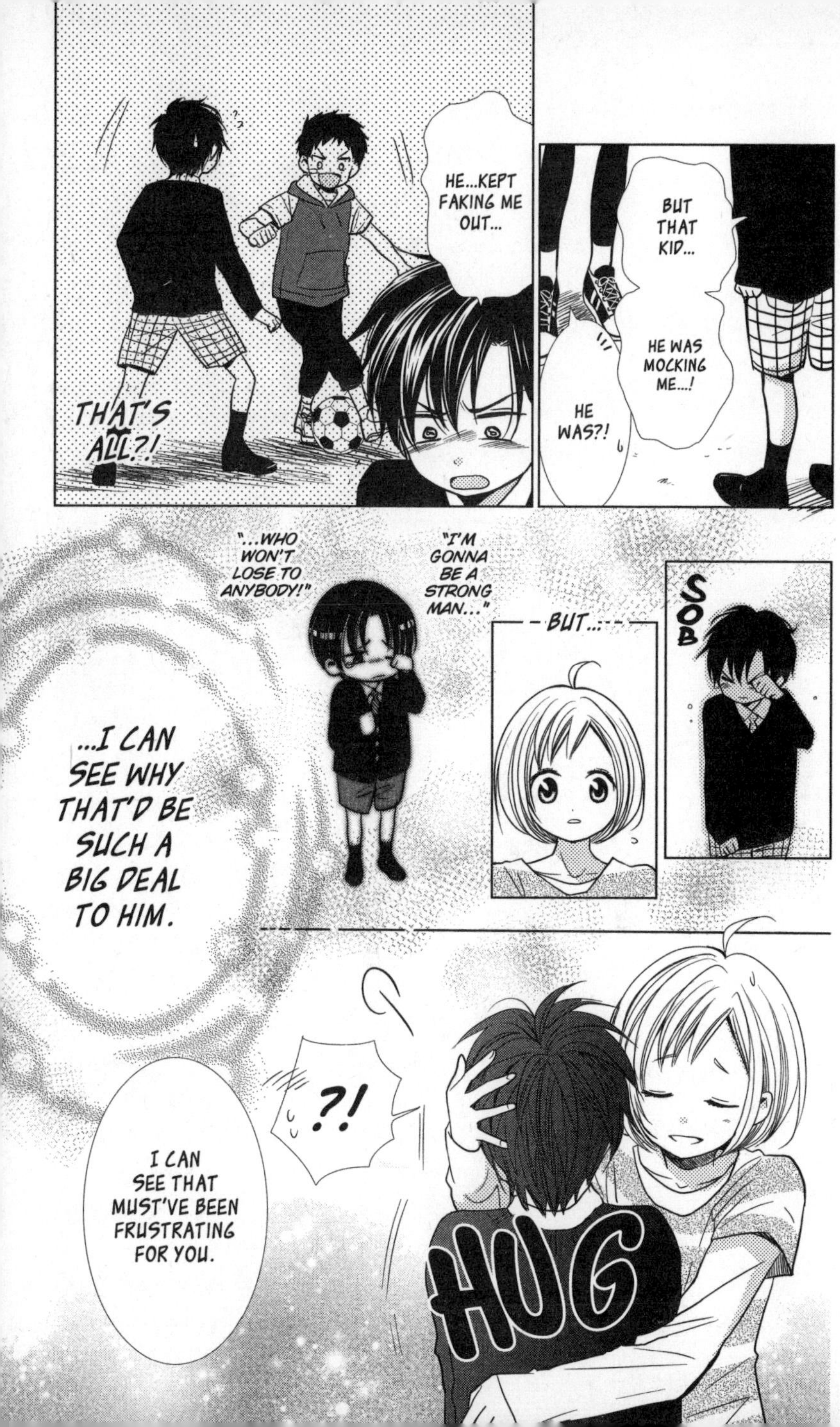
BUT THAT KID...
HE WAS MOCKING ME...!
HE WAS?!
HE...KEPT FAKING ME OUT...
THAT'S ALL?!
SOB
--BUT...:--
"I'M GONNA BE A STRONG MAN..."
"...WHO WON'T LOSE TO ANYBODY!"
...I CAN SEE WHY THAT'D BE SUCH A BIG DEAL TO HIM.
?!
HUG
I CAN SEE THAT MUST'VE BEEN FRUSTRATING FOR YOU.

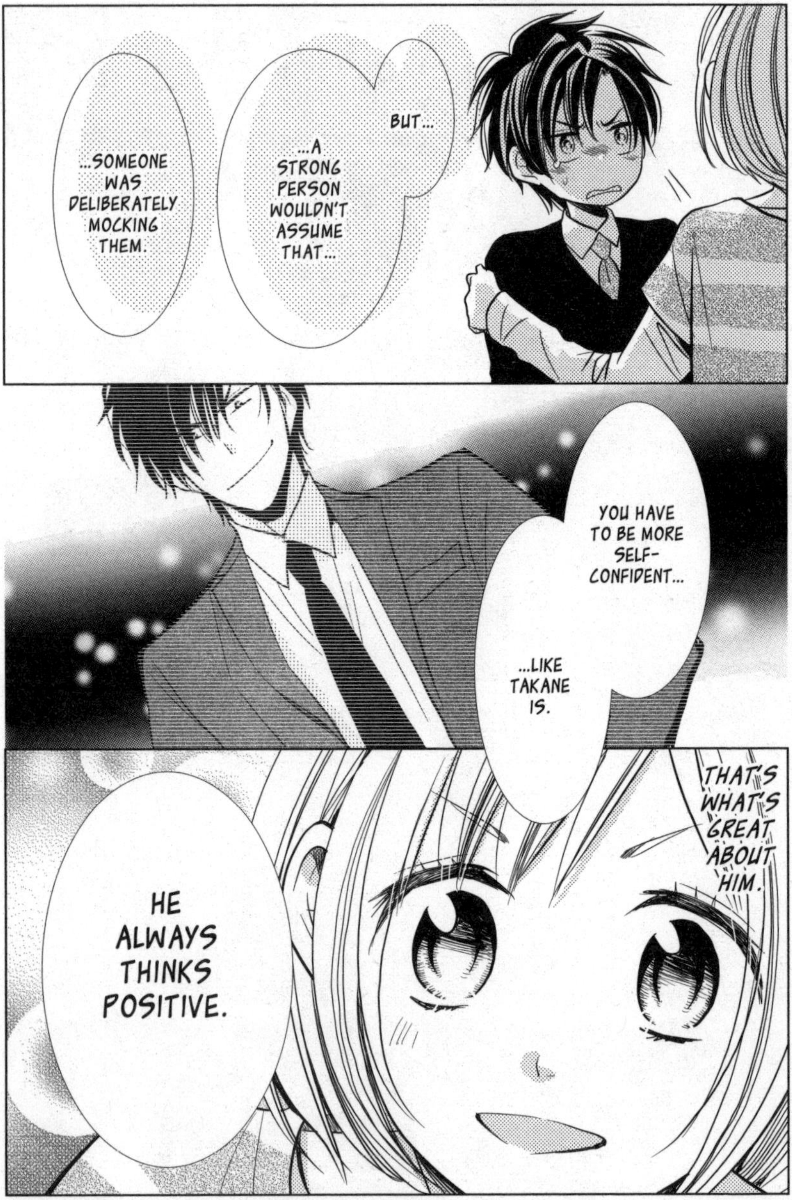
BUT...
...A STRONG PERSON WOULDN'T ASSUME THAT...
...SOMEONE WAS DELIBERATELY MOCKING THEM.
YOU HAVE TO BE MORE SELF-CONFIDENT...
...LIKE TAKANE IS.
THAT'S WHAT'S GREAT ABOUT HIM.
HE ALWAYS THINKS POSITIVE.

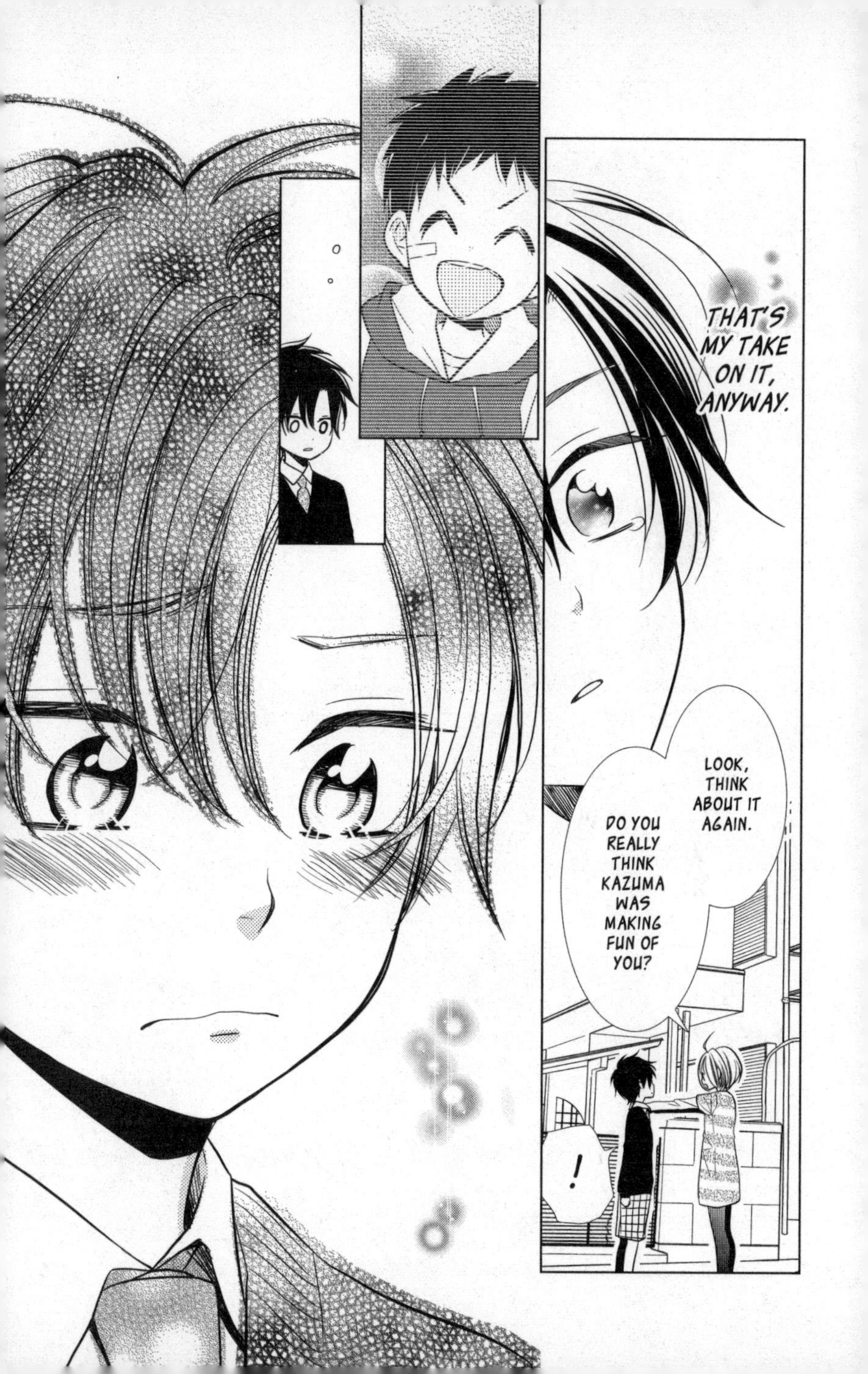
THAT'S MY TAKE ON IT, ANYWAY.
LOOK, THINK ABOUT IT AGAIN.
DO YOU REALLY THINK KAZUMA WAS MAKING FUN OF YOU?
!

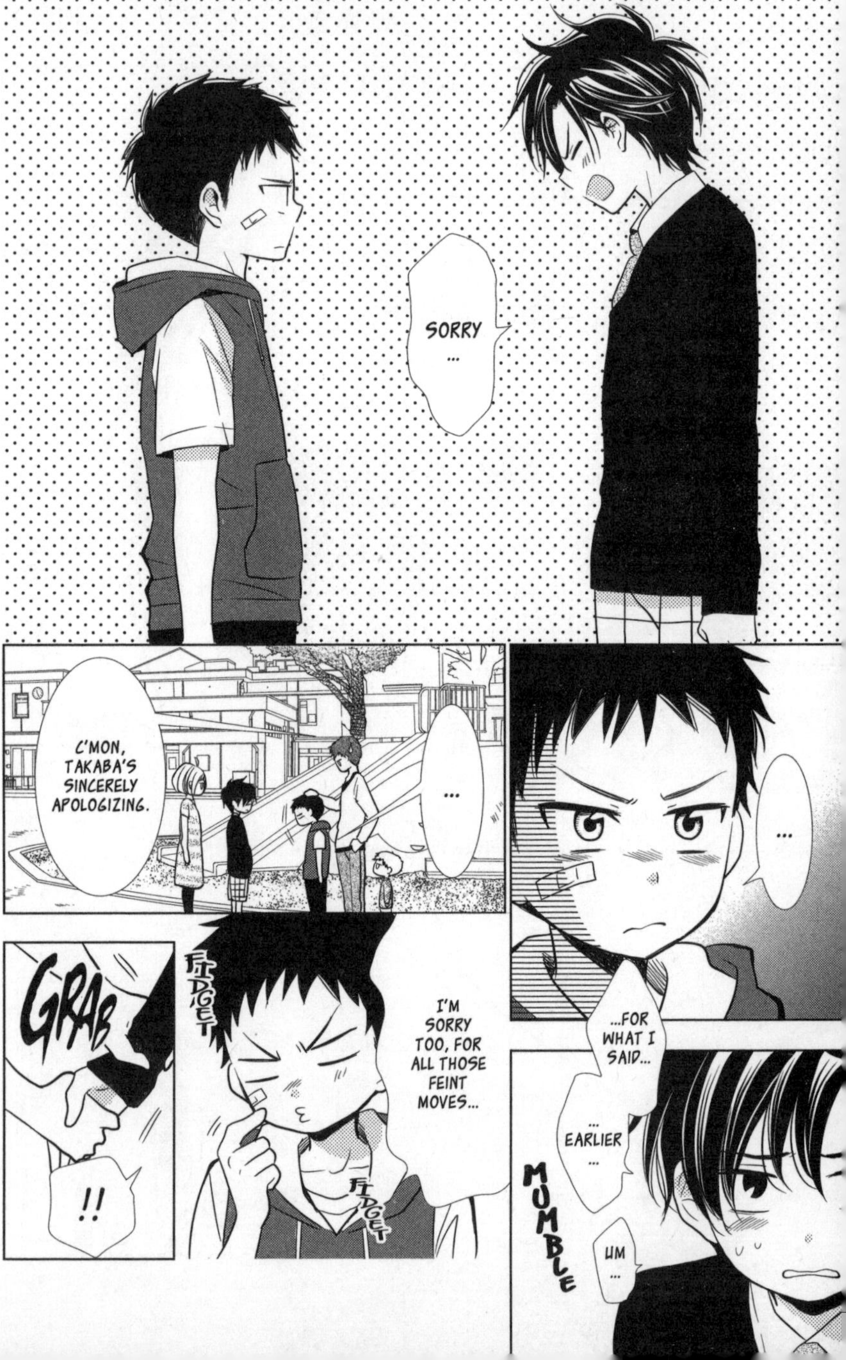
SORRY ...
...
C'MON, TAKABA'S SINCERELY APOLOGIZING.
...
...FOR WHAT I SAID...
... EARLIER ...
MUMBLE
UM ...
FIDGET
I'M SORRY TOO, FOR ALL THOSE FEINT MOVES...
FIDGET
GRAB
!!

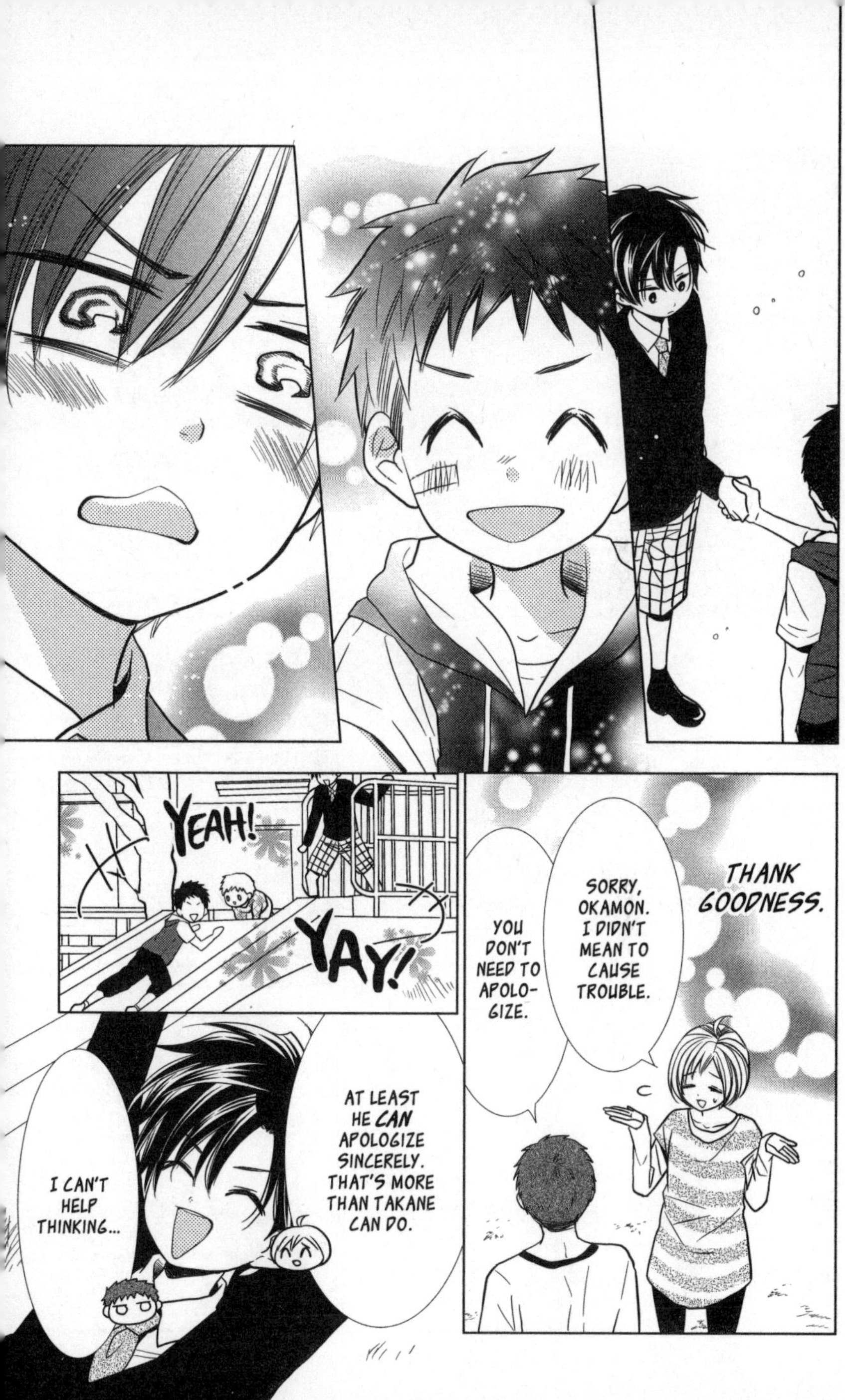
THANK GOODNESS.
SORRY, OKAMON. I DIDN'T MEAN TO CAUSE TROUBLE.
YOU DON'T NEED TO APOLO-GIZE.
YEAH!
YAY!
AT LEAST HE *CAN* APOLOGIZE SINCERELY. THAT'S MORE THAN TAKANE CAN DO.
I CAN'T HELP THINKING...

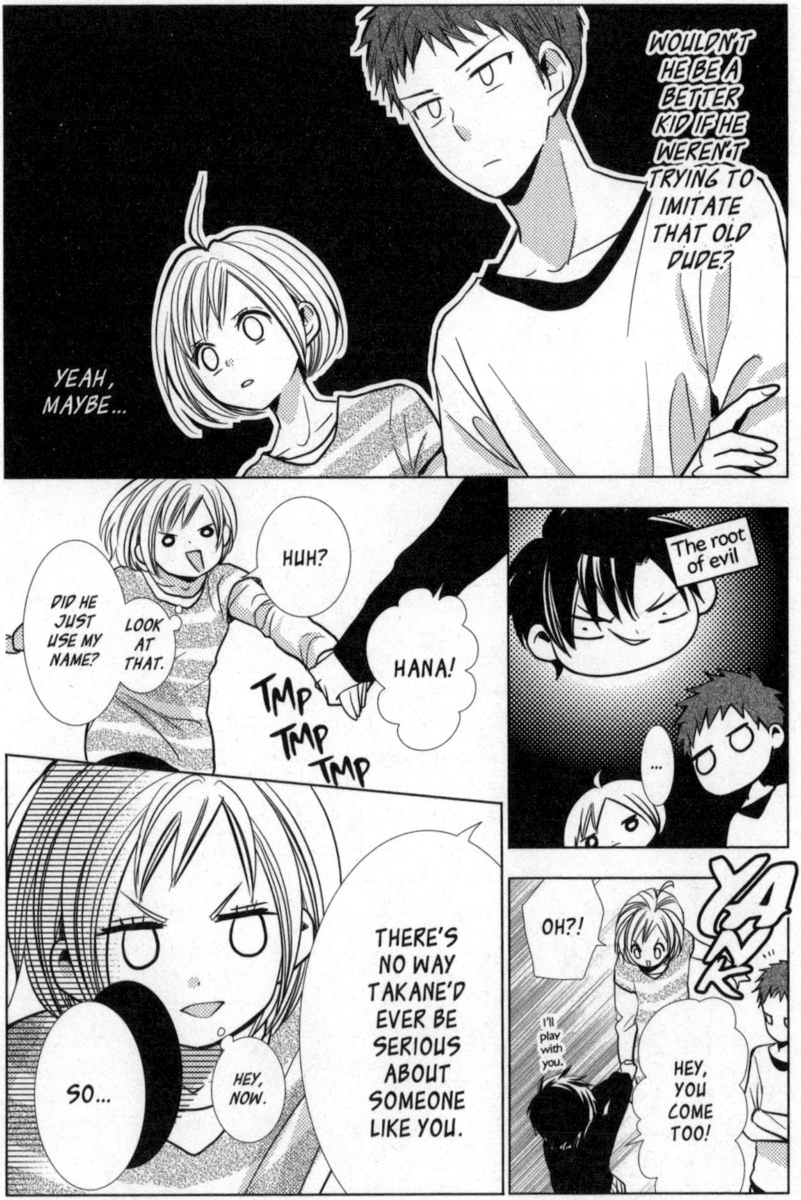
WOULDN'T HE BE A BETTER KID IF HE WEREN'T TRYING TO IMITATE THAT OLD DUDE?
YEAH, MAYBE...
HANA!
TMP TMP TMP
HUH?
LOOK AT THAT.
DID HE JUST USE MY NAME?
The root of evil
...
YANK
OH?!
HEY, YOU COME TOO!
I'll play with you.
THERE'S NO WAY TAKANE'D EVER BE SERIOUS ABOUT SOMEONE LIKE YOU.
HEY, NOW.
SO...

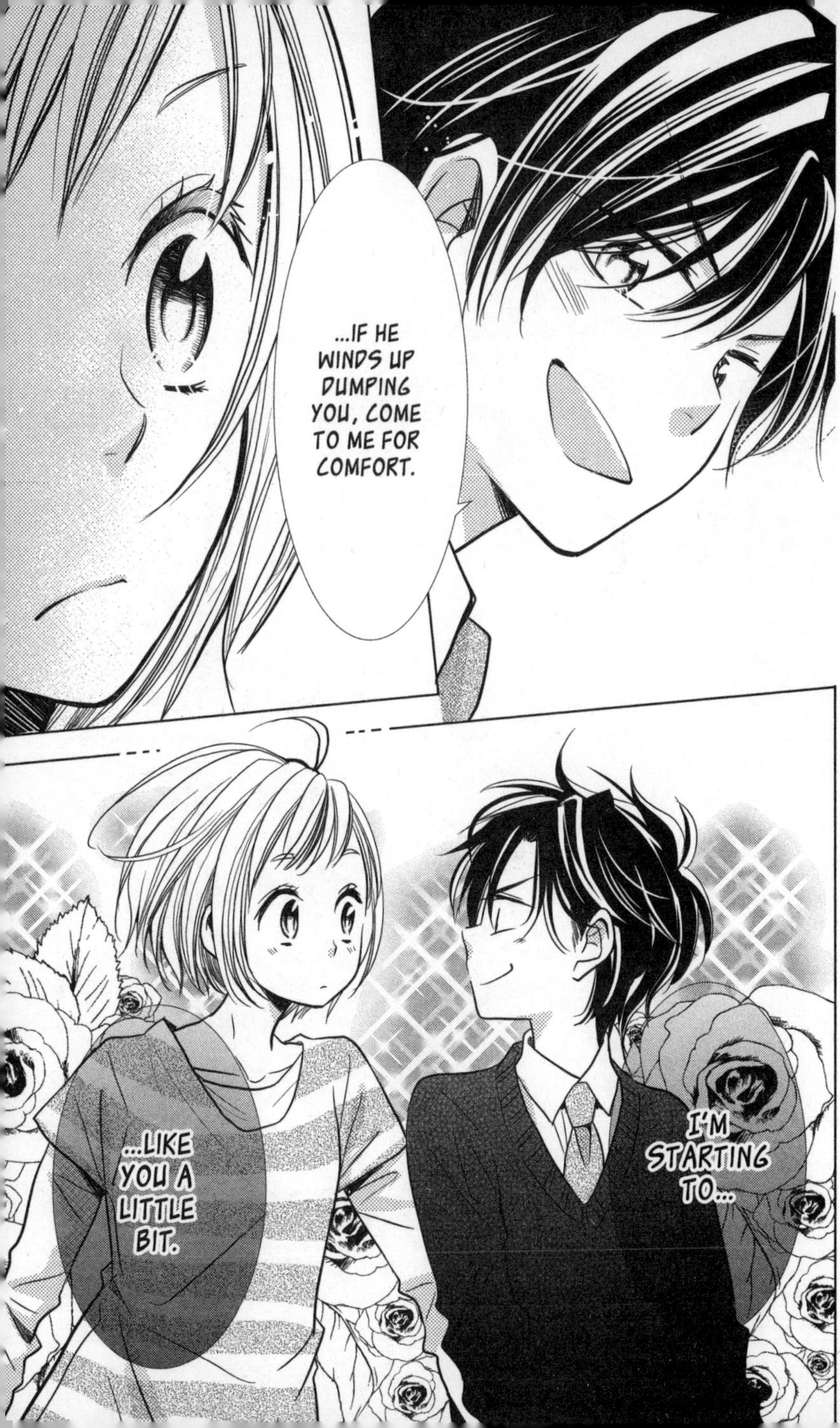
...IF HE WINDS UP DUMPING YOU, COME TO ME FOR COMFORT.
I'M STARTING TO...
...LIKE YOU A LITTLE BIT.

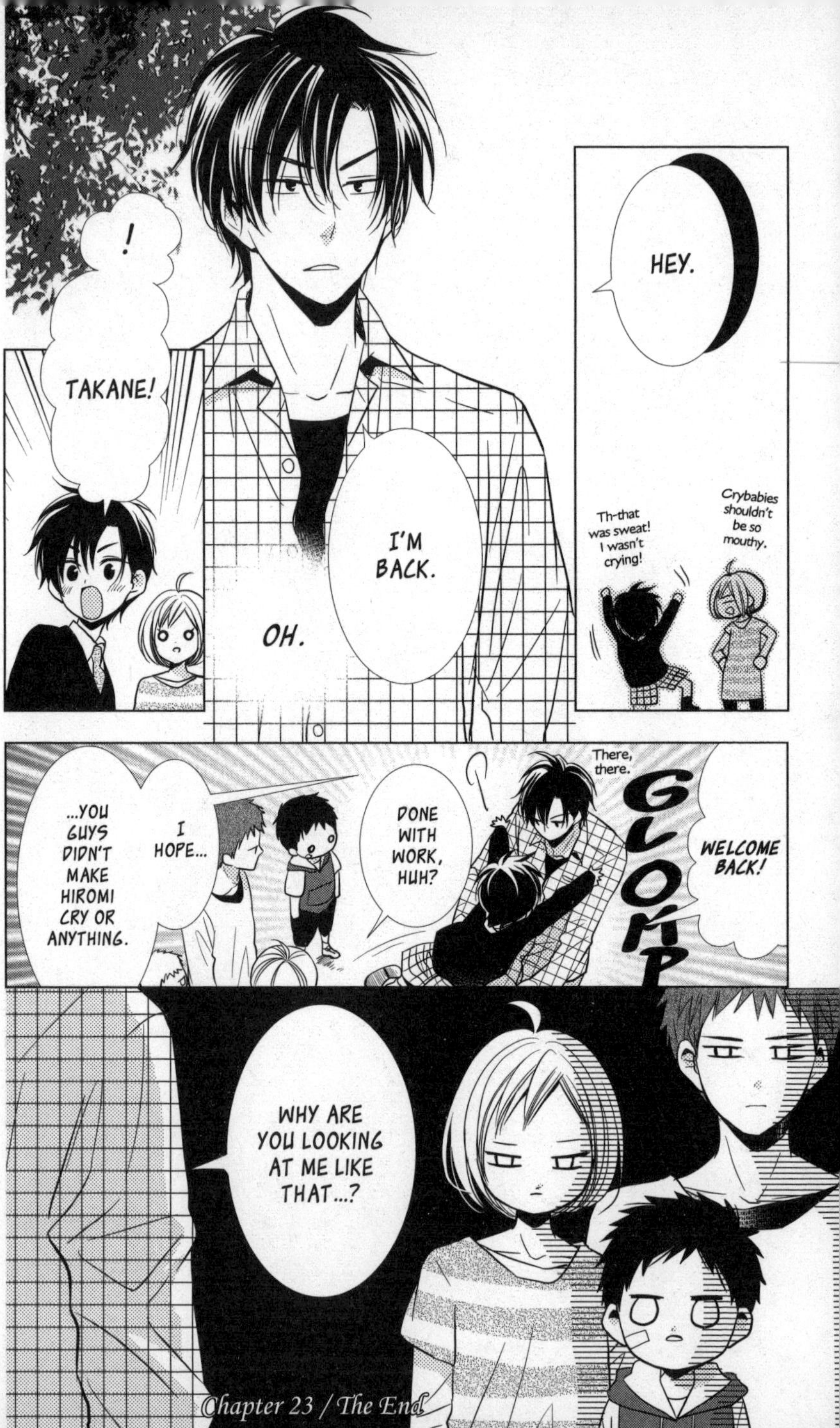
HEY.
Crybabies shouldn't be so mouthy.
Th-that was sweat! I wasn't crying!
I'M BACK.
OH.
!
TAKANE!
WELCOME BACK!
GLOMP
There, there.
DONE WITH WORK, HUH?
I HOPE...
...YOU GUYS DIDN'T MAKE HIROMI CRY OR ANYTHING.
WHY ARE YOU LOOKING AT ME LIKE THAT...?

Chapter 23 / The End

Chapter 24

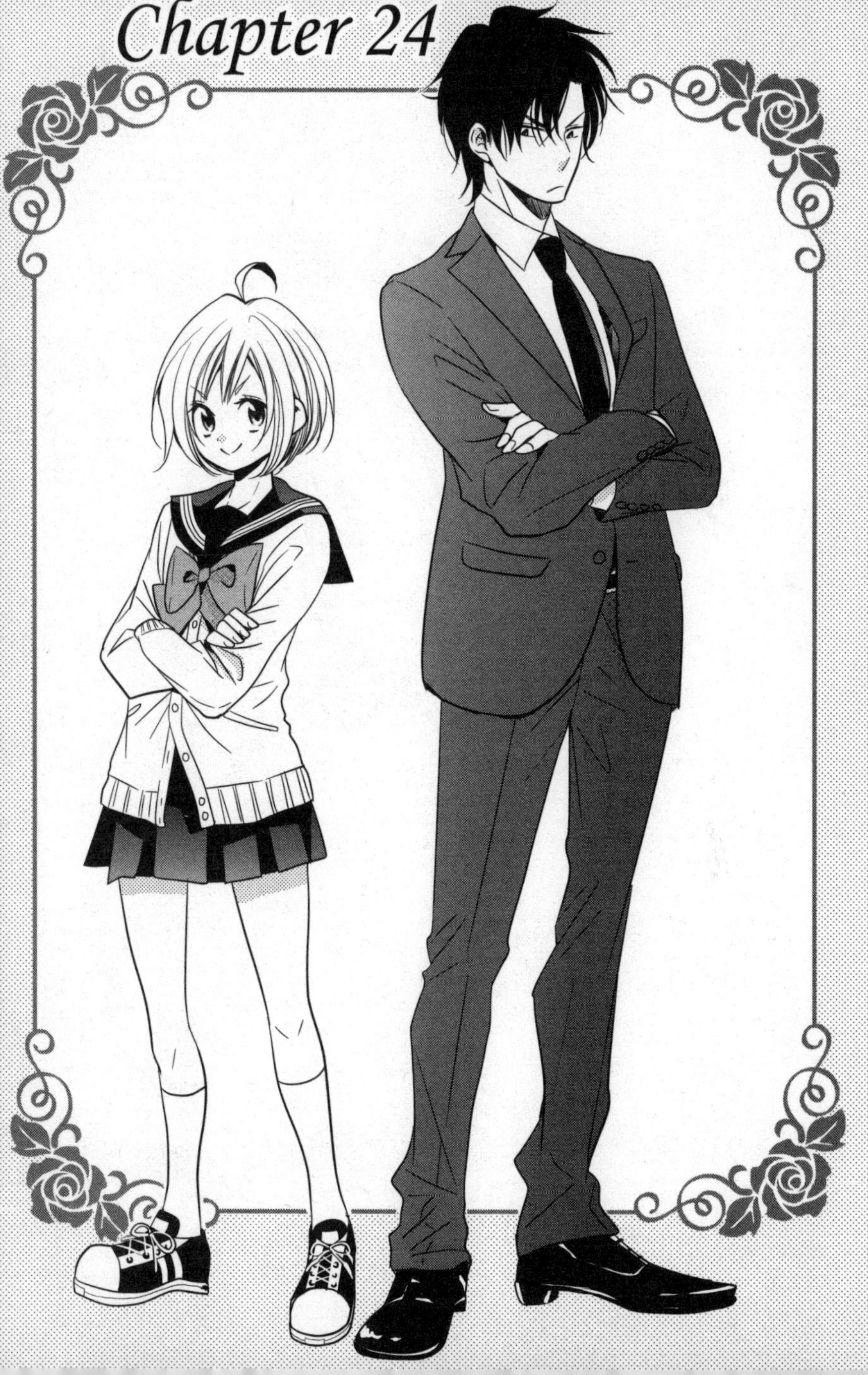

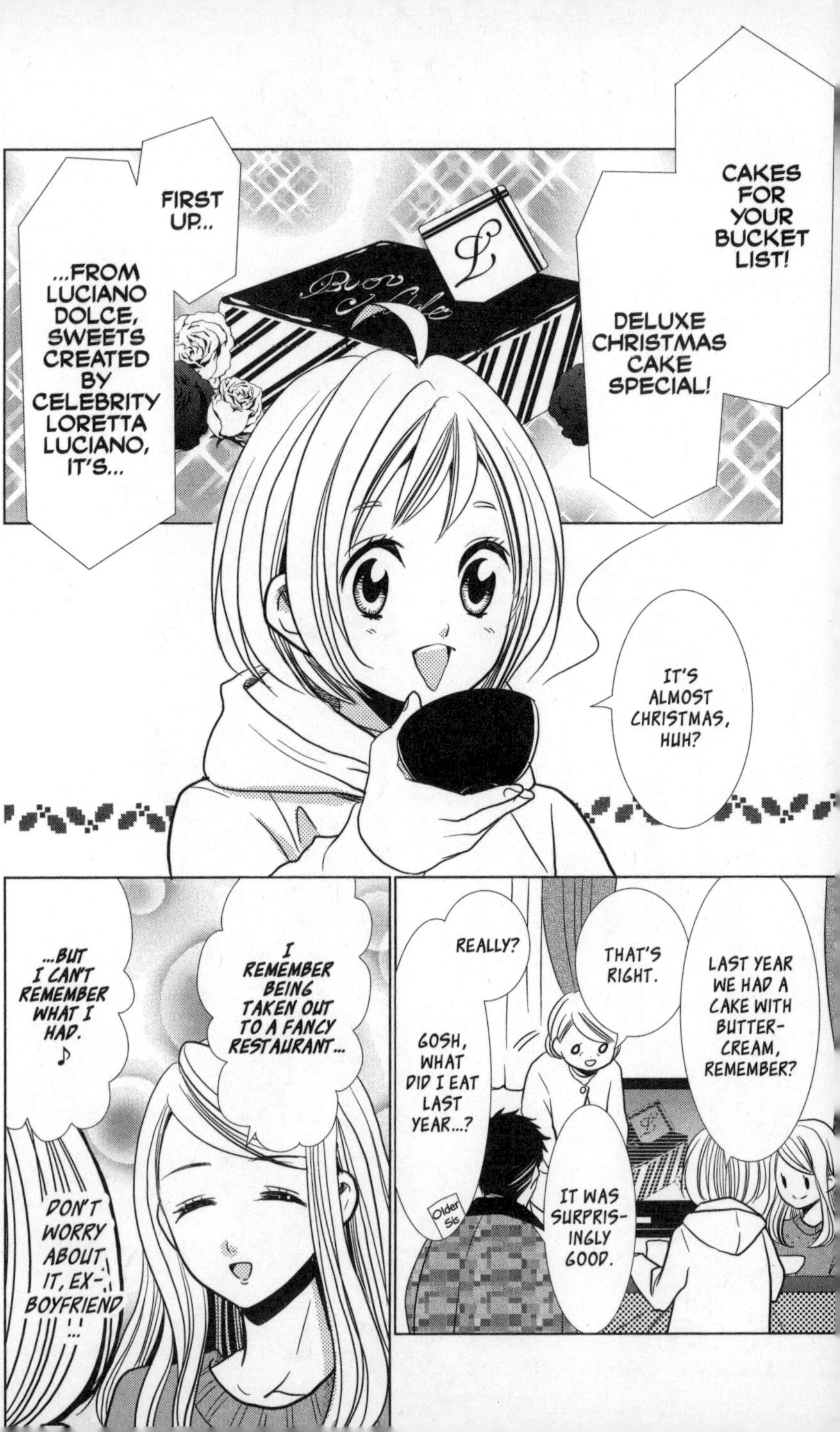
CAKES FOR YOUR BUCKET LIST!
DELUXE CHRISTMAS CAKE SPECIAL!
FIRST UP...
...FROM LUCIANO DOLCE, SWEETS CREATED BY CELEBRITY LORETTA LUCIANO, IT'S...
IT'S ALMOST CHRISTMAS, HUH?
LAST YEAR WE HAD A CAKE WITH BUTTER-CREAM, REMEMBER?
THAT'S RIGHT.
REALLY?
IT WAS SURPRIS-INGLY GOOD.
GOSH, WHAT DID I EAT LAST YEAR...?
Older Sis
I REMEMBER BEING TAKEN OUT TO A FANCY RESTAURANT...
...BUT I CAN'T REMEMBER WHAT I HAD. ♪
DON'T WORRY ABOUT IT, EX-BOYFRIEND!!...

Hiromi Takaba

Takane's cousin. Fourth grader. He puts a lot of effort into styling his hair every day so that he can be like Takane. Takane has naturally wavy hair, but Hiromi's is completely straight, so he has trouble getting the look.

When Hiromi's trying to act like Takane, he uses the pronoun *ore* for "I" (commonly used by men in Japan), but when he's just being himself, he uses *boku* (a more age-appropriate pronoun). He also tries to mimic Takane's way of talking down to people, but his own vocabulary is more limited, so he just winds up sounding too blunt.

I've always wanted to draw a child character, so this is a dream come true. I debated until the last minute about whether he'd be a boy or a girl.

Drawing kids is fun!

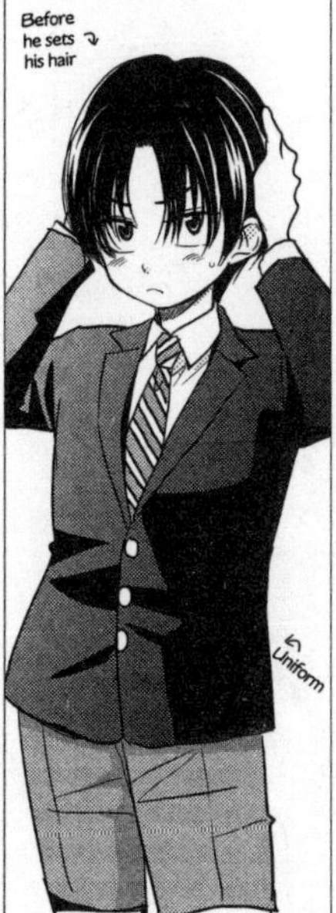
Before he sets his hair
Uniform

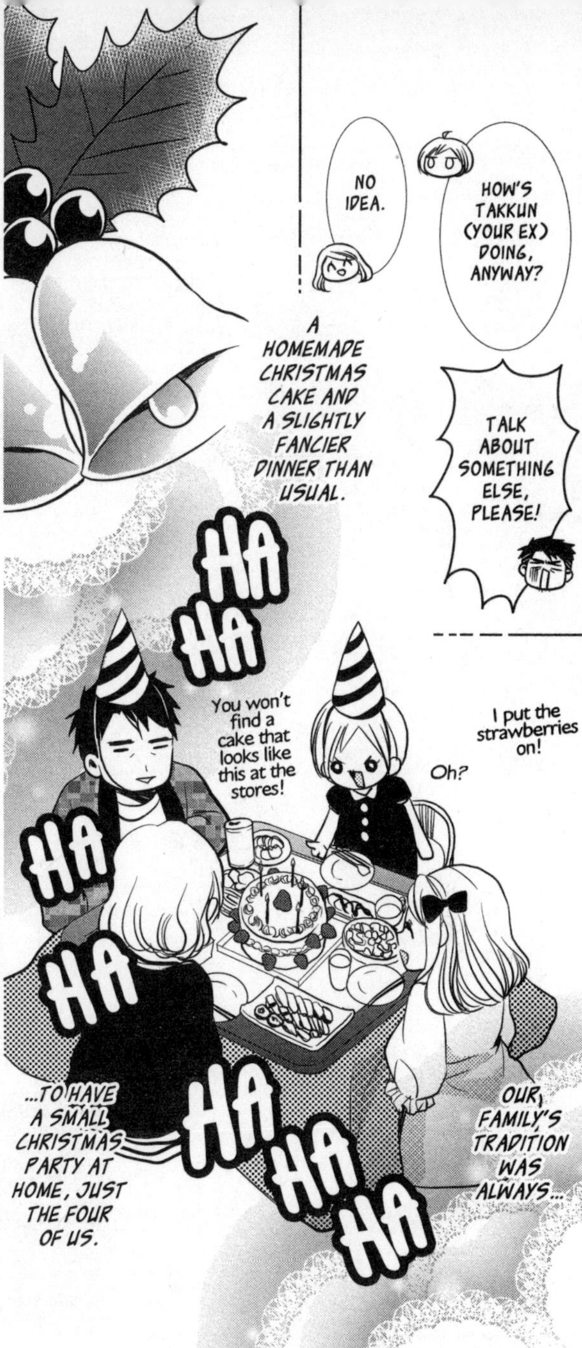
OUR FAMILY'S TRADITION WAS ALWAYS...
...TO HAVE A SMALL CHRISTMAS PARTY AT HOME, JUST THE FOUR OF US.
A HOMEMADE CHRISTMAS CAKE AND A SLIGHTLY FANCIER DINNER THAN USUAL.
I put the strawberries on!
Oh?
You won't find a cake that looks like this at the stores!
HA HA
HA HA
HA HA HA
HOW'S TAKKUN (YOUR EX) DOING, ANYWAY?
NO IDEA.
TALK ABOUT SOMETHING ELSE, PLEASE!

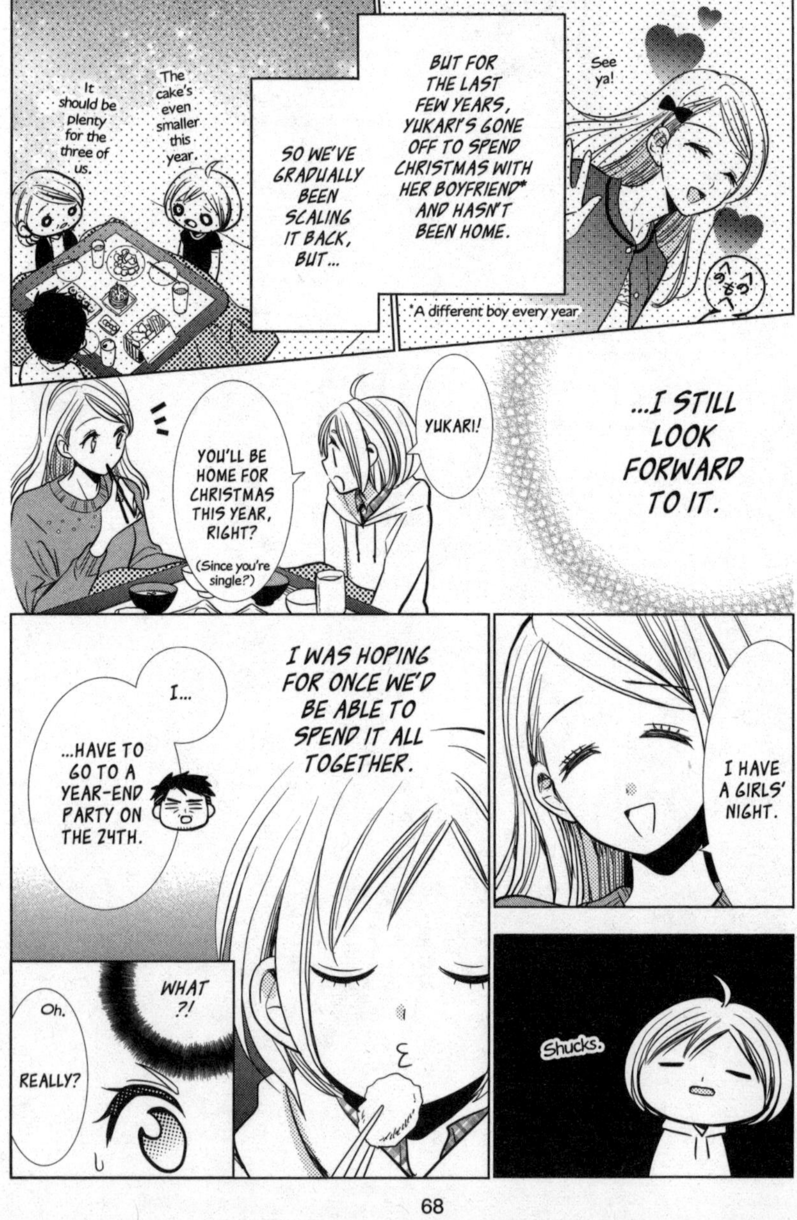
See ya!
But for the last few years, Yukari's gone off to spend Christmas with her boyfriend* and hasn't been home.
*A different boy every year.
So we've gradually been scaling it back, but...
The cake's even smaller this year.
It should be plenty for the three of us.
...I still look forward to it.
Yukari!
You'll be home for Christmas this year, right?
(Since you're single?)
I have a girls' night.
I was hoping for once we'd be able to spend it all together.
I...
...have to go to a year-end party on the 24th.
Shucks.
What?!
Oh.
Really?

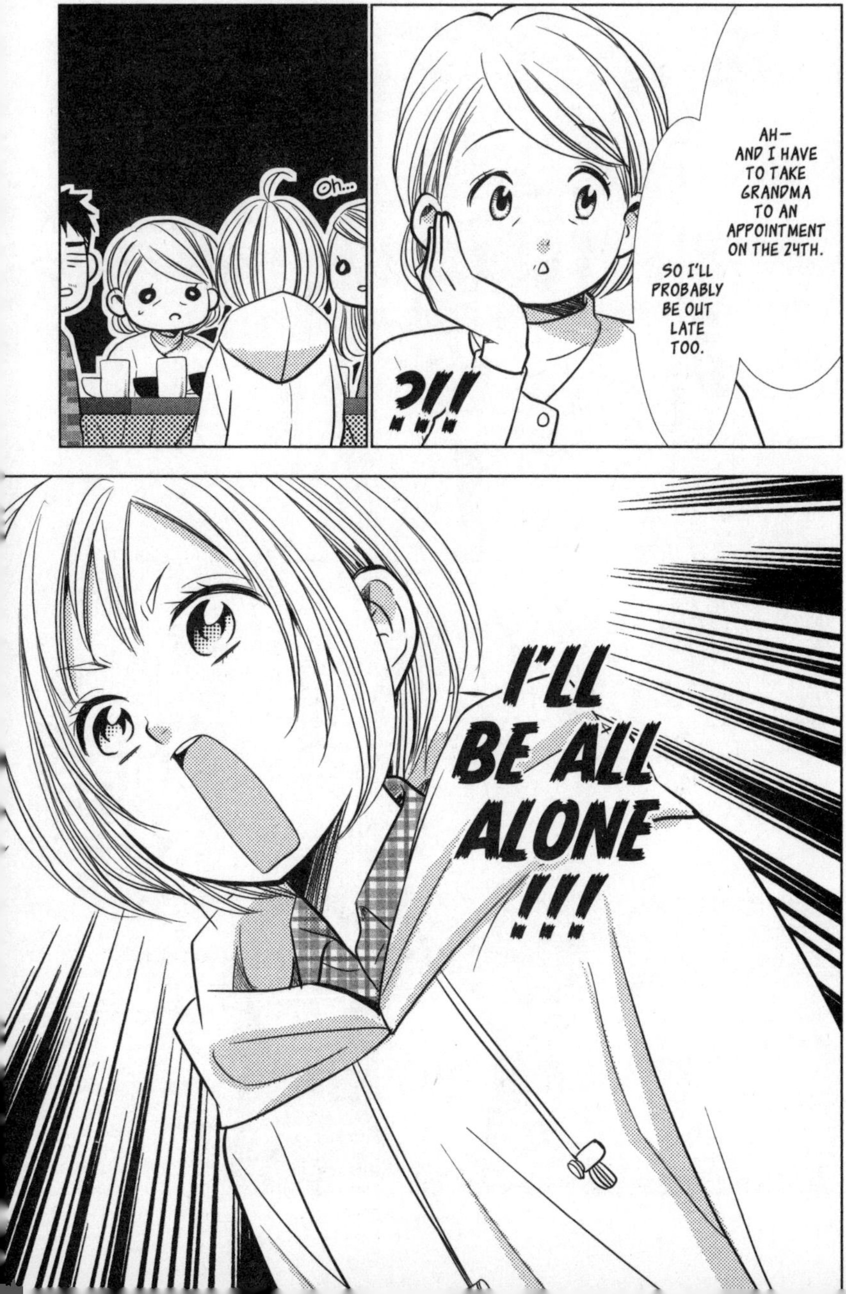
AH— AND I HAVE TO TAKE GRANDMA TO AN APPOINTMENT ON THE 24TH.
SO I'LL PROBABLY BE OUT LATE TOO.
?!!
Oh...
I'LL BE ALL ALONE!!!

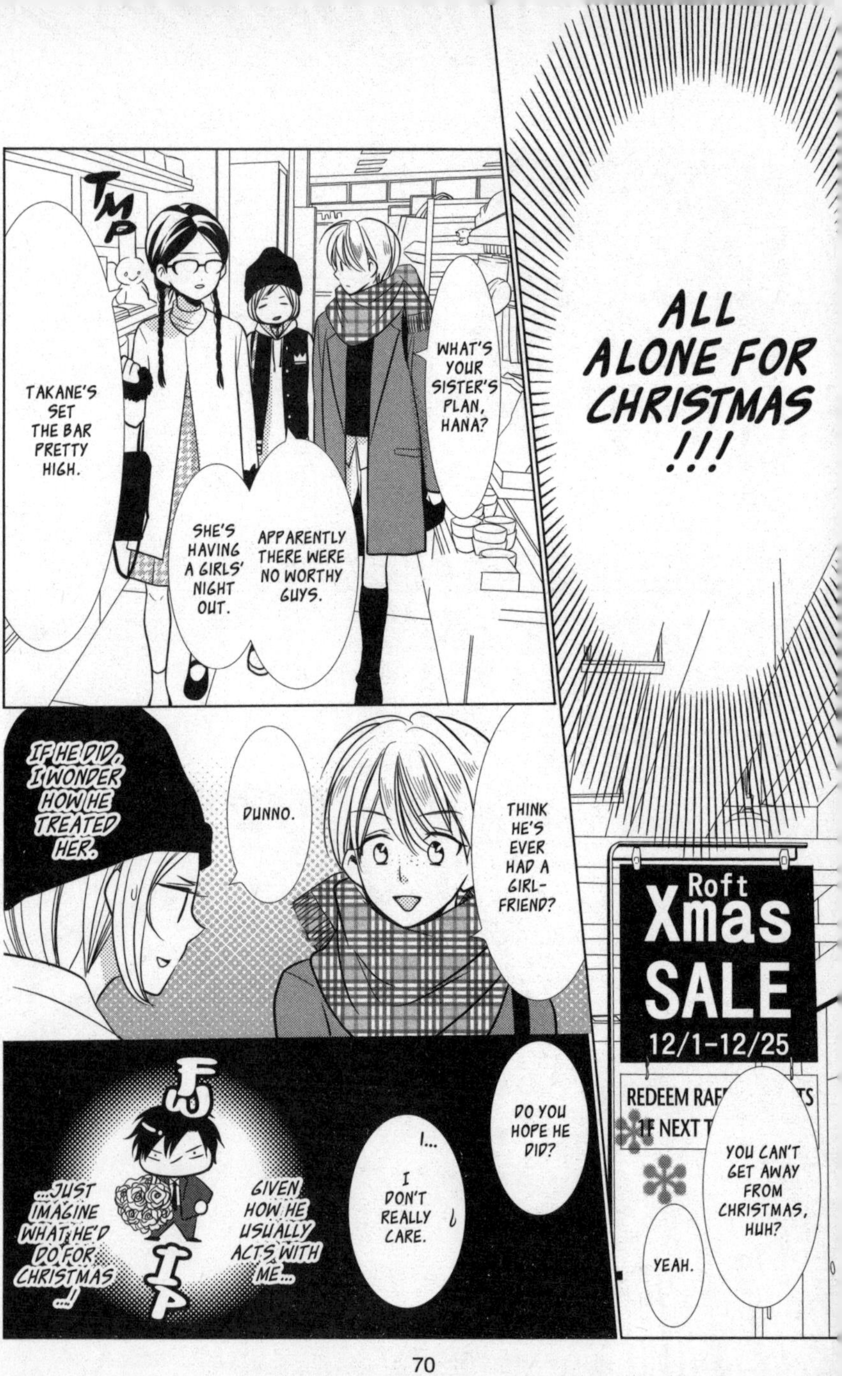
ALL ALONE FOR CHRISTMAS!!!
Roft
Xmas
SALE
12/1-12/25
YOU CAN'T GET AWAY FROM CHRISTMAS, HUH?
YEAH.
TMP
WHAT'S YOUR SISTER'S PLAN, HANA?
APPARENTLY THERE WERE NO WORTHY GUYS.
SHE'S HAVING A GIRLS' NIGHT OUT.
TAKANE'S SET THE BAR PRETTY HIGH.
THINK HE'S EVER HAD A GIRLFRIEND?
DUNNO.
IF HE DID, I WONDER HOW HE TREATED HER.
DO YOU HOPE HE DID?
I... I DON'T REALLY CARE.
GIVEN HOW HE USUALLY ACTS WITH ME...
...JUST IMAGINE WHAT HE'D DO FOR CHRISTMAS...!
FU
IP

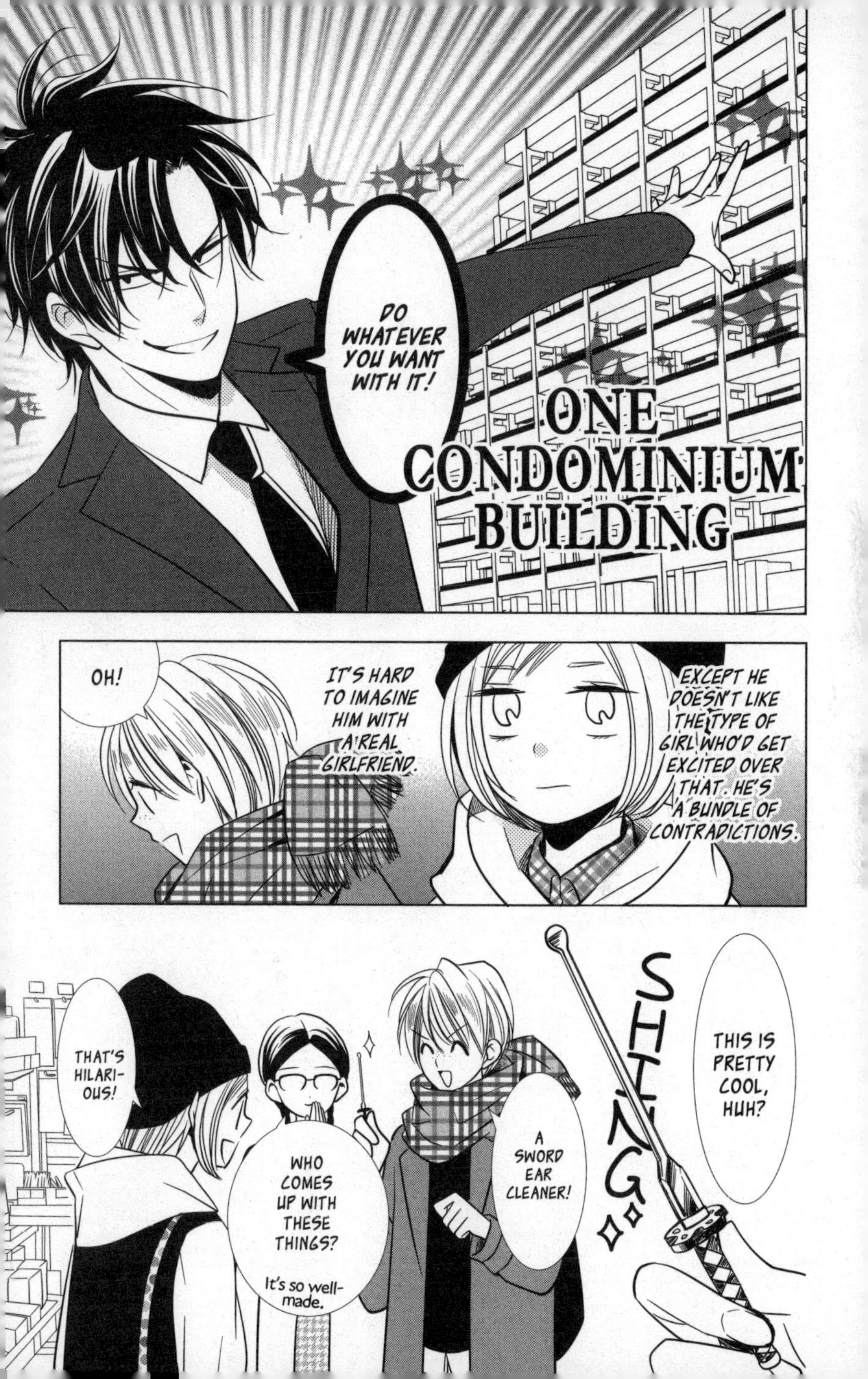
DO WHATEVER YOU WANT WITH IT!
ONE CONDOMINIUM BUILDING
EXCEPT HE DOESN'T LIKE THE TYPE OF GIRL WHO'D GET EXCITED OVER THAT. HE'S A BUNDLE OF CONTRADICTIONS.
IT'S HARD TO IMAGINE HIM WITH A REAL GIRLFRIEND.
OH!
THIS IS PRETTY COOL, HUH?
SHING
A SWORD EAR CLEANER!
THAT'S HILARI-OUS!
WHO COMES UP WITH THESE THINGS?
It's so well-made.

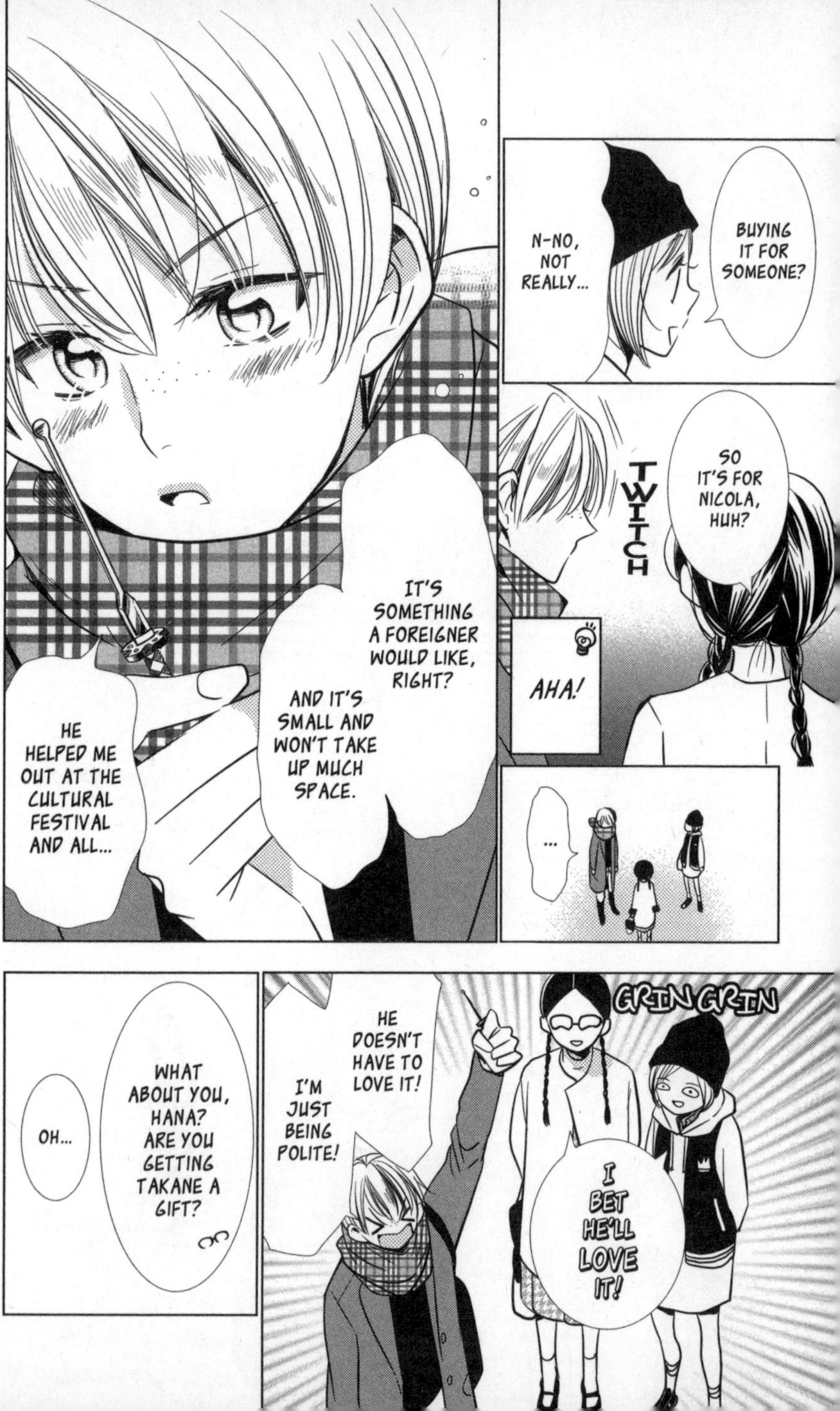
BUYING IT FOR SOMEONE?
N-NO, NOT REALLY...
SO IT'S FOR NICOLA, HUH?
TWITCH
AHA!
...
IT'S SOMETHING A FOREIGNER WOULD LIKE, RIGHT?
AND IT'S SMALL AND WON'T TAKE UP MUCH SPACE.
HE HELPED ME OUT AT THE CULTURAL FESTIVAL AND ALL...
GRIN GRIN
I BET HE'LL LOVE IT!
HE DOESN'T HAVE TO LOVE IT!
I'M JUST BEING POLITE!
WHAT ABOUT YOU, HANA? ARE YOU GETTING TAKANE A GIFT?
OH...

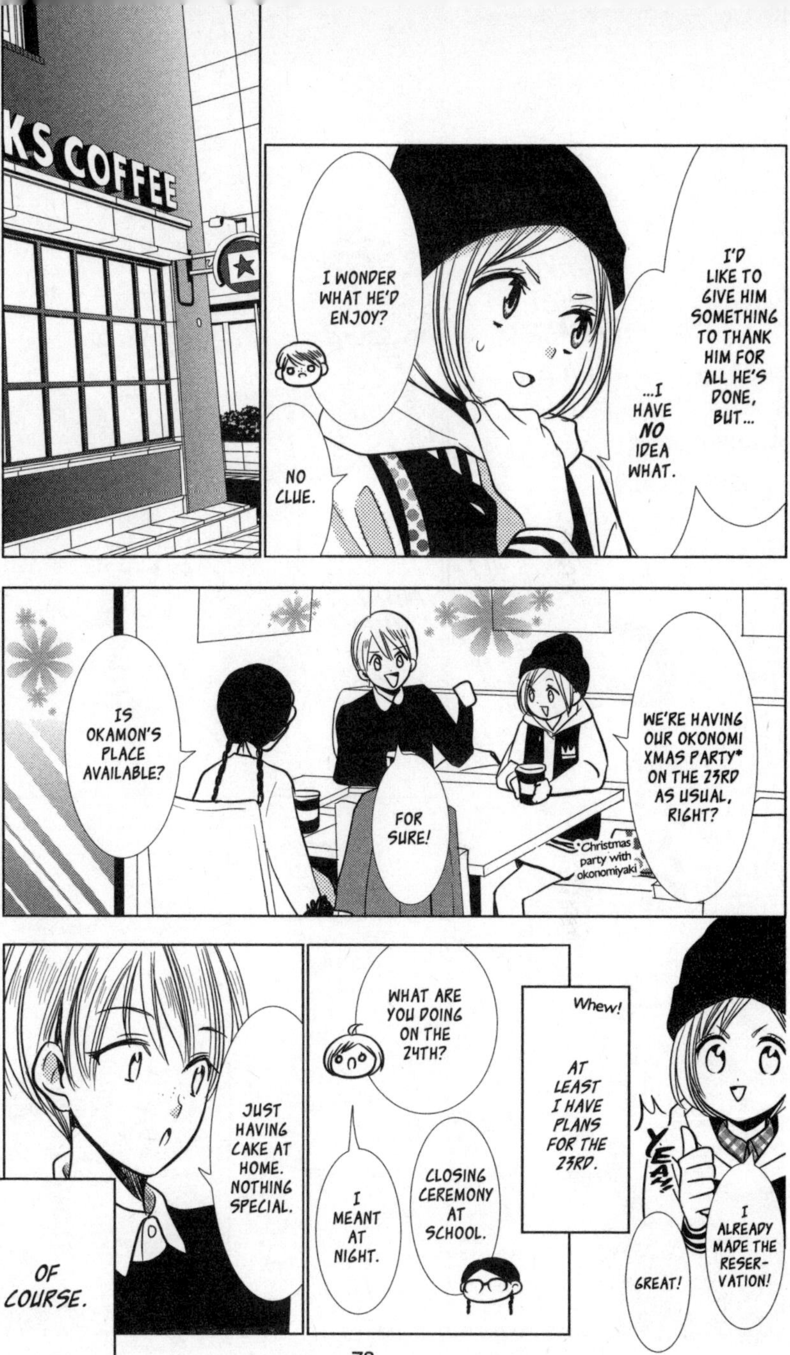
I'D LIKE TO GIVE HIM SOMETHING TO THANK HIM FOR ALL HE'S DONE, BUT...
...I HAVE NO IDEA WHAT.
I WONDER WHAT HE'D ENJOY?
NO CLUE.
KS COFFEE
WE'RE HAVING OUR OKONOMI XMAS PARTY* ON THE 23RD AS USUAL, RIGHT?
*Christmas party with okonomiyaki
IS OKAMON'S PLACE AVAILABLE?
FOR SURE!
YEAH!
I ALREADY MADE THE RESER-VATION!
GREAT!
Whew!
AT LEAST I HAVE PLANS FOR THE 23RD.
WHAT ARE YOU DOING ON THE 24TH?
CLOSING CEREMONY AT SCHOOL.
I MEANT AT NIGHT.
JUST HAVING CAKE AT HOME. NOTHING SPECIAL.
OF COURSE.

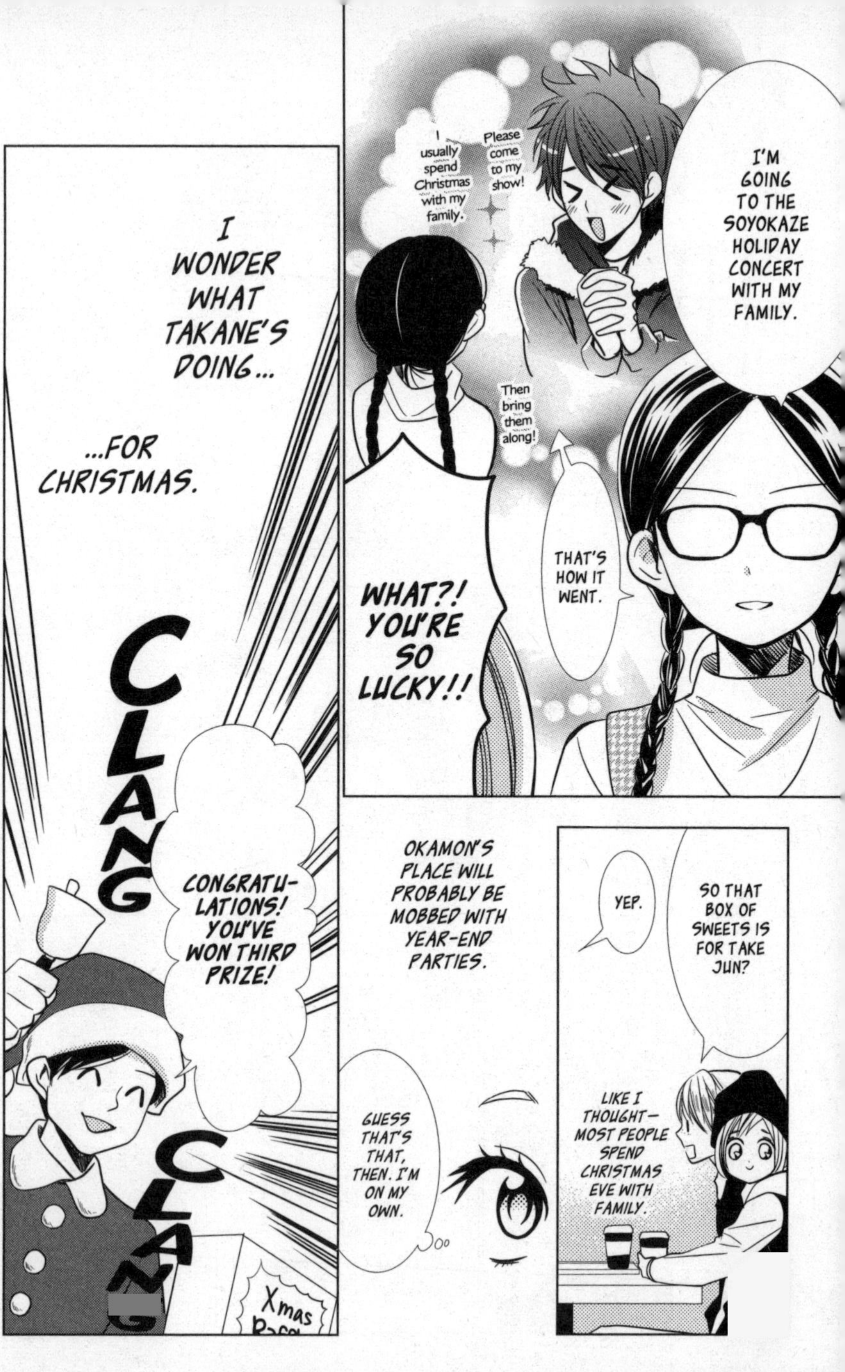
I'M GOING TO THE SOYOKAZE HOLIDAY CONCERT WITH MY FAMILY.
Please come to my show!
I usually spend Christmas with my family.
Then bring them along!
THAT'S HOW IT WENT.
WHAT?! YOU'RE SO LUCKY!!
SO THAT BOX OF SWEETS IS FOR TAKE JUN?
YEP.
LIKE I THOUGHT— MOST PEOPLE SPEND CHRISTMAS EVE WITH FAMILY.
OKAMON'S PLACE WILL PROBABLY BE MOBBED WITH YEAR-END PARTIES.
GUESS THAT'S THAT, THEN. I'M ON MY OWN.
I WONDER WHAT TAKANE'S DOING...
...FOR CHRISTMAS.
CLANG
CONGRATU-LATIONS! YOU'VE WON THIRD PRIZE!
CLANG

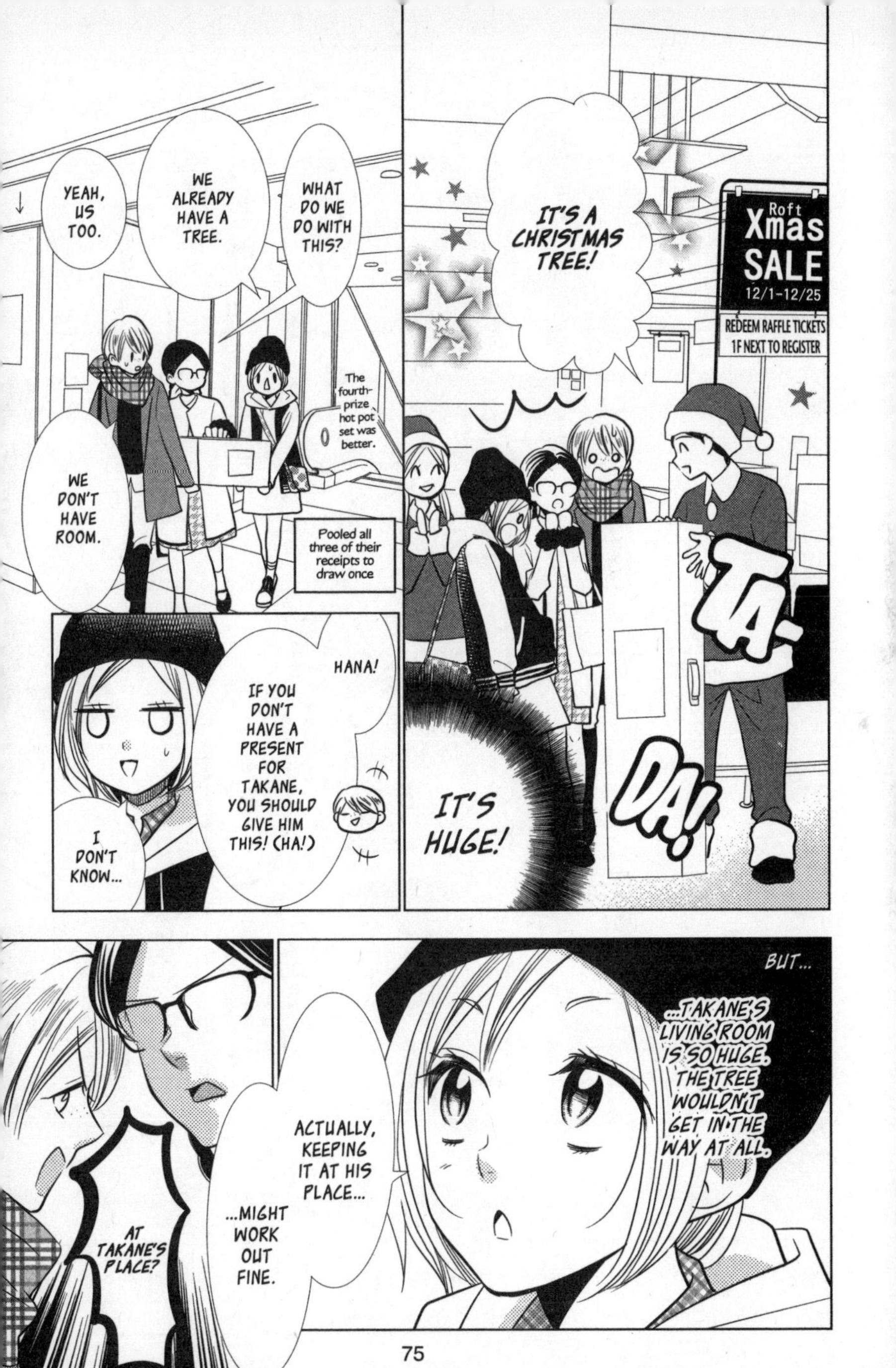
IT'S A CHRISTMAS TREE!
Roft Xmas SALE 12/1-12/25
REDEEM RAFFLE TICKETS 1F NEXT TO REGISTER
TA-DA!
IT'S HUGE!
WHAT DO WE DO WITH THIS?
WE ALREADY HAVE A TREE.
YEAH, US TOO.
The fourth-prize hot pot set was better.
WE DON'T HAVE ROOM.
Pooled all three of their receipts to draw once
HANA!
IF YOU DON'T HAVE A PRESENT FOR TAKANE, YOU SHOULD GIVE HIM THIS! (HA!)
I DON'T KNOW...
BUT...
...TAKANE'S LIVING ROOM IS SO HUGE. THE TREE WOULDN'T GET IN THE WAY AT ALL.
ACTUALLY, KEEPING IT AT HIS PLACE...
...MIGHT WORK OUT FINE.
AT TAKANE'S PLACE?

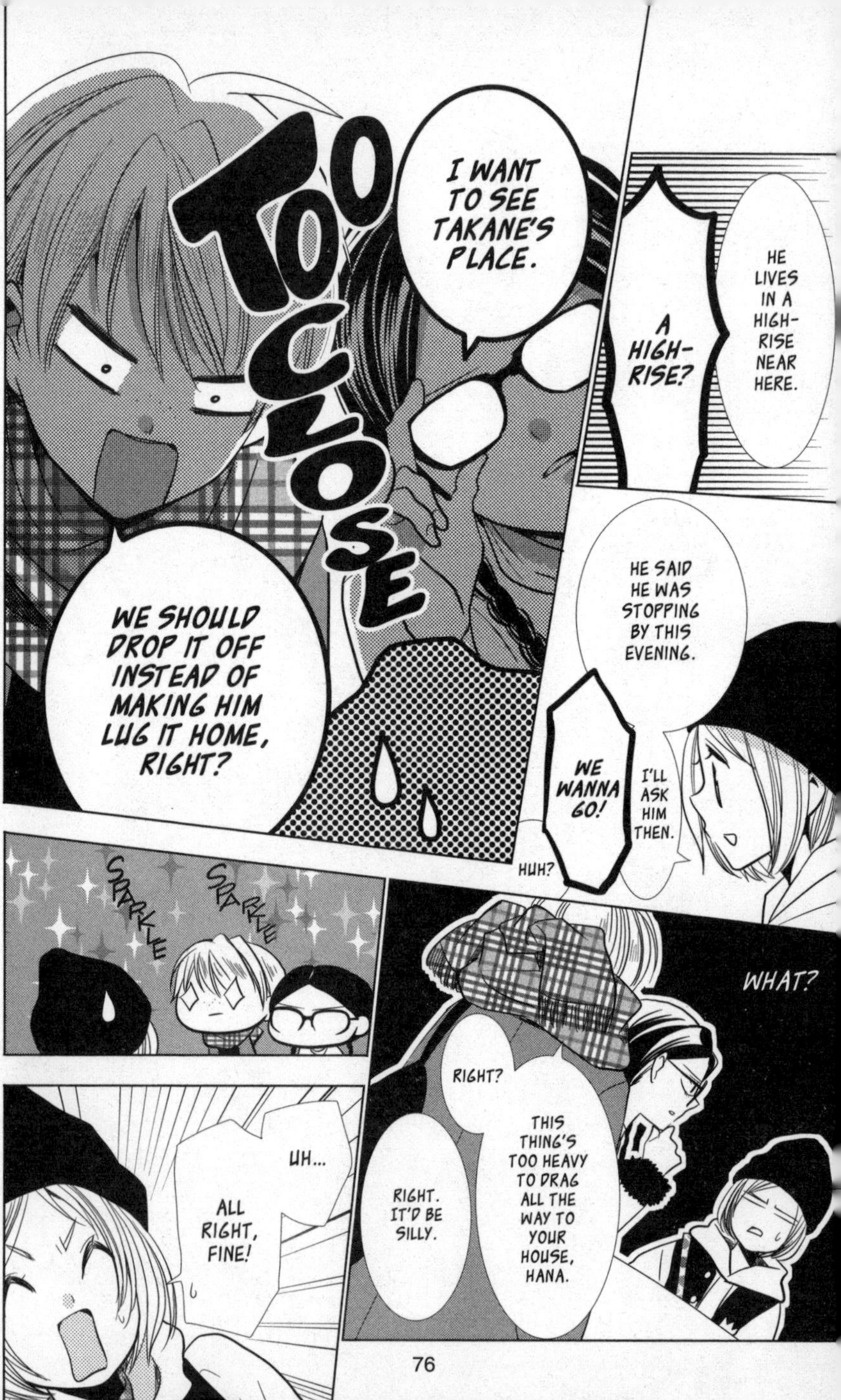
HE LIVES IN A HIGH-RISE NEAR HERE.
A HIGH-RISE?
HE SAID HE WAS STOPPING BY THIS EVENING.
I'LL ASK HIM THEN.
WE WANNA GO!
HUH?
I WANT TO SEE TAKANE'S PLACE.
TOO CLOSE
WE SHOULD DROP IT OFF INSTEAD OF MAKING HIM LUG IT HOME, RIGHT?
WHAT?
RIGHT?
THIS THING'S TOO HEAVY TO DRAG ALL THE WAY TO YOUR HOUSE, HANA.
RIGHT. IT'D BE SILLY.
SPARKLE
SPARKLE
UH...
ALL RIGHT, FINE!

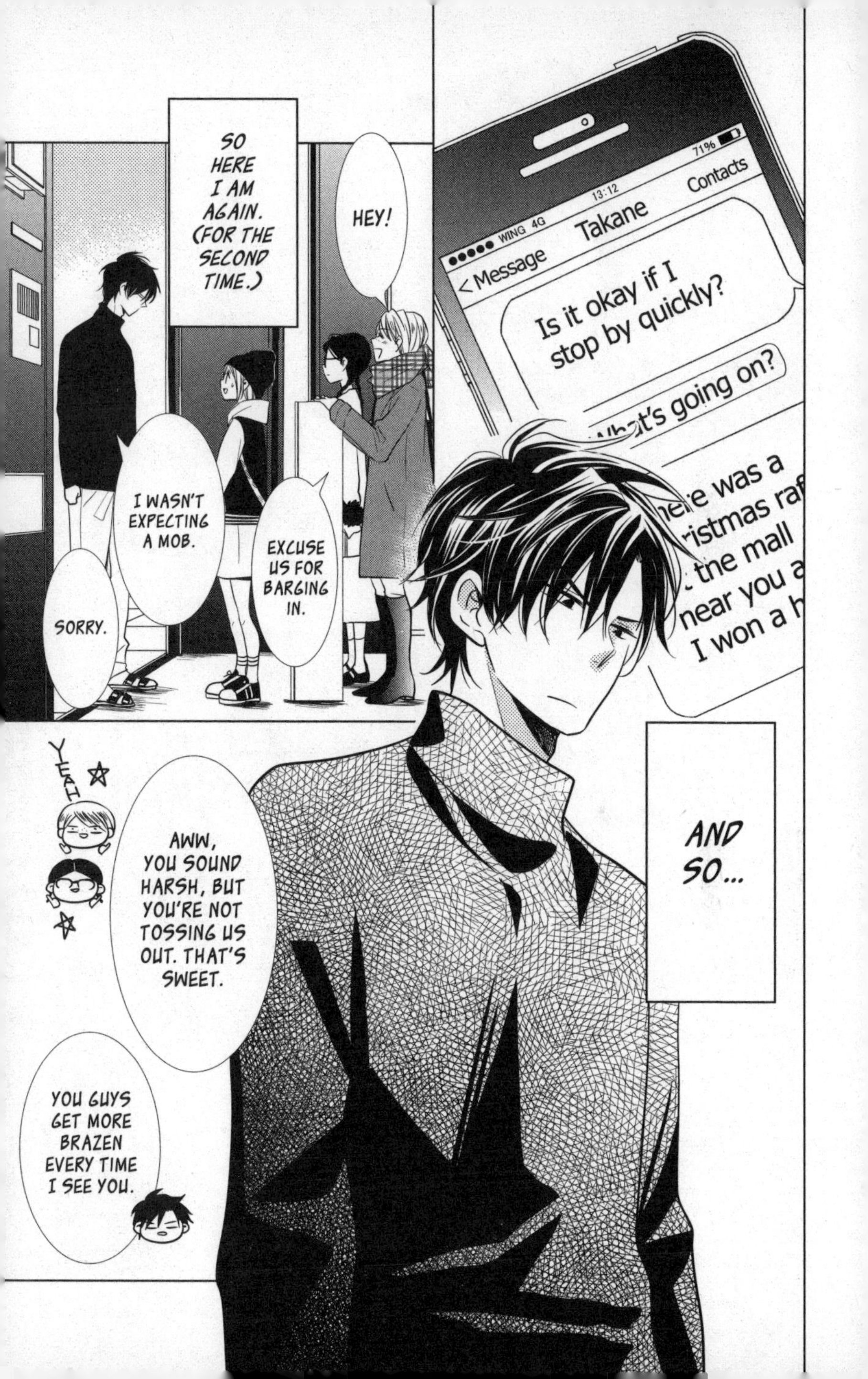
WING 4G
13:12
71%
< Message
Takane
Contacts
Is it okay if I stop by quickly?
AND SO...
SO HERE I AM AGAIN. (FOR THE SECOND TIME.)
HEY!
EXCUSE US FOR BARGING IN.
I WASN'T EXPECTING A MOB.
SORRY.
AWW, YOU SOUND HARSH, BUT YOU'RE NOT TOSSING US OUT. THAT'S SWEET.
YEAH ☆
YOU GUYS GET MORE BRAZEN EVERY TIME I SEE YOU.

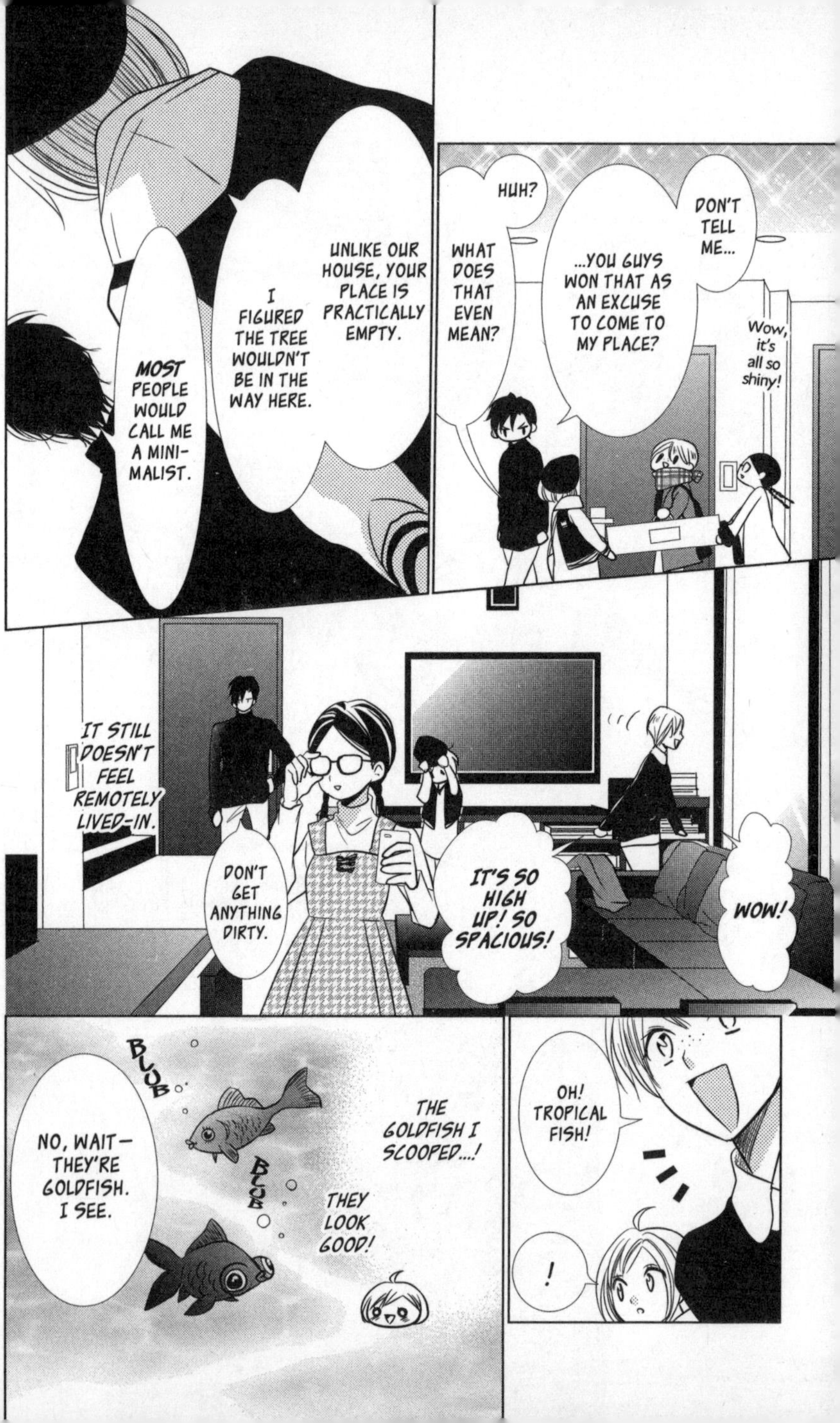
DON'T TELL ME...
...YOU GUYS WON THAT AS AN EXCUSE TO COME TO MY PLACE?
Wow, it's all so shiny!
HUH?
WHAT DOES THAT EVEN MEAN?
UNLIKE OUR HOUSE, YOUR PLACE IS PRACTICALLY EMPTY.
I FIGURED THE TREE WOULDN'T BE IN THE WAY HERE.
MOST PEOPLE WOULD CALL ME A MINI-MALIST.
WOW!
IT'S SO HIGH UP! SO SPACIOUS!
DON'T GET ANYTHING DIRTY.
IT STILL DOESN'T FEEL REMOTELY LIVED-IN.
OH! TROPICAL FISH!
!
THE GOLDFISH I SCOOPED...!
THEY LOOK GOOD!
BLUB
BLUB
NO, WAIT— THEY'RE GOLDFISH. I SEE.

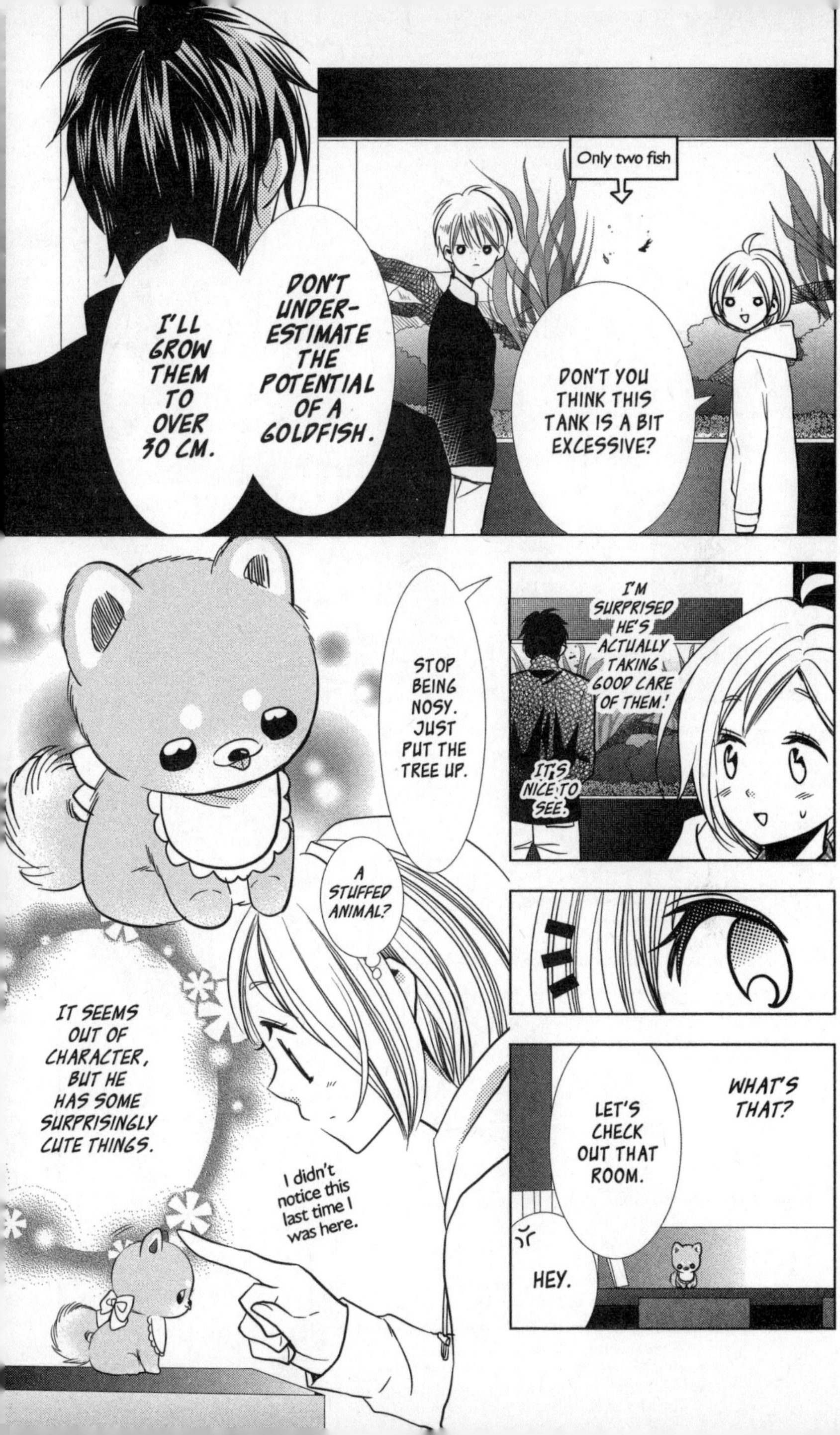
Only two fish
DON'T YOU THINK THIS TANK IS A BIT EXCESSIVE?
DON'T UNDER-ESTIMATE THE POTENTIAL OF A GOLDFISH.
I'LL GROW THEM TO OVER 30 CM.
I'M SURPRISED HE'S ACTUALLY TAKING GOOD CARE OF THEM.
IT'S NICE TO SEE.
WHAT'S THAT?
LET'S CHECK OUT THAT ROOM.
HEY.
STOP BEING NOSY. JUST PUT THE TREE UP.
A STUFFED ANIMAL?
I didn't notice this last time I was here.
IT SEEMS OUT OF CHARACTER, BUT HE HAS SOME SURPRISINGLY CUTE THINGS.

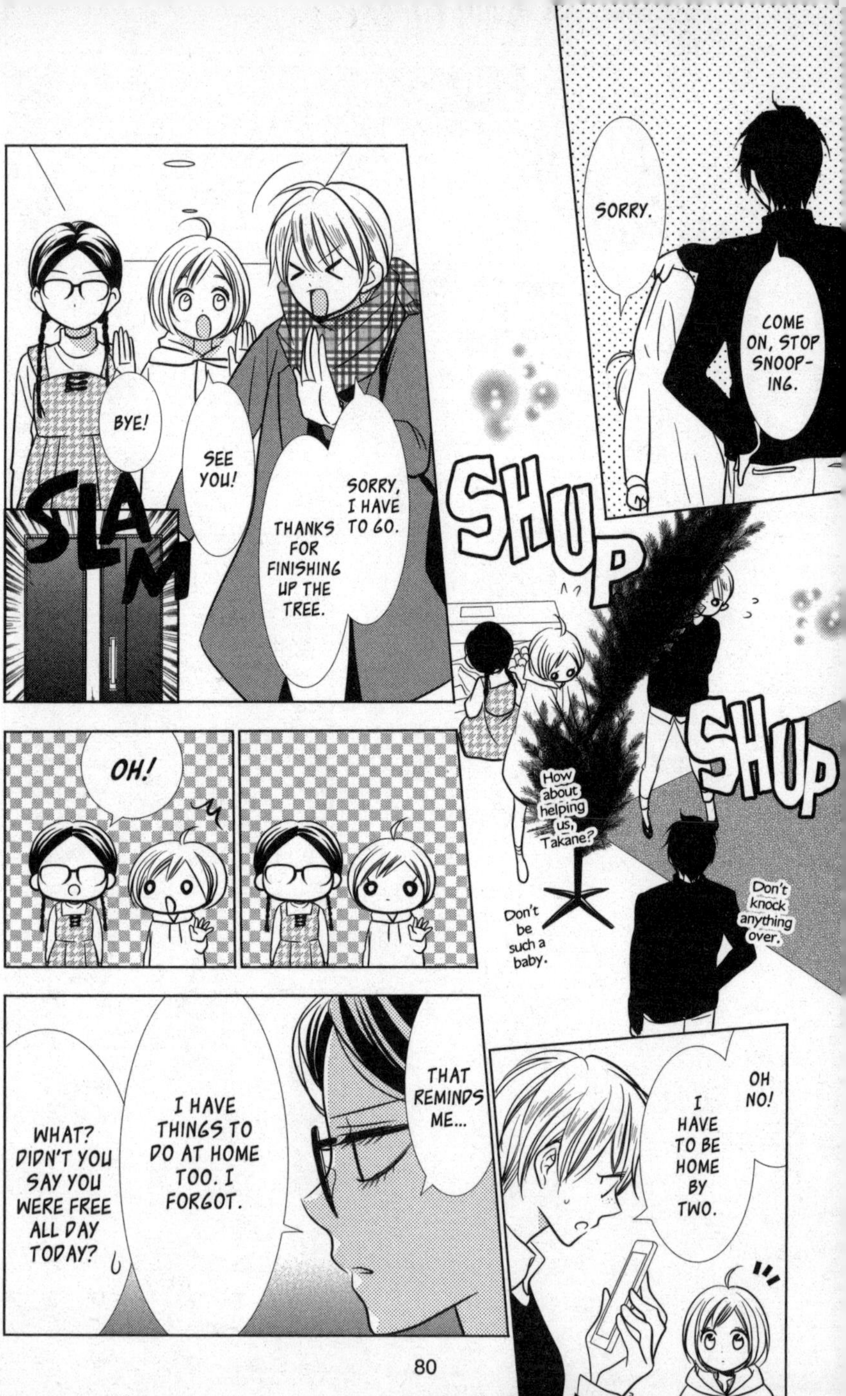
SORRY.
COME ON, STOP SNOOPING.
SHUP
How about helping us, Takane?
Don't knock anything over.
Don't be such a baby.
SHUP
SORRY, I HAVE TO GO.
THANKS FOR FINISHING UP THE TREE.
SEE YOU!
BYE!
SLAM
OH!
OH NO!
I HAVE TO BE HOME BY TWO.
THAT REMINDS ME...
I HAVE THINGS TO DO AT HOME TOO. I FORGOT.
WHAT? DIDN'T YOU SAY YOU WERE FREE ALL DAY TODAY?

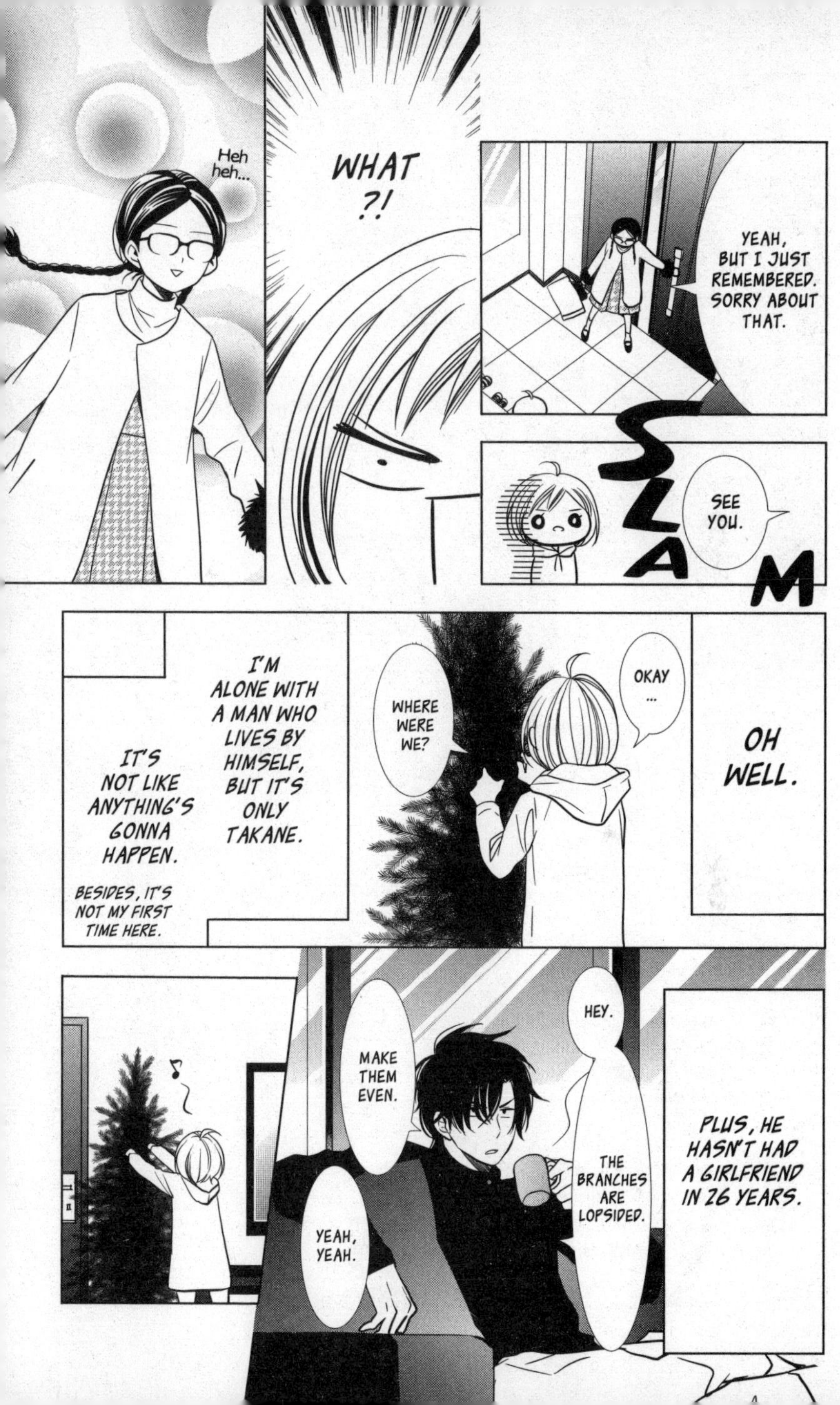
YEAH, BUT I JUST REMEMBERED. SORRY ABOUT THAT.
SLAM
SEE YOU.
WHAT ?!
Heh heh...
OH WELL.
OKAY ...
WHERE WERE WE?
I'M ALONE WITH A MAN WHO LIVES BY HIMSELF, BUT IT'S ONLY TAKANE.
IT'S NOT LIKE ANYTHING'S GONNA HAPPEN.
BESIDES, IT'S NOT MY FIRST TIME HERE.
PLUS, HE HASN'T HAD A GIRLFRIEND IN 26 YEARS.
HEY.
THE BRANCHES ARE LOPSIDED.
MAKE THEM EVEN.
YEAH, YEAH.

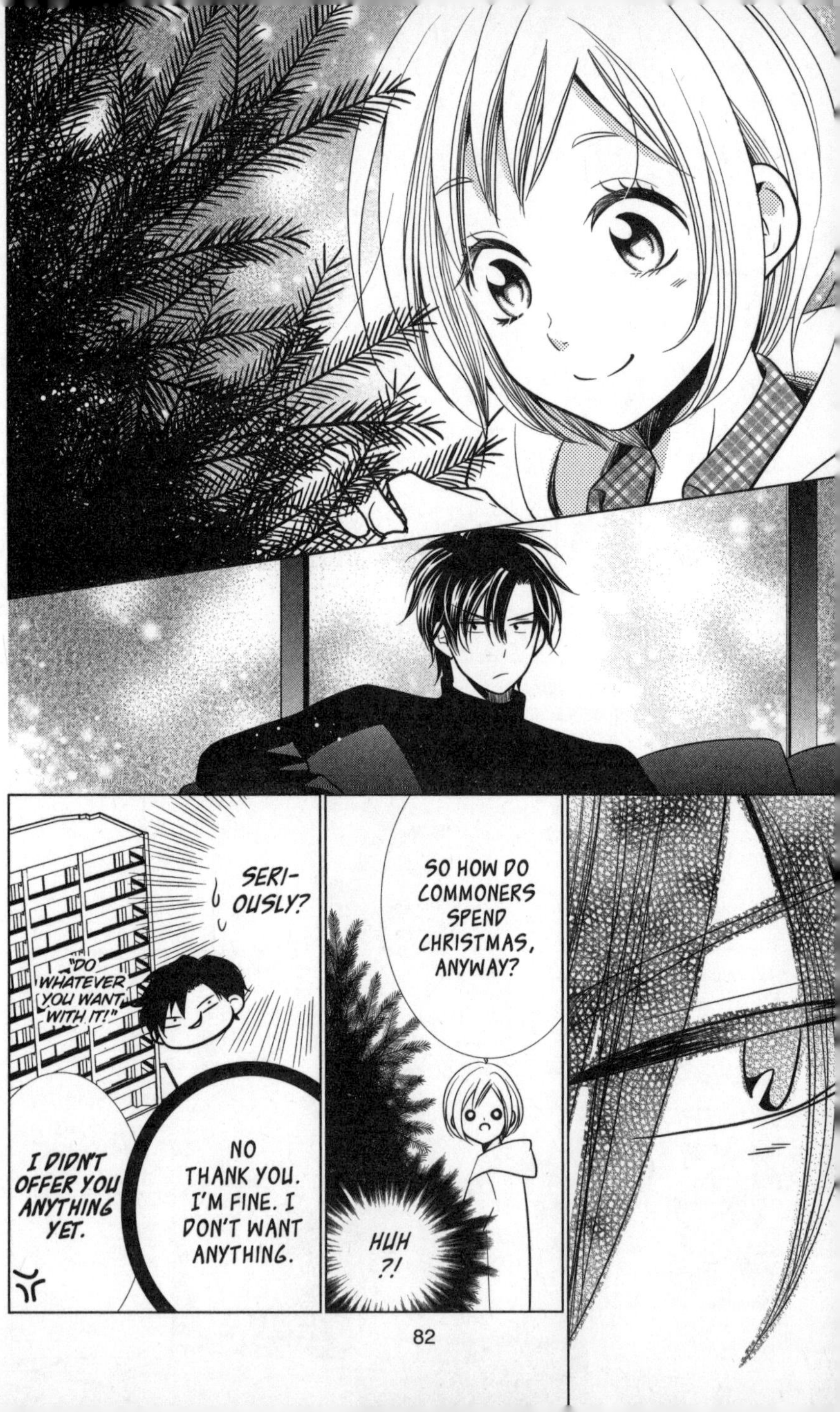
SO HOW DO COMMONERS SPEND CHRISTMAS, ANYWAY?
HUH ?!
SERI-OUSLY?
"DO WHATEVER YOU WANT WITH IT!"
NO THANK YOU. I'M FINE. I DON'T WANT ANYTHING.
I DIDN'T OFFER YOU ANYTHING YET.

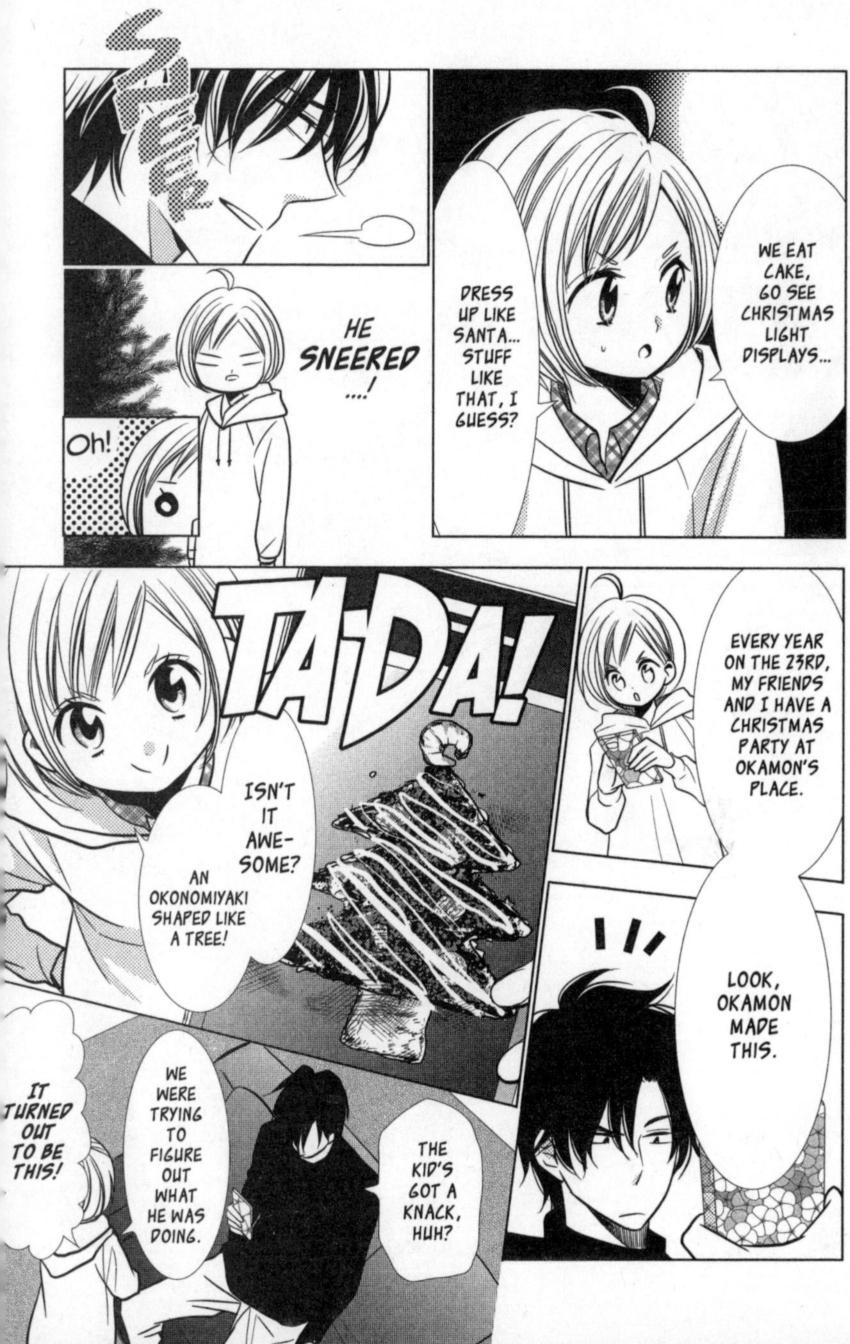
WE EAT CAKE, GO SEE CHRISTMAS LIGHT DISPLAYS...
DRESS UP LIKE SANTA... STUFF LIKE THAT, I GUESS?
HE SNEERED ...!
Oh!
EVERY YEAR ON THE 23RD, MY FRIENDS AND I HAVE A CHRISTMAS PARTY AT OKAMON'S PLACE.
LOOK, OKAMON MADE THIS.
TA-DA!
ISN'T IT AWESOME?
AN OKONOMIYAKI SHAPED LIKE A TREE!
THE KID'S GOT A KNACK, HUH?
WE WERE TRYING TO FIGURE OUT WHAT HE WAS DOING.
IT TURNED OUT TO BE THIS!

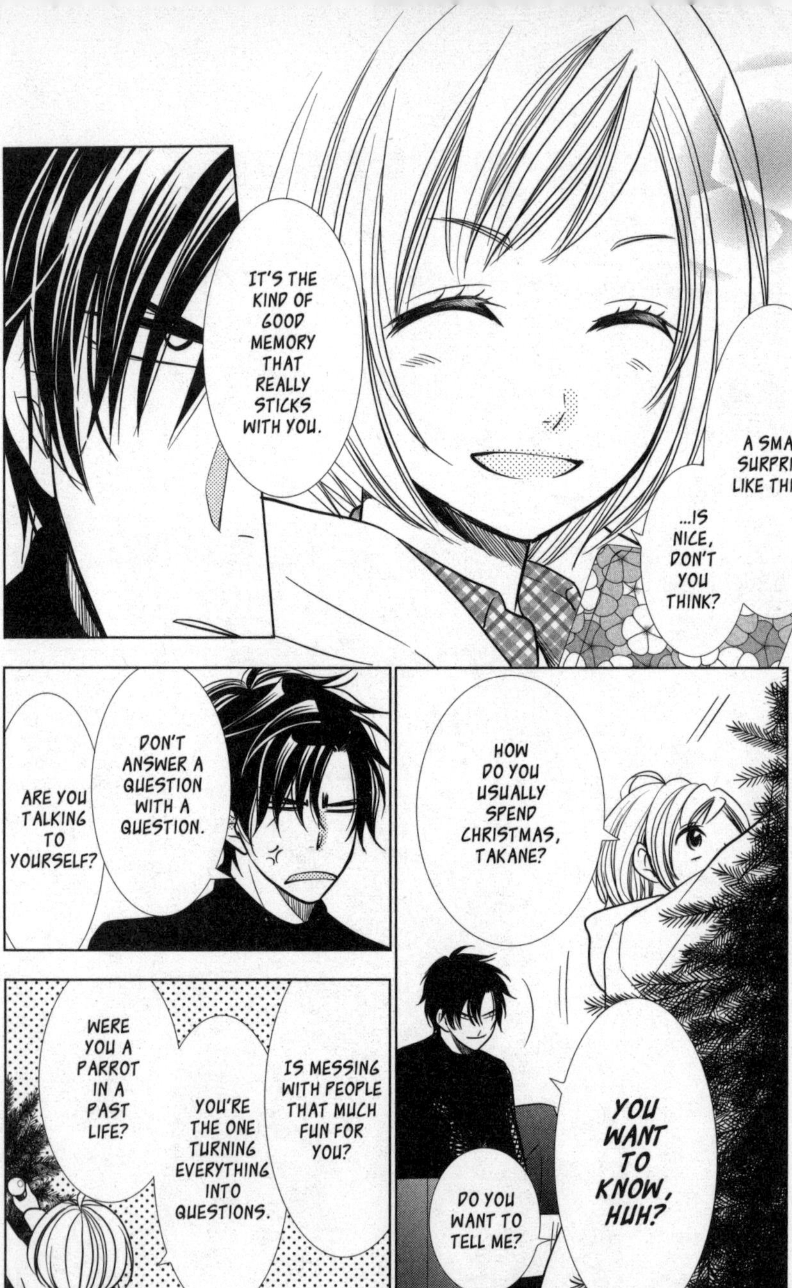
A SMALL SURPRISE LIKE THIS...
...IS NICE, DON'T YOU THINK?
IT'S THE KIND OF GOOD MEMORY THAT REALLY STICKS WITH YOU.
HOW DO YOU USUALLY SPEND CHRISTMAS, TAKANE?
YOU WANT TO KNOW, HUH?
DO YOU WANT TO TELL ME?
DON'T ANSWER A QUESTION WITH A QUESTION.
ARE YOU TALKING TO YOURSELF?
IS MESSING WITH PEOPLE THAT MUCH FUN FOR YOU?
YOU'RE THE ONE TURNING EVERYTHING INTO QUESTIONS.
WERE YOU A PARROT IN A PAST LIFE?

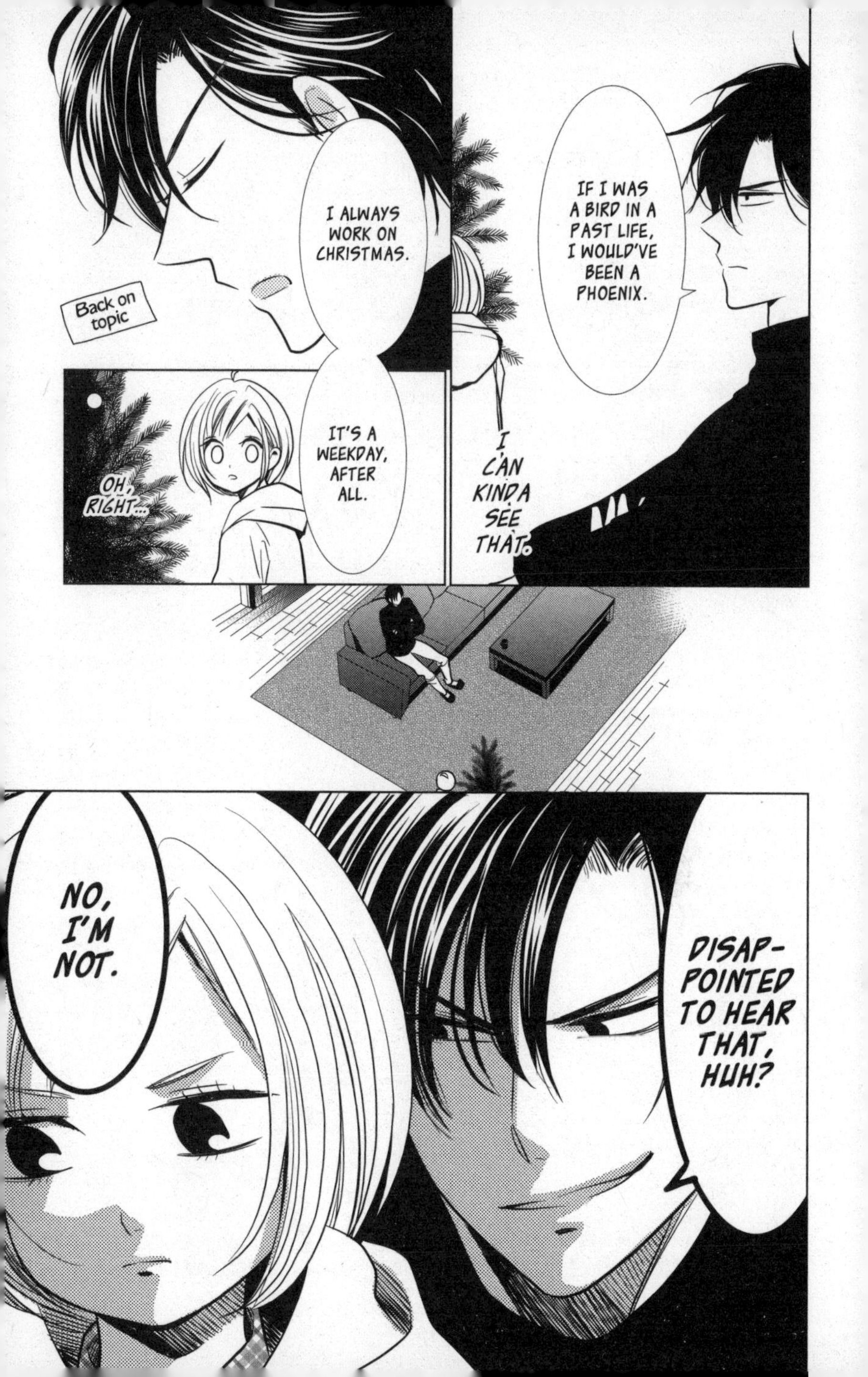
IF I WAS A BIRD IN A PAST LIFE, I WOULD'VE BEEN A PHOENIX.
I CAN KINDA SEE THAT.
I ALWAYS WORK ON CHRISTMAS.
Back on topic
IT'S A WEEKDAY, AFTER ALL.
OH, RIGHT...
DISAP-POINTED TO HEAR THAT, HUH?
NO, I'M NOT.

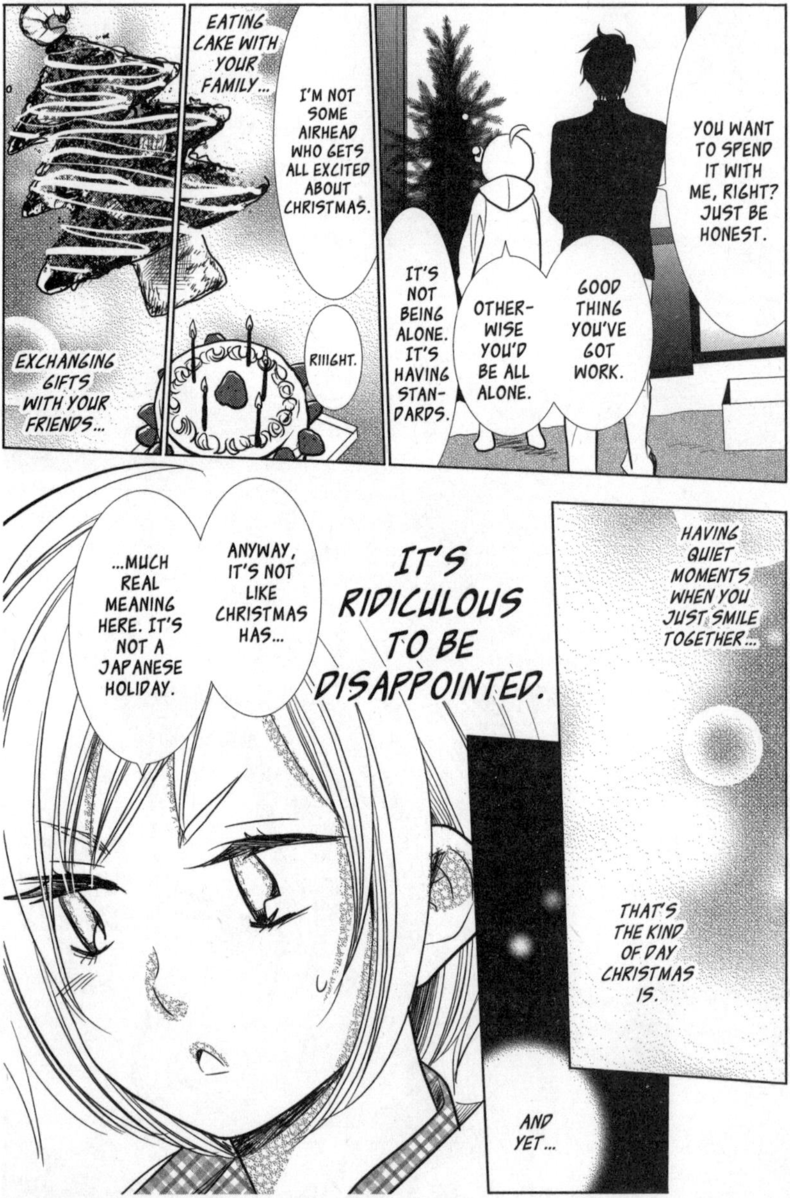
YOU WANT TO SPEND IT WITH ME, RIGHT? JUST BE HONEST.
GOOD THING YOU'VE GOT WORK.
OTHER-WISE YOU'D BE ALL ALONE.
IT'S NOT BEING ALONE. IT'S HAVING STAN-DARDS.
EATING CAKE WITH YOUR FAMILY...
I'M NOT SOME AIRHEAD WHO GETS ALL EXCITED ABOUT CHRISTMAS.
RIIIGHT.
EXCHANGING GIFTS WITH YOUR FRIENDS...
HAVING QUIET MOMENTS WHEN YOU JUST SMILE TOGETHER...
THAT'S THE KIND OF DAY CHRISTMAS IS.
AND YET...
IT'S RIDICULOUS TO BE DISAPPOINTED.
ANYWAY, IT'S NOT LIKE CHRISTMAS HAS...
...MUCH REAL MEANING HERE. IT'S NOT A JAPANESE HOLIDAY.

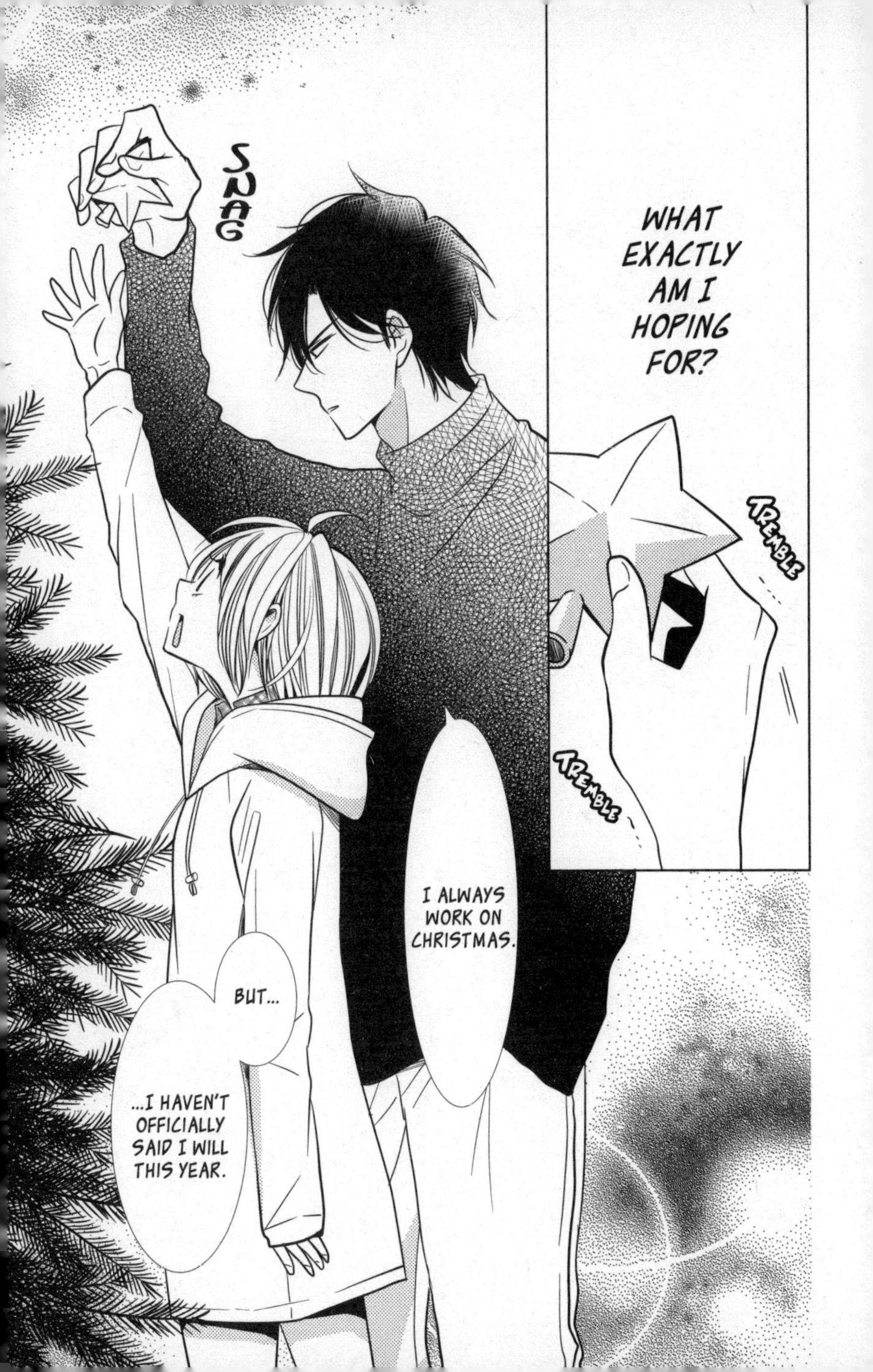
WHAT EXACTLY AM I HOPING FOR?
TREMBLE
TREMBLE
SNAG
I ALWAYS WORK ON CHRISTMAS.
BUT...
...I HAVEN'T OFFICIALLY SAID I WILL THIS YEAR.

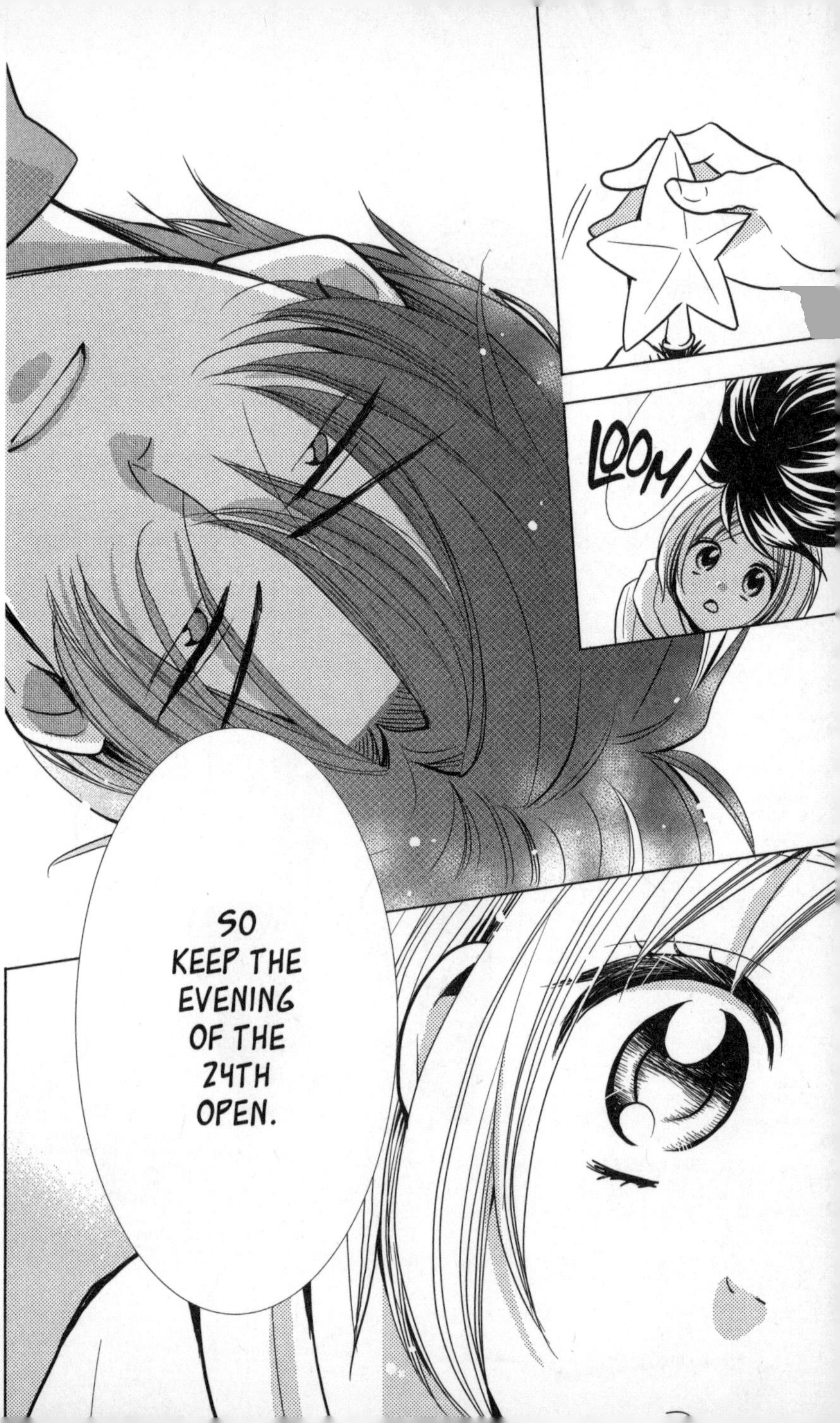
LOOM
SO KEEP THE EVENING OF THE 24TH OPEN.

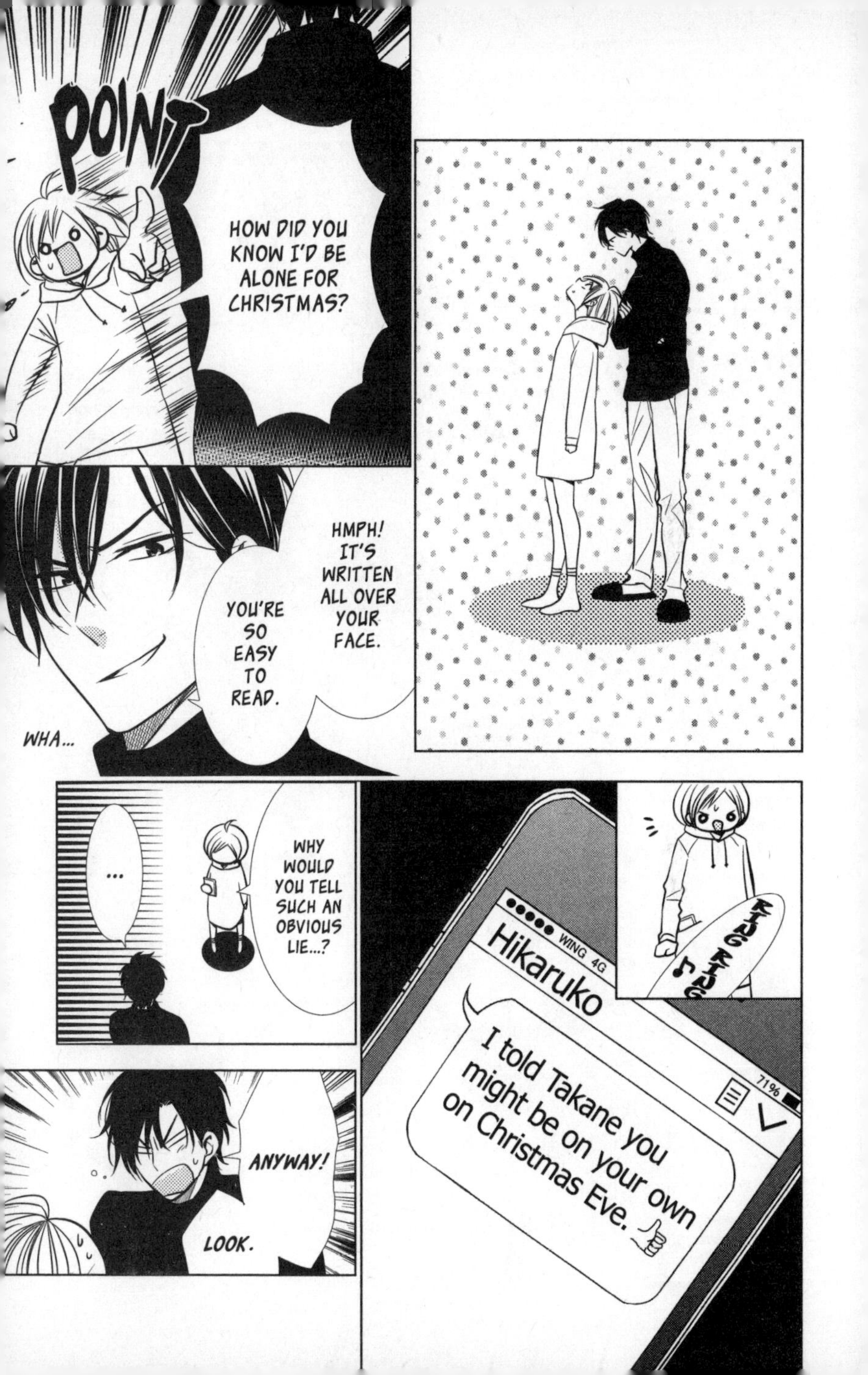
POINT
HOW DID YOU KNOW I'D BE ALONE FOR CHRISTMAS?
HMPH! IT'S WRITTEN ALL OVER YOUR FACE.
YOU'RE SO EASY TO READ.
WHA...
RING RING ♪
Hikaruko
WING 4G
71%
I told Takane you might be on your own on Christmas Eve.
...
WHY WOULD YOU TELL SUCH AN OBVIOUS LIE...?
ANYWAY!
LOOK.

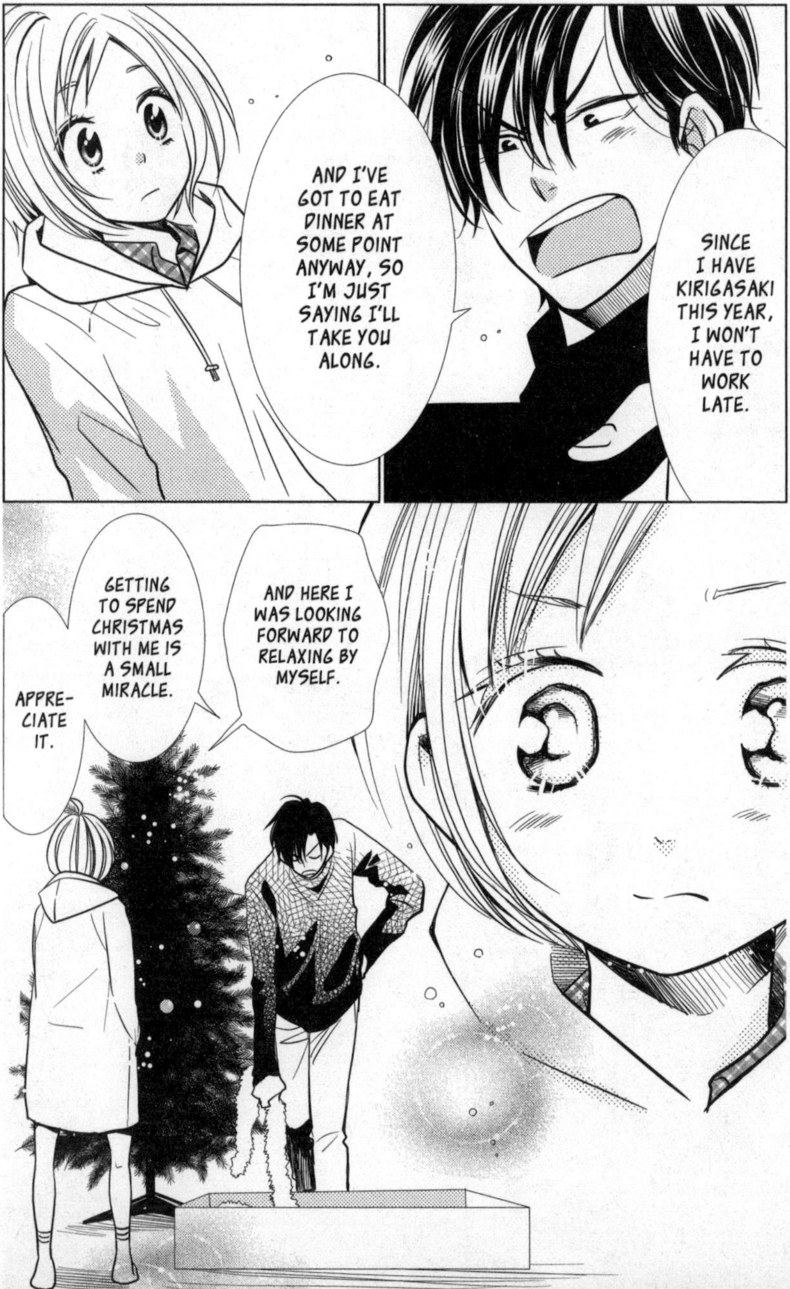
SINCE I HAVE KIRIGASAKI THIS YEAR, I WON'T HAVE TO WORK LATE.
AND I'VE GOT TO EAT DINNER AT SOME POINT ANYWAY, SO I'M JUST SAYING I'LL TAKE YOU ALONG.
AND HERE I WAS LOOKING FORWARD TO RELAXING BY MYSELF.
GETTING TO SPEND CHRISTMAS WITH ME IS A SMALL MIRACLE.
APPRE-CIATE IT.

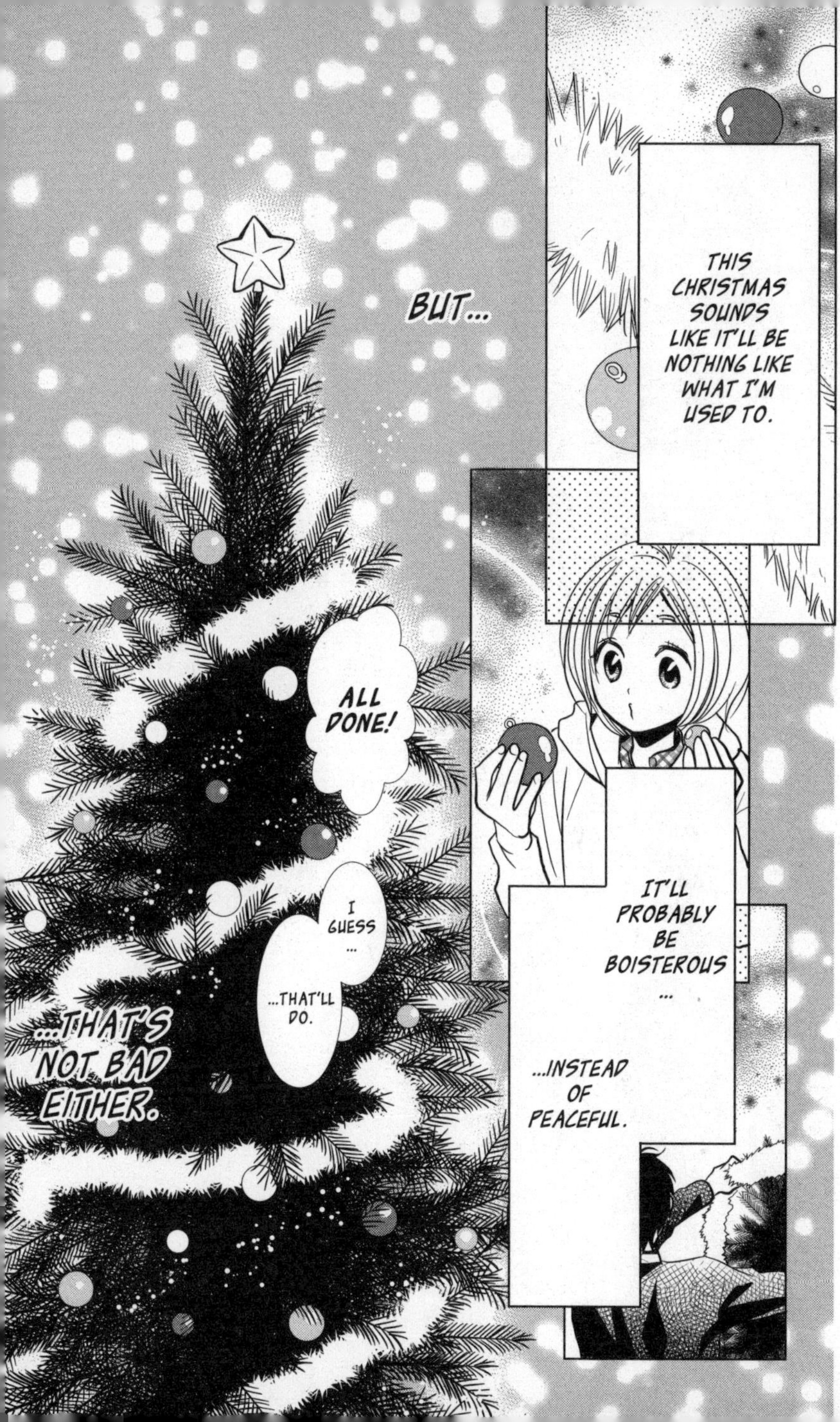
THIS CHRISTMAS SOUNDS LIKE IT'LL BE NOTHING LIKE WHAT I'M USED TO.
IT'LL PROBABLY BE BOISTEROUS...
...INSTEAD OF PEACEFUL.
BUT...
ALL DONE!
I GUESS...
...THAT'LL DO.
...THAT'S NOT BAD EITHER.

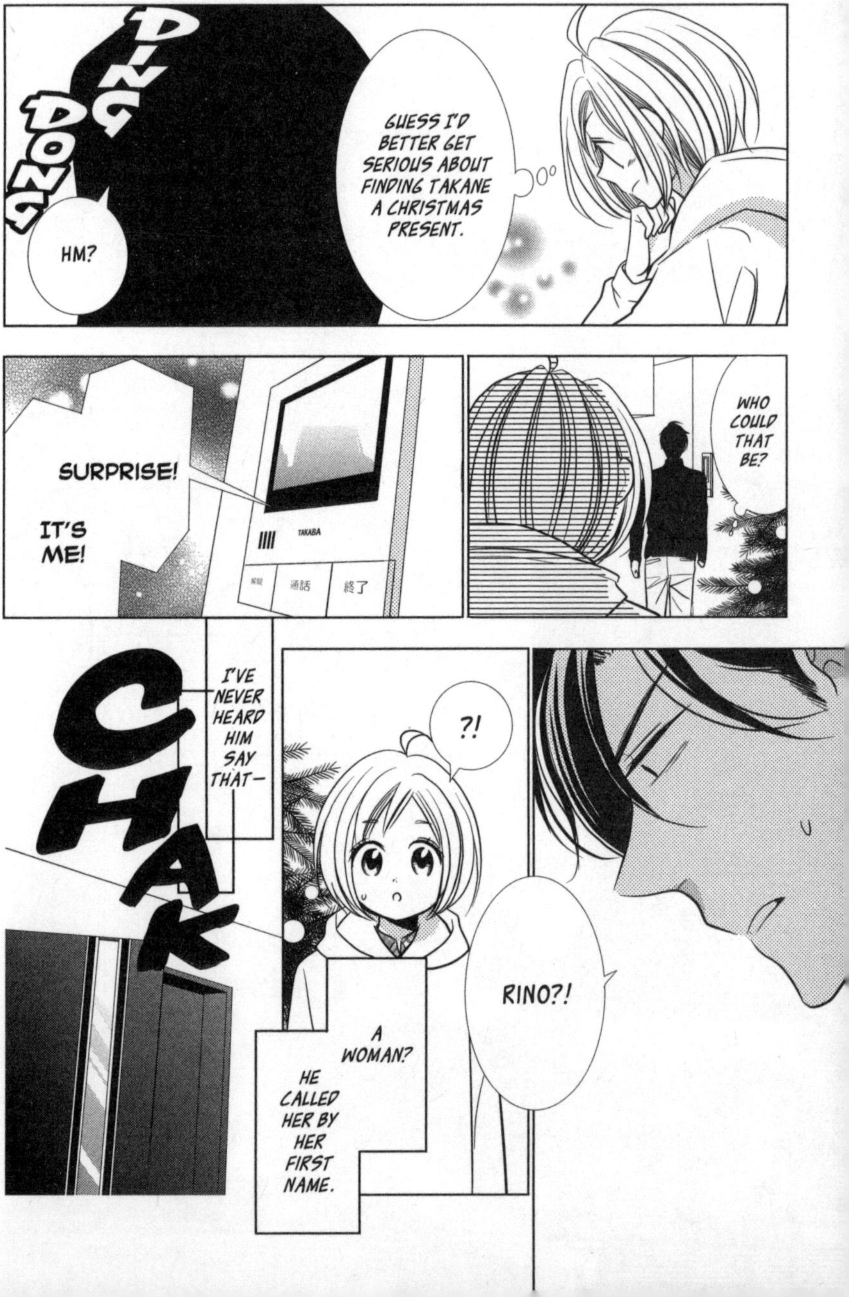
GUESS I'D BETTER GET SERIOUS ABOUT FINDING TAKANE A CHRISTMAS PRESENT.
DING DONG
HM?
WHO COULD THAT BE?
SURPRISE!
IT'S ME!
TAKABA
通話
終了
RINO?!
?!
I'VE NEVER HEARD HIM SAY THAT—
A WOMAN?
HE CALLED HER BY HER FIRST NAME.
CHAK

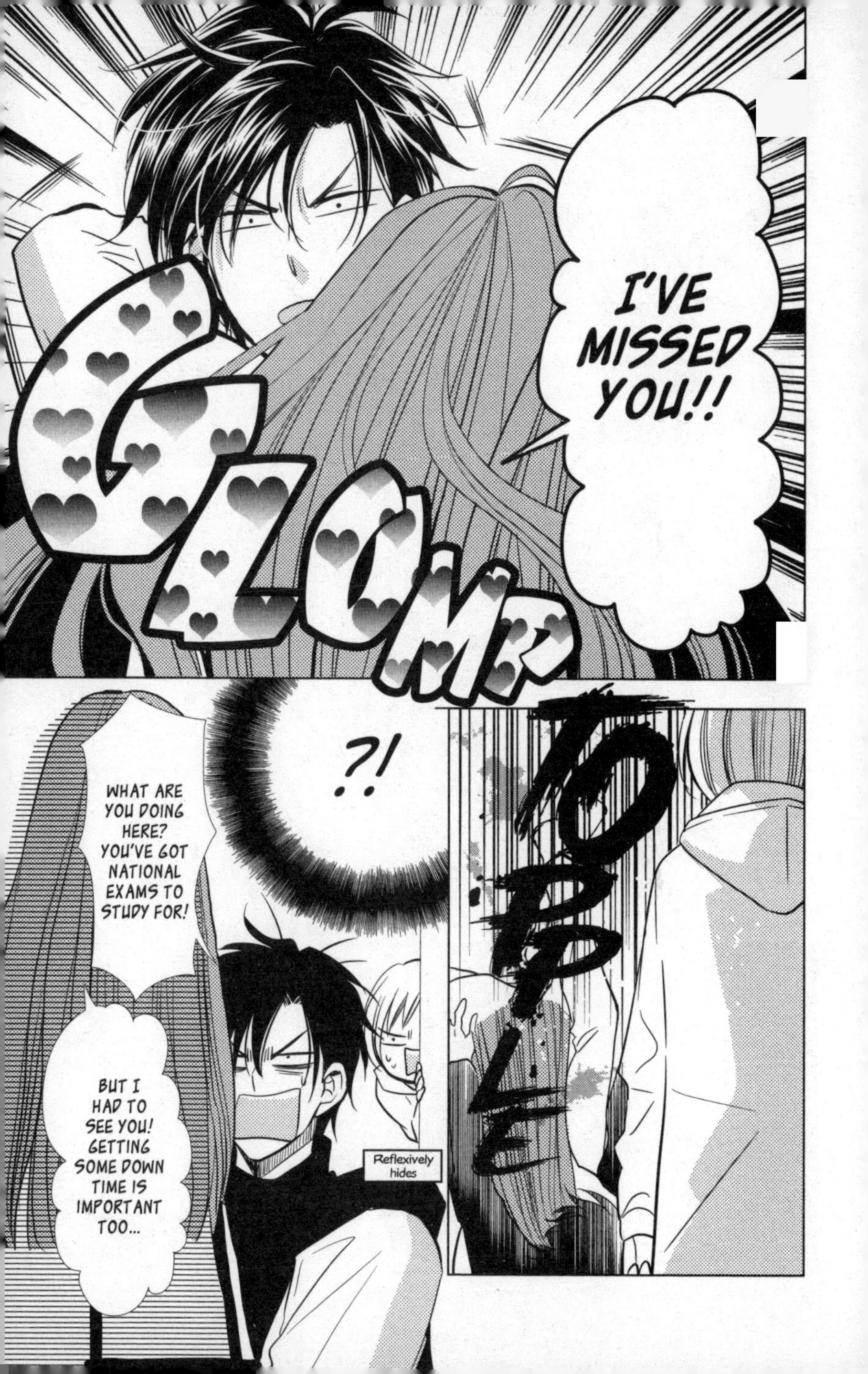
I'VE MISSED YOU!!
GLOMP
TOPPLE
?!
WHAT ARE YOU DOING HERE? YOU'VE GOT NATIONAL EXAMS TO STUDY FOR!
BUT I HAD TO SEE YOU! GETTING SOME DOWN TIME IS IMPORTANT TOO...
Reflexively hides

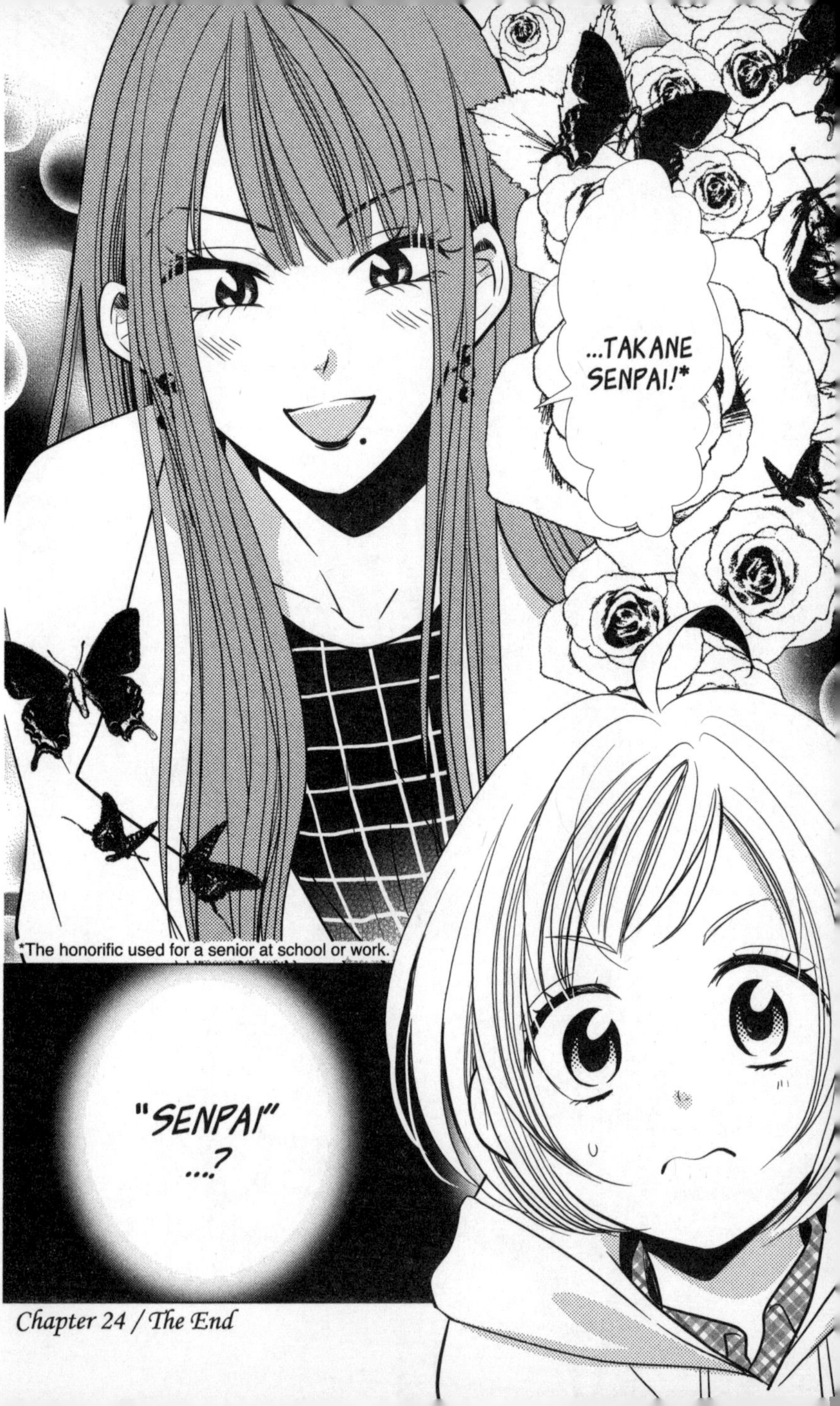

Chapter 24 / The End

Eiji Kirigasaki's Job Responsibilities ①

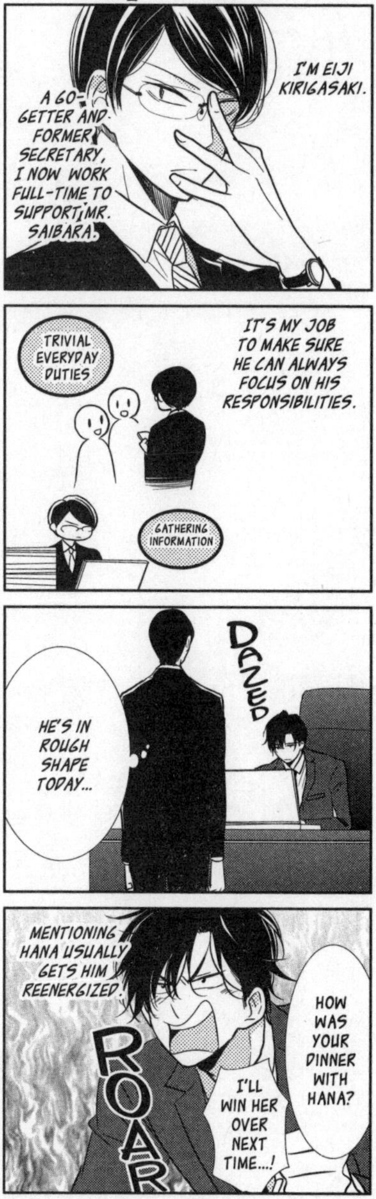
I'M EIJI KIRIGASAKI.
A GO-GETTER AND FORMER SECRETARY, I NOW WORK FULL-TIME TO SUPPORT MR. SAIBARA.
IT'S MY JOB TO MAKE SURE HE CAN ALWAYS FOCUS ON HIS RESPONSIBILITIES.
TRIVIAL EVERYDAY DUTIES
GATHERING INFORMATION
DAZED
HE'S IN ROUGH SHAPE TODAY...
HOW WAS YOUR DINNER WITH HANA?
MENTIONING HANA USUALLY GETS HIM REENERGIZED.
I'LL WIN HER OVER NEXT TIME...!
ROAR

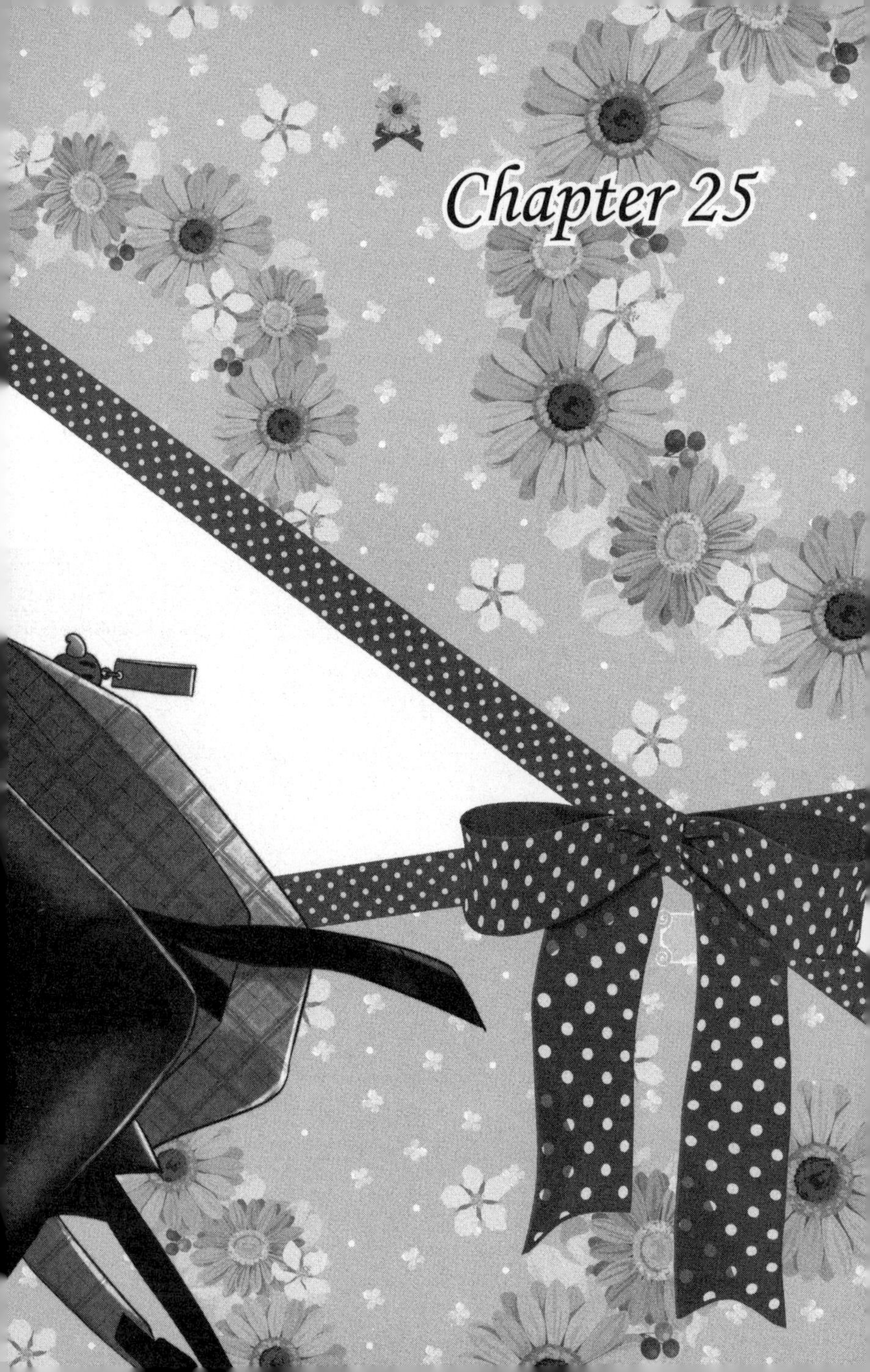
Chapter 25

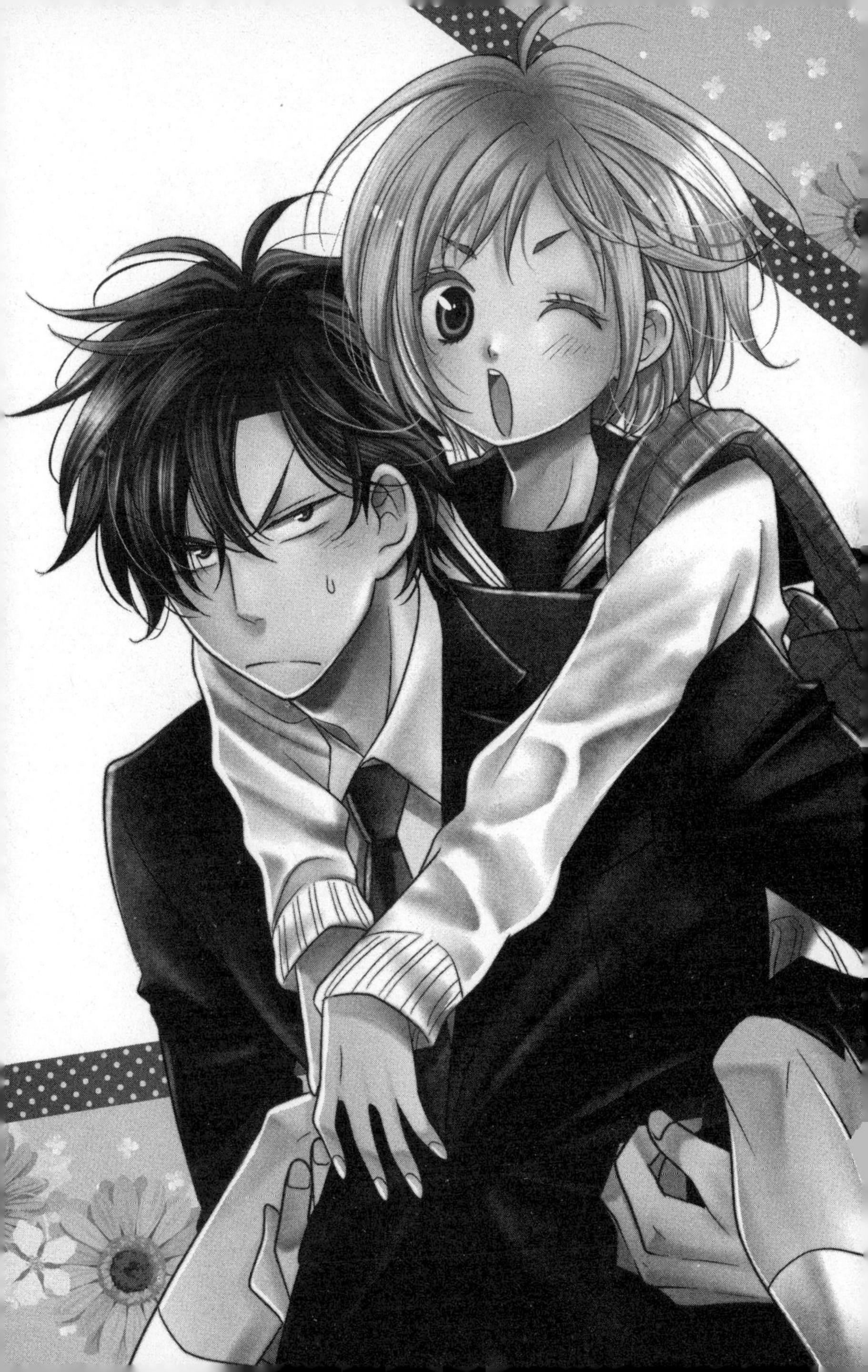

Eiji Kirigasaki's Job Responsibilities ②

I'M EIJI KIRIGASAKI.

A GO-GETTER AND FORMER SECRETARY, I NOW WORK FULL-TIME TO SUPPORT MR. SAIBARA.

HE'S IN ESPECIALLY BAD SHAPE TODAY...

OUT OF IT

TAKANE-NIP!

A cowlick!

Let me grab it!

That cowlick!

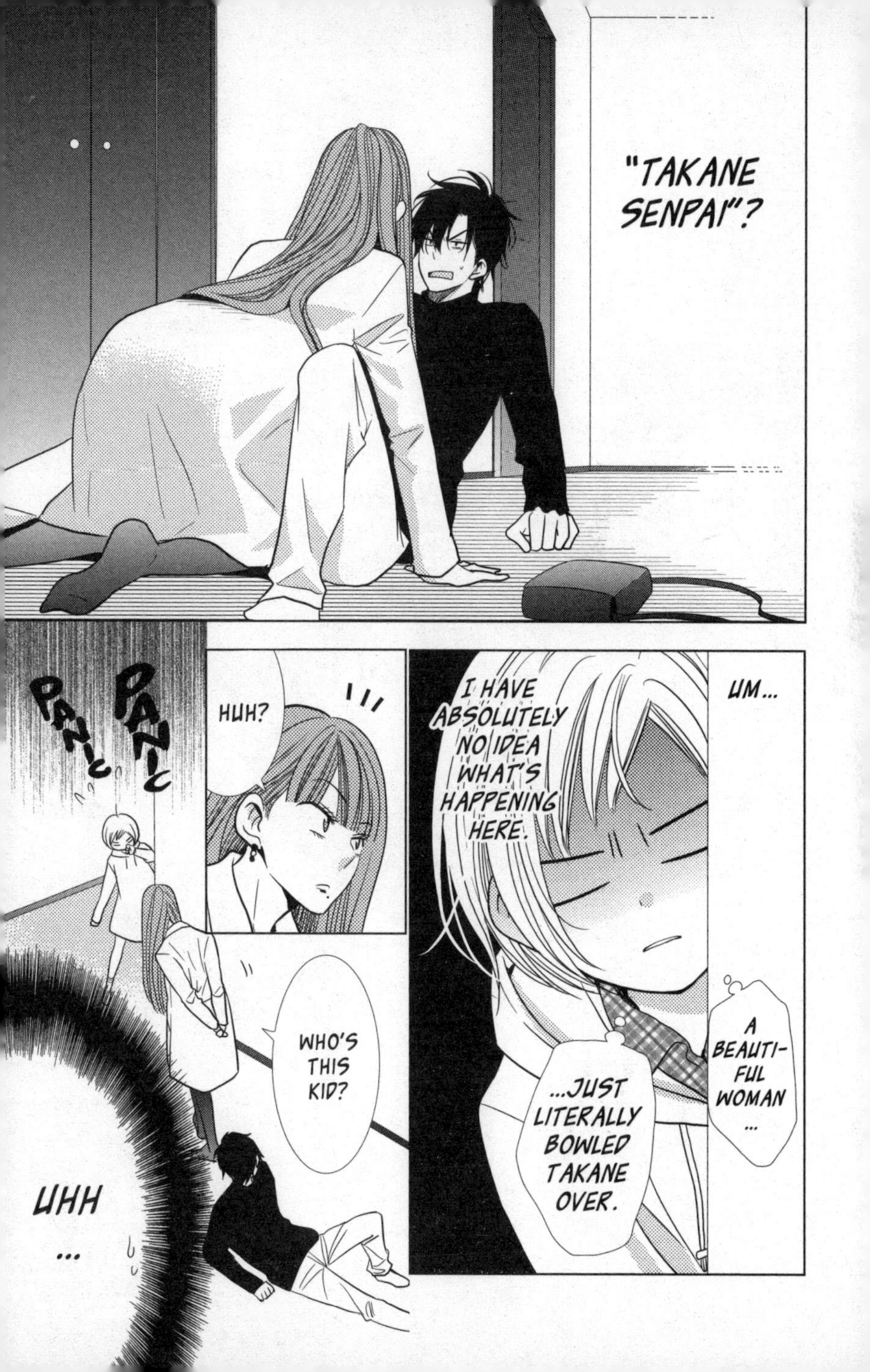
"TAKANE SENPAI"?
UM...
I HAVE ABSOLUTELY NO IDEA WHAT'S HAPPENING HERE.
A BEAUTIFUL WOMAN...
...JUST LITERALLY BOWLED TAKANE OVER.
HUH?
PANIC PANIC
WHO'S THIS KID?
UHH...

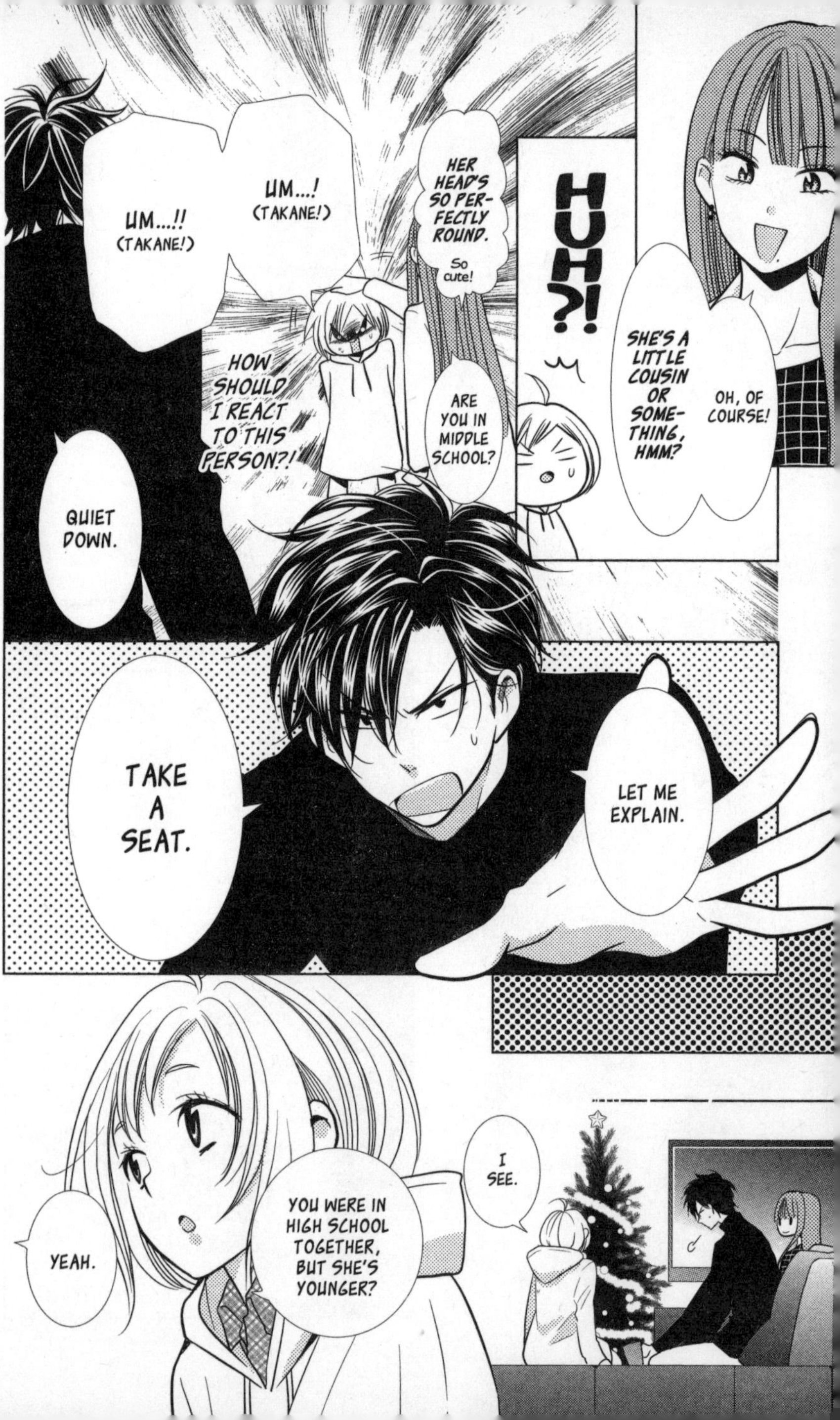
OH, OF COURSE!
SHE'S A LITTLE COUSIN OR SOMETHING, HMM?
HUH?!
HER HEAD'S SO PERFECTLY ROUND.
So cute!
ARE YOU IN MIDDLE SCHOOL?
UM...! (TAKANE!)
UM...!! (TAKANE!)
HOW SHOULD I REACT TO THIS PERSON?!
QUIET DOWN.
LET ME EXPLAIN.
TAKE A SEAT.
I SEE.
YOU WERE IN HIGH SCHOOL TOGETHER, BUT SHE'S YOUNGER?
YEAH.

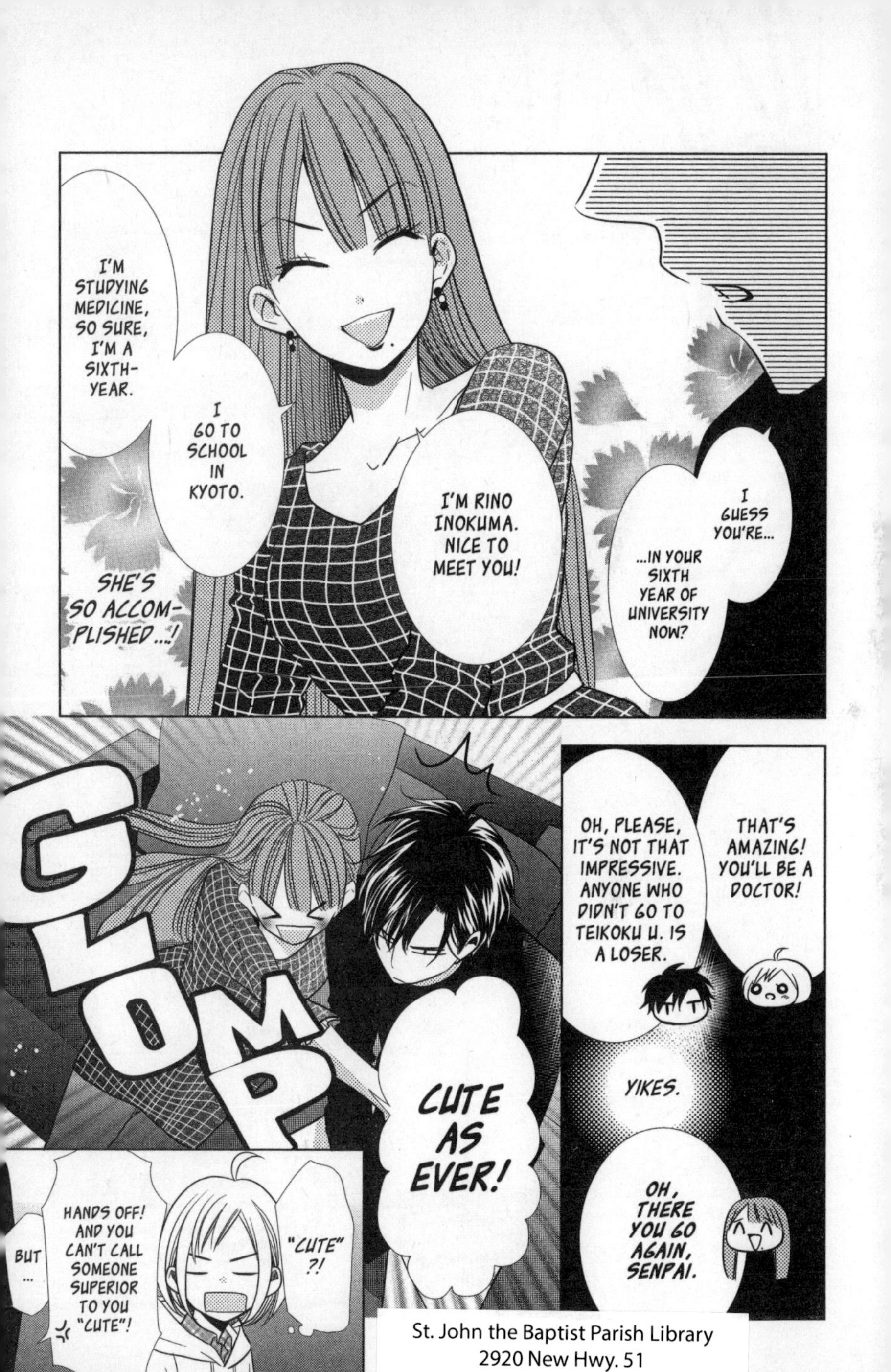
I GUESS YOU'RE...
...IN YOUR SIXTH YEAR OF UNIVERSITY NOW?
I'M RINO INOKUMA. NICE TO MEET YOU!
I GO TO SCHOOL IN KYOTO.
I'M STUDYING MEDICINE, SO SURE, I'M A SIXTH-YEAR.
SHE'S SO ACCOMPLISHED...!
THAT'S AMAZING! YOU'LL BE A DOCTOR!
OH, PLEASE, IT'S NOT THAT IMPRESSIVE. ANYONE WHO DIDN'T GO TO TEIKOKU U. IS A LOSER.
YIKES.
OH, THERE YOU GO AGAIN, SENPAI.
CLOMP
CUTE AS EVER!
"CUTE" ?!
HANDS OFF! AND YOU CAN'T CALL SOMEONE SUPERIOR TO YOU "CUTE"!
BUT...

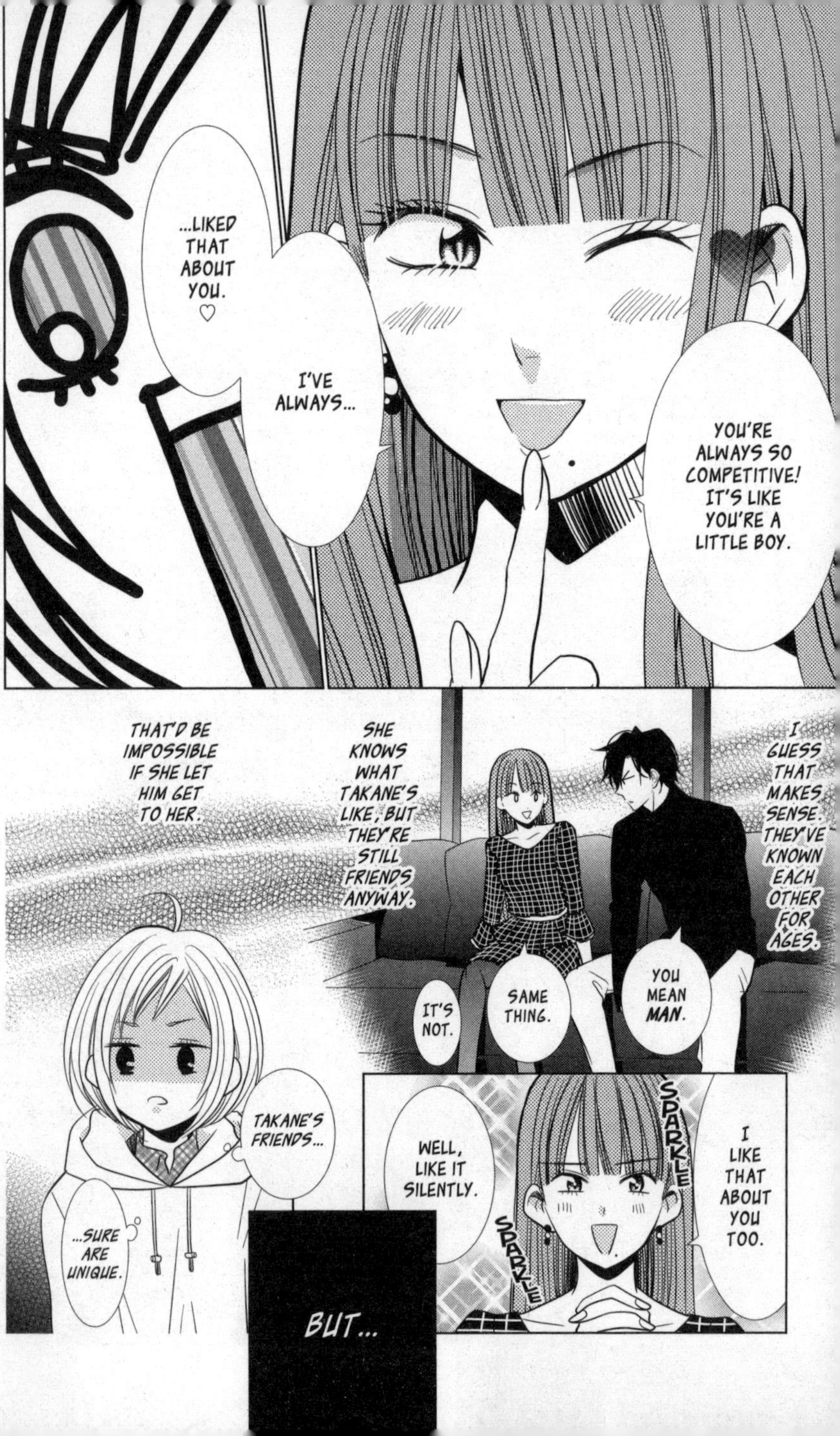

YOU'RE ALWAYS SO COMPETITIVE! IT'S LIKE YOU'RE A LITTLE BOY.
I'VE ALWAYS...
...LIKED THAT ABOUT YOU. ♡
I GUESS THAT MAKES SENSE. THEY'VE KNOWN EACH OTHER FOR AGES.
YOU MEAN MAN.
SAME THING.
IT'S NOT.
SHE KNOWS WHAT TAKANE'S LIKE, BUT THEY'RE STILL FRIENDS ANYWAY.
THAT'D BE IMPOSSIBLE IF SHE LET HIM GET TO HER.
I LIKE THAT ABOUT YOU TOO.
SPARKLE
SPARKLE
WELL, LIKE IT SILENTLY.
TAKANE'S FRIENDS...
...SURE ARE UNIQUE.
BUT...

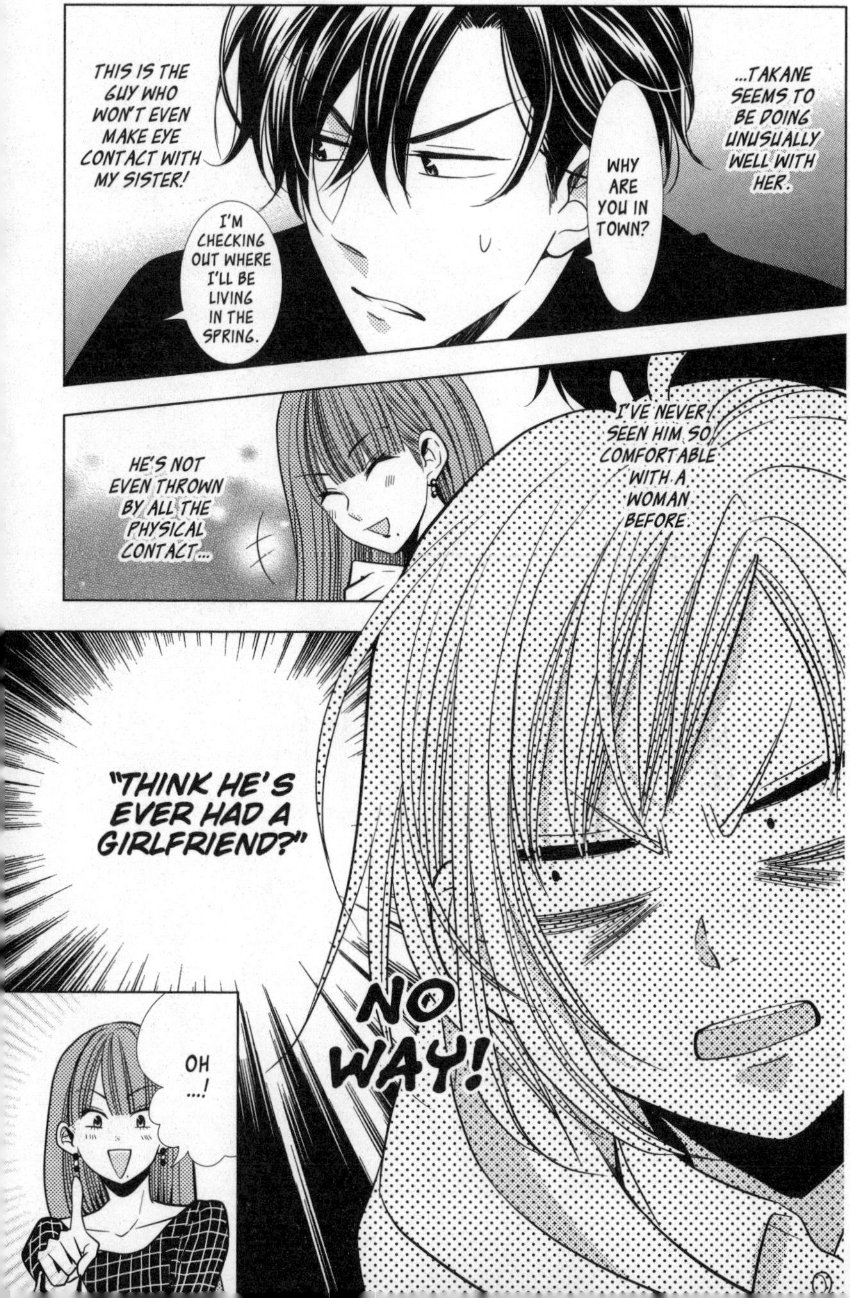
...TAKANE SEEMS TO BE DOING UNUSUALLY WELL WITH HER.
WHY ARE YOU IN TOWN?
THIS IS THE GUY WHO WON'T EVEN MAKE EYE CONTACT WITH MY SISTER!
I'M CHECKING OUT WHERE I'LL BE LIVING IN THE SPRING.
I'VE NEVER SEEN HIM SO COMFORTABLE WITH A WOMAN BEFORE.
HE'S NOT EVEN THROWN BY ALL THE PHYSICAL CONTACT...
"THINK HE'S EVER HAD A GIRLFRIEND?"
NO WAY!
OH ...!

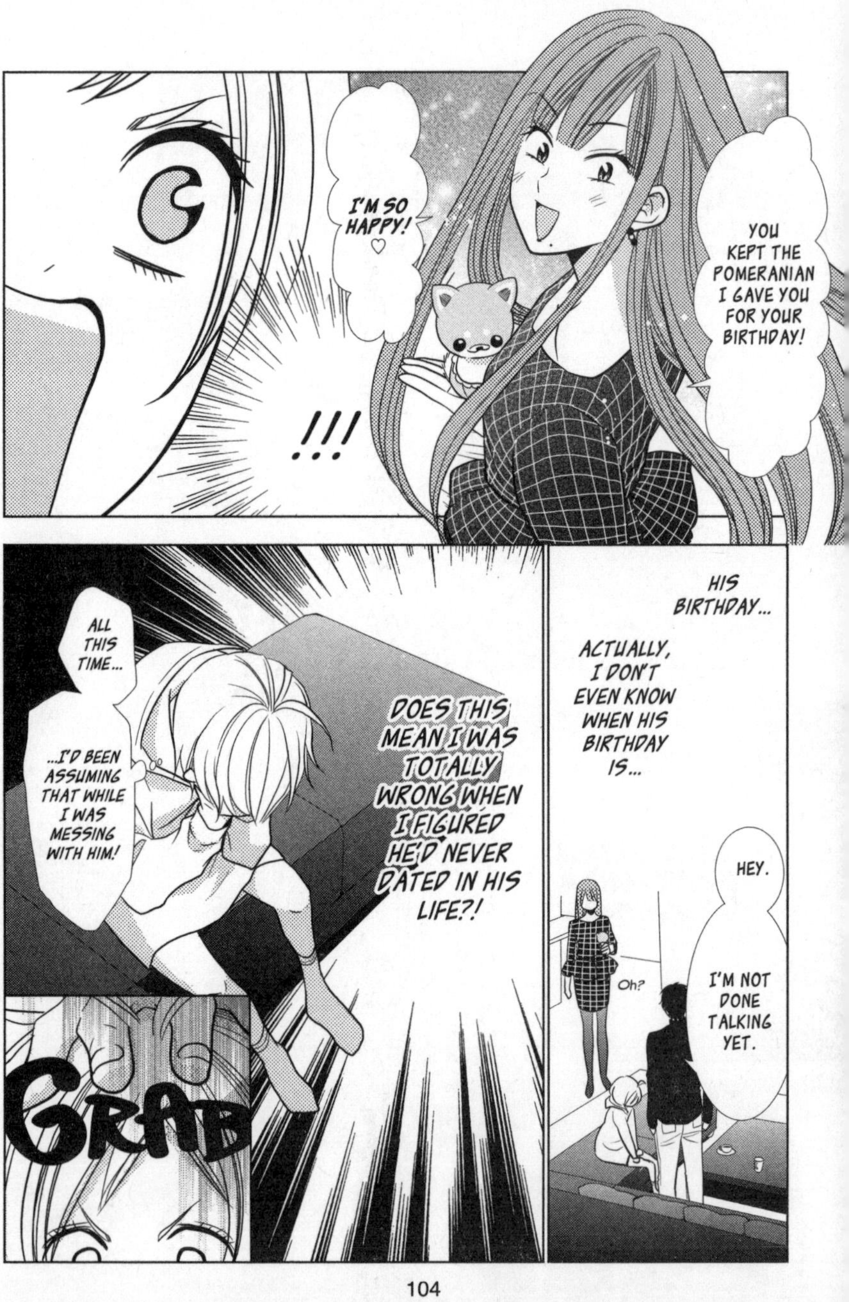
YOU KEPT THE POMERANIAN I GAVE YOU FOR YOUR BIRTHDAY!
I'M SO HAPPY! ♡
!!!
HIS BIRTHDAY...
ACTUALLY, I DON'T EVEN KNOW WHEN HIS BIRTHDAY IS...
HEY.
I'M NOT DONE TALKING YET.
Oh?
DOES THIS MEAN I WAS TOTALLY WRONG WHEN I FIGURED HE'D NEVER DATED IN HIS LIFE?!
ALL THIS TIME...
...I'D BEEN ASSUMING THAT WHILE I WAS MESSING WITH HIM!
GRAB

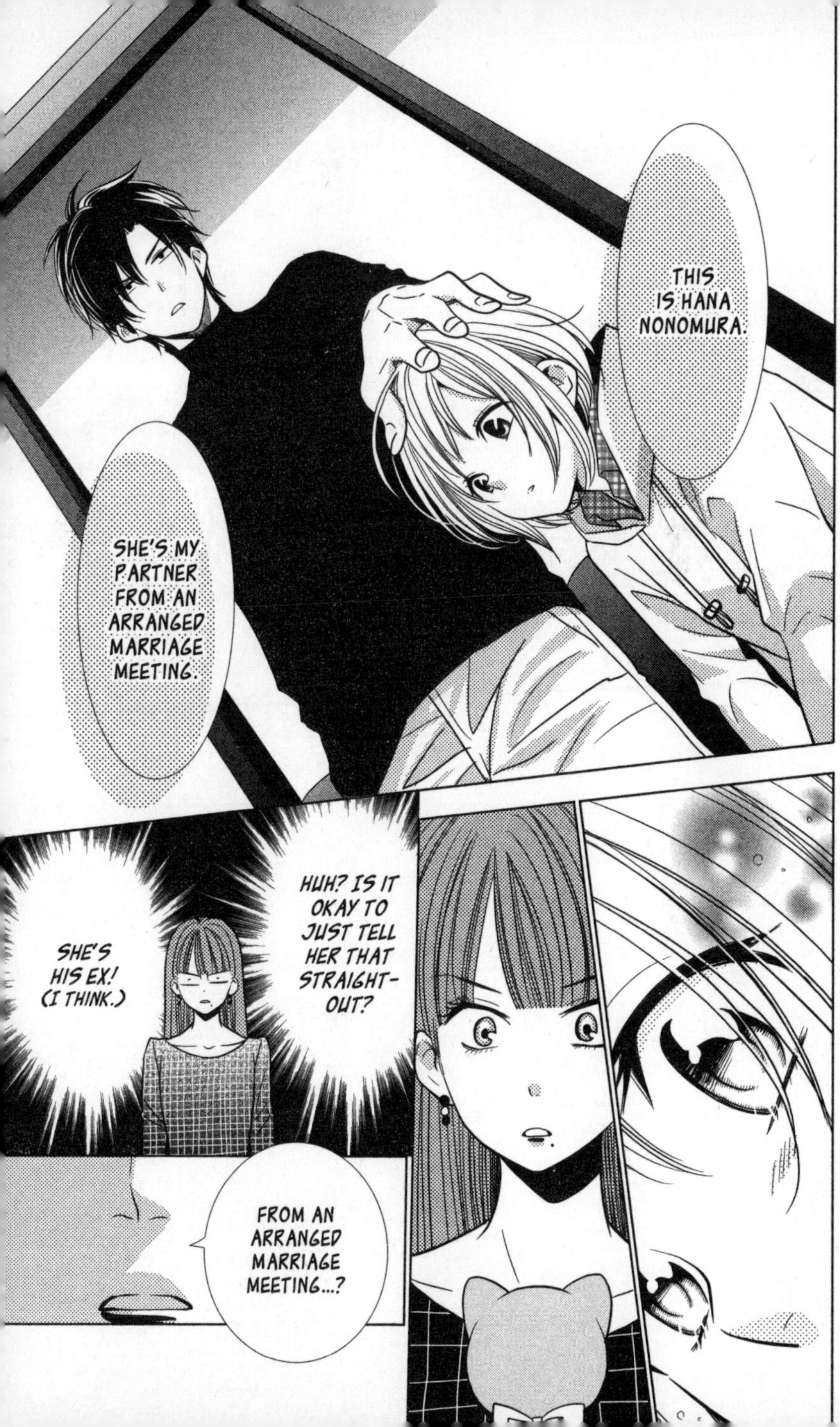
THIS IS HANA NONOMURA.
SHE'S MY PARTNER FROM AN ARRANGED MARRIAGE MEETING.
HUH? IS IT OKAY TO JUST TELL HER THAT STRAIGHT-OUT?
SHE'S HIS EX! (I THINK.)
FROM AN ARRANGED MARRIAGE MEETING...?

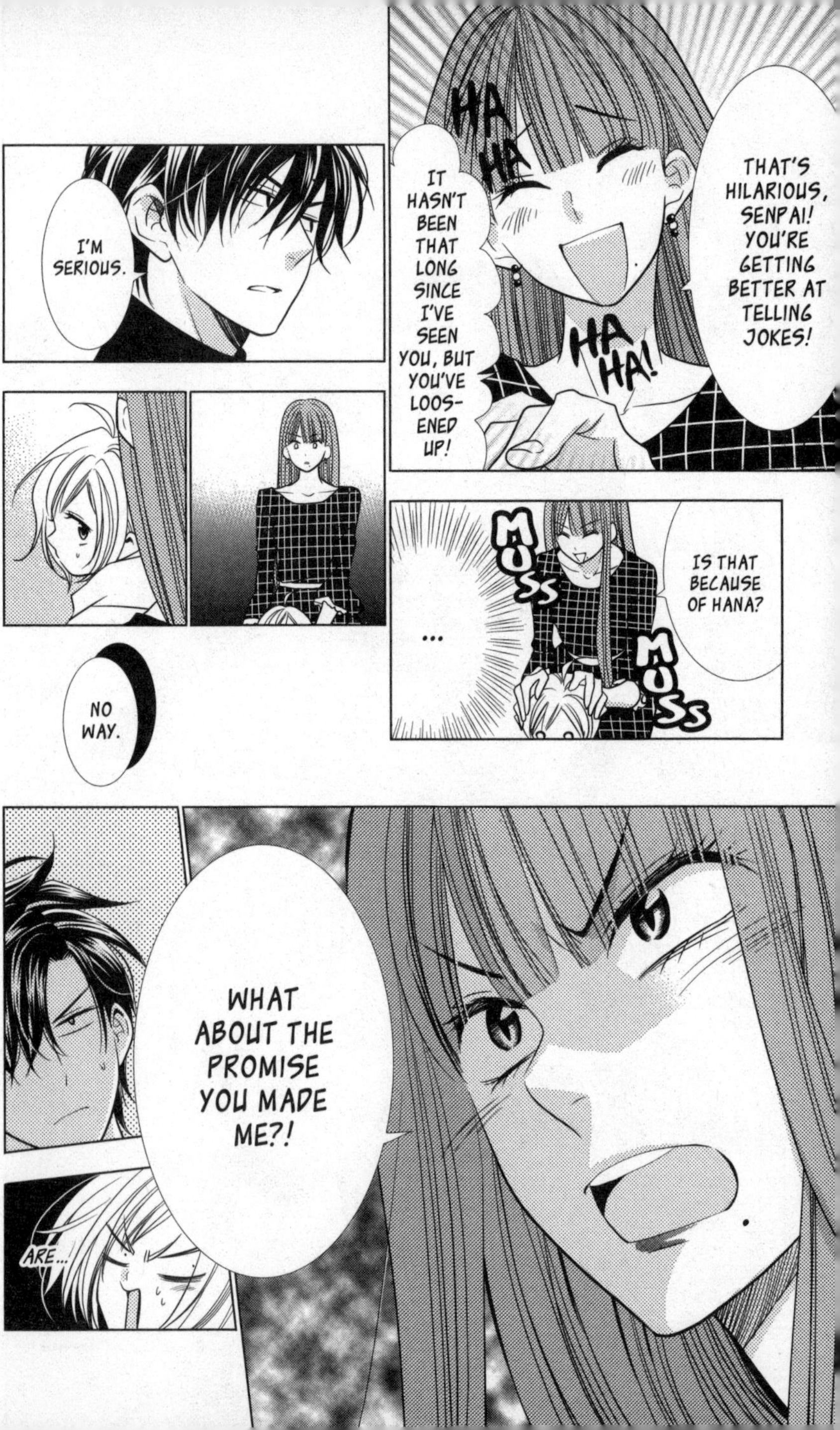
HA HA
THAT'S HILARIOUS, SENPAI! YOU'RE GETTING BETTER AT TELLING JOKES!
HA HA!
IT HASN'T BEEN THAT LONG SINCE I'VE SEEN YOU, BUT YOU'VE LOOS-ENED UP!
I'M SERIOUS.
IS THAT BECAUSE OF HANA?
MUSS
MUSS
...
NO WAY.
WHAT ABOUT THE PROMISE YOU MADE ME?!
ARE...

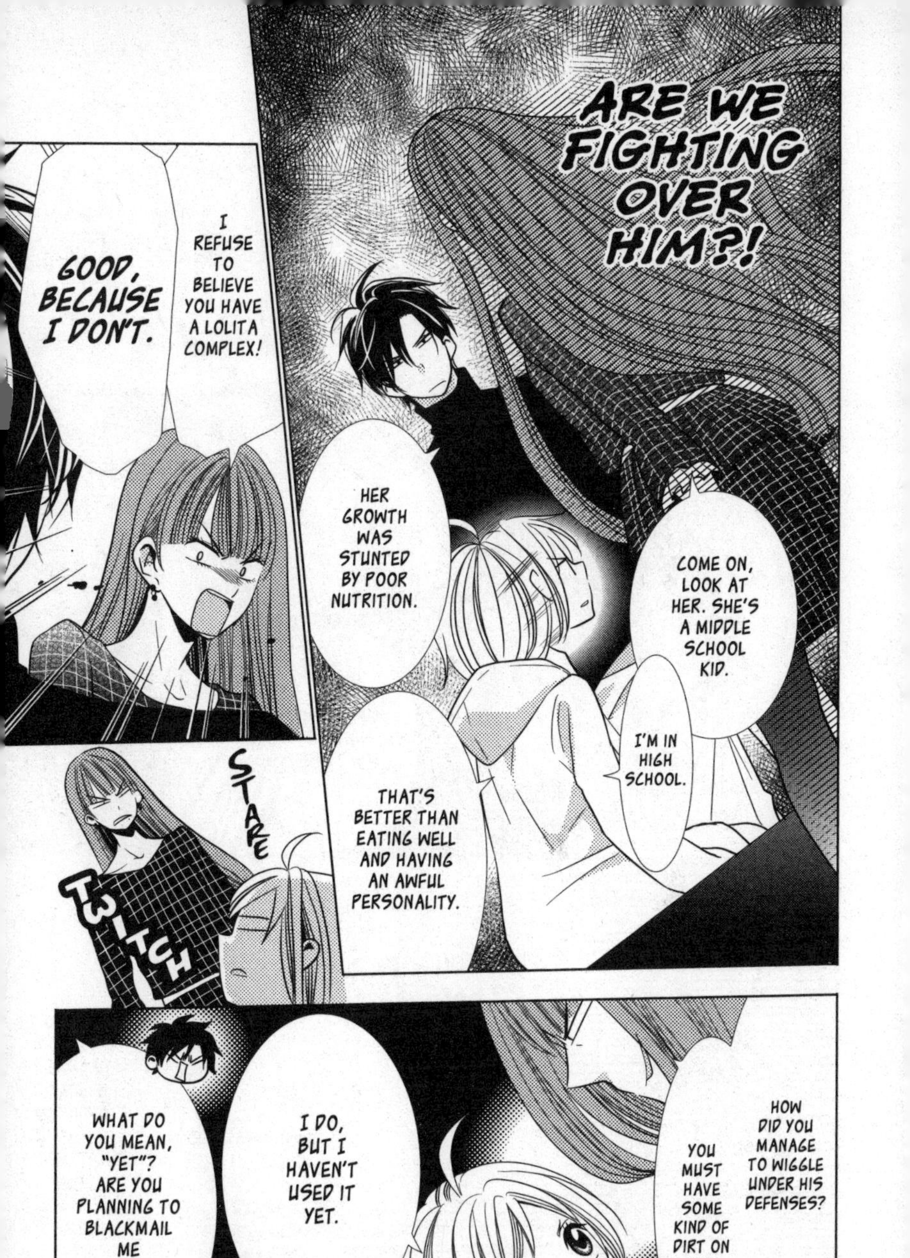
ARE WE FIGHTING OVER HIM?!
COME ON, LOOK AT HER. SHE'S A MIDDLE SCHOOL KID.
I'M IN HIGH SCHOOL.
HER GROWTH WAS STUNTED BY POOR NUTRITION.
THAT'S BETTER THAN EATING WELL AND HAVING AN AWFUL PERSONALITY.
I REFUSE TO BELIEVE YOU HAVE A LOLITA COMPLEX!
GOOD, BECAUSE I DON'T.
STARE
TWITCH
HOW DID YOU MANAGE TO WIGGLE UNDER HIS DEFENSES?
YOU MUST HAVE SOME KIND OF DIRT ON HIM.
I DO, BUT I HAVEN'T USED IT YET.
WHAT DO YOU MEAN, "YET"? ARE YOU PLANNING TO BLACKMAIL ME SOMEDAY?

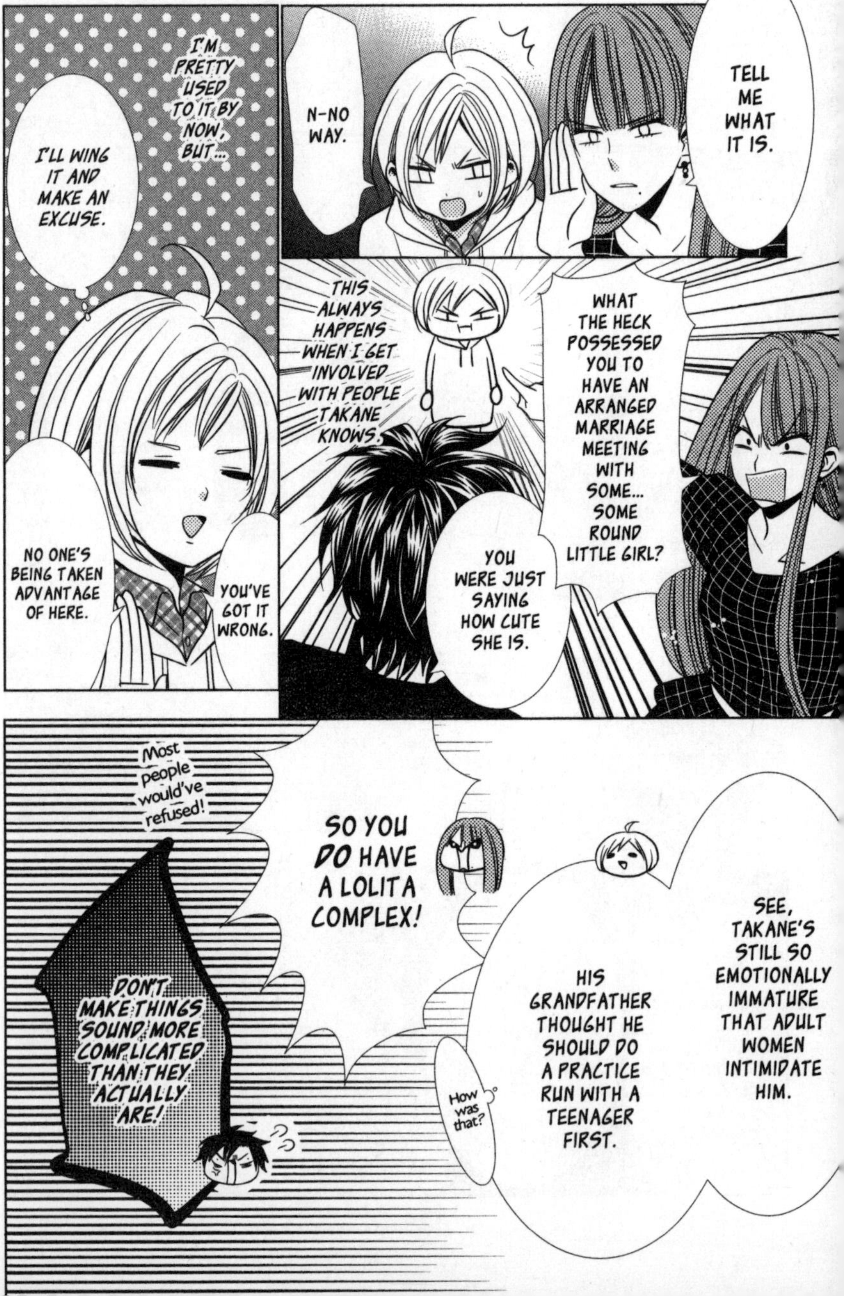
TELL ME WHAT IT IS.
N-NO WAY.
WHAT THE HECK POSSESSED YOU TO HAVE AN ARRANGED MARRIAGE MEETING WITH SOME... SOME ROUND LITTLE GIRL?
THIS ALWAYS HAPPENS WHEN I GET INVOLVED WITH PEOPLE TAKANE KNOWS.
YOU WERE JUST SAYING HOW CUTE SHE IS.
I'M PRETTY USED TO IT BY NOW, BUT...
I'LL WING IT AND MAKE AN EXCUSE.
YOU'VE GOT IT WRONG.
NO ONE'S BEING TAKEN ADVANTAGE OF HERE.
SEE, TAKANE'S STILL SO EMOTIONALLY IMMATURE THAT ADULT WOMEN INTIMIDATE HIM.
HIS GRANDFATHER THOUGHT HE SHOULD DO A PRACTICE RUN WITH A TEENAGER FIRST.
How was that?
SO YOU DO HAVE A LOLITA COMPLEX!
Most people would've refused!
DON'T MAKE THINGS SOUND MORE COMPLICATED THAN THEY ACTUALLY ARE!

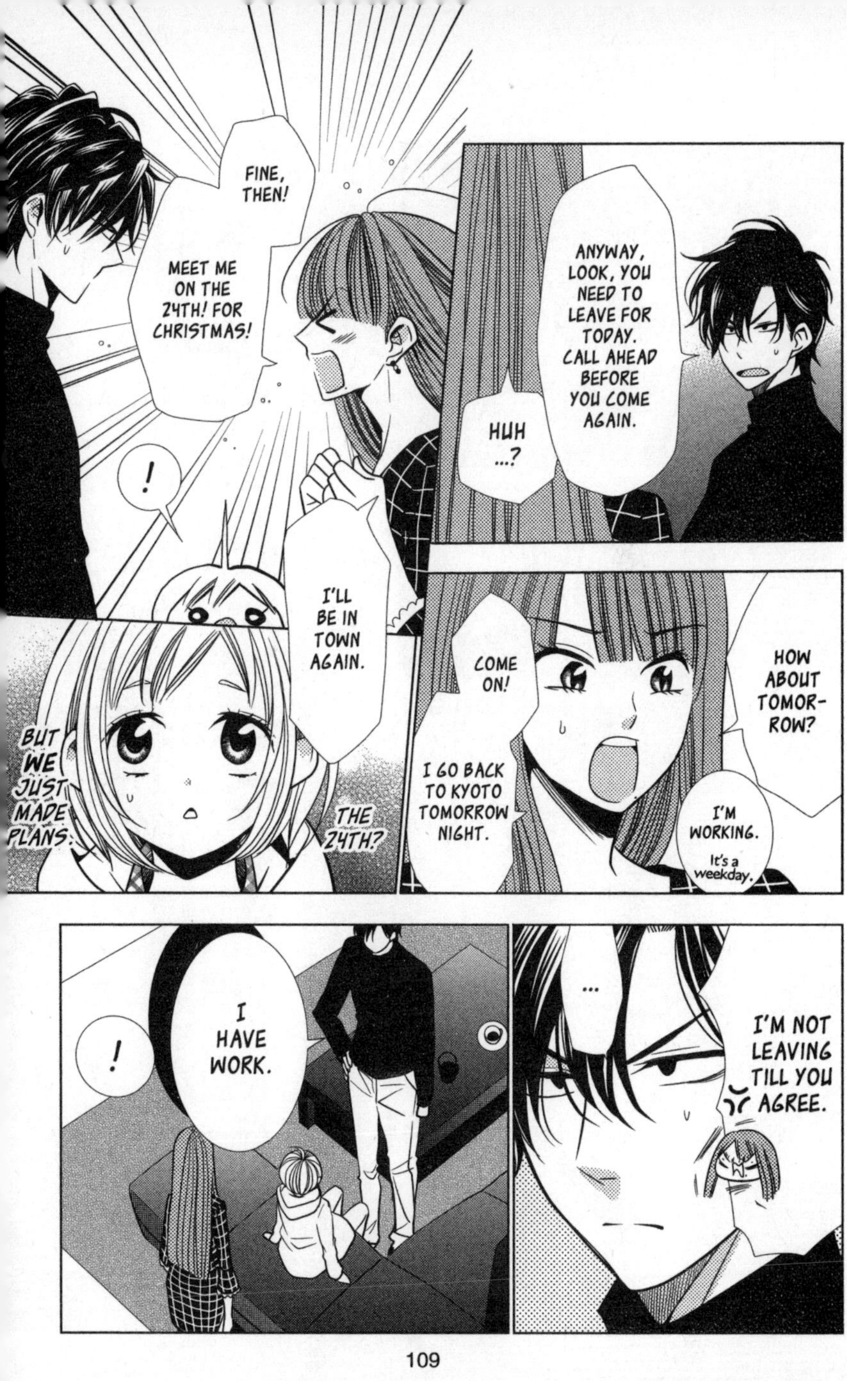
ANYWAY, LOOK, YOU NEED TO LEAVE FOR TODAY. CALL AHEAD BEFORE YOU COME AGAIN.
HUH ...?
HOW ABOUT TOMORROW?
I'M WORKING.
It's a weekday.
COME ON!
I GO BACK TO KYOTO TOMORROW NIGHT.
FINE, THEN!
MEET ME ON THE 24TH! FOR CHRISTMAS!
!
I'LL BE IN TOWN AGAIN.
THE 24TH?
BUT WE JUST MADE PLANS.
...
I'M NOT LEAVING TILL YOU AGREE.
I HAVE WORK.
!

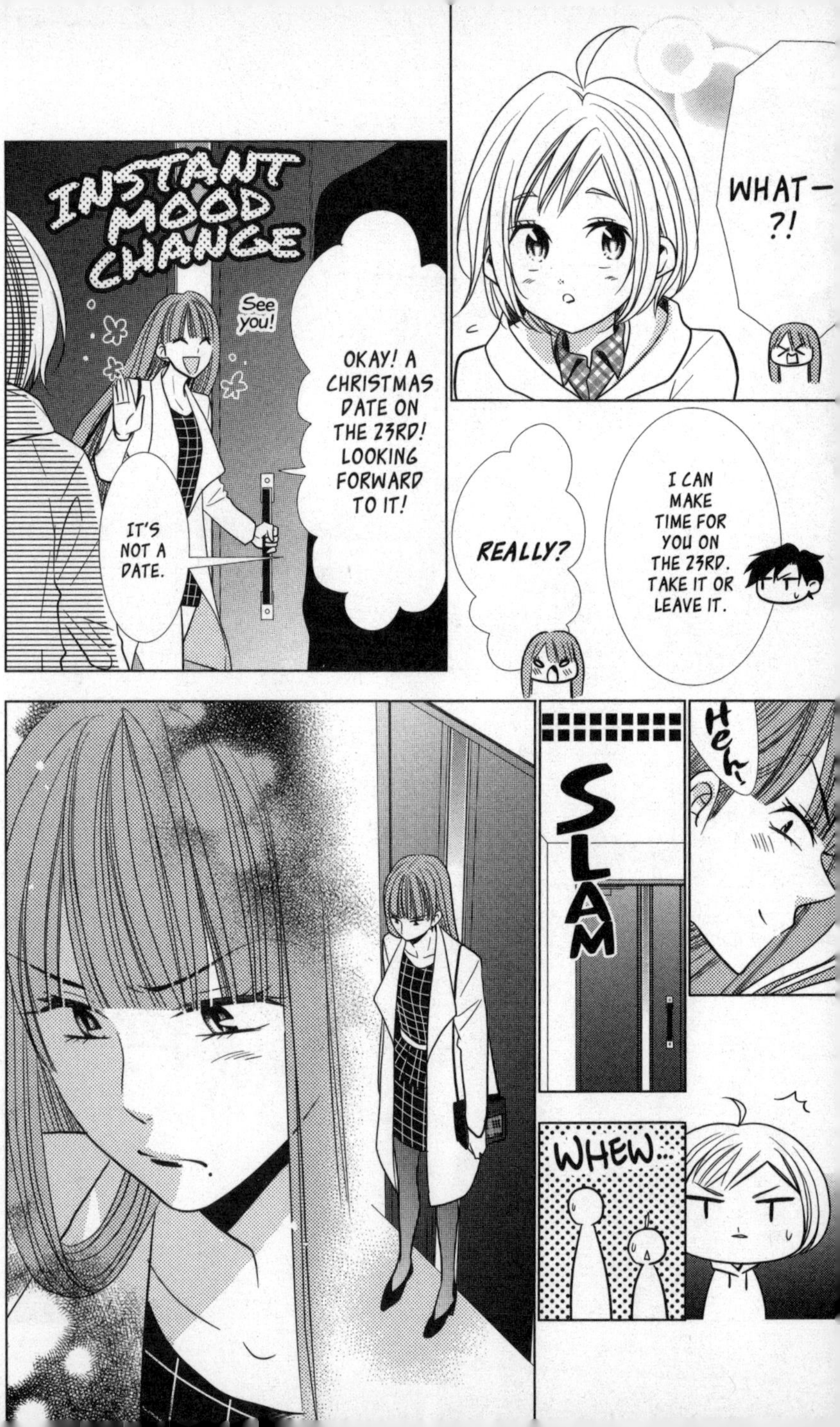
WHAT—?!
I CAN MAKE TIME FOR YOU ON THE 23RD. TAKE IT OR LEAVE IT.
REALLY?
INSTANT MOOD CHANGE
OKAY! A CHRISTMAS DATE ON THE 23RD! LOOKING FORWARD TO IT!
See you!
IT'S NOT A DATE.
Heh.
SLAM
WHEW...

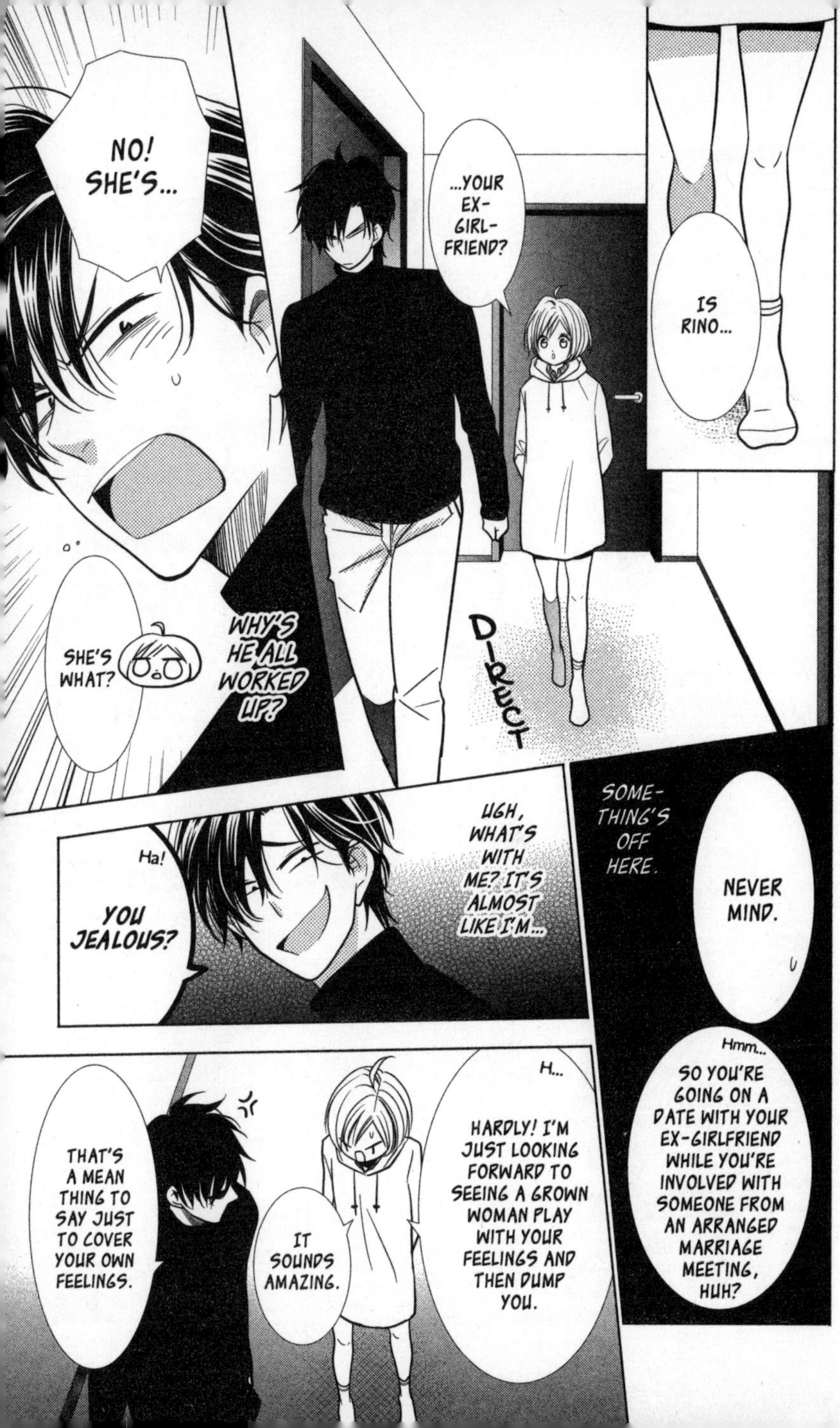
IS RINO...
...YOUR EX-GIRLFRIEND?
DIRECT
NO! SHE'S...
SHE'S WHAT?
WHY'S HE ALL WORKED UP?
SOMETHING'S OFF HERE.
NEVER MIND.
Hmm...
SO YOU'RE GOING ON A DATE WITH YOUR EX-GIRLFRIEND WHILE YOU'RE INVOLVED WITH SOMEONE FROM AN ARRANGED MARRIAGE MEETING, HUH?
Ha!
YOU JEALOUS?
UGH, WHAT'S WITH ME? IT'S ALMOST LIKE I'M...
H...
HARDLY! I'M JUST LOOKING FORWARD TO SEEING A GROWN WOMAN PLAY WITH YOUR FEELINGS AND THEN DUMP YOU.
IT SOUNDS AMAZING.
THAT'S A MEAN THING TO SAY JUST TO COVER YOUR OWN FEELINGS.

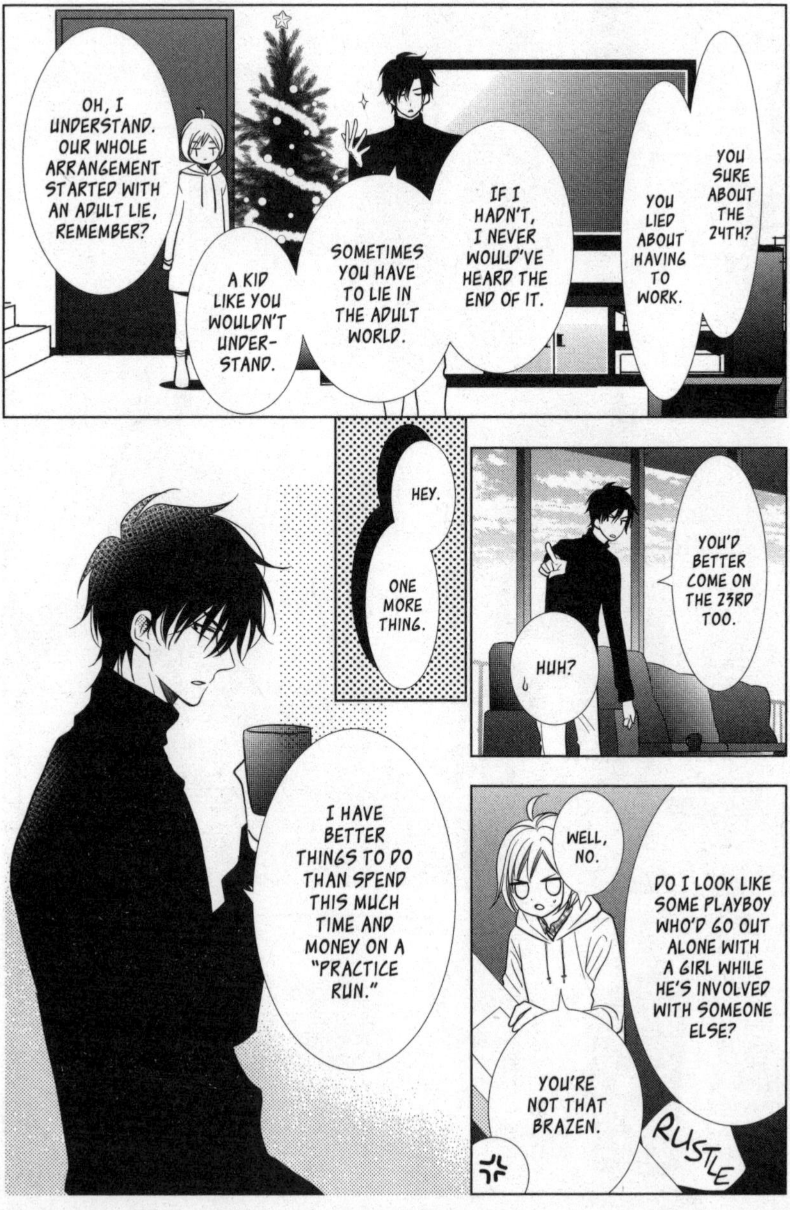
YOU SURE ABOUT THE 24TH?
YOU LIED ABOUT HAVING TO WORK.
IF I HADN'T, I NEVER WOULD'VE HEARD THE END OF IT.
SOMETIMES YOU HAVE TO LIE IN THE ADULT WORLD.
A KID LIKE YOU WOULDN'T UNDER-STAND.
OH, I UNDERSTAND. OUR WHOLE ARRANGEMENT STARTED WITH AN ADULT LIE, REMEMBER?
HEY.
ONE MORE THING.
YOU'D BETTER COME ON THE 23RD TOO.
HUH?
I HAVE BETTER THINGS TO DO THAN SPEND THIS MUCH TIME AND MONEY ON A "PRACTICE RUN."
DO I LOOK LIKE SOME PLAYBOY WHO'D GO OUT ALONE WITH A GIRL WHILE HE'S INVOLVED WITH SOMEONE ELSE?
WELL, NO.
YOU'RE NOT THAT BRAZEN.
RUSTLE

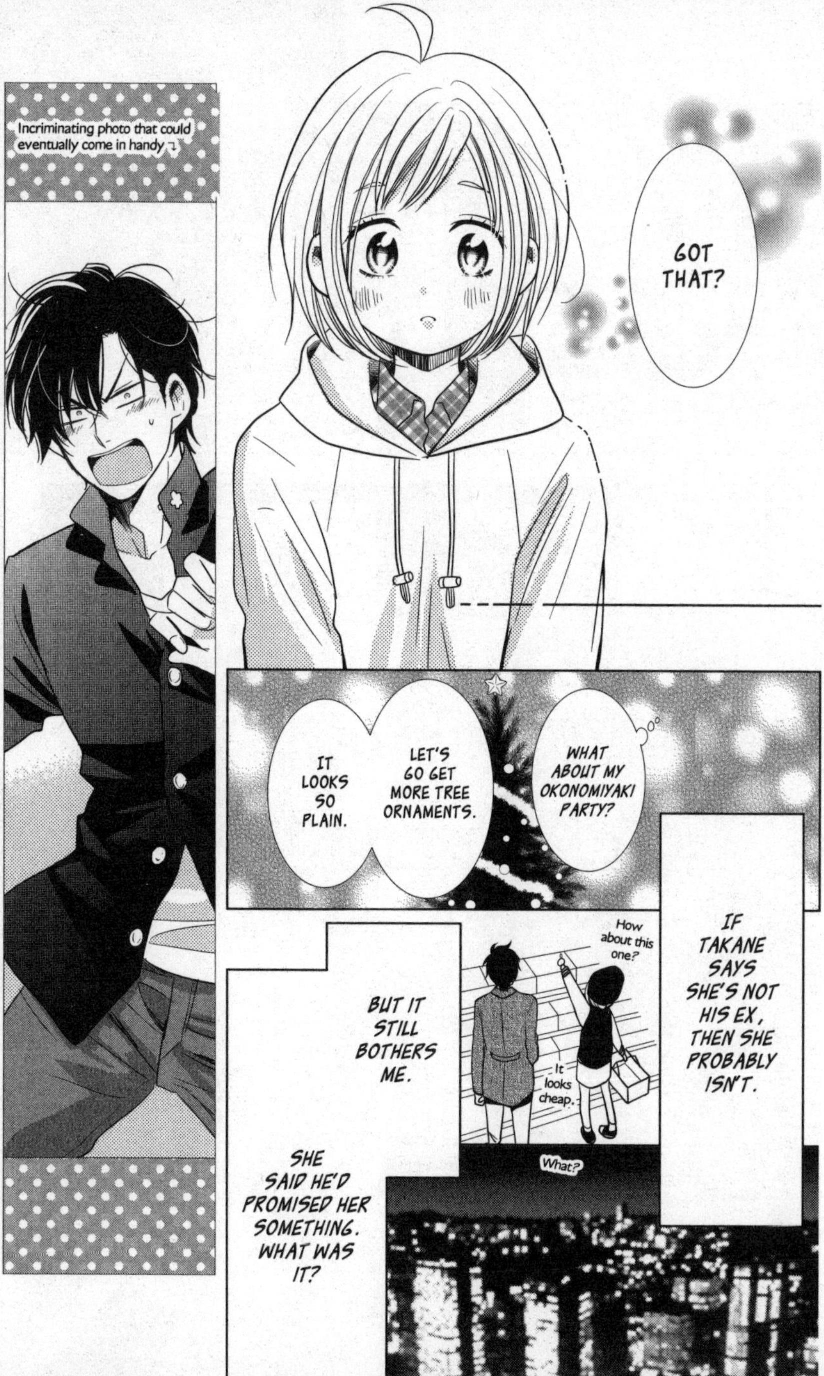
GOT THAT?
WHAT ABOUT MY OKONOMIYAKI PARTY?
LET'S GO GET MORE TREE ORNAMENTS.
IT LOOKS SO PLAIN.
IF TAKANE SAYS SHE'S NOT HIS EX, THEN SHE PROBABLY ISN'T.
How about this one?
It looks cheap.
BUT IT STILL BOTHERS ME.
What?
SHE SAID HE'D PROMISED HER SOMETHING. WHAT WAS IT?
Incriminating photo that could eventually come in handy ↴

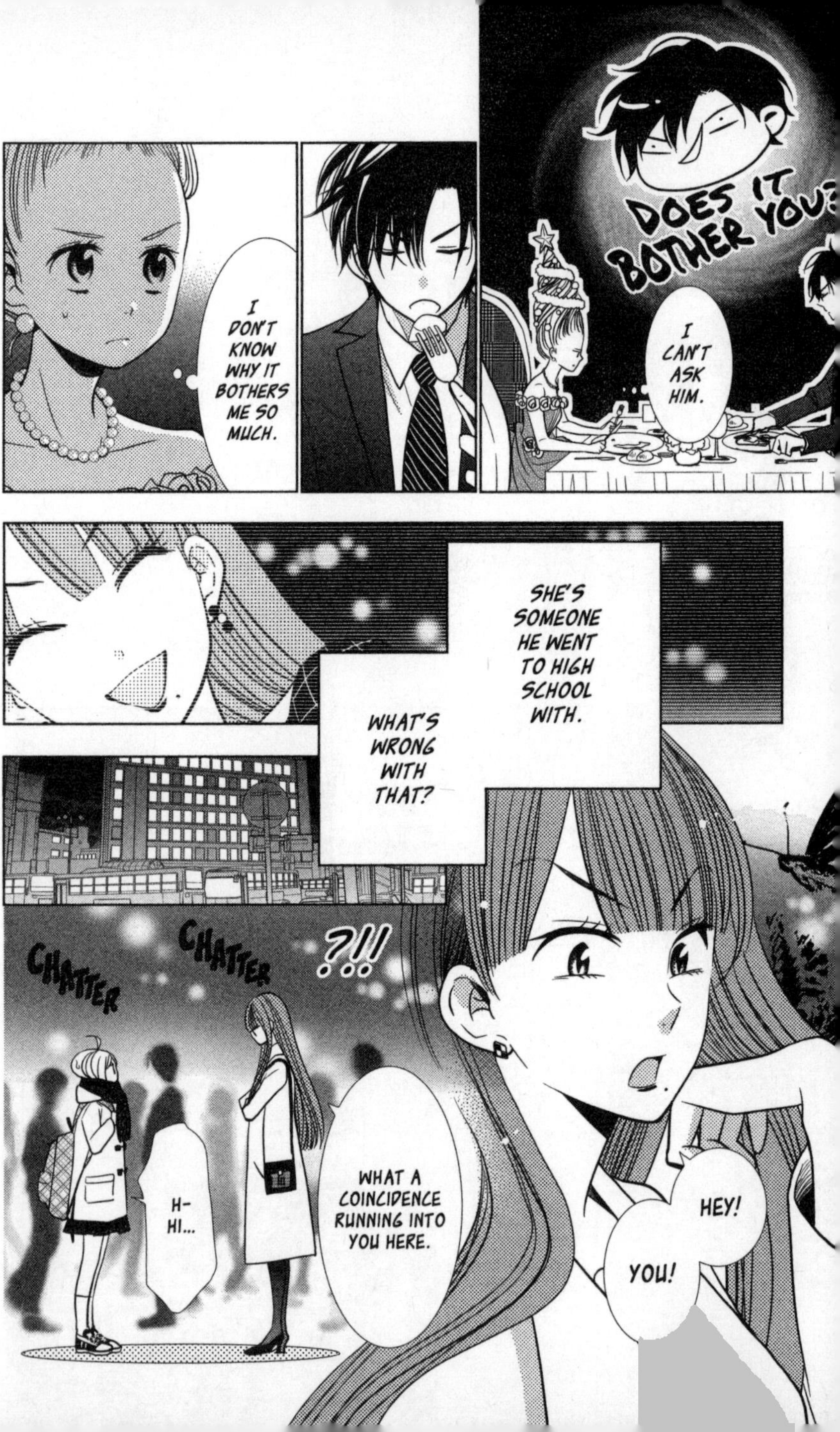
DOES IT BOTHER YOU?
I CAN'T ASK HIM.
I DON'T KNOW WHY IT BOTHERS ME SO MUCH.
SHE'S SOMEONE HE WENT TO HIGH SCHOOL WITH.
WHAT'S WRONG WITH THAT?
HEY!
YOU!
?!!
CHATTER
CHATTER
WHAT A COINCIDENCE RUNNING INTO YOU HERE.
H-HI...

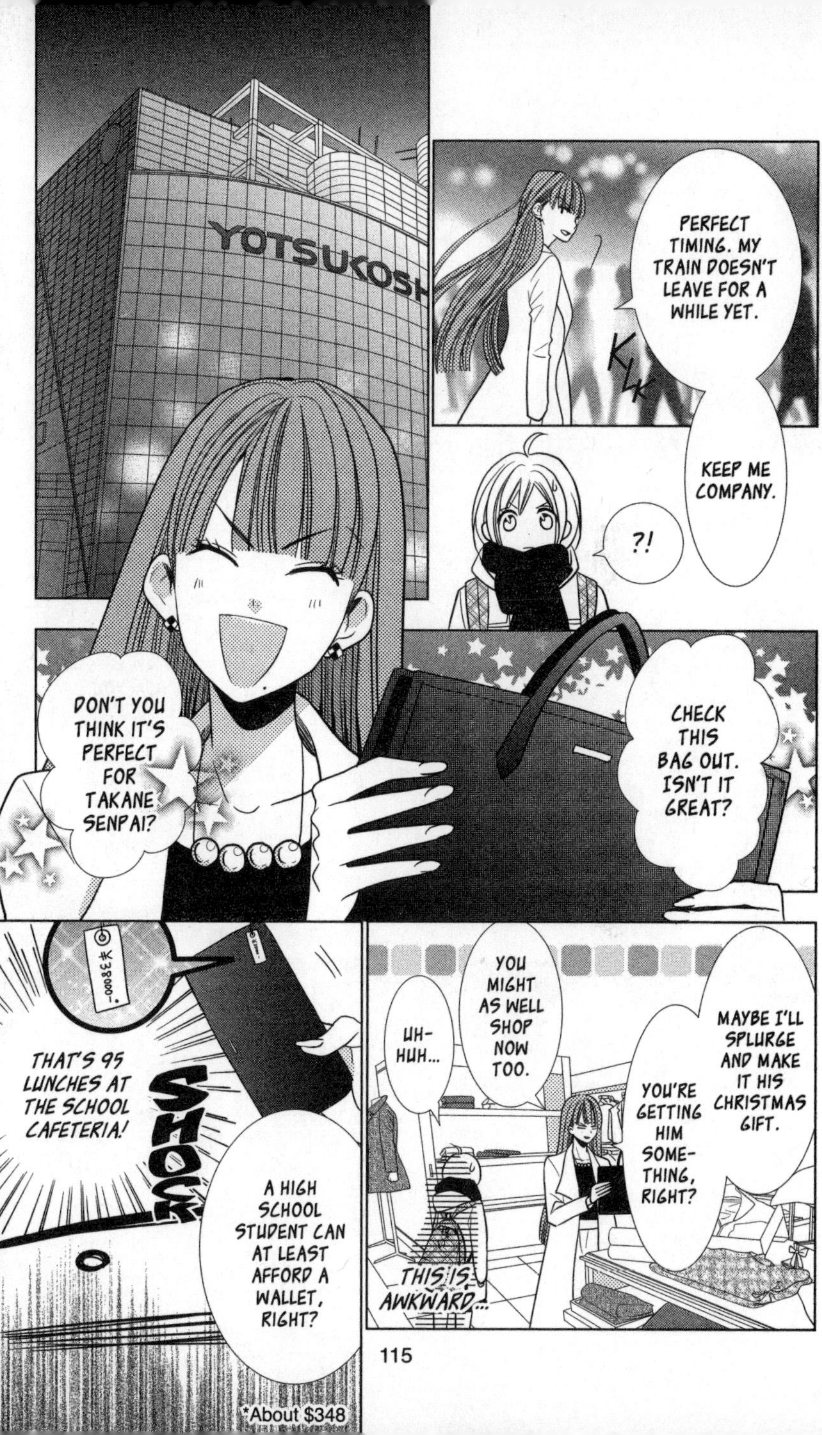

PERFECT TIMING. MY TRAIN DOESN'T LEAVE FOR A WHILE YET.
KLIK
KEEP ME COMPANY.
?!
CHECK THIS BAG OUT. ISN'T IT GREAT?
DON'T YOU THINK IT'S PERFECT FOR TAKANE SENPAI?
MAYBE I'LL SPLURGE AND MAKE IT HIS CHRISTMAS GIFT.
YOU'RE GETTING HIM SOMETHING, RIGHT?
YOU MIGHT AS WELL SHOP NOW TOO.
UH-HUH...
THIS IS AWKWARD...
¥38000-*
A HIGH SCHOOL STUDENT CAN AT LEAST AFFORD A WALLET, RIGHT?
THAT'S 95 LUNCHES AT THE SCHOOL CAFETERIA!
SHOCK

*About $348

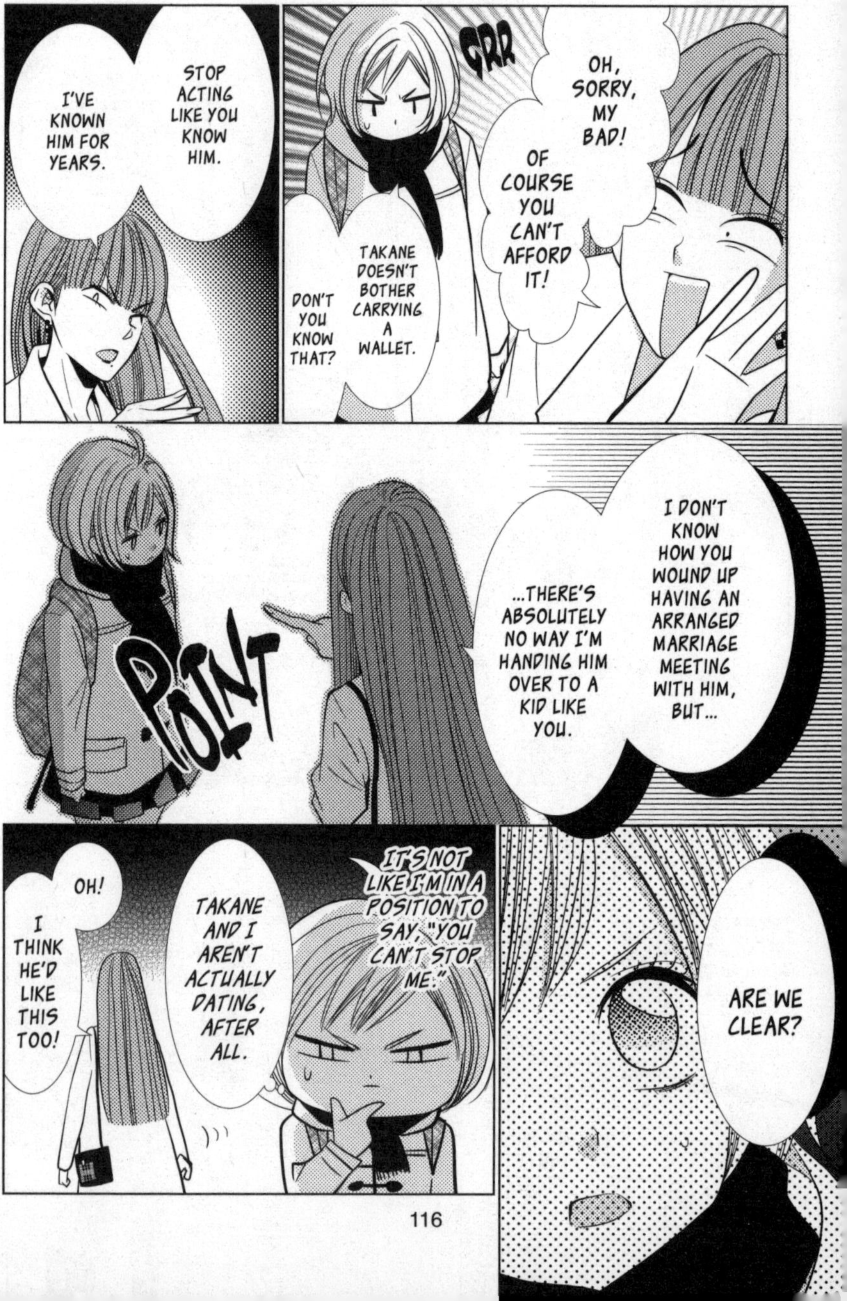
OH, SORRY, MY BAD!
OF COURSE YOU CAN'T AFFORD IT!
GRR
TAKANE DOESN'T BOTHER CARRYING A WALLET.
DON'T YOU KNOW THAT?
STOP ACTING LIKE YOU KNOW HIM.
I'VE KNOWN HIM FOR YEARS.
I DON'T KNOW HOW YOU WOUND UP HAVING AN ARRANGED MARRIAGE MEETING WITH HIM, BUT...
...THERE'S ABSOLUTELY NO WAY I'M HANDING HIM OVER TO A KID LIKE YOU.
POINT
ARE WE CLEAR?
IT'S NOT LIKE I'M IN A POSITION TO SAY, "YOU CAN'T STOP ME."
TAKANE AND I AREN'T ACTUALLY DATING, AFTER ALL.
OH!
I THINK HE'D LIKE THIS TOO!

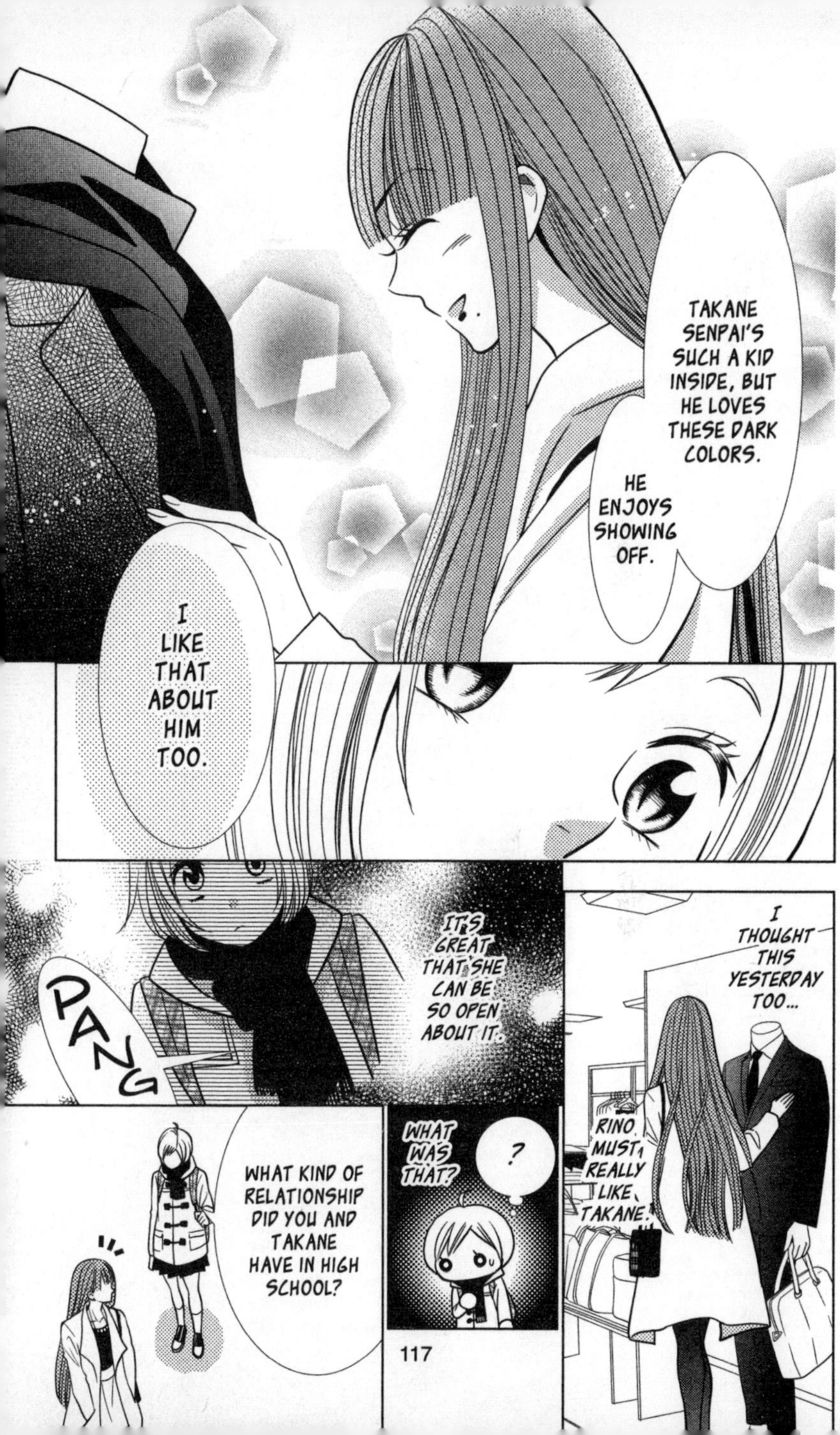
TAKANE SENPAI'S SUCH A KID INSIDE, BUT HE LOVES THESE DARK COLORS.
HE ENJOYS SHOWING OFF.
I LIKE THAT ABOUT HIM TOO.
I THOUGHT THIS YESTERDAY TOO...
RINO MUST REALLY LIKE TAKANE.
IT'S GREAT THAT SHE CAN BE SO OPEN ABOUT IT.
PANG
WHAT WAS THAT?
?
WHAT KIND OF RELATIONSHIP DID YOU AND TAKANE HAVE IN HIGH SCHOOL?

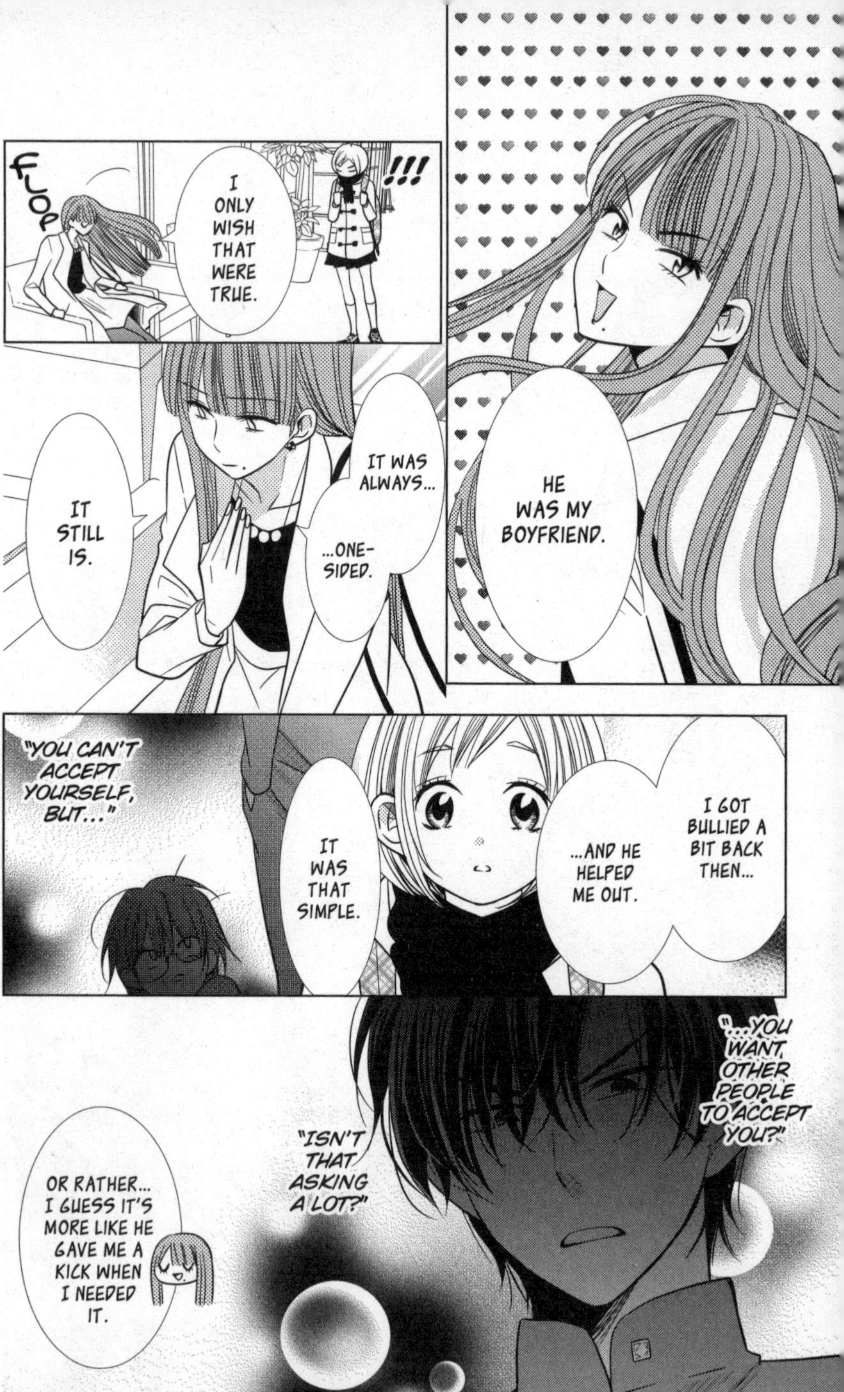
HE WAS MY BOYFRIEND.
!!!
FLOP
I ONLY WISH THAT WERE TRUE.
IT WAS ALWAYS...
...ONE-SIDED.
IT STILL IS.
I GOT BULLIED A BIT BACK THEN...
...AND HE HELPED ME OUT.
IT WAS THAT SIMPLE.
"YOU CAN'T ACCEPT YOURSELF, BUT..."
"...YOU WANT OTHER PEOPLE TO ACCEPT YOU?"
"ISN'T THAT ASKING A LOT?"
OR RATHER... I GUESS IT'S MORE LIKE HE GAVE ME A KICK WHEN I NEEDED IT.

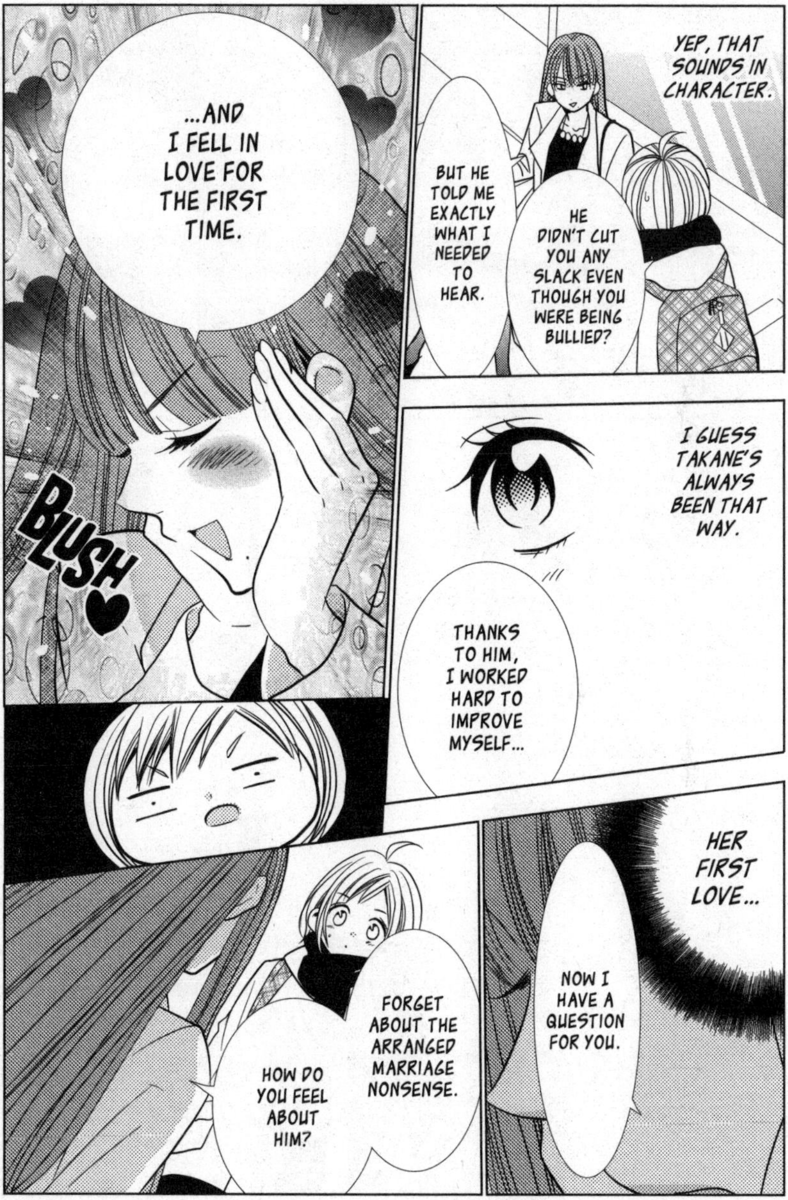
YEP, THAT SOUNDS IN CHARACTER.
HE DIDN'T CUT YOU ANY SLACK EVEN THOUGH YOU WERE BEING BULLIED?
BUT HE TOLD ME EXACTLY WHAT I NEEDED TO HEAR.
I GUESS TAKANE'S ALWAYS BEEN THAT WAY.
THANKS TO HIM, I WORKED HARD TO IMPROVE MYSELF...
...AND I FELL IN LOVE FOR THE FIRST TIME.
BLUSH
HER FIRST LOVE...
NOW I HAVE A QUESTION FOR YOU.
FORGET ABOUT THE ARRANGED MARRIAGE NONSENSE.
HOW DO YOU FEEL ABOUT HIM?

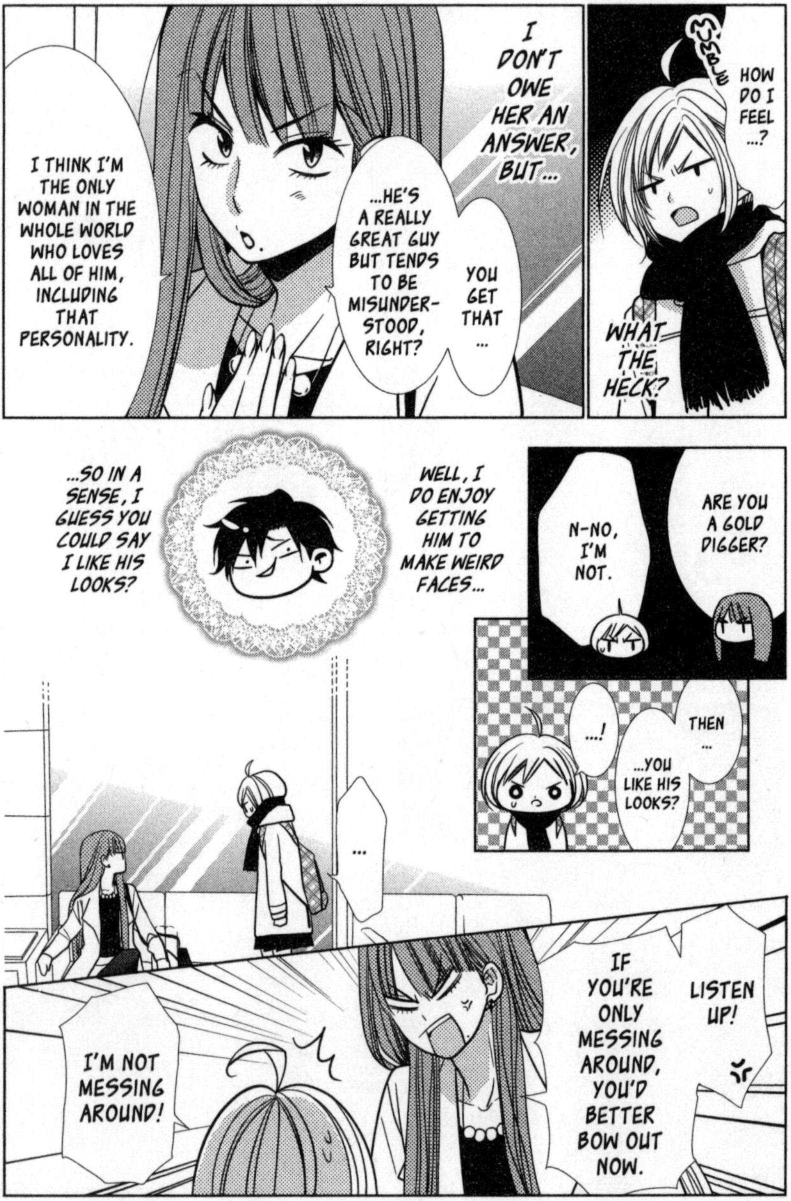
MUMBLE
HOW DO I FEEL ...?
WHAT THE HECK?
I DON'T OWE HER AN ANSWER, BUT...
YOU GET THAT ...
...HE'S A REALLY GREAT GUY BUT TENDS TO BE MISUNDER-STOOD, RIGHT?
I THINK I'M THE ONLY WOMAN IN THE WHOLE WORLD WHO LOVES ALL OF HIM, INCLUDING THAT PERSONALITY.
ARE YOU A GOLD DIGGER?
N-NO, I'M NOT.
THEN ...
...YOU LIKE HIS LOOKS?
...!
WELL, I DO ENJOY GETTING HIM TO MAKE WEIRD FACES...
...SO IN A SENSE, I GUESS YOU COULD SAY I LIKE HIS LOOKS?
...
LISTEN UP!
IF YOU'RE ONLY MESSING AROUND, YOU'D BETTER BOW OUT NOW.
I'M NOT MESSING AROUND!

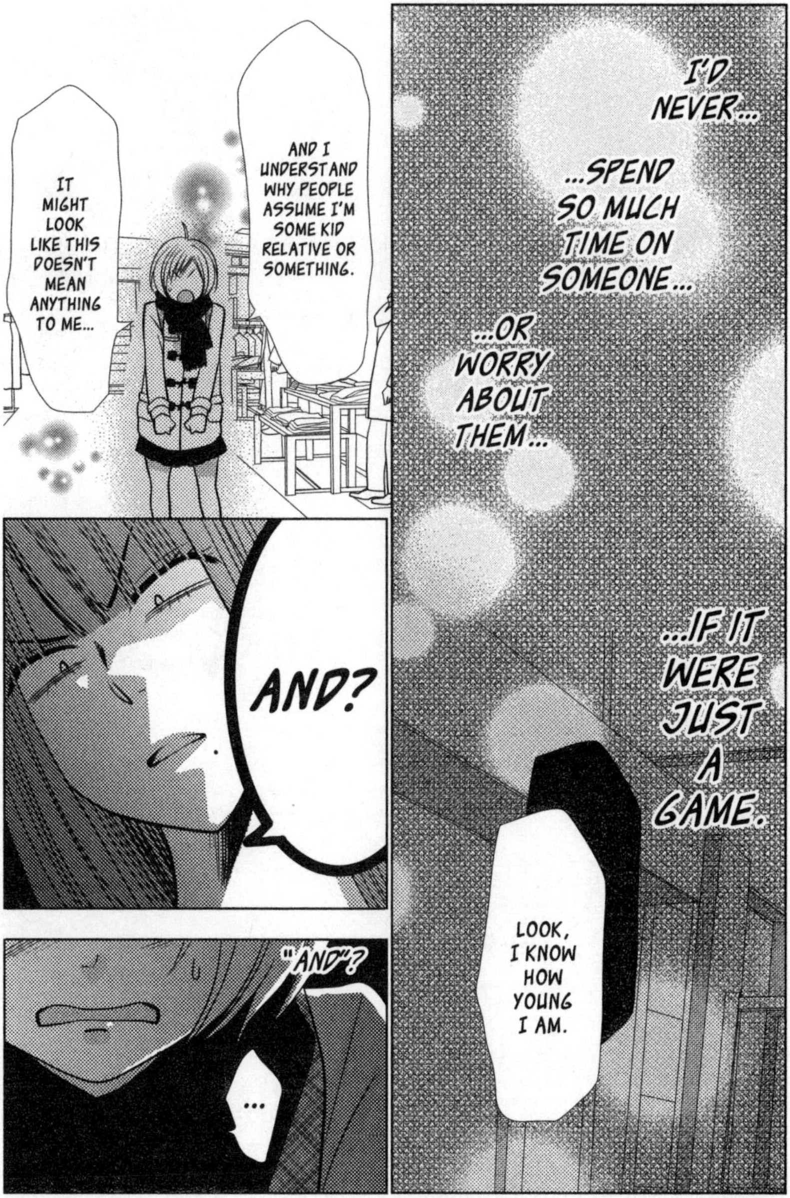
IT MIGHT LOOK LIKE THIS DOESN'T MEAN ANYTHING TO ME...
AND I UNDERSTAND WHY PEOPLE ASSUME I'M SOME KID RELATIVE OR SOMETHING.
AND?
"AND"?
...
LOOK, I KNOW HOW YOUNG I AM.
I'D NEVER...
...SPEND SO MUCH TIME ON SOMEONE...
...OR WORRY ABOUT THEM...
...IF IT WERE JUST A GAME.

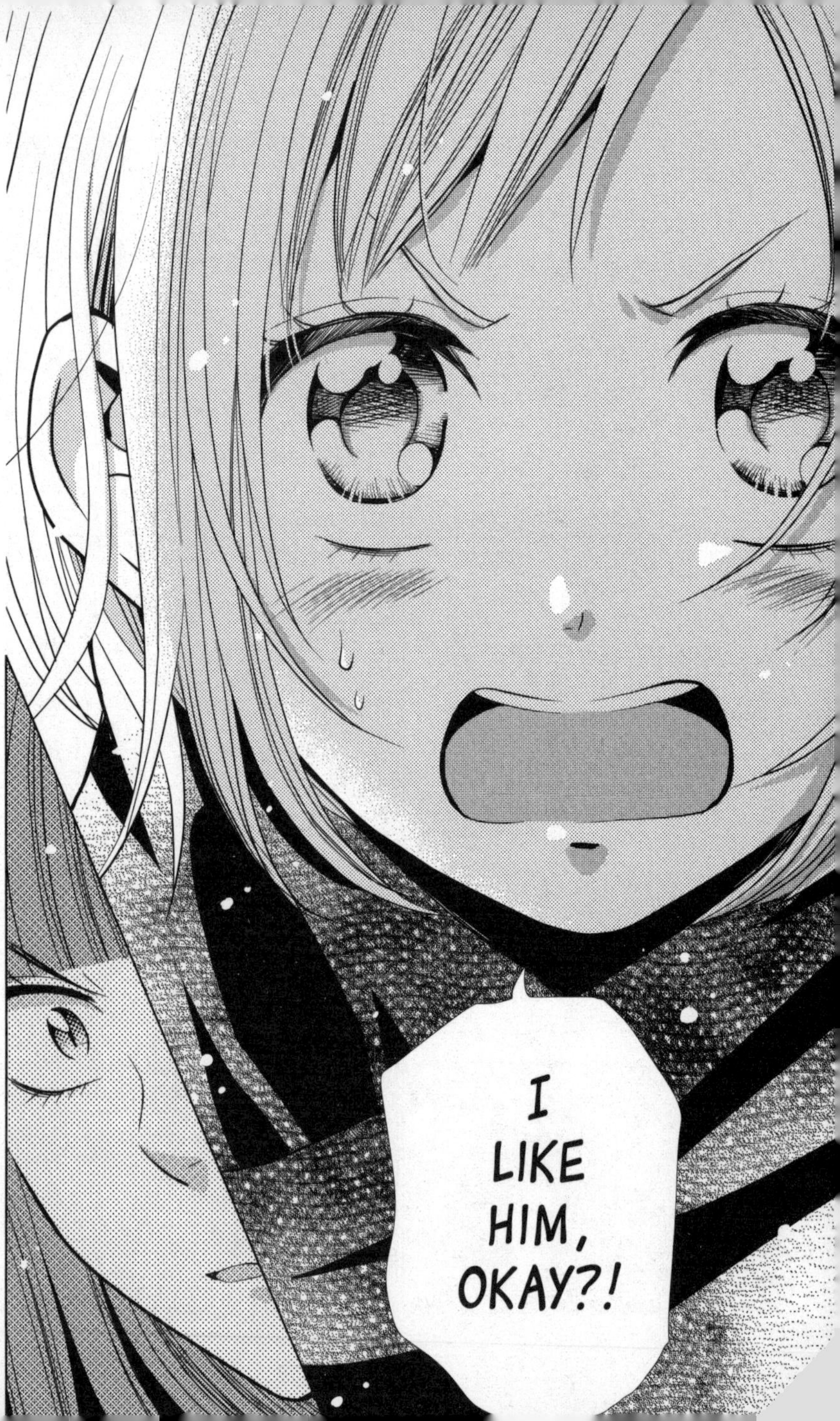
I LIKE HIM, OKAY?!

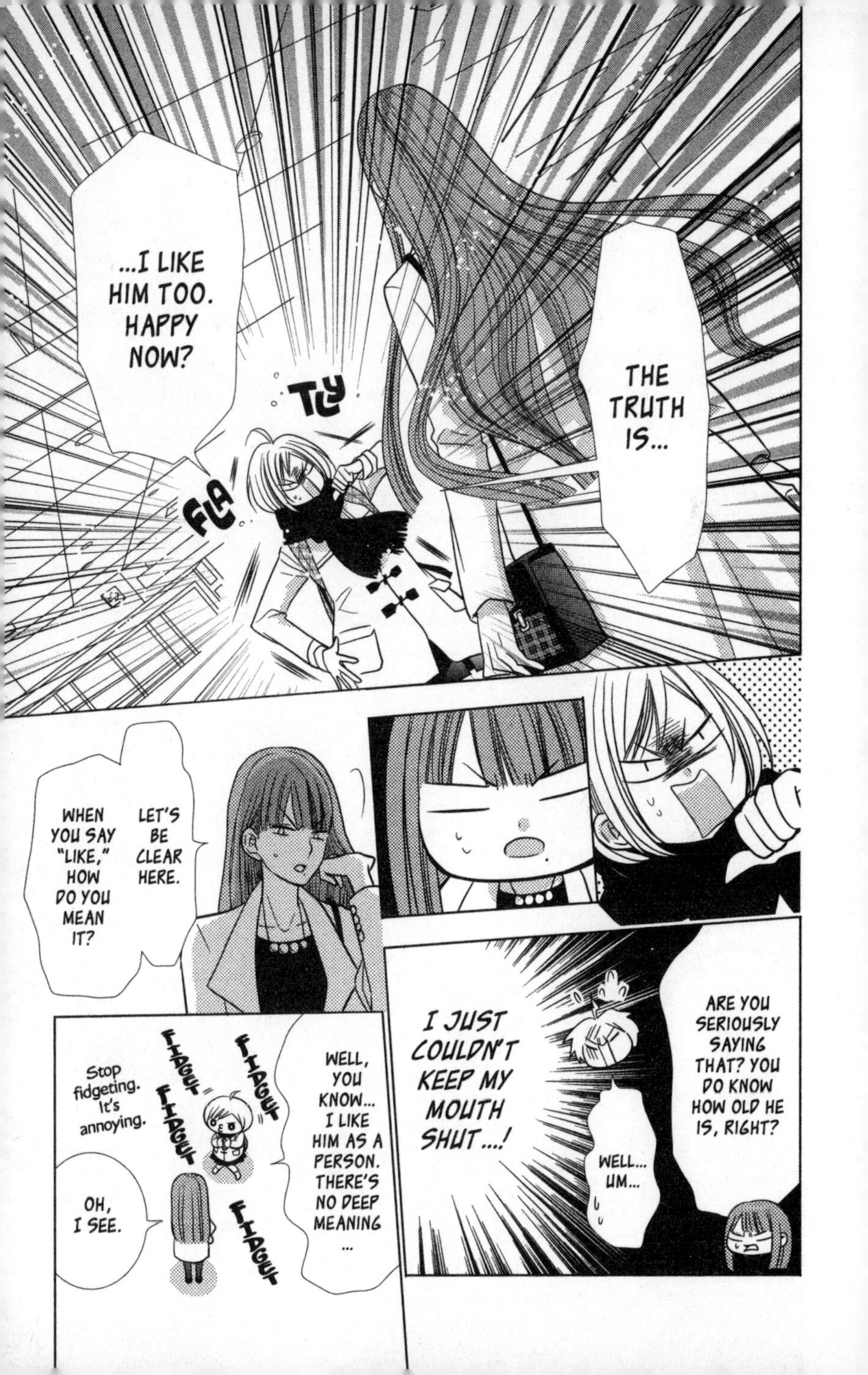
THE TRUTH IS...
...I LIKE HIM TOO. HAPPY NOW?
LET'S BE CLEAR HERE.
WHEN YOU SAY "LIKE," HOW DO YOU MEAN IT?
ARE YOU SERIOUSLY SAYING THAT? YOU DO KNOW HOW OLD HE IS, RIGHT?
WELL... UM...
I JUST COULDN'T KEEP MY MOUTH SHUT...!
WELL, YOU KNOW... I LIKE HIM AS A PERSON. THERE'S NO DEEP MEANING...
FIDGET
FIDGET
FIDGET
FIDGET
Stop fidgeting. It's annoying.
OH, I SEE.

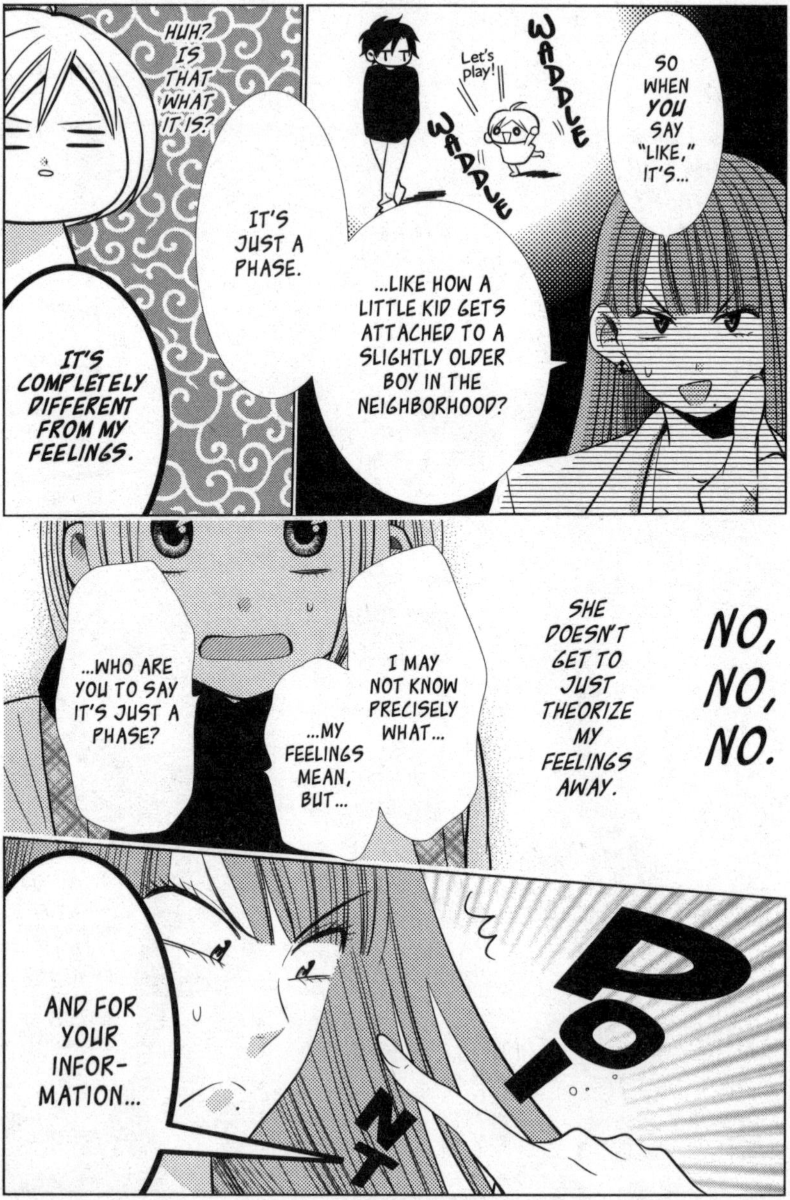
SO WHEN YOU SAY "LIKE," IT'S...
Let's play!
WADDLE
WADDLE
...LIKE HOW A LITTLE KID GETS ATTACHED TO A SLIGHTLY OLDER BOY IN THE NEIGHBORHOOD?
IT'S JUST A PHASE.
HUH? IS THAT WHAT IT IS?
IT'S COMPLETELY DIFFERENT FROM MY FEELINGS.
NO, NO, NO.
SHE DOESN'T GET TO JUST THEORIZE MY FEELINGS AWAY.
I MAY NOT KNOW PRECISELY WHAT...
...MY FEELINGS MEAN, BUT...
...WHO ARE YOU TO SAY IT'S JUST A PHASE?
POINT
AND FOR YOUR INFORMATION...

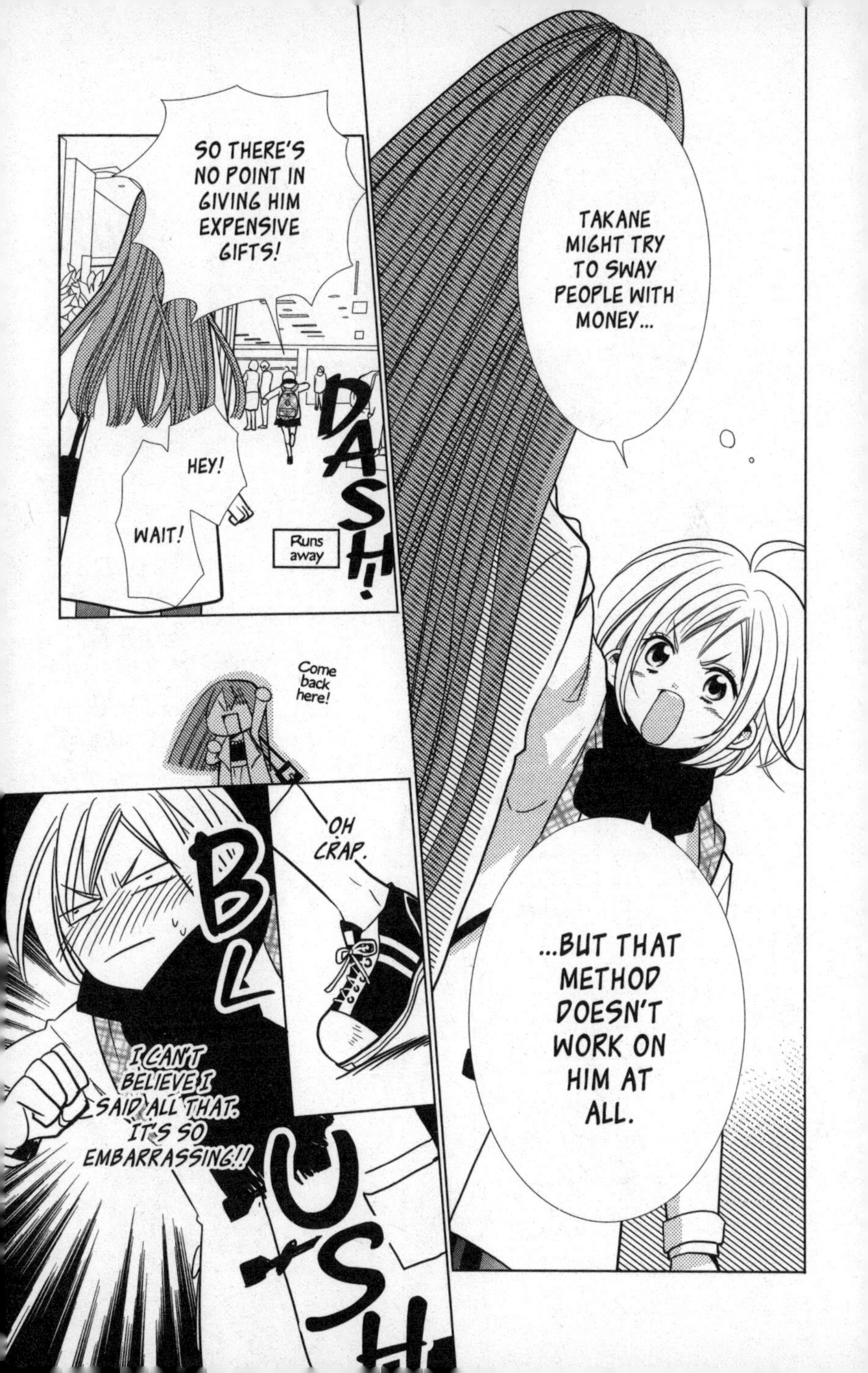
TAKANE MIGHT TRY TO SWAY PEOPLE WITH MONEY...
...BUT THAT METHOD DOESN'T WORK ON HIM AT ALL.
SO THERE'S NO POINT IN GIVING HIM EXPENSIVE GIFTS!
DASH!
Runs away
HEY!
WAIT!
Come back here!
OH CRAP.
BLUSH
I CAN'T BELIEVE I SAID ALL THAT. IT'S SO EMBARRASSING!!

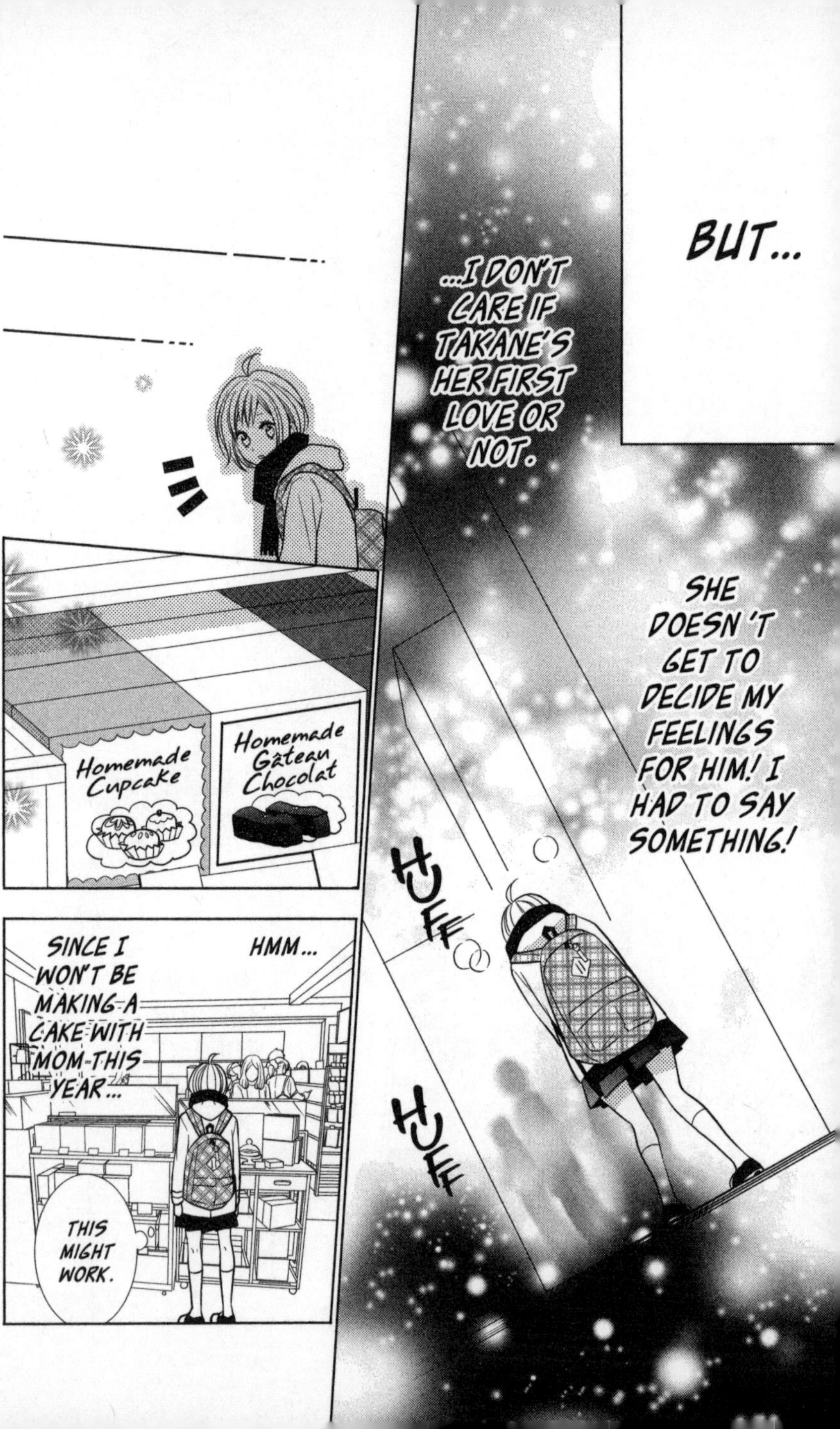
BUT...
...I DON'T CARE IF TAKANE'S HER FIRST LOVE OR NOT.
SHE DOESN'T GET TO DECIDE MY FEELINGS FOR HIM! I HAD TO SAY SOMETHING!
HUFF
HUFF
Homemade Gâteau Chocolat
Homemade Cupcake
HMM...
SINCE I WON'T BE MAKING A CAKE WITH MOM THIS YEAR...
THIS MIGHT WORK.

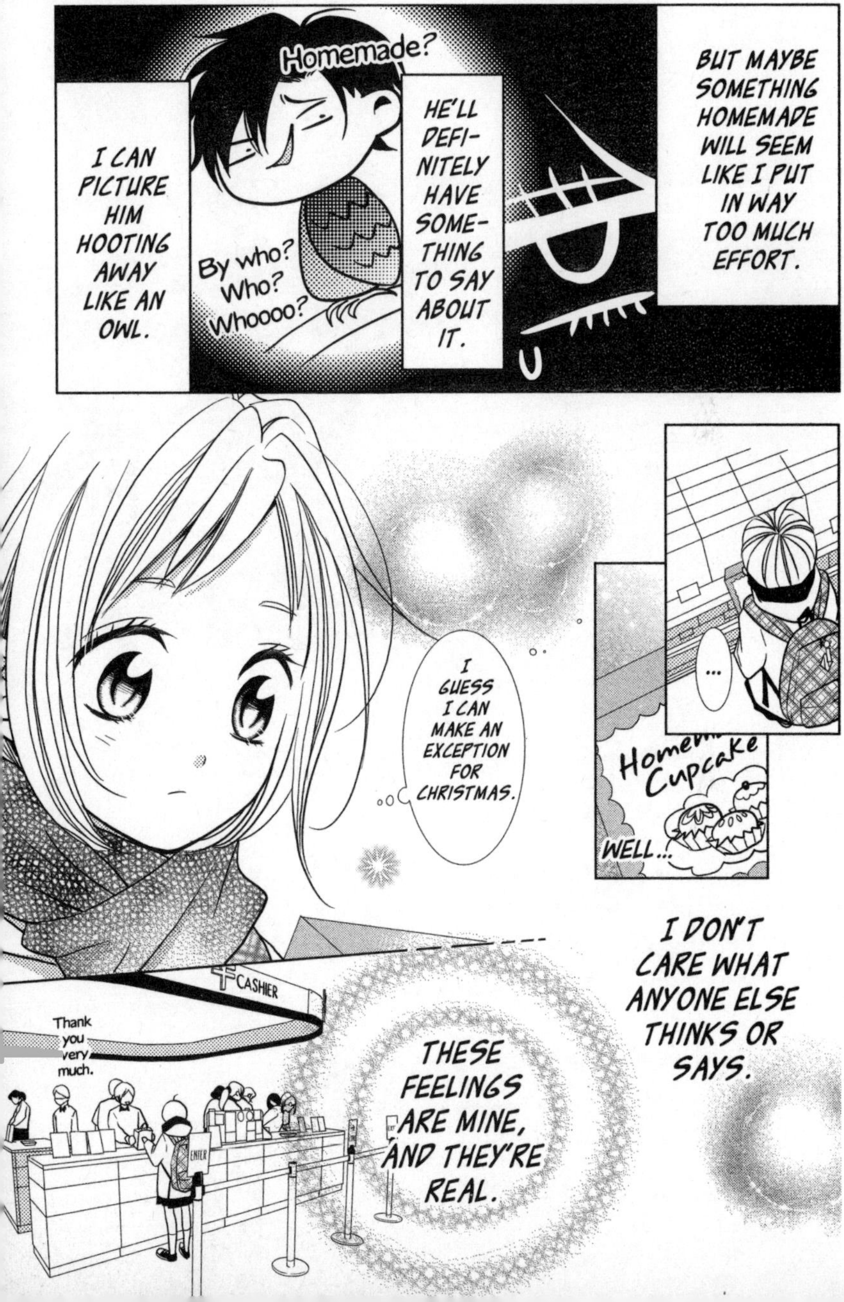
BUT MAYBE SOMETHING HOMEMADE WILL SEEM LIKE I PUT IN WAY TOO MUCH EFFORT.
HE'LL DEFINITELY HAVE SOMETHING TO SAY ABOUT IT.
Homemade?
By who? Who? Whoooo?
I CAN PICTURE HIM HOOTING AWAY LIKE AN OWL.
...
Homem Cupcake
WELL...
I GUESS I CAN MAKE AN EXCEPTION FOR CHRISTMAS.
I DON'T CARE WHAT ANYONE ELSE THINKS OR SAYS.
THESE FEELINGS ARE MINE, AND THEY'RE REAL.
CASHIER
ENTER
Thank you very much.

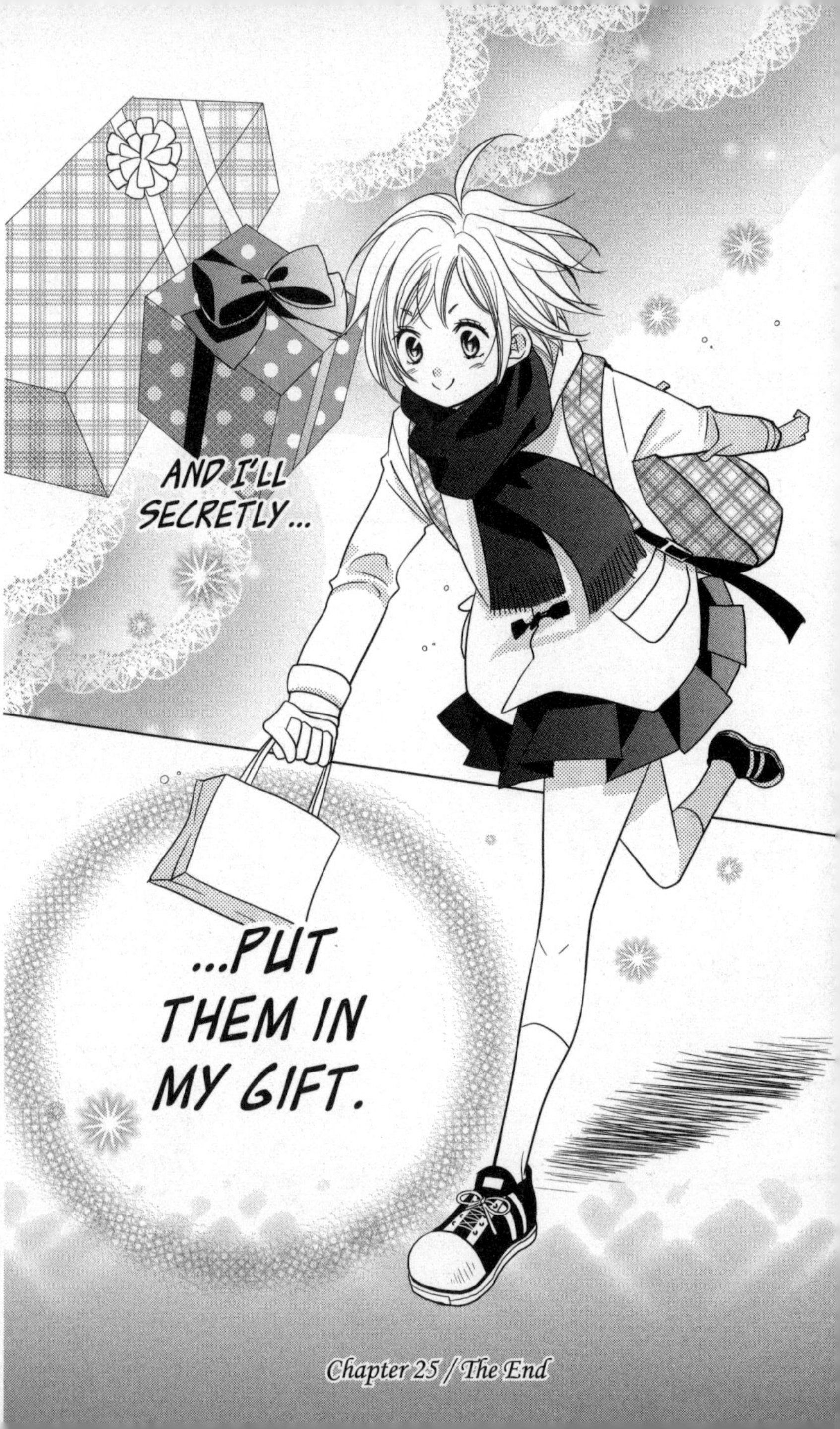
AND I'LL SECRETLY...
...PUT THEM IN MY GIFT.

Chapter 25 / The End

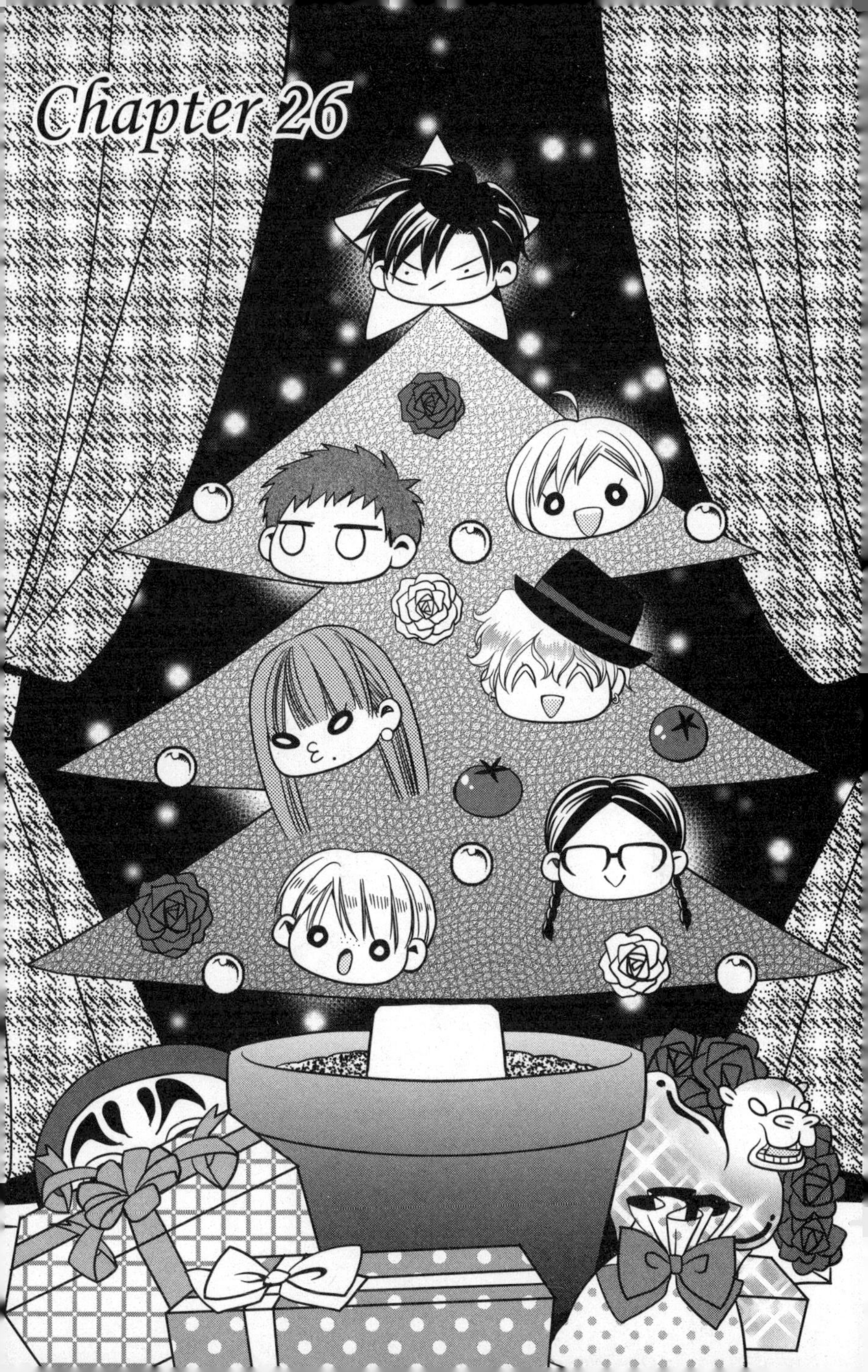
Chapter 26

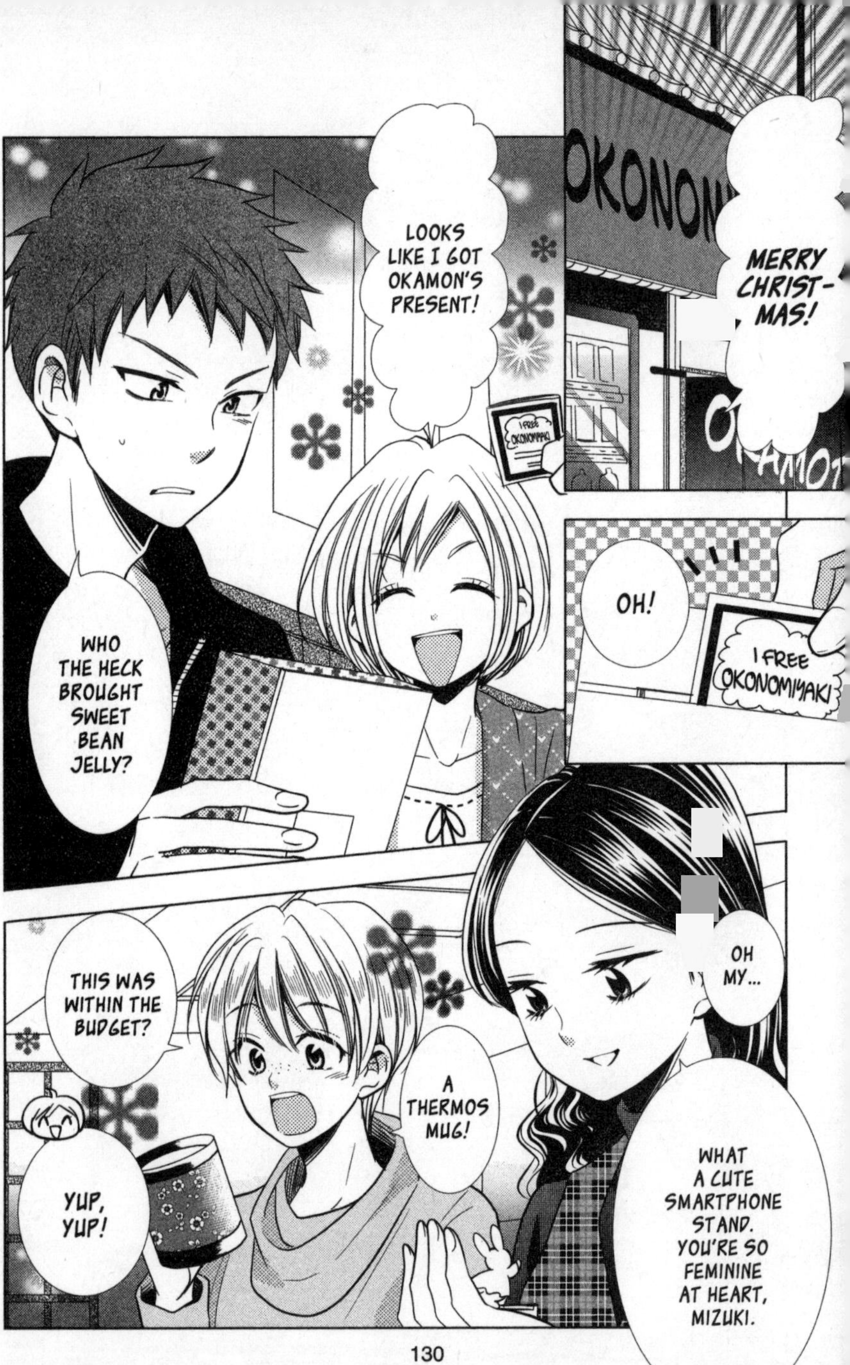
MERRY CHRISTMAS!
OH!
I FREE OKONOMIYAKI
LOOKS LIKE I GOT OKAMON'S PRESENT!
WHO THE HECK BROUGHT SWEET BEAN JELLY?
OH MY...
WHAT A CUTE SMARTPHONE STAND. YOU'RE SO FEMININE AT HEART, MIZUKI.
A THERMOS MUG!
THIS WAS WITHIN THE BUDGET?
YUP, YUP!

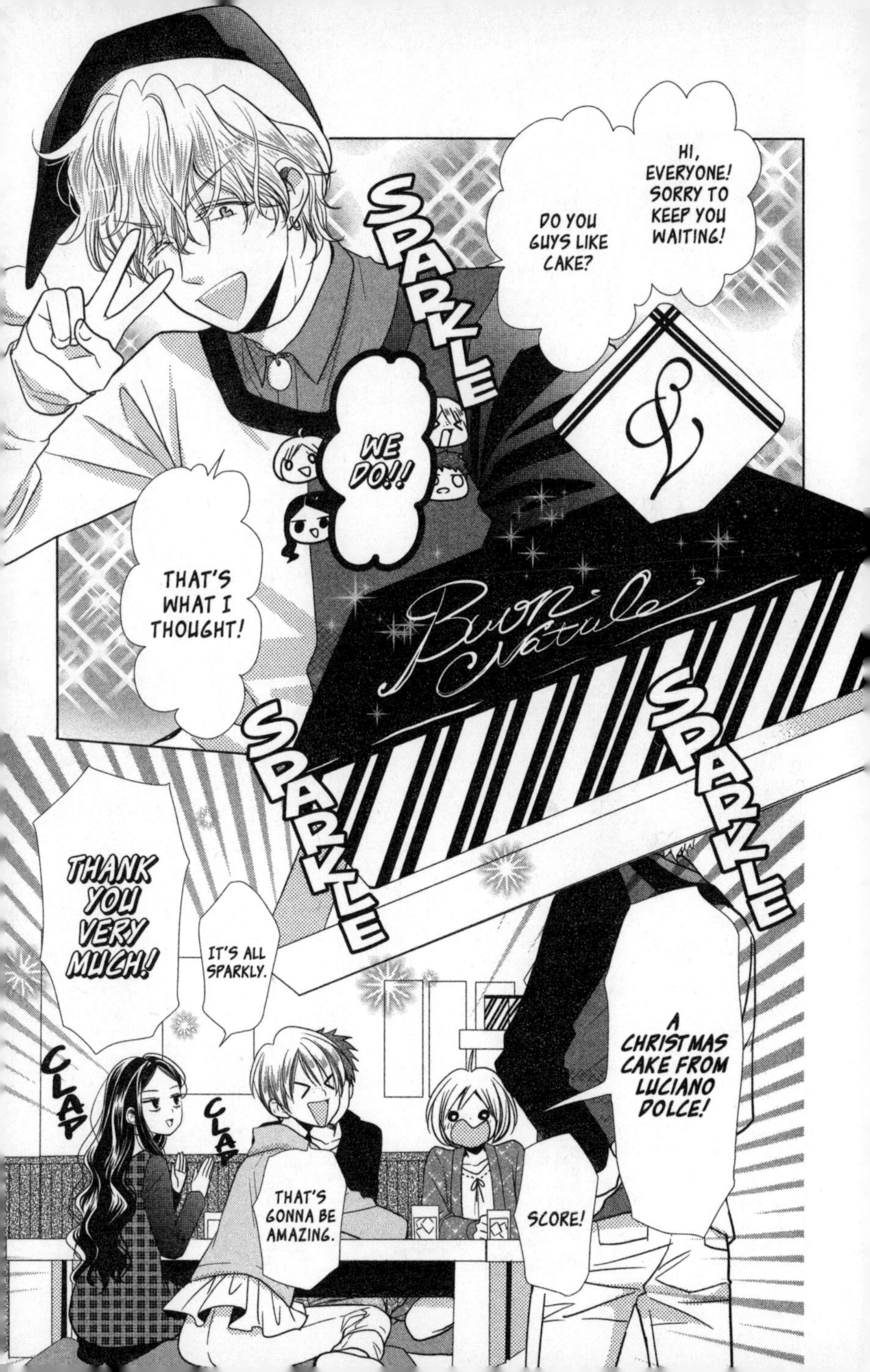
HI, EVERYONE! SORRY TO KEEP YOU WAITING!
DO YOU GUYS LIKE CAKE?
SPARKLE
WE DO!!
THAT'S WHAT I THOUGHT!
Buon Natale
SPARKLE
SPARKLE
A CHRISTMAS CAKE FROM LUCIANO DOLCE!
SCORE!
THAT'S GONNA BE AMAZING.
CLAP
CLAP
IT'S ALL SPARKLY.
THANK YOU VERY MUCH!

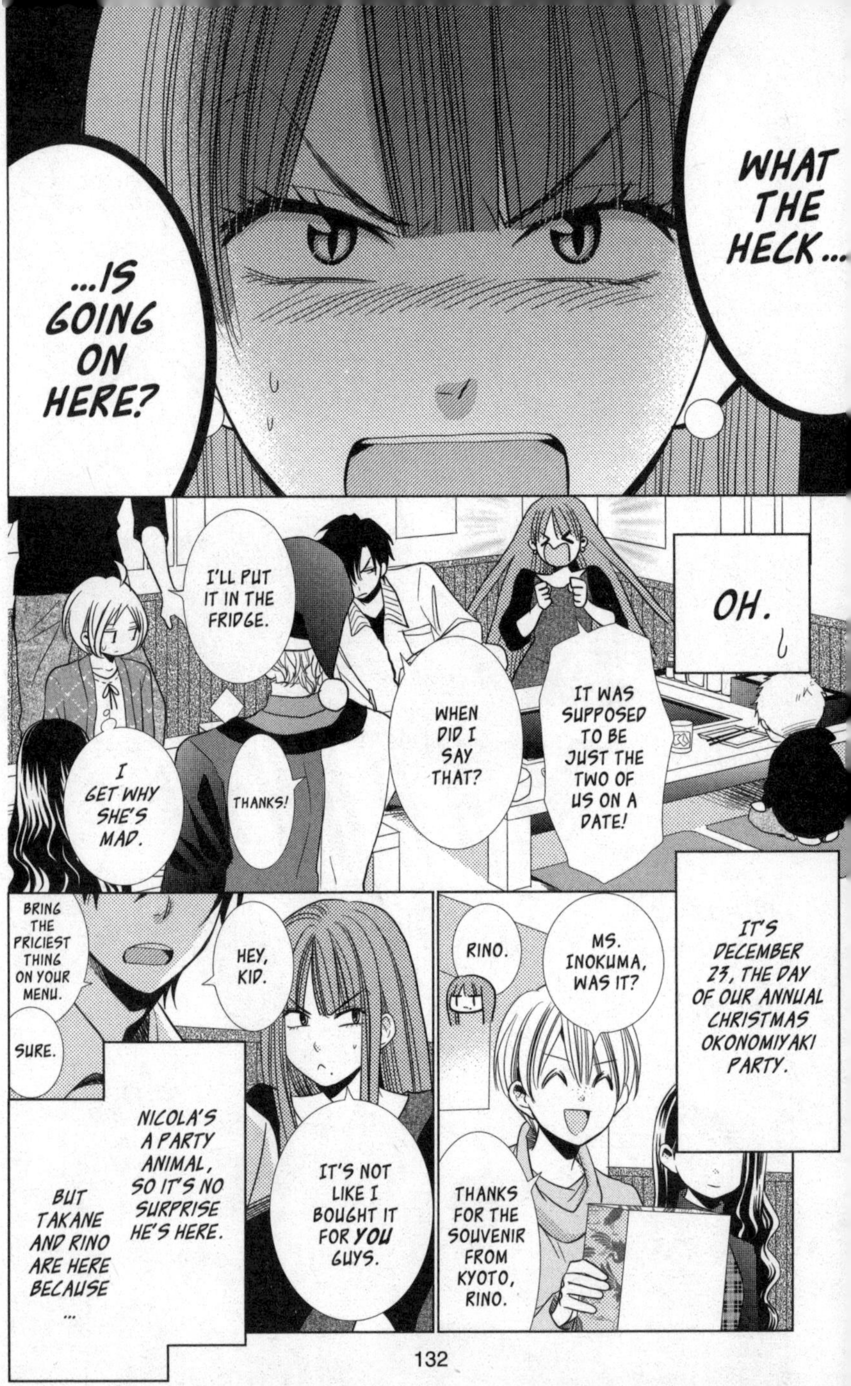
WHAT THE HECK...
...IS GOING ON HERE?
OH.
IT WAS SUPPOSED TO BE JUST THE TWO OF US ON A DATE!
WHEN DID I SAY THAT?
I'LL PUT IT IN THE FRIDGE.
THANKS!
I GET WHY SHE'S MAD.
IT'S DECEMBER 23, THE DAY OF OUR ANNUAL CHRISTMAS OKONOMIYAKI PARTY.
MS. INOKUMA, WAS IT?
RINO.
THANKS FOR THE SOUVENIR FROM KYOTO, RINO.
HEY, KID.
BRING THE PRICIEST THING ON YOUR MENU.
SURE.
IT'S NOT LIKE I BOUGHT IT FOR YOU GUYS.
NICOLA'S A PARTY ANIMAL, SO IT'S NO SURPRISE HE'S HERE.
BUT TAKANE AND RINO ARE HERE BECAUSE ...

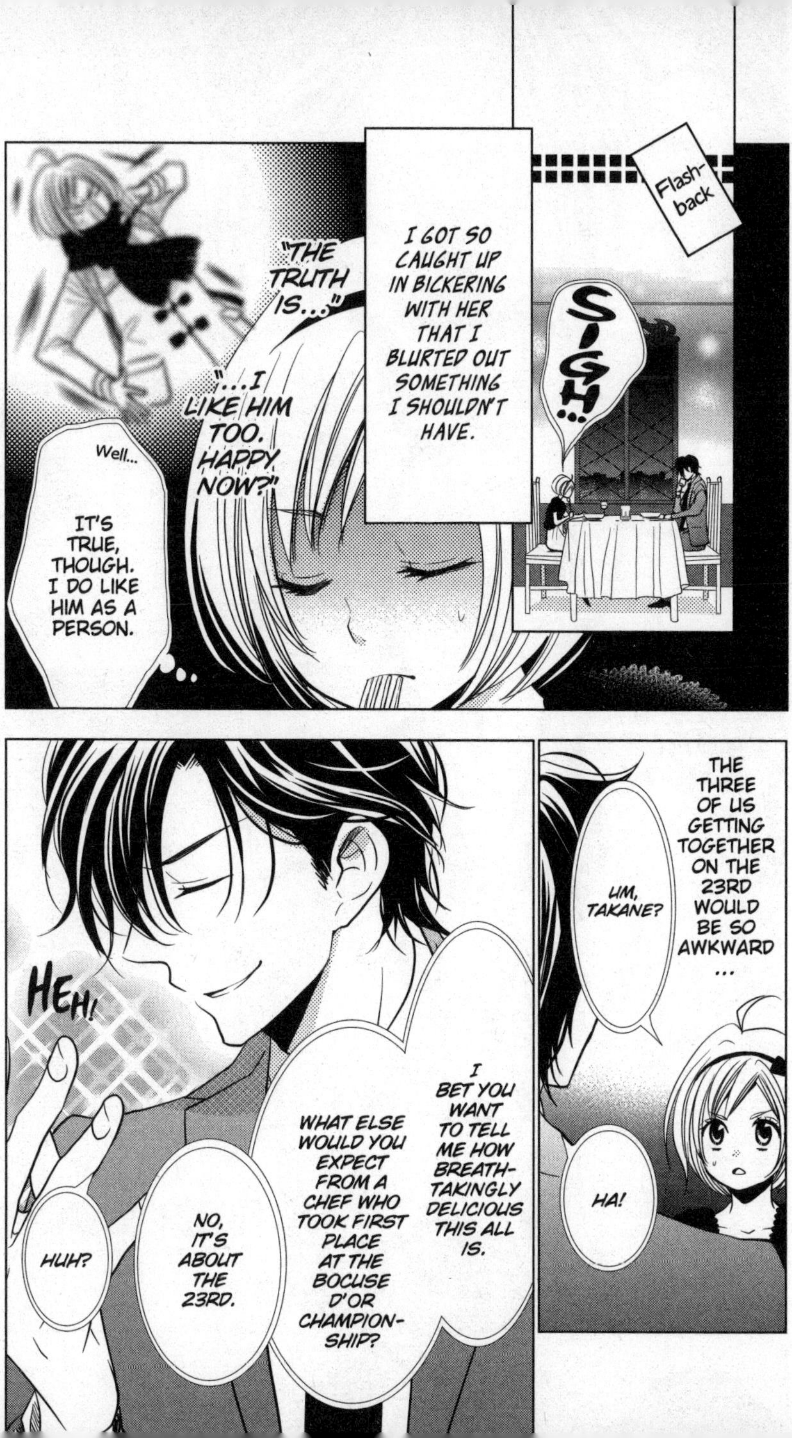
Flash-back
I GOT SO CAUGHT UP IN BICKERING WITH HER THAT I BLURTED OUT SOMETHING I SHOULDN'T HAVE.
SIGH!!
"THE TRUTH IS..."
"...I LIKE HIM TOO. HAPPY NOW?"
Well...
IT'S TRUE, THOUGH. I DO LIKE HIM AS A PERSON.
THE THREE OF US GETTING TOGETHER ON THE 23RD WOULD BE SO AWKWARD...
UM, TAKANE?
HA!
HEH!
I BET YOU WANT TO TELL ME HOW BREATH-TAKINGLY DELICIOUS THIS ALL IS.
WHAT ELSE WOULD YOU EXPECT FROM A CHEF WHO TOOK FIRST PLACE AT THE BOCUSE D'OR CHAMPION-SHIP?
NO, IT'S ABOUT THE 23RD.
HUH?

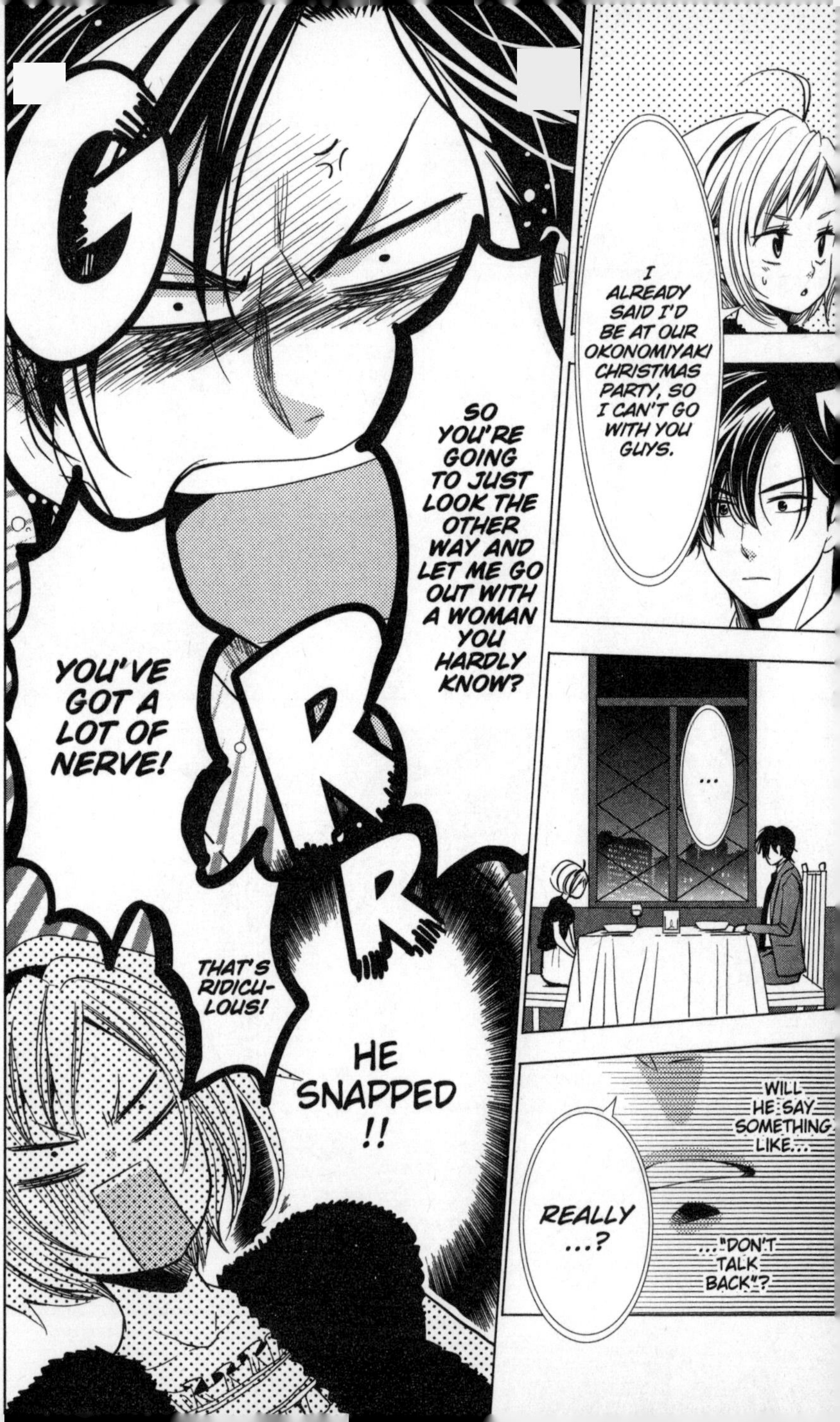
I ALREADY SAID I'D BE AT OUR OKONOMIYAKI CHRISTMAS PARTY, SO I CAN'T GO WITH YOU GUYS.
...
WILL HE SAY SOMETHING LIKE...
REALLY ...?
..."DON'T TALK BACK"?
GRR
SO YOU'RE GOING TO JUST LOOK THE OTHER WAY AND LET ME GO OUT WITH A WOMAN YOU HARDLY KNOW?
YOU'VE GOT A LOT OF NERVE!
THAT'S RIDICU-LOUS!
HE SNAPPED !!

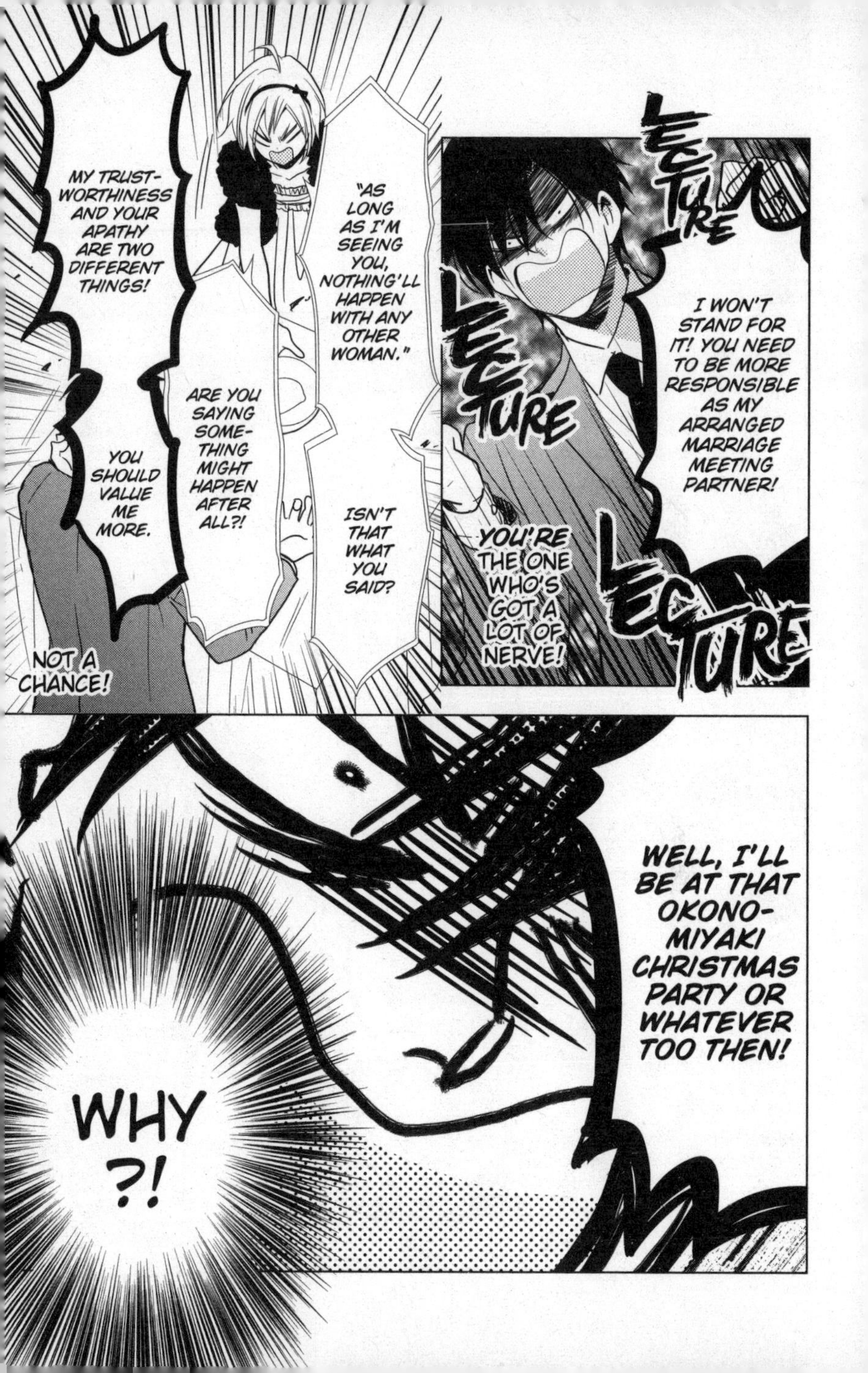
LECTURE
I WON'T STAND FOR IT! YOU NEED TO BE MORE RESPONSIBLE AS MY ARRANGED MARRIAGE MEETING PARTNER!
LECTURE
LECTURE
YOU'RE THE ONE WHO'S GOT A LOT OF NERVE!
"AS LONG AS I'M SEEING YOU, NOTHING'LL HAPPEN WITH ANY OTHER WOMAN."
ISN'T THAT WHAT YOU SAID?
MY TRUST-WORTHINESS AND YOUR APATHY ARE TWO DIFFERENT THINGS!
ARE YOU SAYING SOME-THING MIGHT HAPPEN AFTER ALL?!
YOU SHOULD VALUE ME MORE.
NOT A CHANCE!
WELL, I'LL BE AT THAT OKONO-MIYAKI CHRISTMAS PARTY OR WHATEVER TOO THEN!
WHY ?!

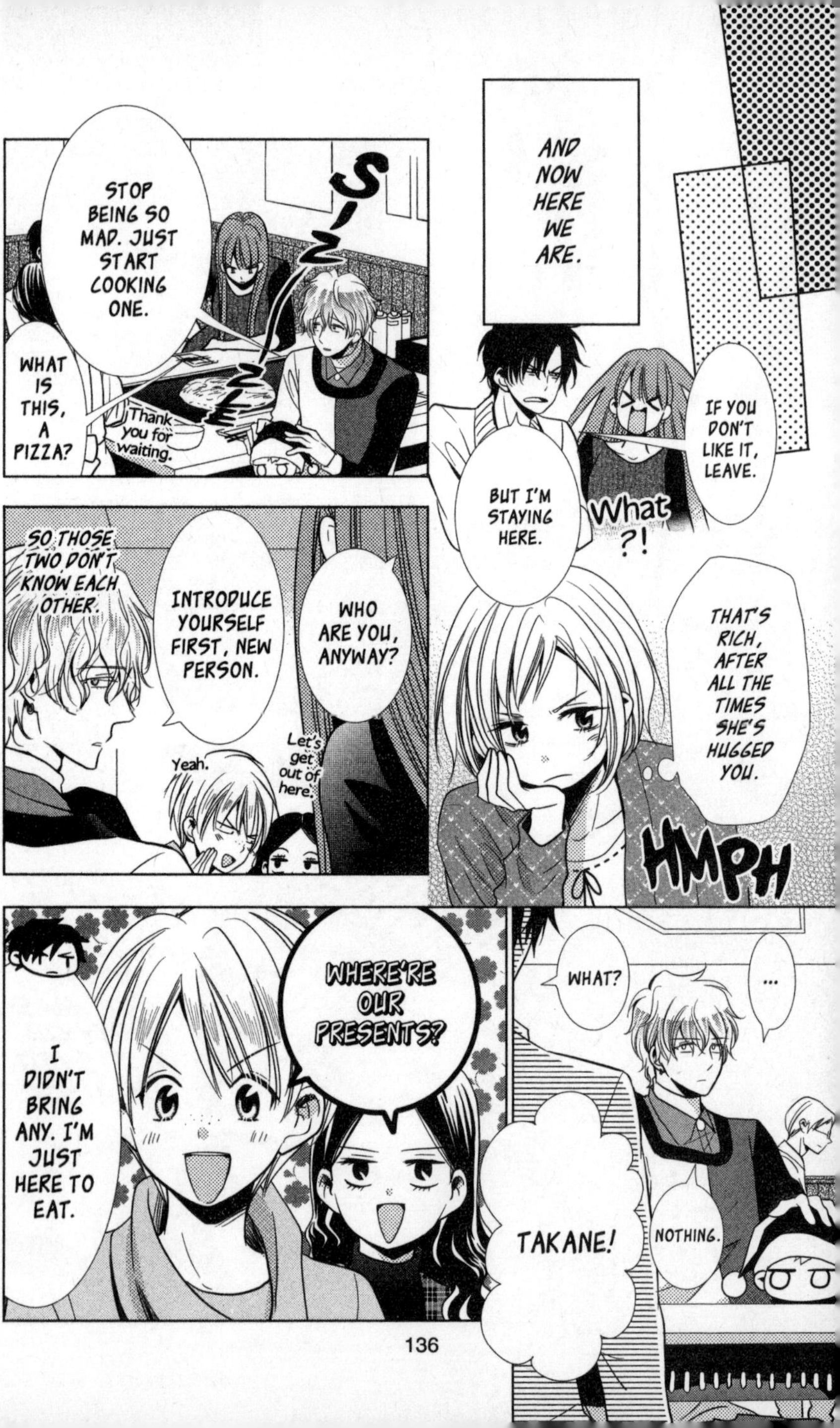
AND NOW HERE WE ARE.
IF YOU DON'T LIKE IT, LEAVE.
What?!
BUT I'M STAYING HERE.
STOP BEING SO MAD. JUST START COOKING ONE.
WHAT IS THIS, A PIZZA?
Thank you for waiting.
THAT'S RICH, AFTER ALL THE TIMES SHE'S HUGGED YOU.
HMPH
WHO ARE YOU, ANYWAY?
INTRODUCE YOURSELF FIRST, NEW PERSON.
SO THOSE TWO DON'T KNOW EACH OTHER.
Let's get out of here.
Yeah.
...
WHAT?
NOTHING.
TAKANE!
WHERE'RE OUR PRESENTS?
I DIDN'T BRING ANY. I'M JUST HERE TO EAT.

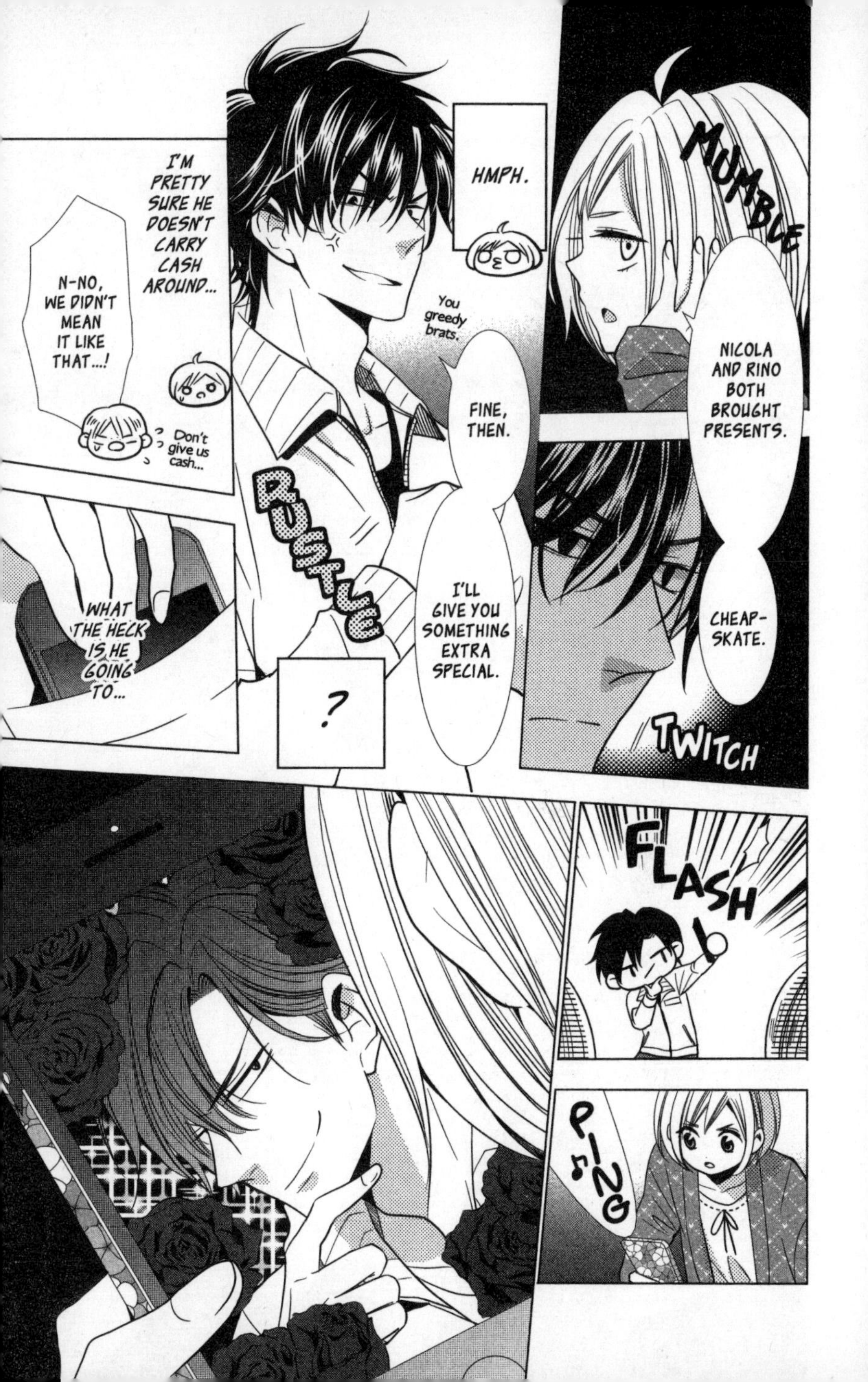
MUMBLE
NICOLA AND RINO BOTH BROUGHT PRESENTS.
CHEAP-SKATE.
TWITCH
HMPH.
You greedy brats.
FINE, THEN.
RUSTLE
I'LL GIVE YOU SOMETHING EXTRA SPECIAL.
?
I'M PRETTY SURE HE DOESN'T CARRY CASH AROUND...
N-NO, WE DIDN'T MEAN IT LIKE THAT...!
Don't give us cash...
WHAT THE HECK IS HE GOING TO...
FLASH
PING

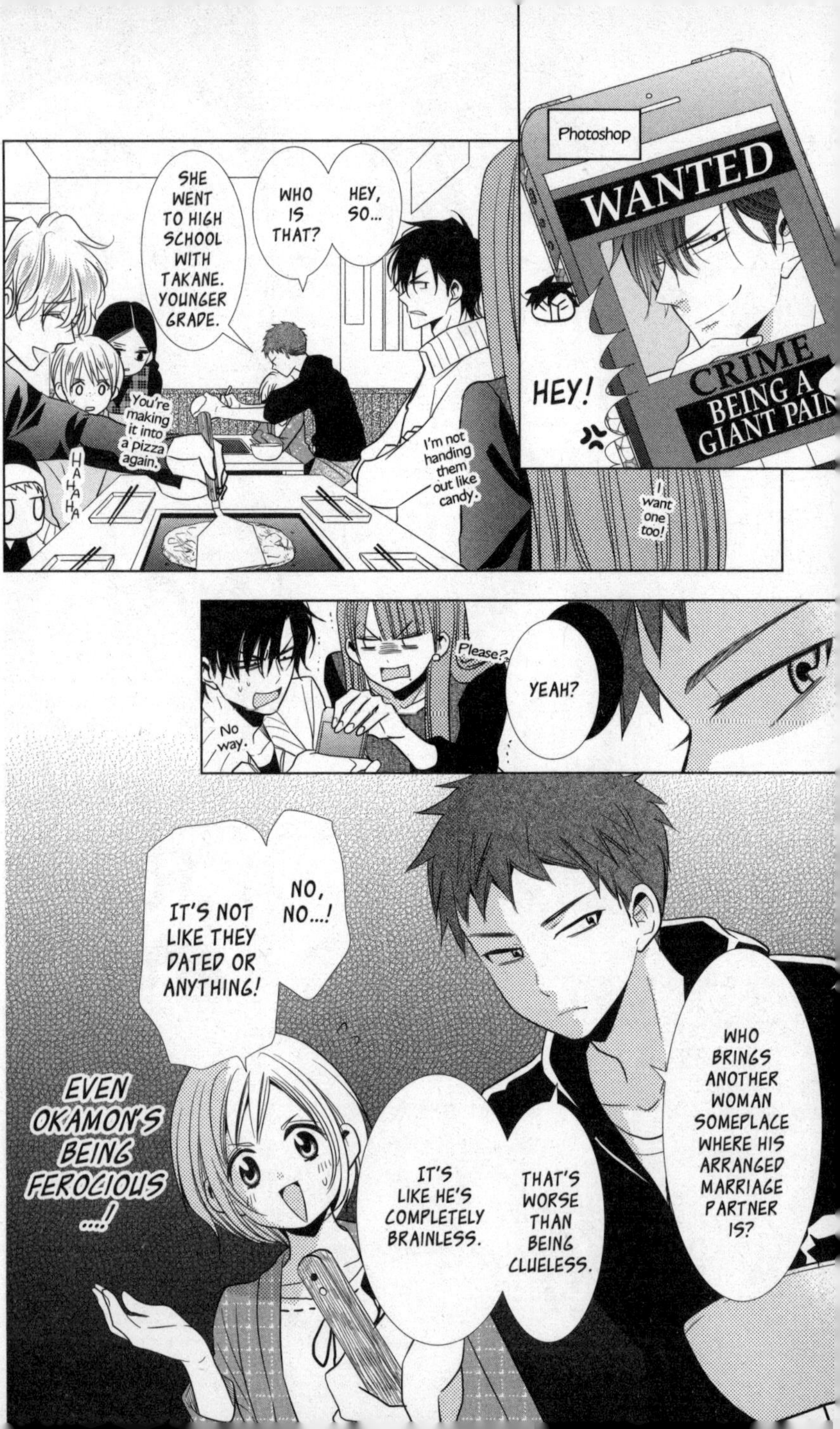
Photoshop
WANTED
CRIME
BEING A GIANT PAIN
HEY!
I want one too!
HEY, SO...
WHO IS THAT?
SHE WENT TO HIGH SCHOOL WITH TAKANE. YOUNGER GRADE.
I'm not handing them out like candy.
You're making it into a pizza again.
HAHAHA
YEAH?
Please?
No way.
NO, NO...!
IT'S NOT LIKE THEY DATED OR ANYTHING!
WHO BRINGS ANOTHER WOMAN SOMEPLACE WHERE HIS ARRANGED MARRIAGE PARTNER IS?
THAT'S WORSE THAN BEING CLUELESS.
IT'S LIKE HE'S COMPLETELY BRAINLESS.
EVEN OKAMON'S BEING FEROCIOUS ...!

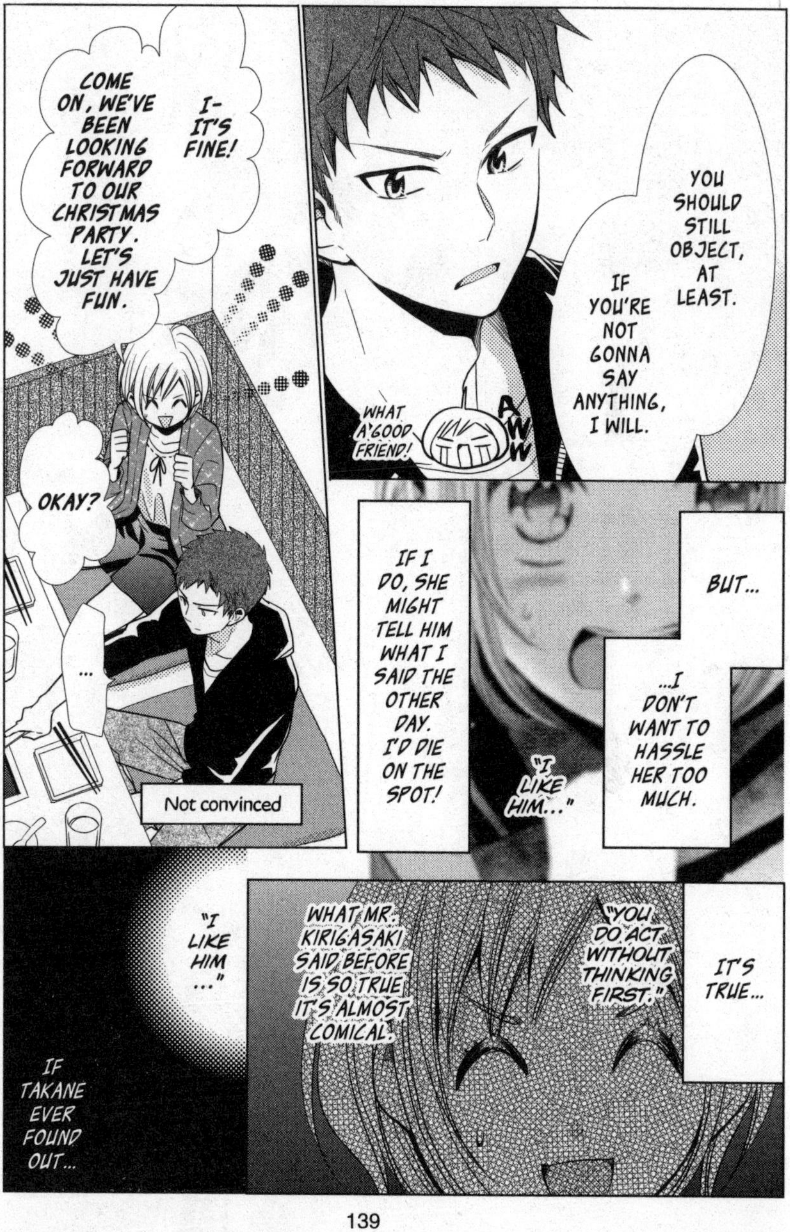
YOU SHOULD STILL OBJECT, AT LEAST.
IF YOU'RE NOT GONNA SAY ANYTHING, I WILL.
WHAT A GOOD FRIEND!
AWW
BUT...
...I DON'T WANT TO HASSLE HER TOO MUCH.
"I LIKE HIM..."
IF I DO, SHE MIGHT TELL HIM WHAT I SAID THE OTHER DAY. I'D DIE ON THE SPOT!
I- IT'S FINE!
COME ON, WE'VE BEEN LOOKING FORWARD TO OUR CHRISTMAS PARTY. LET'S JUST HAVE FUN.
OKAY?
...
Not convinced
IT'S TRUE...
"YOU DO ACT WITHOUT THINKING FIRST."
WHAT MR. KIRIGASAKI SAID BEFORE IS SO TRUE IT'S ALMOST COMICAL.
"I LIKE HIM..."
IF TAKANE EVER FOUND OUT...

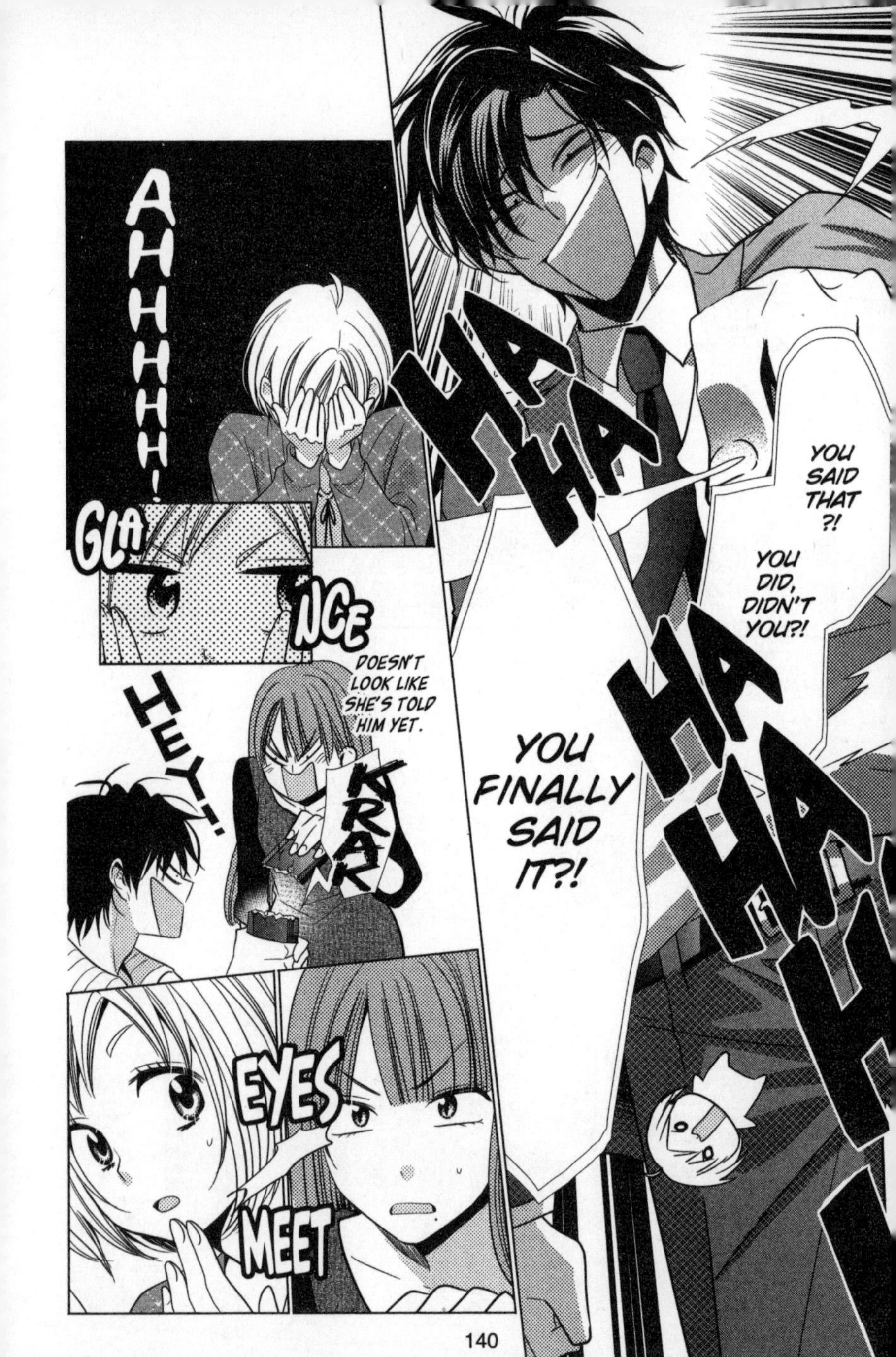
HA HA
YOU SAID THAT?!
YOU DID, DIDN'T YOU?!
HA HA HA HA
YOU FINALLY SAID IT?!
AHHHHHH!
GLANCE
HEY?!
DOESN'T LOOK LIKE SHE'S TOLD HIM YET.
KRAR
EYES MEET

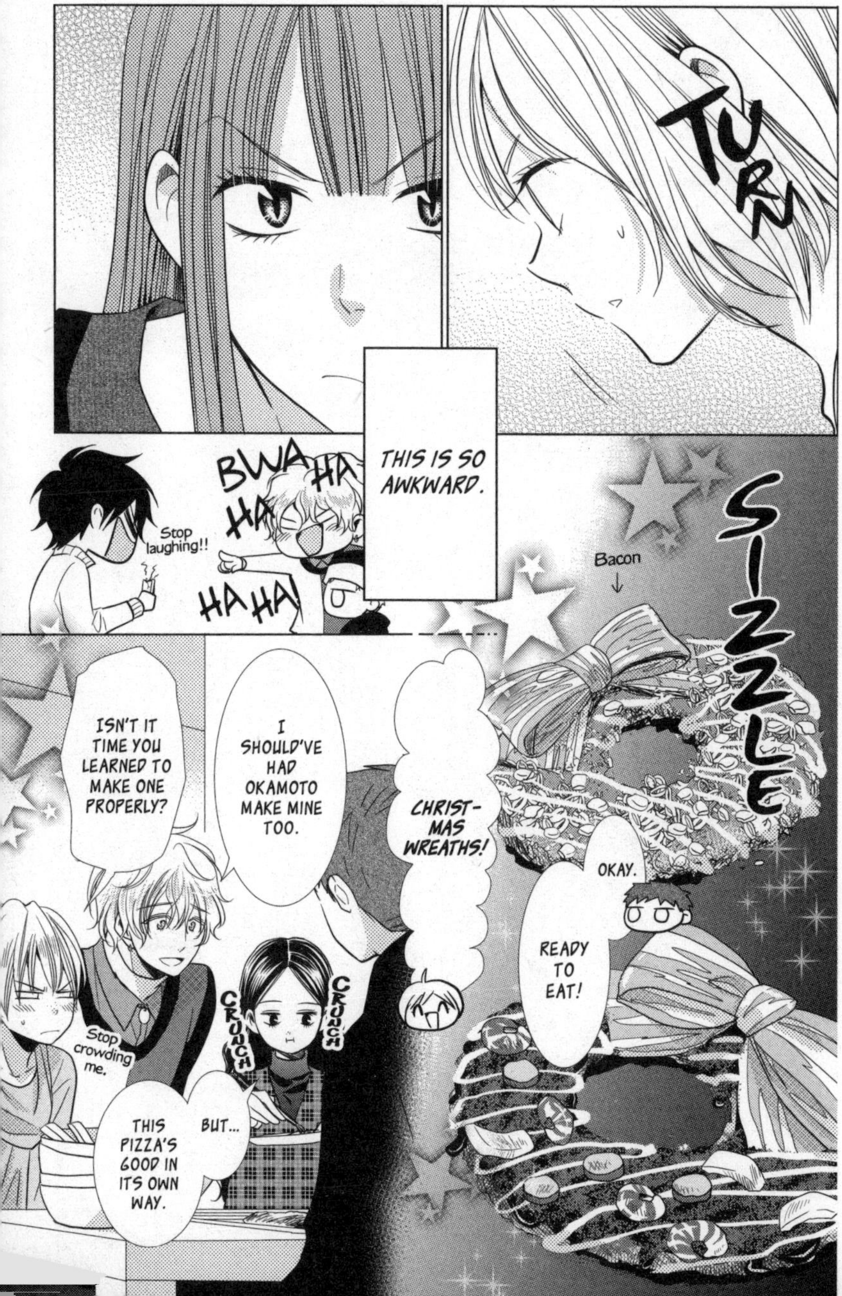
TURN
THIS IS SO AWKWARD.
BWA HA HA HA HA HA!
Stop laughing!!
SIZZLE
Bacon
CHRIST-MAS WREATHS!
READY TO EAT!
OKAY.
I SHOULD'VE HAD OKAMOTO MAKE MINE TOO.
ISN'T IT TIME YOU LEARNED TO MAKE ONE PROPERLY?
Stop crowding me.
CRUNCH CRUNCH
CRUNCH
BUT...
THIS PIZZA'S GOOD IN ITS OWN WAY.

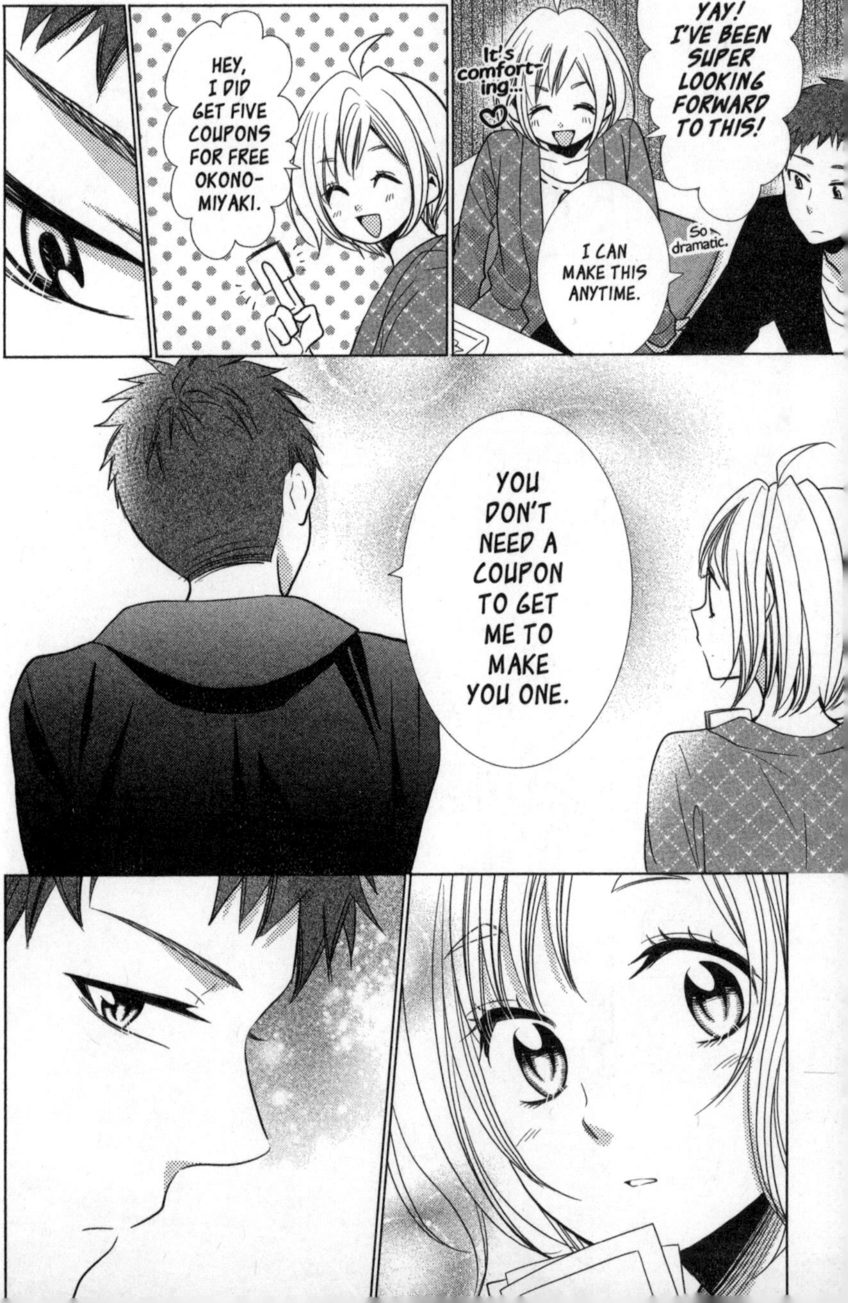
YAY! I'VE BEEN SUPER LOOKING FORWARD TO THIS!
It's comforting...
So dramatic.
I CAN MAKE THIS ANYTIME.
HEY, I DID GET FIVE COUPONS FOR FREE OKONOMIYAKI.
YOU DON'T NEED A COUPON TO GET ME TO MAKE YOU ONE.

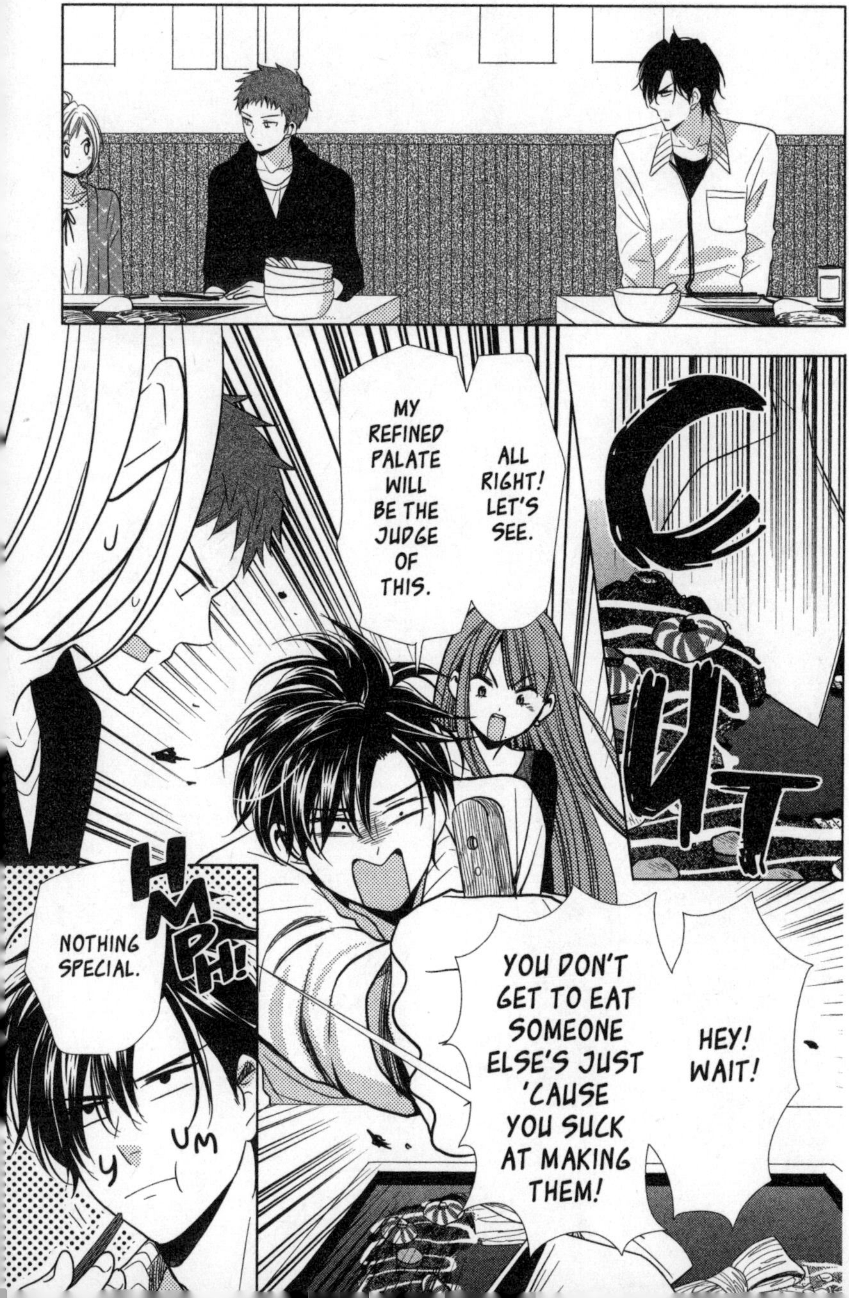
CUT
ALL RIGHT! LET'S SEE.
MY REFINED PALATE WILL BE THE JUDGE OF THIS.
HEY! WAIT!
YOU DON'T GET TO EAT SOMEONE ELSE'S JUST 'CAUSE YOU SUCK AT MAKING THEM!
HMPH!
NOTHING SPECIAL.
YUM

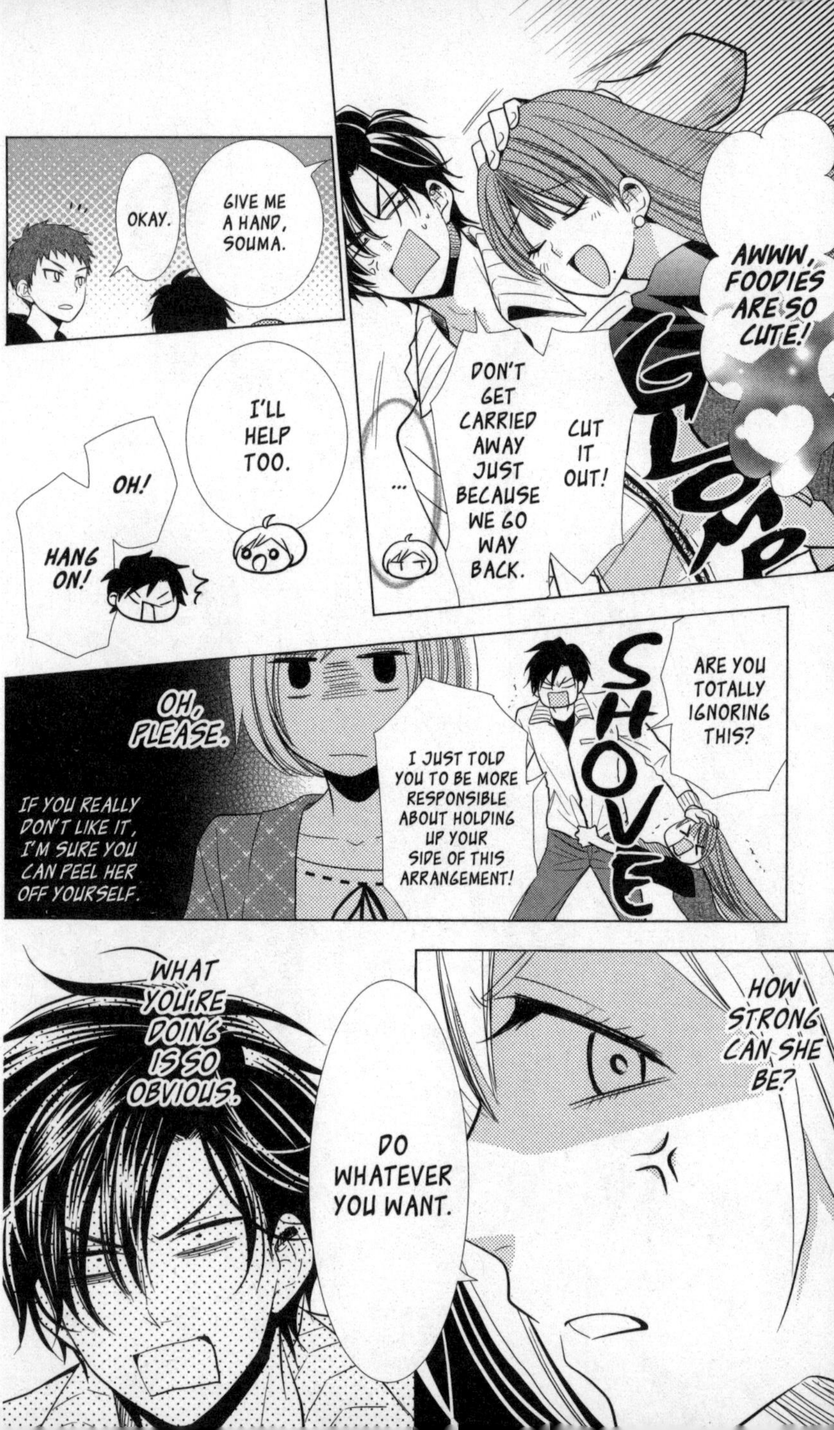
AWWW, FOODIES ARE SO CUTE!
CUT IT OUT!
DON'T GET CARRIED AWAY JUST BECAUSE WE GO WAY BACK.
...
GIVE ME A HAND, SOUMA.
OKAY.
I'LL HELP TOO.
OH!
HANG ON!
ARE YOU TOTALLY IGNORING THIS?
SHOVE
I JUST TOLD YOU TO BE MORE RESPONSIBLE ABOUT HOLDING UP YOUR SIDE OF THIS ARRANGEMENT!
OH, PLEASE.
IF YOU REALLY DON'T LIKE IT, I'M SURE YOU CAN PEEL HER OFF YOURSELF.
HOW STRONG CAN SHE BE?
DO WHATEVER YOU WANT.
WHAT YOU'RE DOING IS SO OBVIOUS.

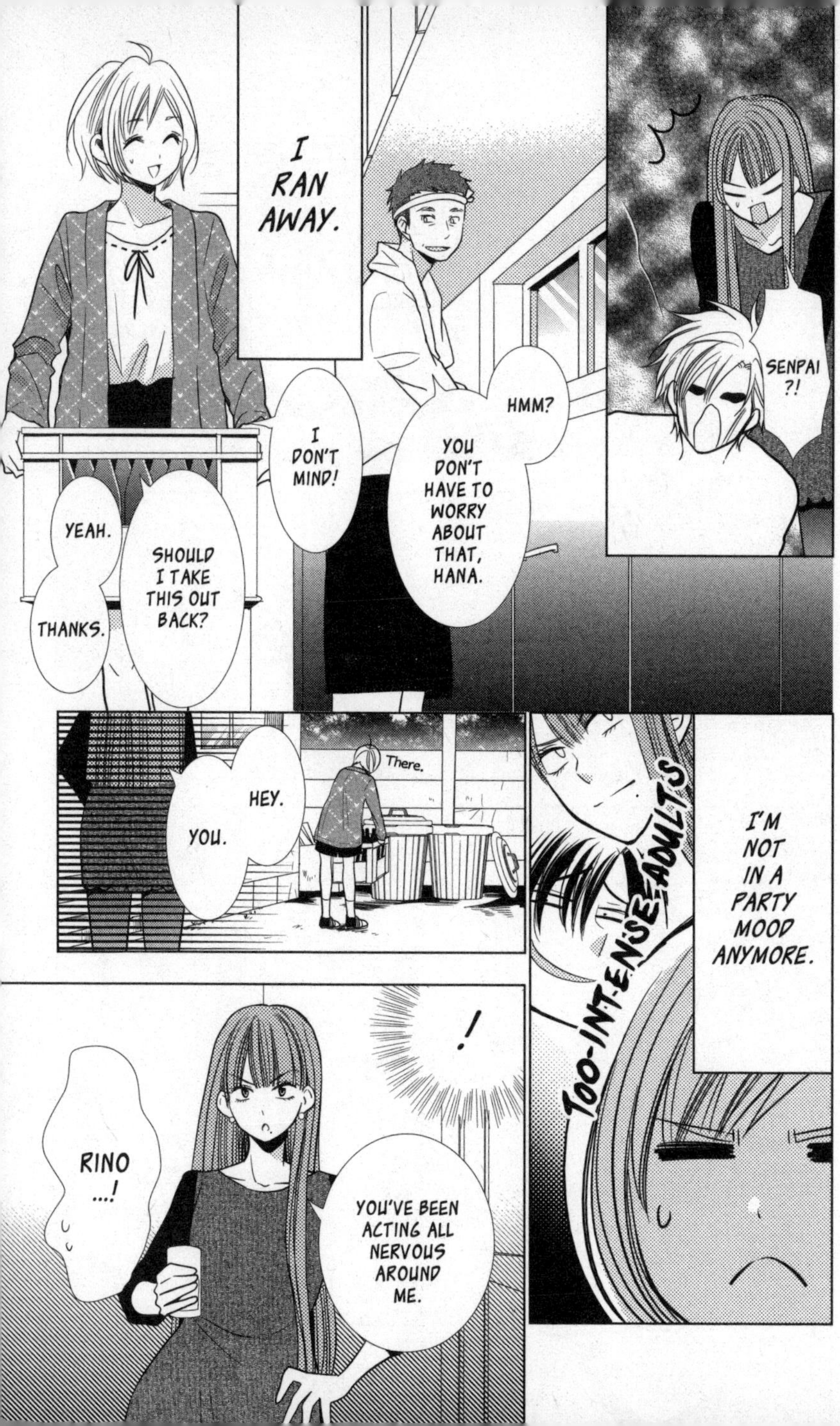
SENPAI ?!
I RAN AWAY.
HMM?
YOU DON'T HAVE TO WORRY ABOUT THAT, HANA.
I DON'T MIND!
SHOULD I TAKE THIS OUT BACK?
YEAH.
THANKS.
I'M NOT IN A PARTY MOOD ANYMORE.
TOO-INTENSE-ADULTS
There.
HEY.
YOU.
!
YOU'VE BEEN ACTING ALL NERVOUS AROUND ME.
RINO ...!

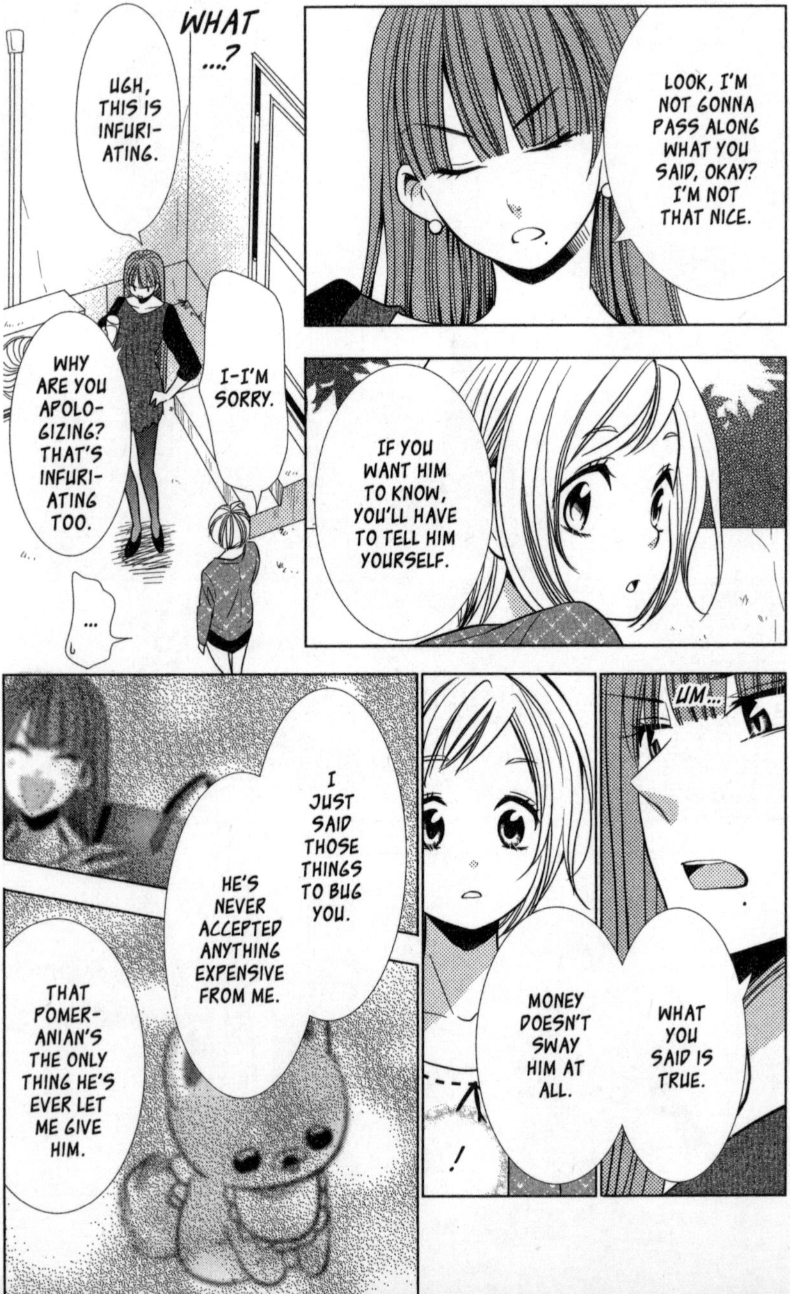
LOOK, I'M NOT GONNA PASS ALONG WHAT YOU SAID, OKAY? I'M NOT THAT NICE.
IF YOU WANT HIM TO KNOW, YOU'LL HAVE TO TELL HIM YOURSELF.
WHAT ...?
UGH, THIS IS INFURI-ATING.
I-I'M SORRY.
WHY ARE YOU APOLO-GIZING? THAT'S INFURI-ATING TOO.
...
UM...
WHAT YOU SAID IS TRUE.
MONEY DOESN'T SWAY HIM AT ALL.
!
I JUST SAID THOSE THINGS TO BUG YOU.
HE'S NEVER ACCEPTED ANYTHING EXPENSIVE FROM ME.
THAT POMER-ANIAN'S THE ONLY THING HE'S EVER LET ME GIVE HIM.

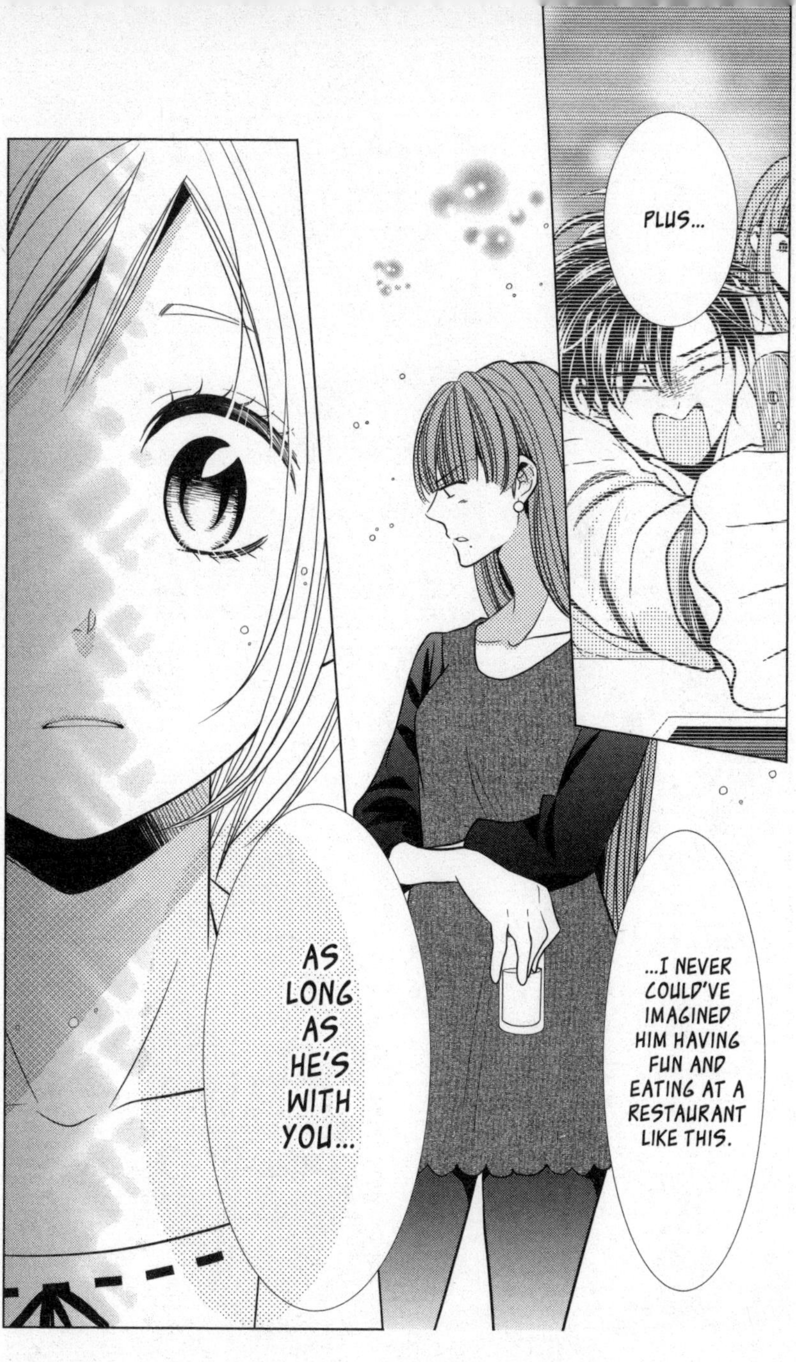
PLUS...
...I NEVER COULD'VE IMAGINED HIM HAVING FUN AND EATING AT A RESTAURANT LIKE THIS.
AS LONG AS HE'S WITH YOU...

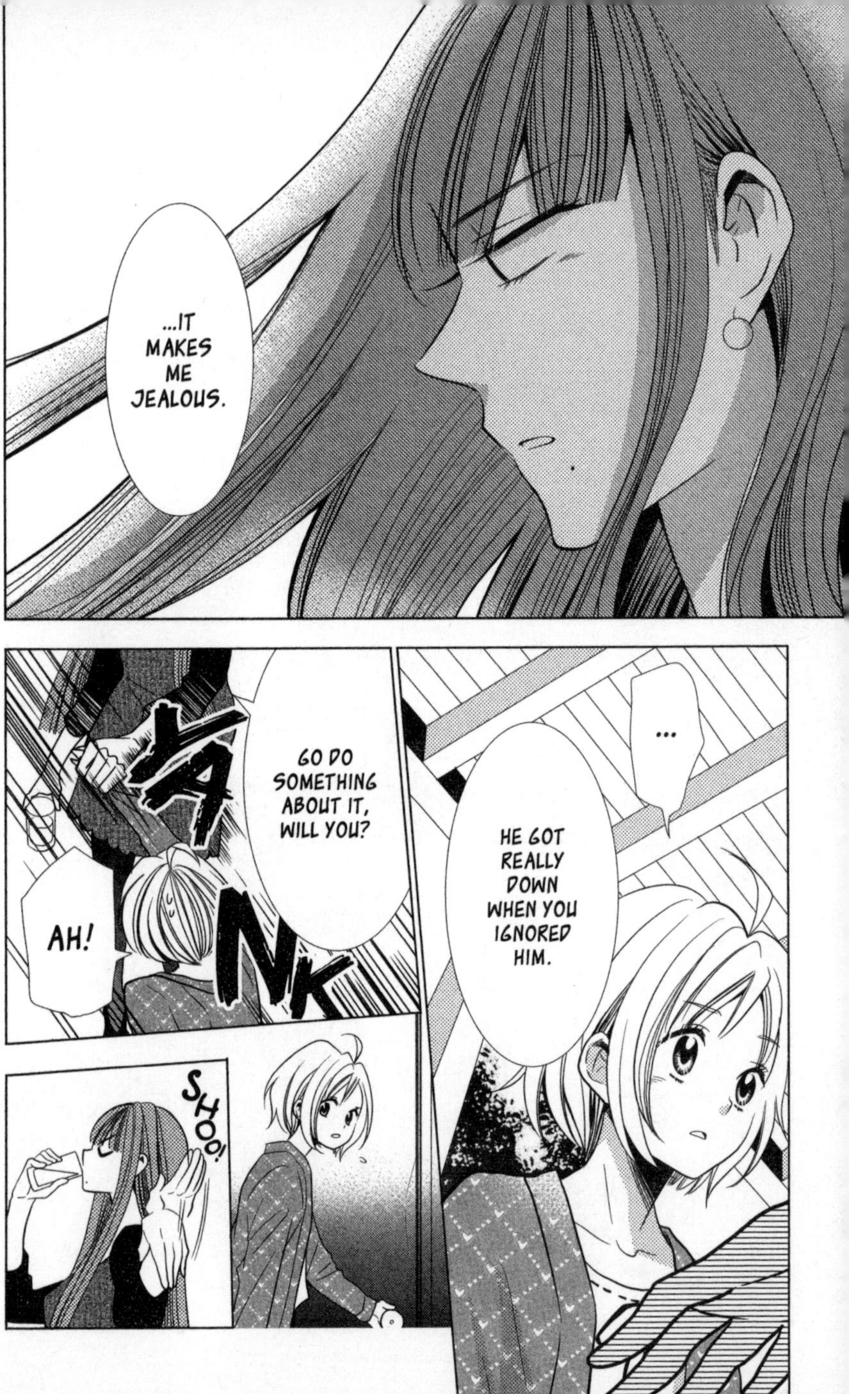
...IT MAKES ME JEALOUS.
...
HE GOT REALLY DOWN WHEN YOU IGNORED HIM.
GO DO SOMETHING ABOUT IT, WILL YOU?
YANK
AH!
SHOO!

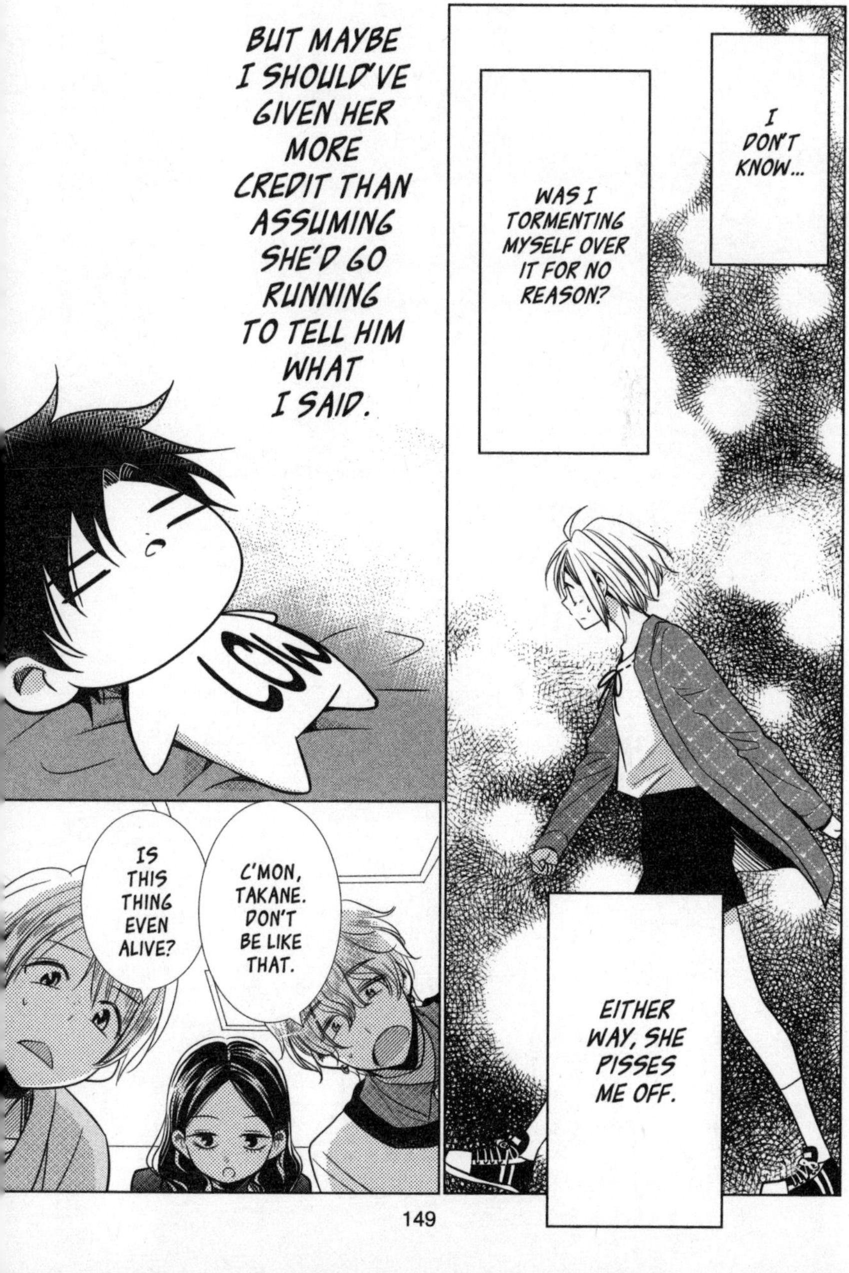
I DON'T KNOW...
WAS I TORMENTING MYSELF OVER IT FOR NO REASON?
EITHER WAY, SHE PISSES ME OFF.
BUT MAYBE I SHOULD'VE GIVEN HER MORE CREDIT THAN ASSUMING SHE'D GO RUNNING TO TELL HIM WHAT I SAID.
C'MON, TAKANE. DON'T BE LIKE THAT.
IS THIS THING EVEN ALIVE?

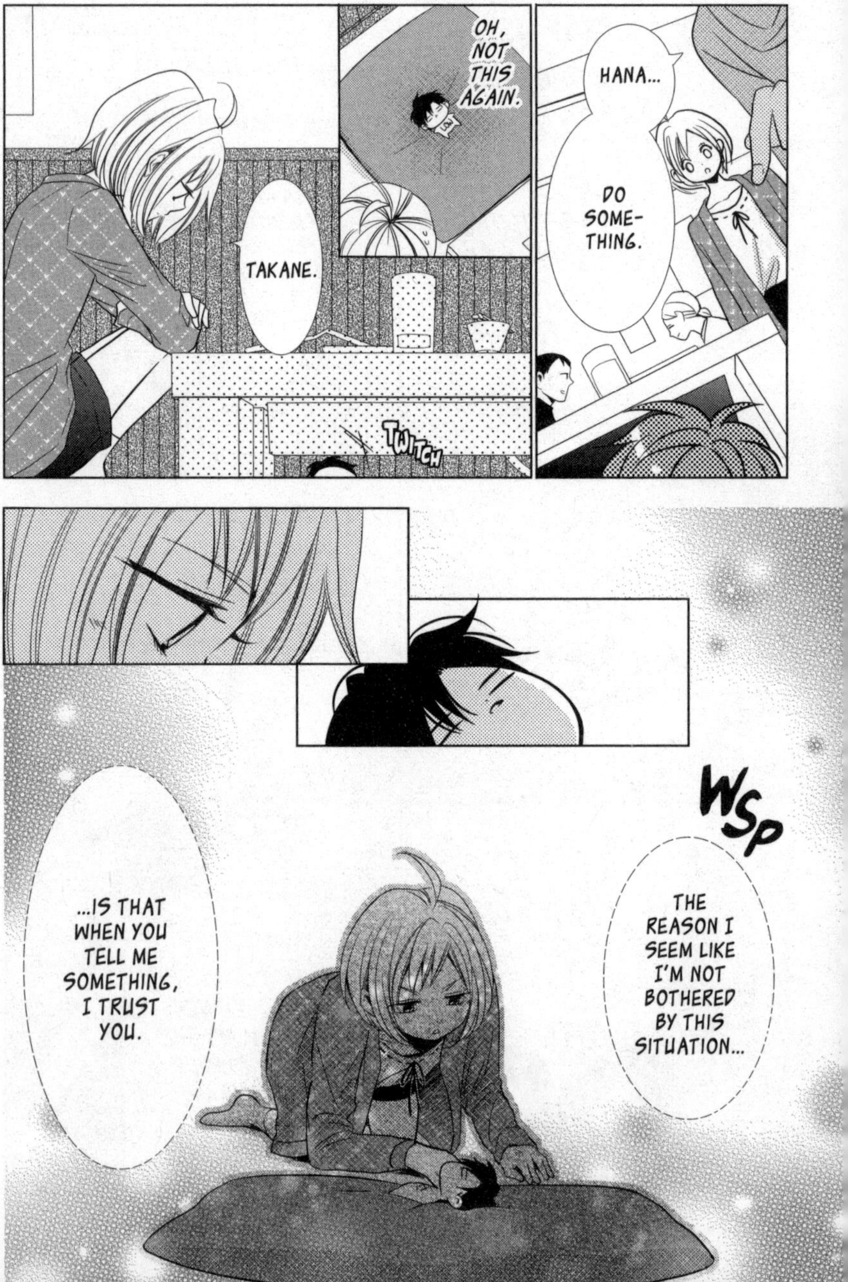
HANA...
DO SOME-THING.
OH, NOT THIS AGAIN.
TAKANE.
TWITCH
WSP
THE REASON I SEEM LIKE I'M NOT BOTHERED BY THIS SITUATION...
...IS THAT WHEN YOU TELL ME SOMETHING, I TRUST YOU.

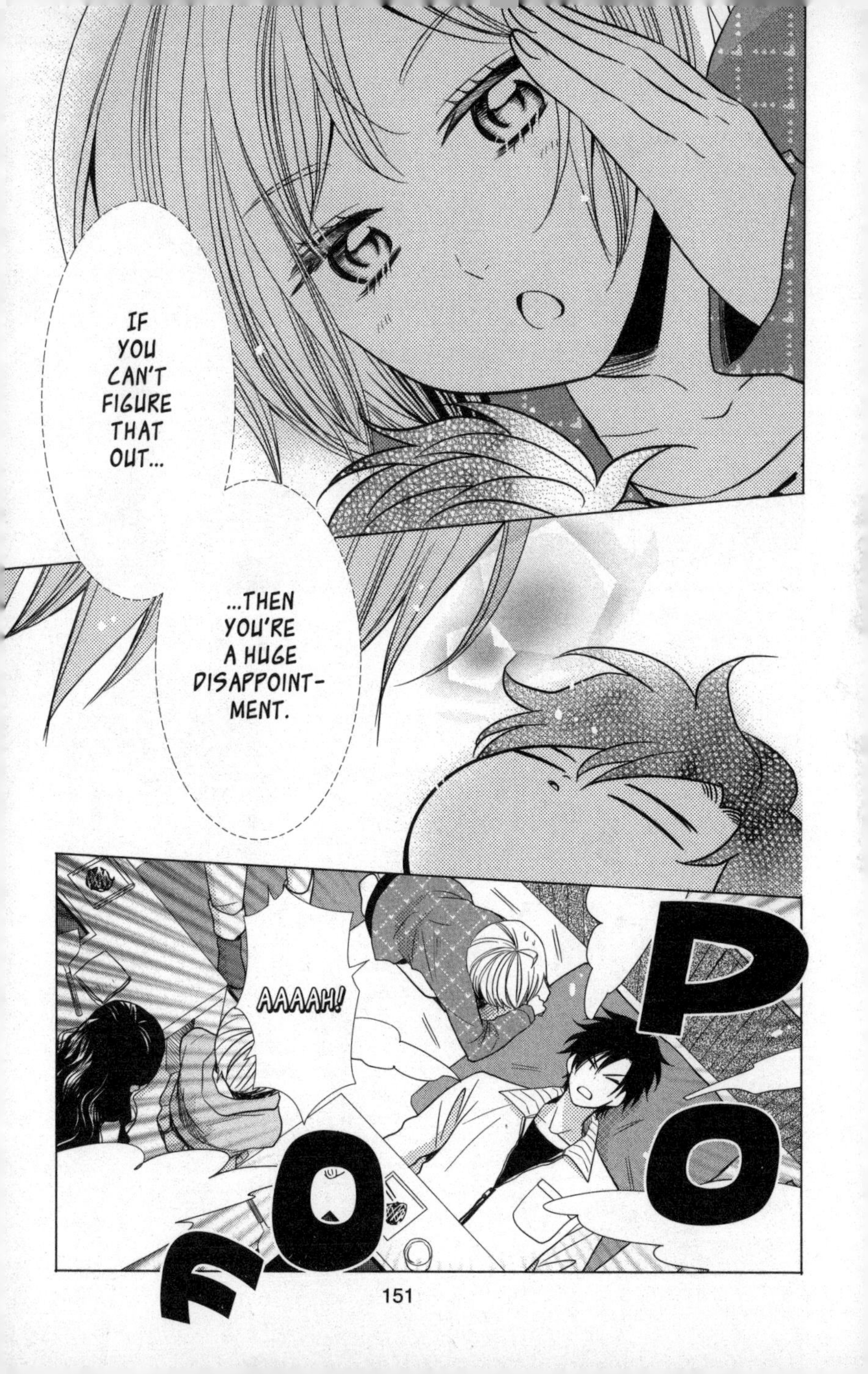
IF YOU CAN'T FIGURE THAT OUT...
...THEN YOU'RE A HUGE DISAPPOINT-MENT.
POOF
AAAAH!

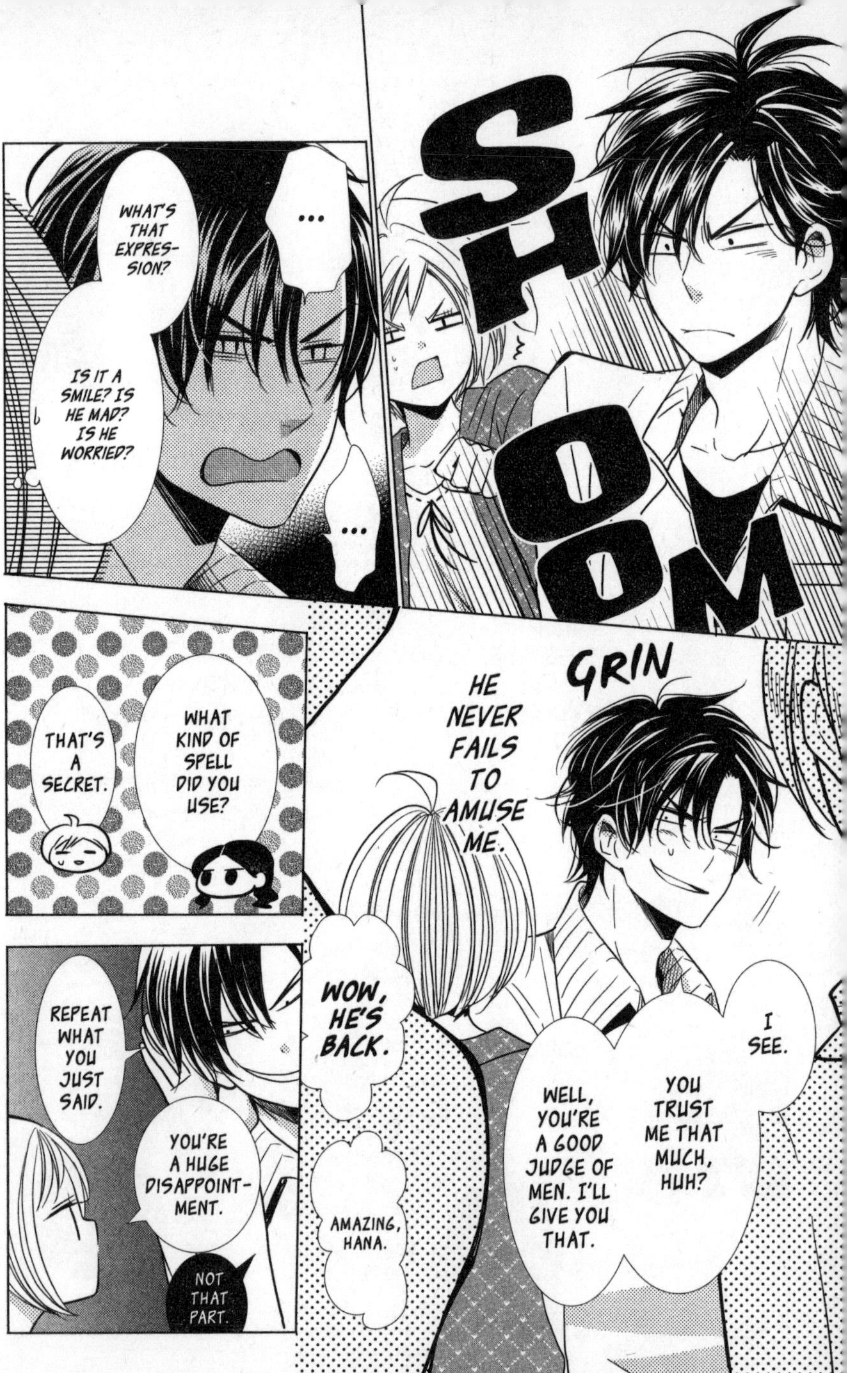
SHOOM
...
WHAT'S THAT EXPRESSION?
IS IT A SMILE? IS HE MAD? IS HE WORRIED?
...
GRIN
HE NEVER FAILS TO AMUSE ME.
I SEE.
YOU TRUST ME THAT MUCH, HUH?
WELL, YOU'RE A GOOD JUDGE OF MEN. I'LL GIVE YOU THAT.
WOW, HE'S BACK.
AMAZING, HANA.
WHAT KIND OF SPELL DID YOU USE?
THAT'S A SECRET.
REPEAT WHAT YOU JUST SAID.
YOU'RE A HUGE DISAPPOINTMENT.
NOT THAT PART.

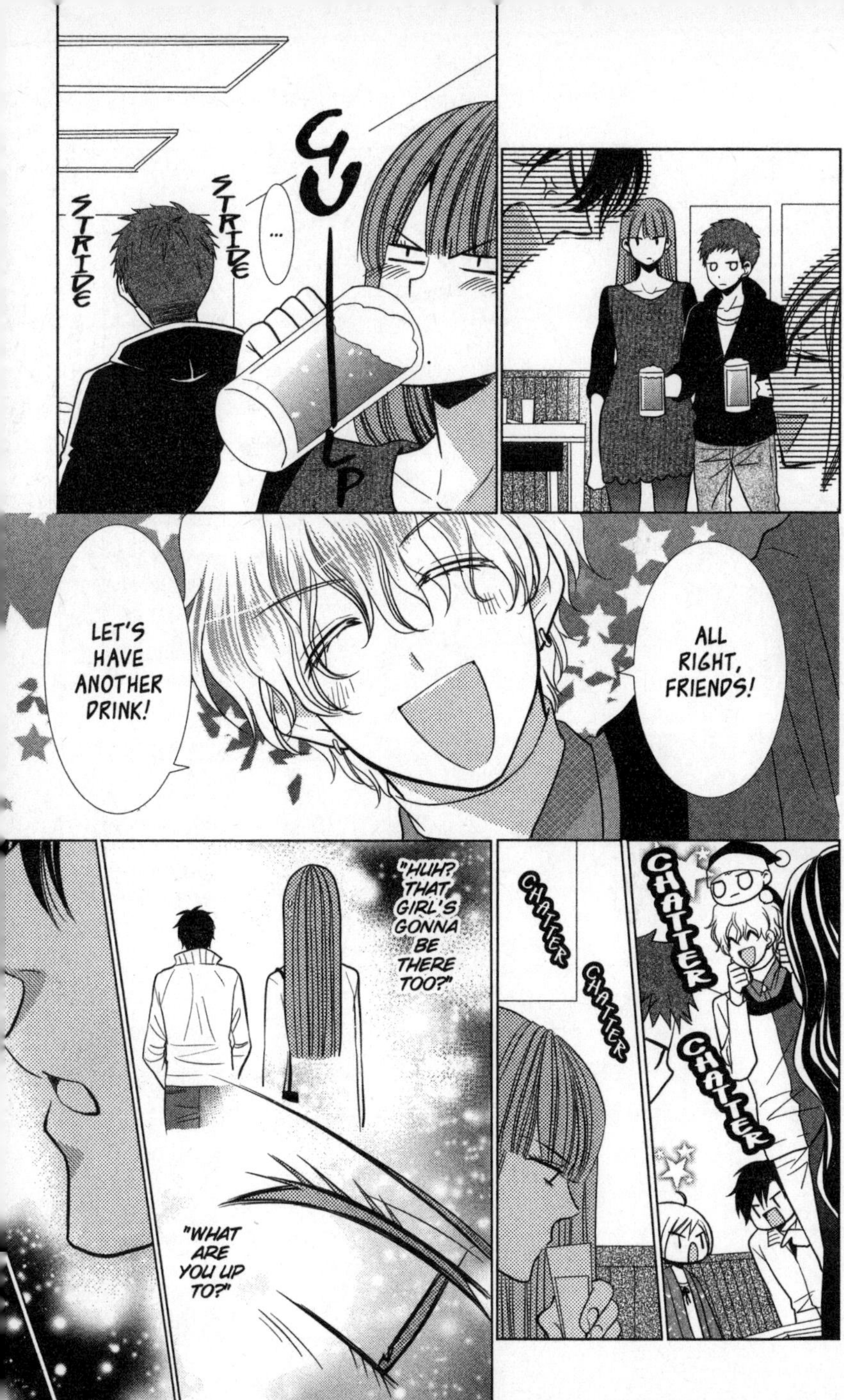
GULP
...
STRIDE
STRIDE
ALL RIGHT, FRIENDS!
LET'S HAVE ANOTHER DRINK!
CHATTER
CHATTER
CHATTER
"HUH? THAT GIRL'S GONNA BE THERE TOO?"
"WHAT ARE YOU UP TO?"

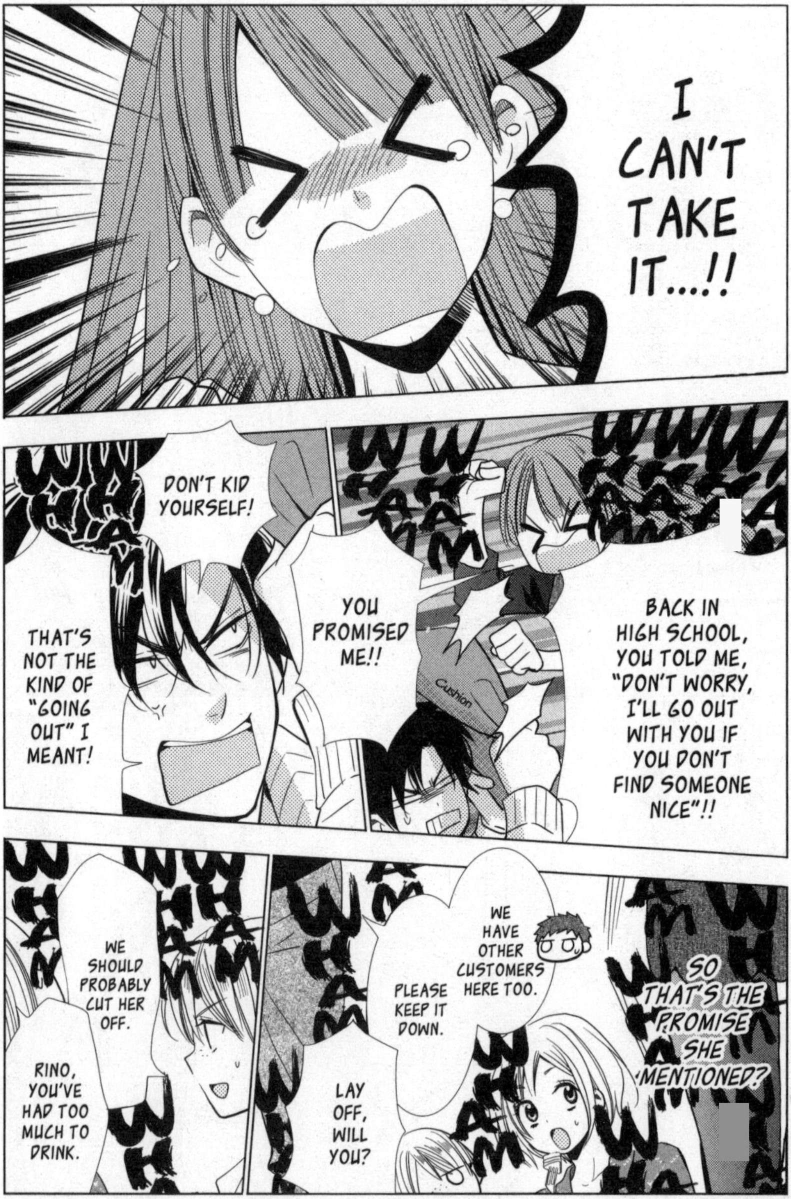
I CAN'T TAKE IT...!!
BACK IN HIGH SCHOOL, YOU TOLD ME, "DON'T WORRY, I'LL GO OUT WITH YOU IF YOU DON'T FIND SOMEONE NICE"!!
YOU PROMISED ME!!
DON'T KID YOURSELF!
THAT'S NOT THE KIND OF "GOING OUT" I MEANT!
SO THAT'S THE PROMISE SHE MENTIONED?
WE HAVE OTHER CUSTOMERS HERE TOO.
PLEASE KEEP IT DOWN.
LAY OFF, WILL YOU?
WE SHOULD PROBABLY CUT HER OFF.
RINO, YOU'VE HAD TOO MUCH TO DRINK.

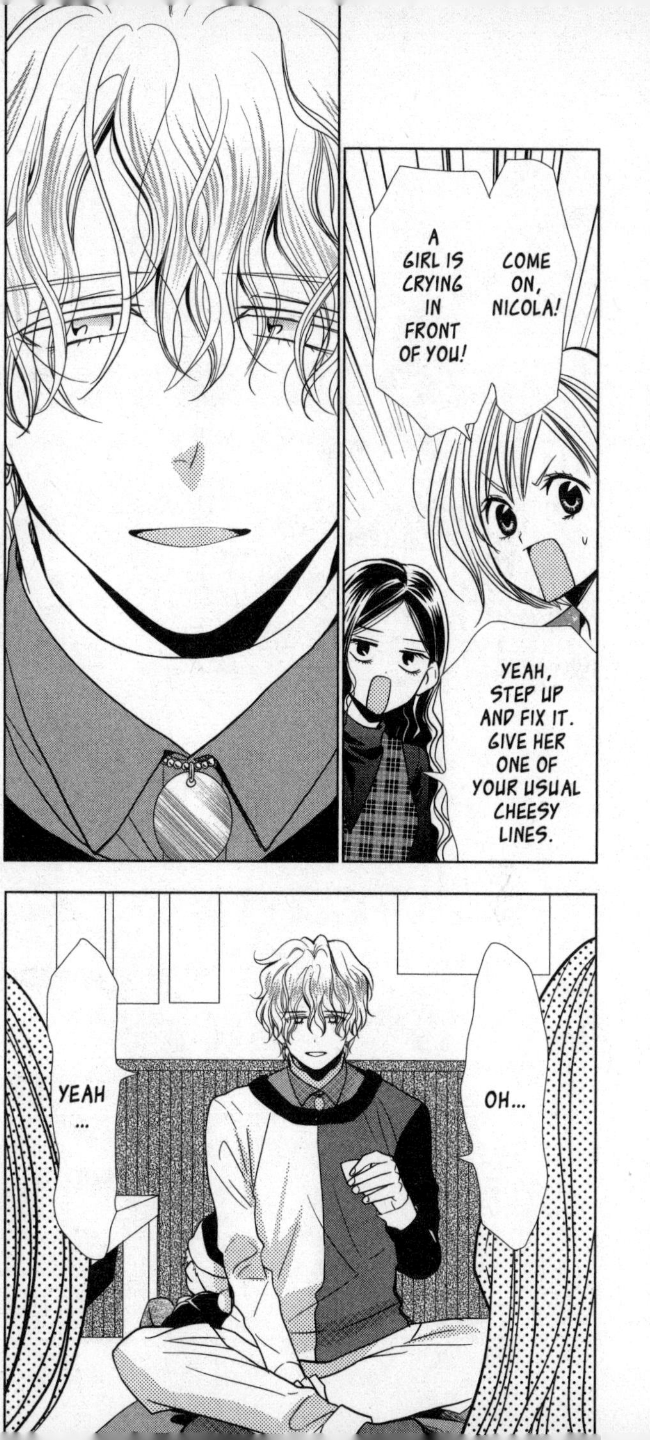
COME ON, NICOLA!
A GIRL IS CRYING IN FRONT OF YOU!
YEAH, STEP UP AND FIX IT. GIVE HER ONE OF YOUR USUAL CHEESY LINES.
OH...
YEAH ...

• Kazuma Okamoto •

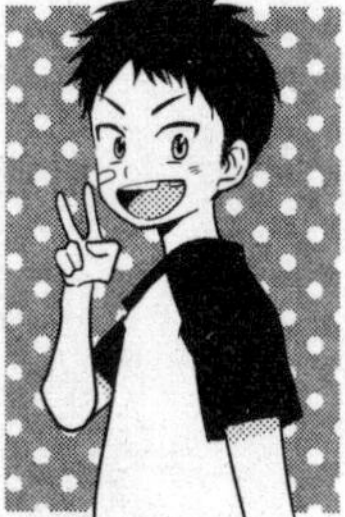

Second son of the Okamoto family. He's in fourth grade. From his first appearance in the flower-viewing chapter, I've portrayed him as a rambunctious kid, but who would've expected he'd have such a big role here? He's got a loud voice. He's happy and carefree, and he plays soccer just like his older brother. He's the ultimate kid.

• Tenma Okamoto •

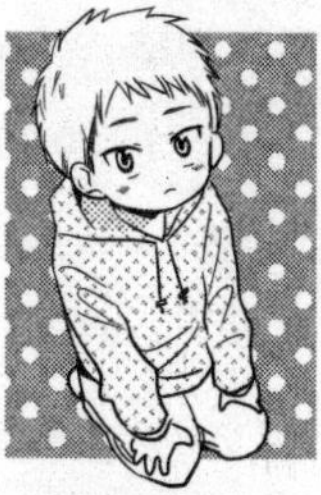

The first time in a while that I've drawn a proper face. Third son of the Okamoto family. Goes to kindergarten. He's a spoiled crybaby. He's pretty quiet and is always clinging to someone. He's become very attached to Luciano.

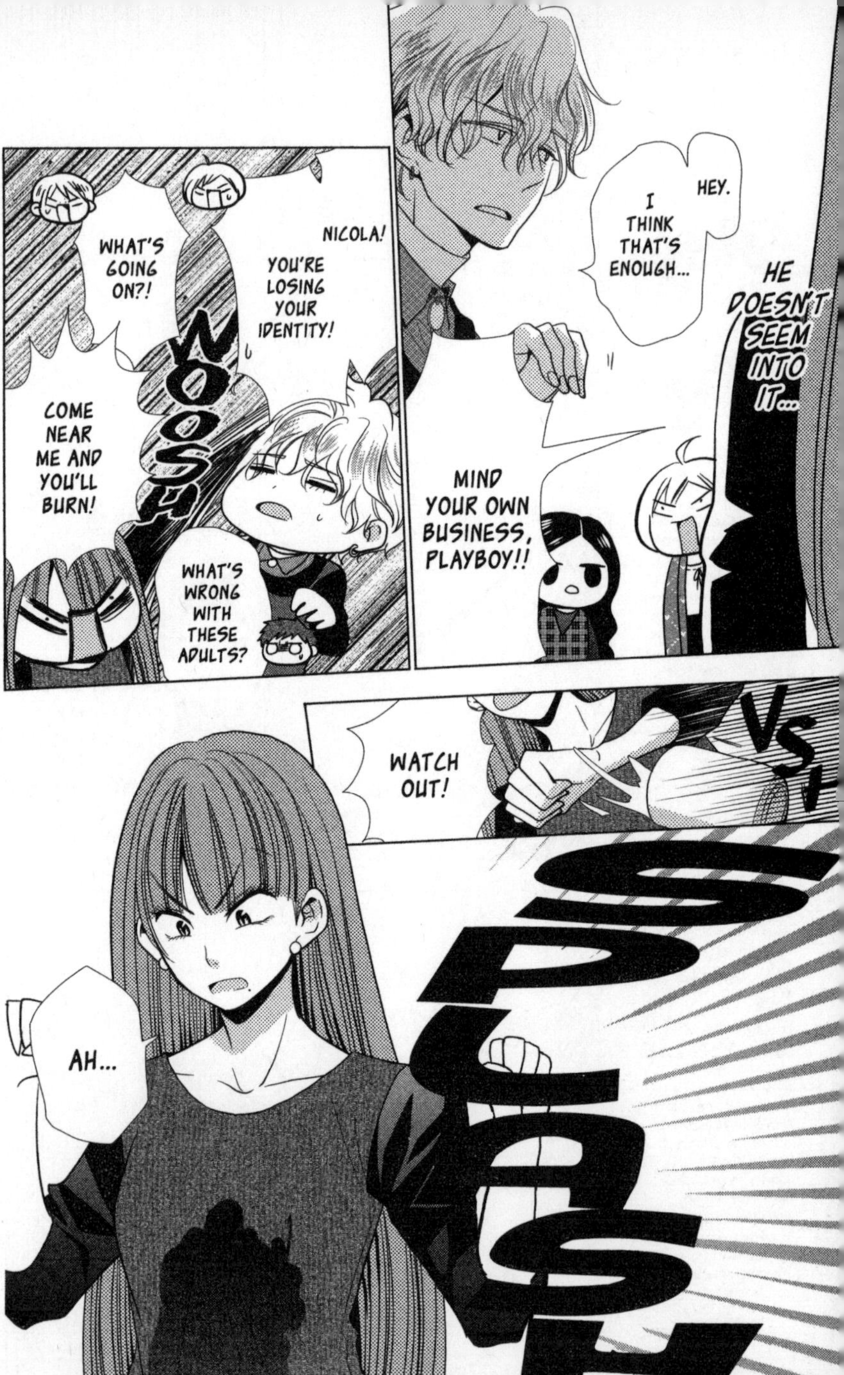
HEY.
I THINK THAT'S ENOUGH...
HE DOESN'T SEEM INTO IT...
MIND YOUR OWN BUSINESS, PLAYBOY!!
NICOLA! YOU'RE LOSING YOUR IDENTITY!
WHAT'S GOING ON?!
WOOSH
COME NEAR ME AND YOU'LL BURN!
WHAT'S WRONG WITH THESE ADULTS?
VSH
WATCH OUT!
SPLASH
AH...

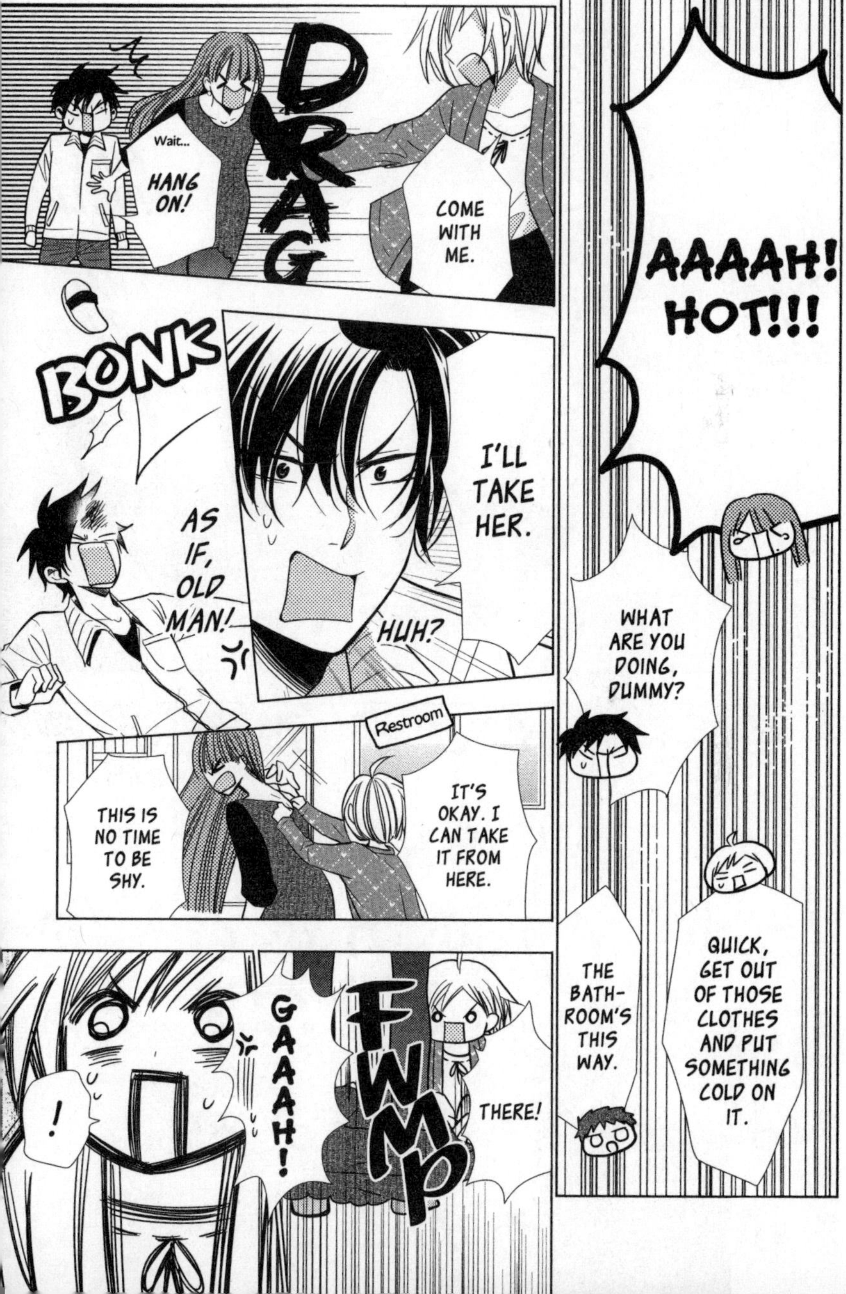
AAAAH! HOT!!!
WHAT ARE YOU DOING, DUMMY?
QUICK, GET OUT OF THOSE CLOTHES AND PUT SOMETHING COLD ON IT.
THE BATH-ROOM'S THIS WAY.
DRAG
COME WITH ME.
Wait... HANG ON!
BONK
I'LL TAKE HER.
HUH?
AS IF, OLD MAN!
Restroom
IT'S OKAY. I CAN TAKE IT FROM HERE.
THIS IS NO TIME TO BE SHY.
FWMP
THERE!
GAAAH!
!

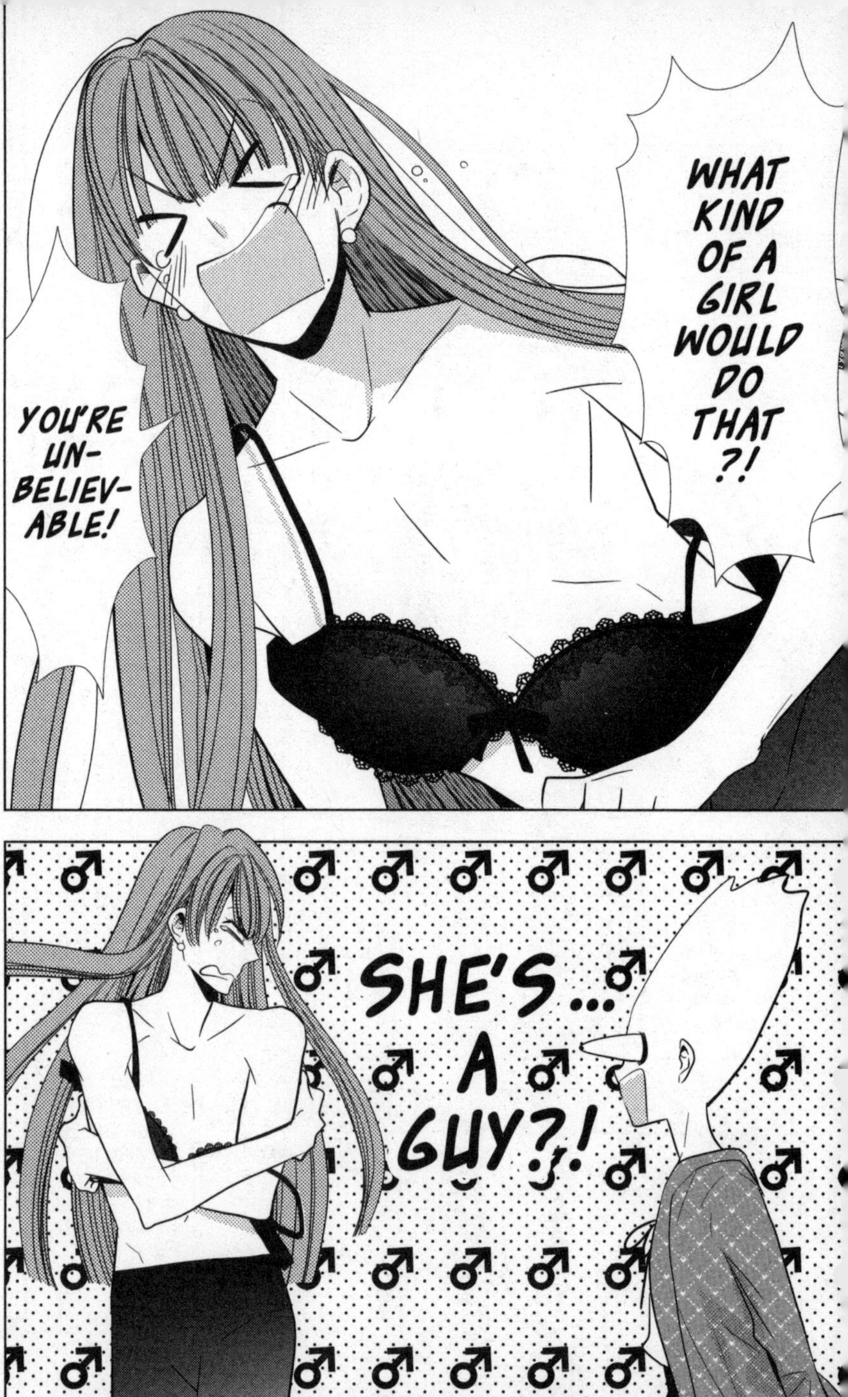
WHAT KIND OF A GIRL WOULD DO THAT?!
YOU'RE UN-BELIEV-ABLE!
SHE'S... A GUY?!
Chapter 26 / The End

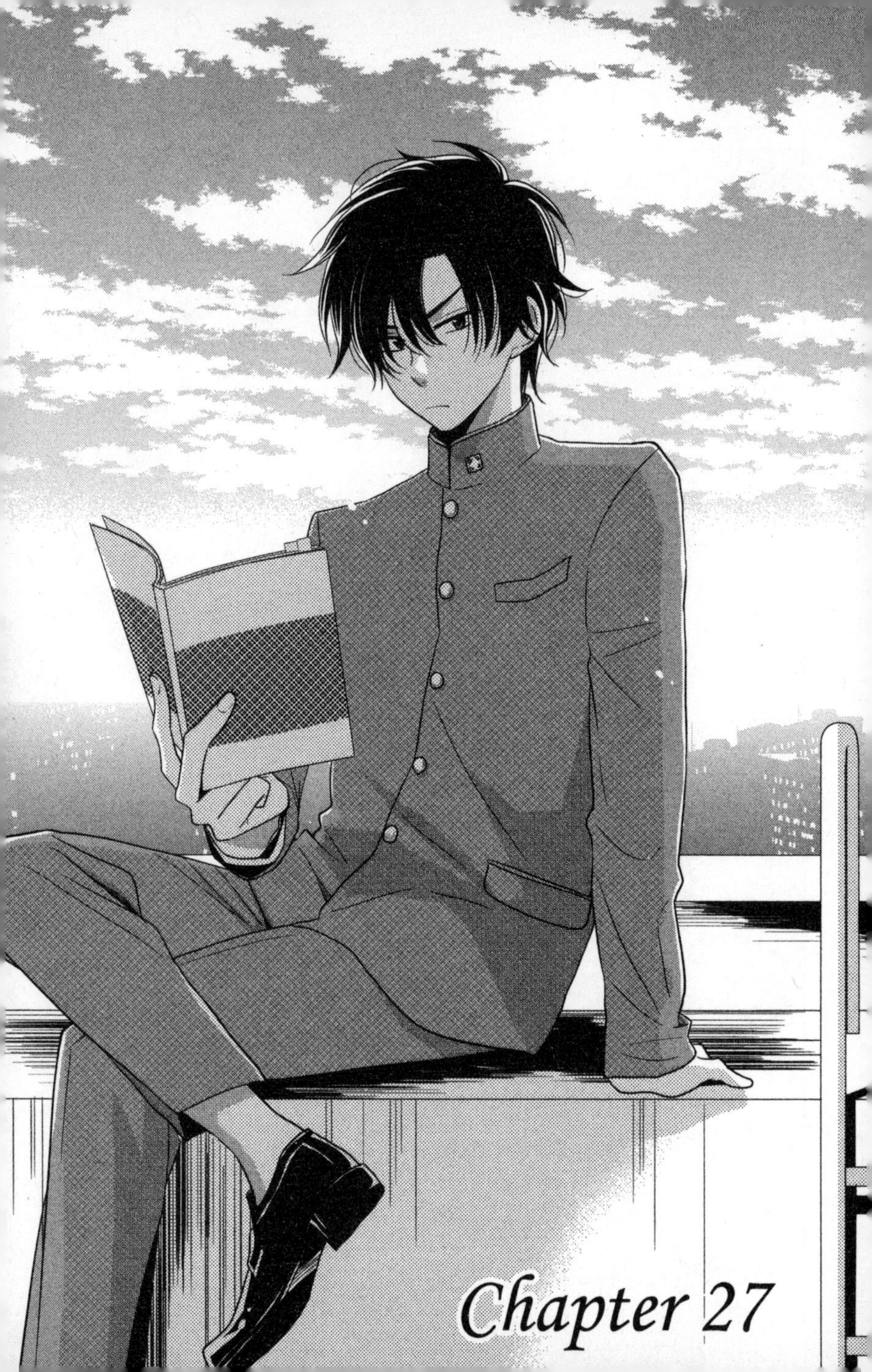
Chapter 27

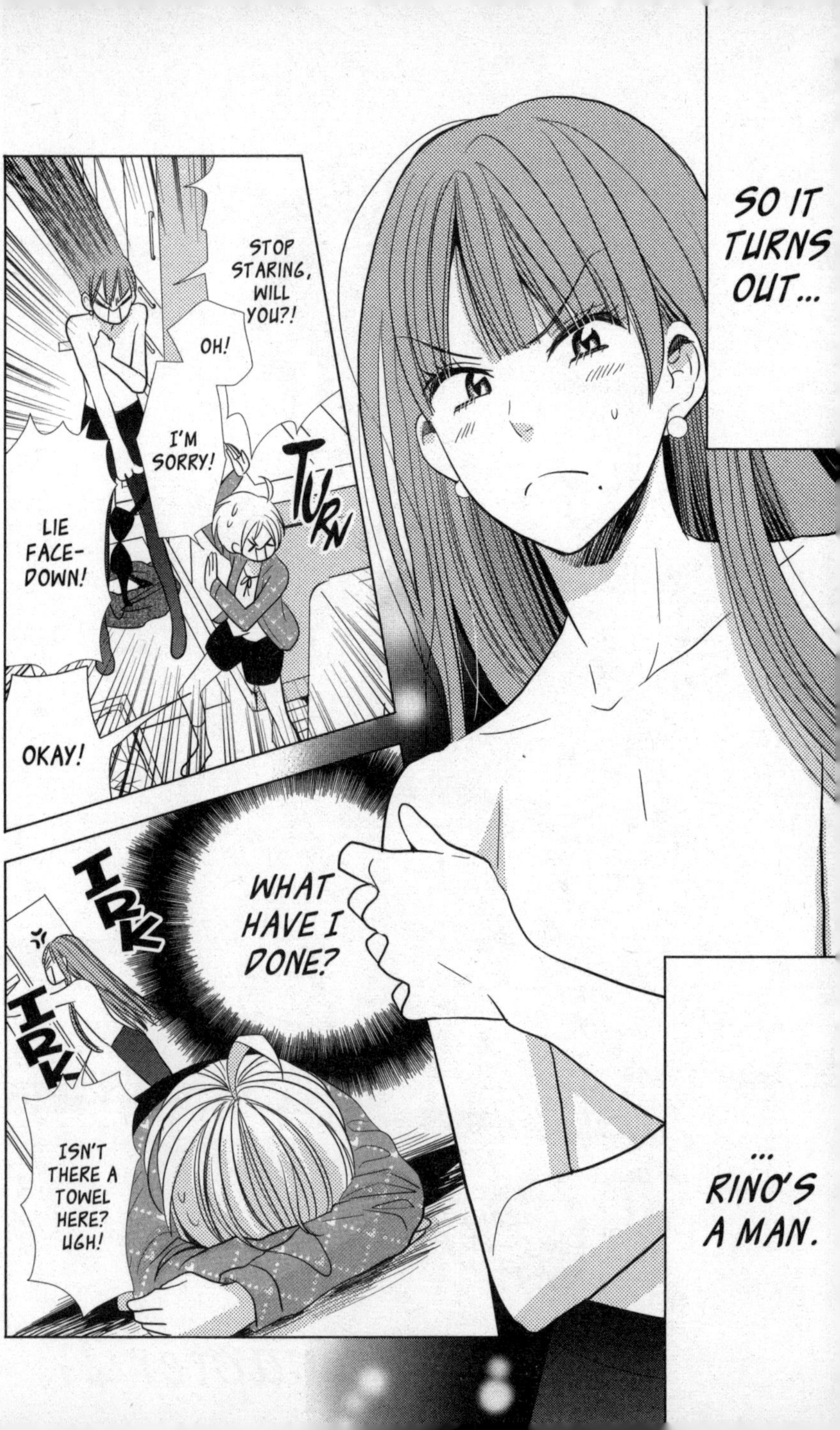
SO IT TURNS OUT...
... RINO'S A MAN.
STOP STARING, WILL YOU?!
OH!
I'M SORRY!
TURN
LIE FACE-DOWN!
OKAY!
WHAT HAVE I DONE?
IRK
IRK
ISN'T THERE A TOWEL HERE? UGH!

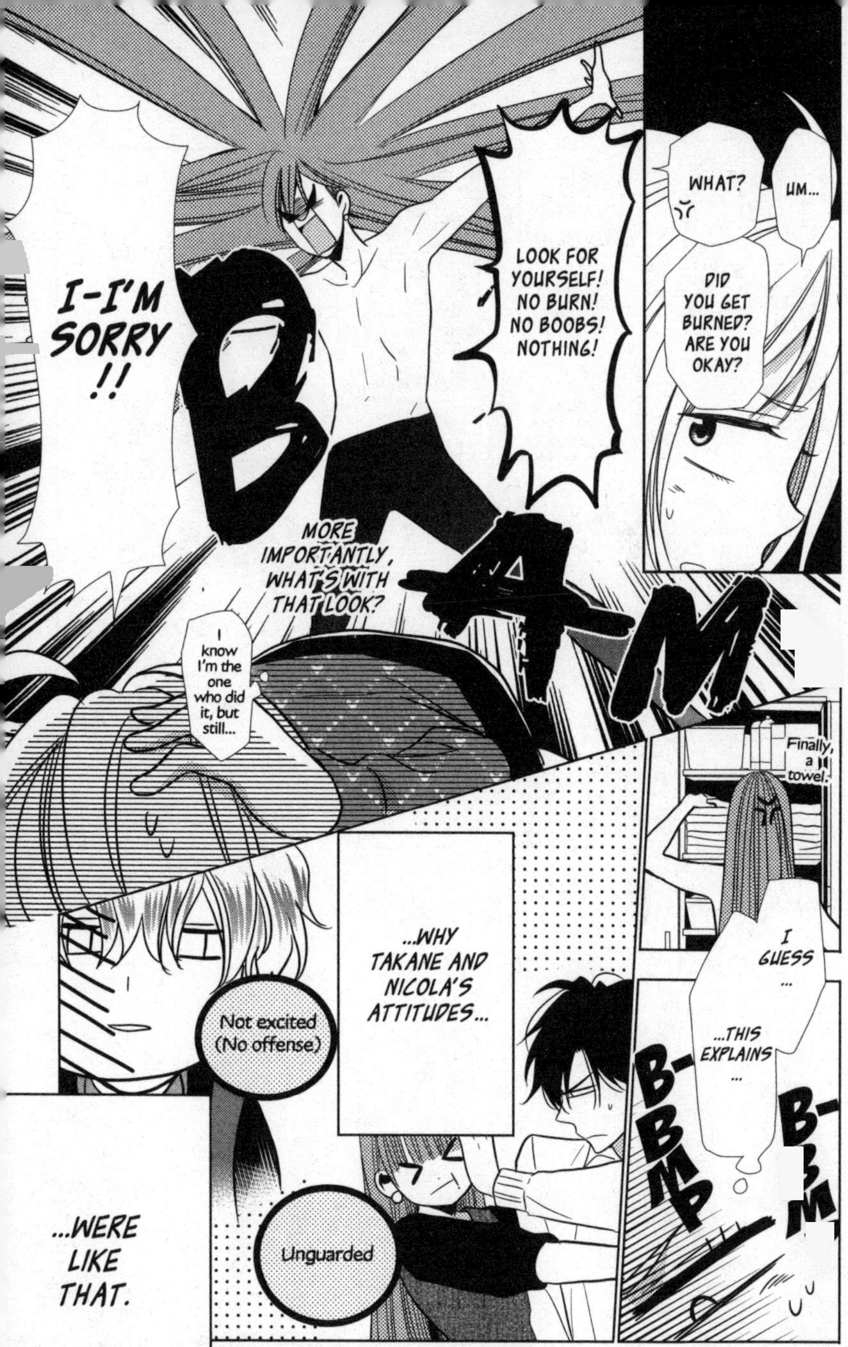
UM...
WHAT?
DID YOU GET BURNED? ARE YOU OKAY?
LOOK FOR YOURSELF! NO BURN! NO BOOBS! NOTHING!
I-I'M SORRY!!
BAM
MORE IMPORTANTLY, WHAT'S WITH THAT LOOK?
I know I'm the one who did it, but still...
Finally, a towel.
I GUESS...
...THIS EXPLAINS...
B-BMP
...WHY TAKANE AND NICOLA'S ATTITUDES...
Not excited (No offense)
Unguarded
...WERE LIKE THAT.

A pretty outrageous plot

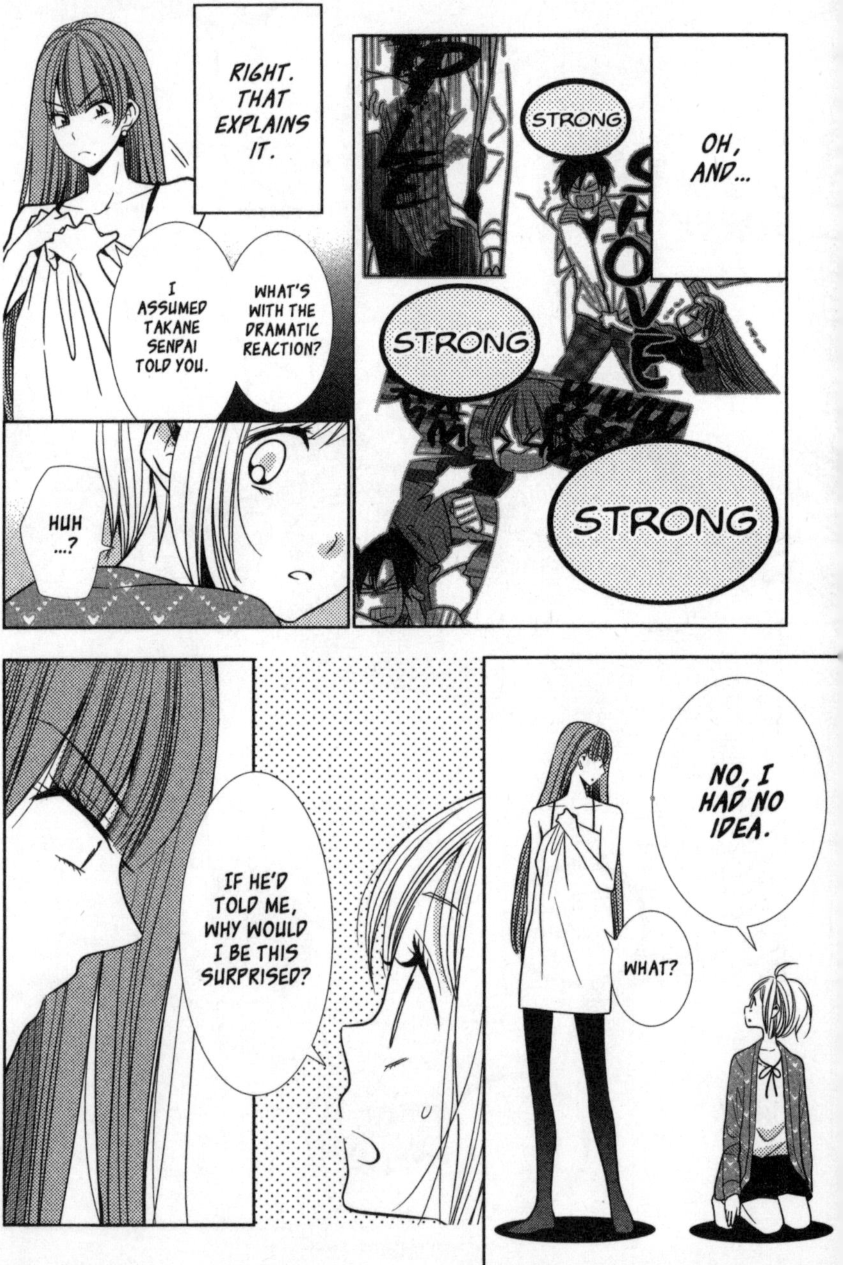
OH, AND...
STRONG
SHOVE
STRONG
STRONG
RIGHT. THAT EXPLAINS IT.
WHAT'S WITH THE DRAMATIC REACTION?
I ASSUMED TAKANE SENPAI TOLD YOU.
HUH ...?
NO, I HAD NO IDEA.
WHAT?
IF HE'D TOLD ME, WHY WOULD I BE THIS SURPRISED?

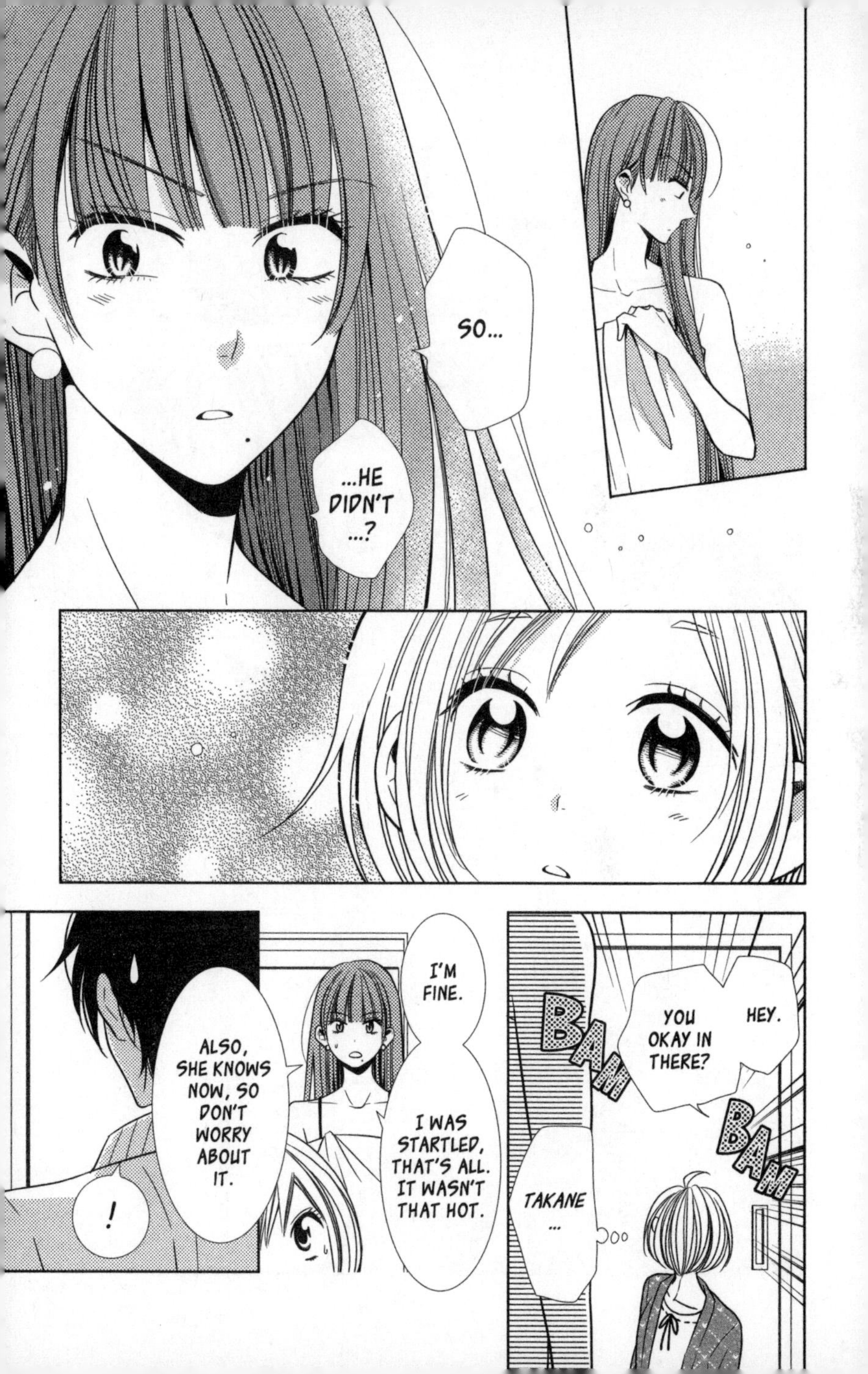
SO...
...HE DIDN'T ...?
HEY.
YOU OKAY IN THERE?
BAM
BAM
TAKANE ...
I'M FINE.
I WAS STARTLED, THAT'S ALL. IT WASN'T THAT HOT.
ALSO, SHE KNOWS NOW, SO DON'T WORRY ABOUT IT.
!

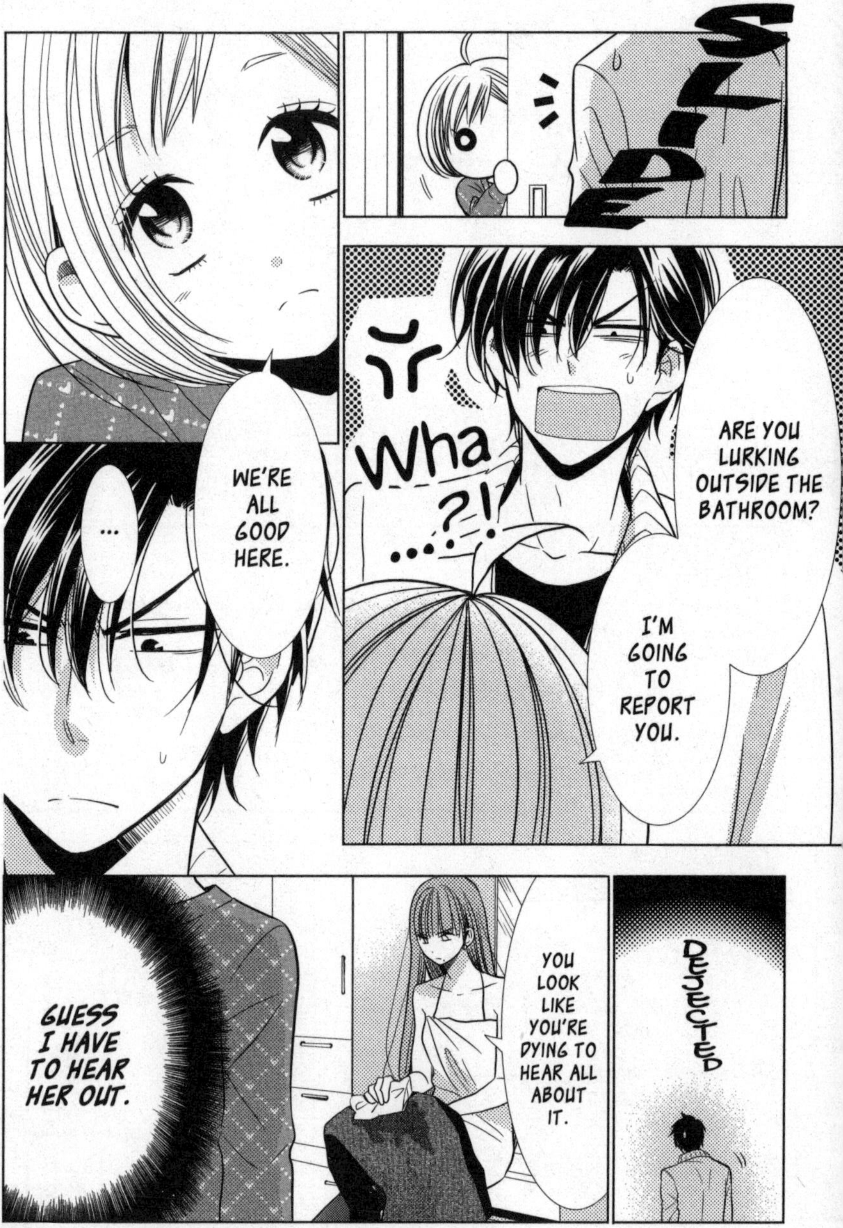
SLIDE
ARE YOU LURKING OUTSIDE THE BATHROOM?
Wha...?!
I'M GOING TO REPORT YOU.
WE'RE ALL GOOD HERE.
...
DEJECTED
YOU LOOK LIKE YOU'RE DYING TO HEAR ALL ABOUT IT.
GUESS I HAVE TO HEAR HER OUT.

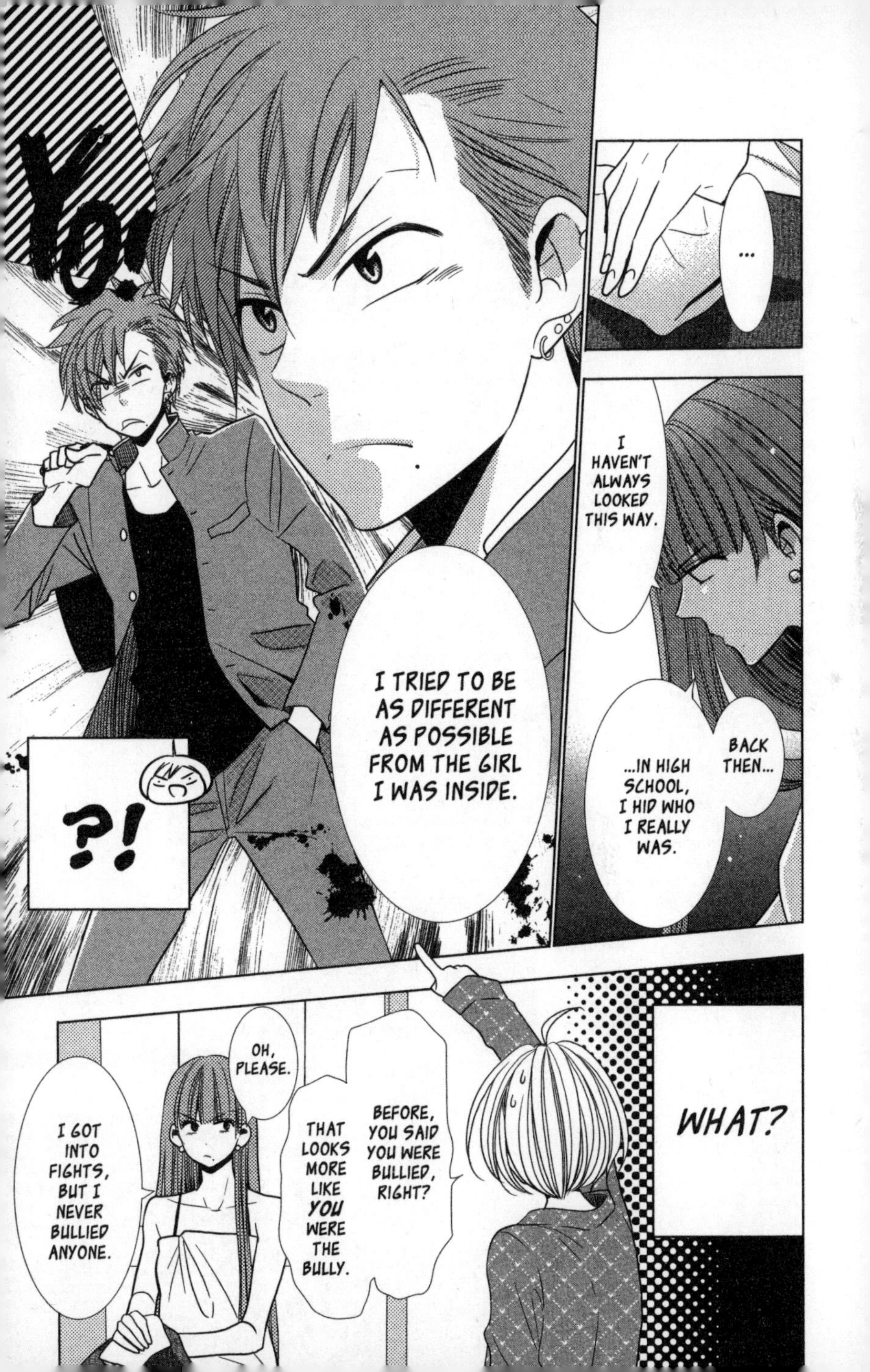
...
I HAVEN'T ALWAYS LOOKED THIS WAY.
BACK THEN...
...IN HIGH SCHOOL, I HID WHO I REALLY WAS.
I TRIED TO BE AS DIFFERENT AS POSSIBLE FROM THE GIRL I WAS INSIDE.
?!
WHAT?
BEFORE, YOU SAID YOU WERE BULLIED, RIGHT?
THAT LOOKS MORE LIKE *YOU* WERE THE BULLY.
OH, PLEASE.
I GOT INTO FIGHTS, BUT I NEVER BULLIED ANYONE.

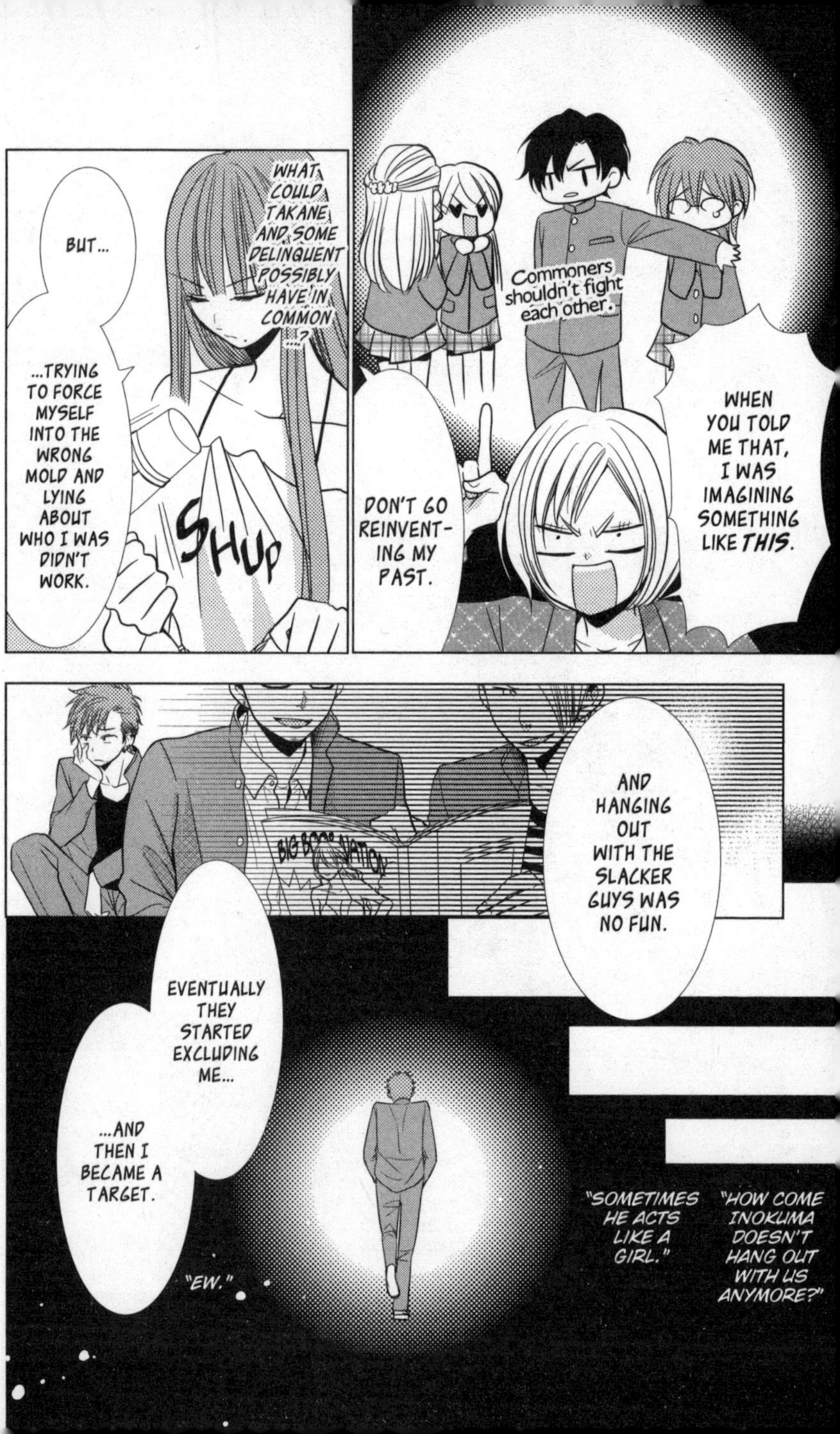
Commoners shouldn't fight each other.
WHEN YOU TOLD ME THAT, I WAS IMAGINING SOMETHING LIKE *THIS*.
DON'T GO REINVENTING MY PAST.
WHAT COULD TAKANE AND SOME DELINQUENT POSSIBLY HAVE IN COMMON ...?
BUT...
...TRYING TO FORCE MYSELF INTO THE WRONG MOLD AND LYING ABOUT WHO I WAS DIDN'T WORK.
SHUP
AND HANGING OUT WITH THE SLACKER GUYS WAS NO FUN.
"HOW COME INOKUMA DOESN'T HANG OUT WITH US ANYMORE?"
"SOMETIMES HE ACTS LIKE A GIRL."
EVENTUALLY THEY STARTED EXCLUDING ME...
...AND THEN I BECAME A TARGET.
"EW."

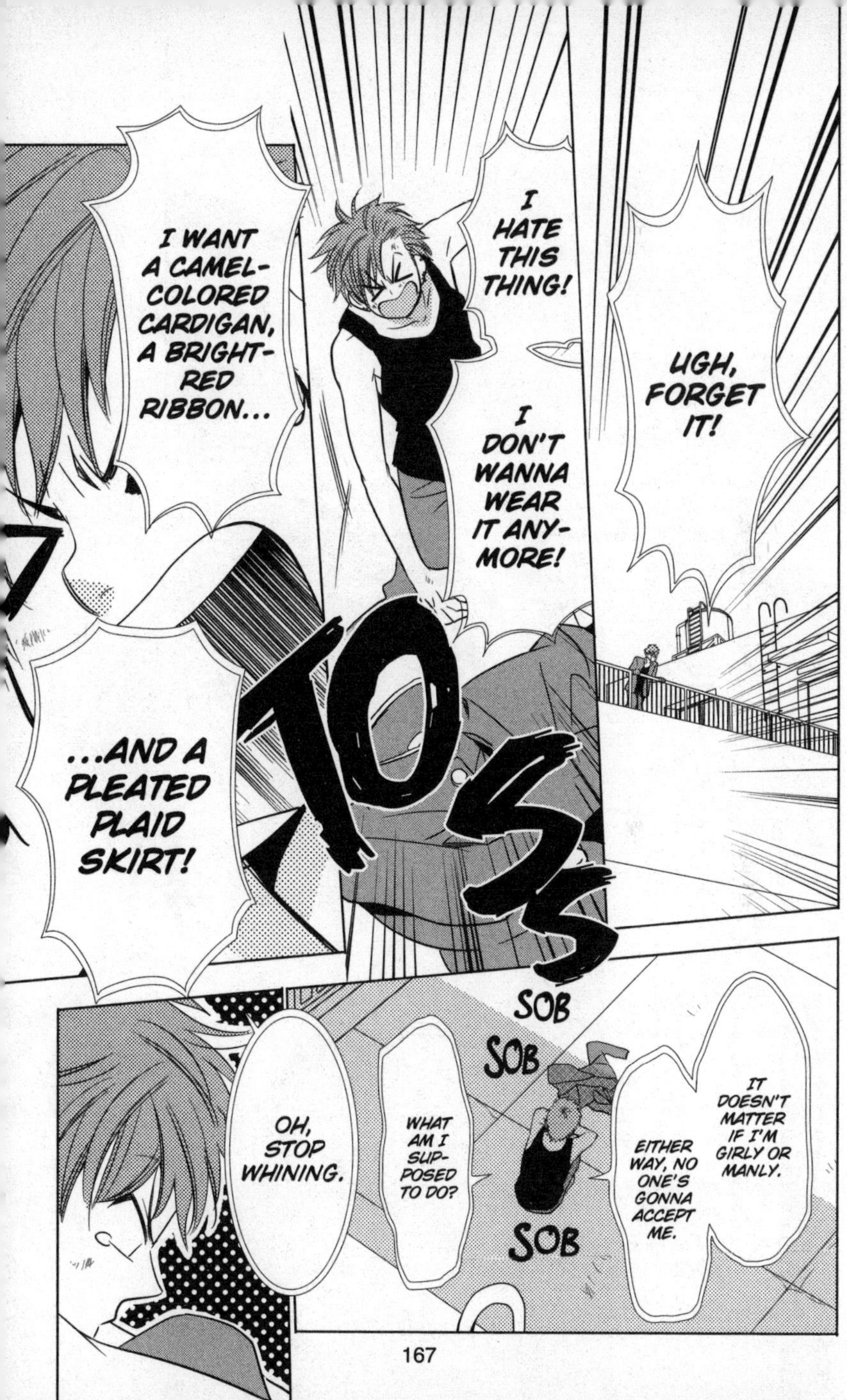
UGH, FORGET IT!
I HATE THIS THING!
I DON'T WANNA WEAR IT ANY-MORE!
TOSS
I WANT A CAMEL-COLORED CARDIGAN, A BRIGHT-RED RIBBON...
...AND A PLEATED PLAID SKIRT!
SOB
SOB
SOB
IT DOESN'T MATTER IF I'M GIRLY OR MANLY.
EITHER WAY, NO ONE'S GONNA ACCEPT ME.
WHAT AM I SUP-POSED TO DO?
OH, STOP WHINING.

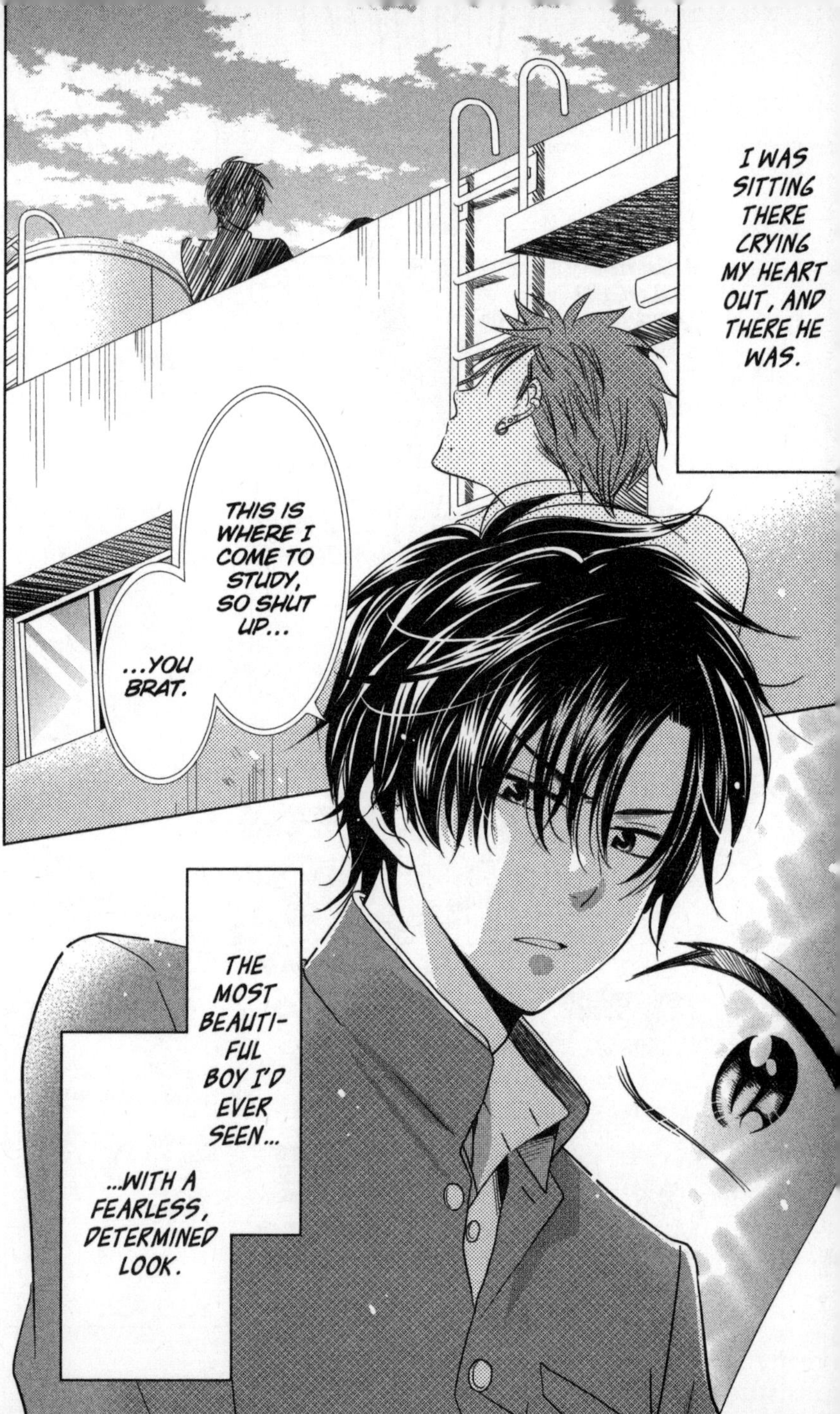
I WAS SITTING THERE CRYING MY HEART OUT, AND THERE HE WAS.
THIS IS WHERE I COME TO STUDY, SO SHUT UP...
...YOU BRAT.
THE MOST BEAUTI-FUL BOY I'D EVER SEEN...
...WITH A FEARLESS, DETERMINED LOOK.

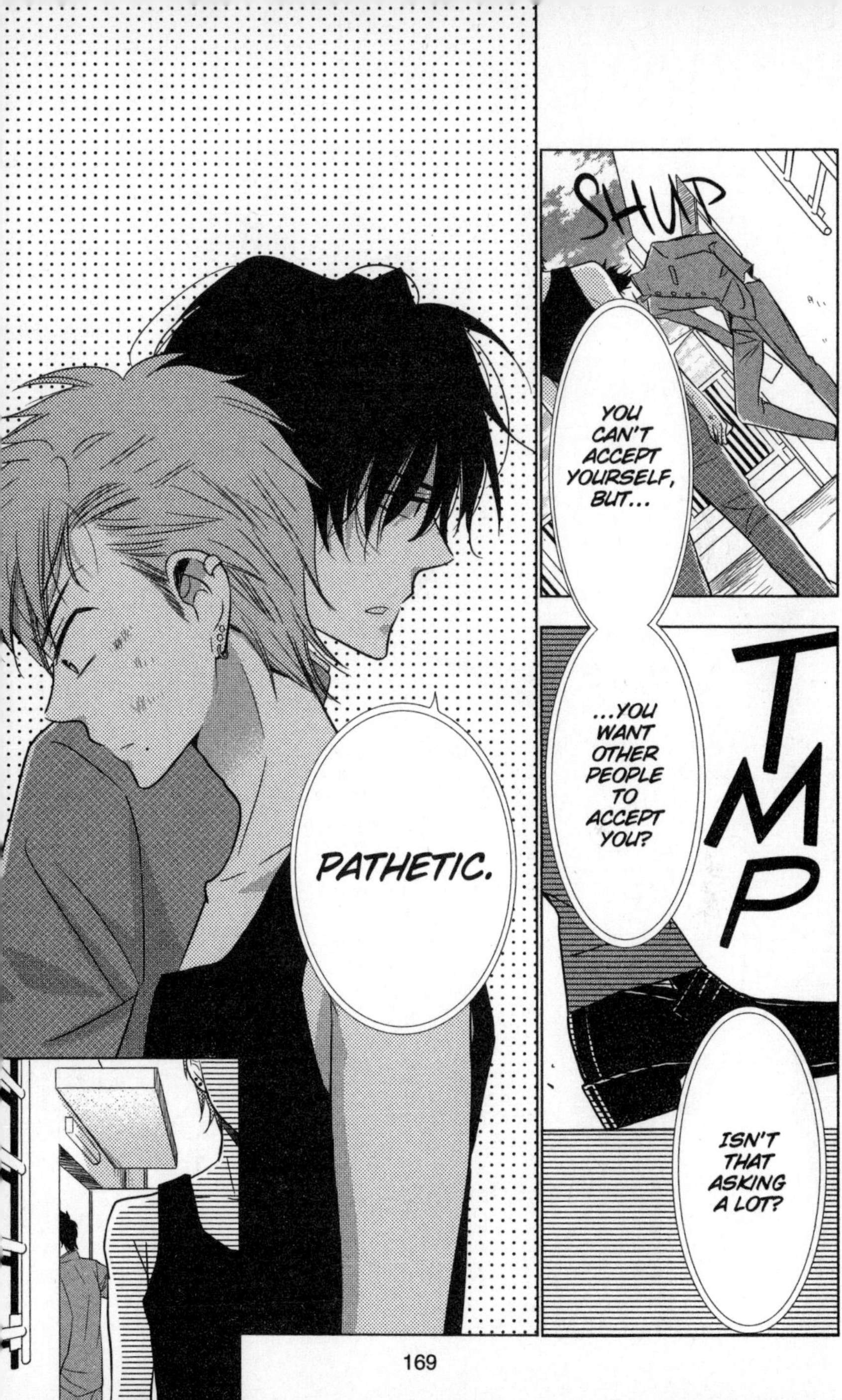
SHUP
YOU CAN'T ACCEPT YOURSELF, BUT...
TMP
...YOU WANT OTHER PEOPLE TO ACCEPT YOU?
ISN'T THAT ASKING A LOT?
PATHETIC.

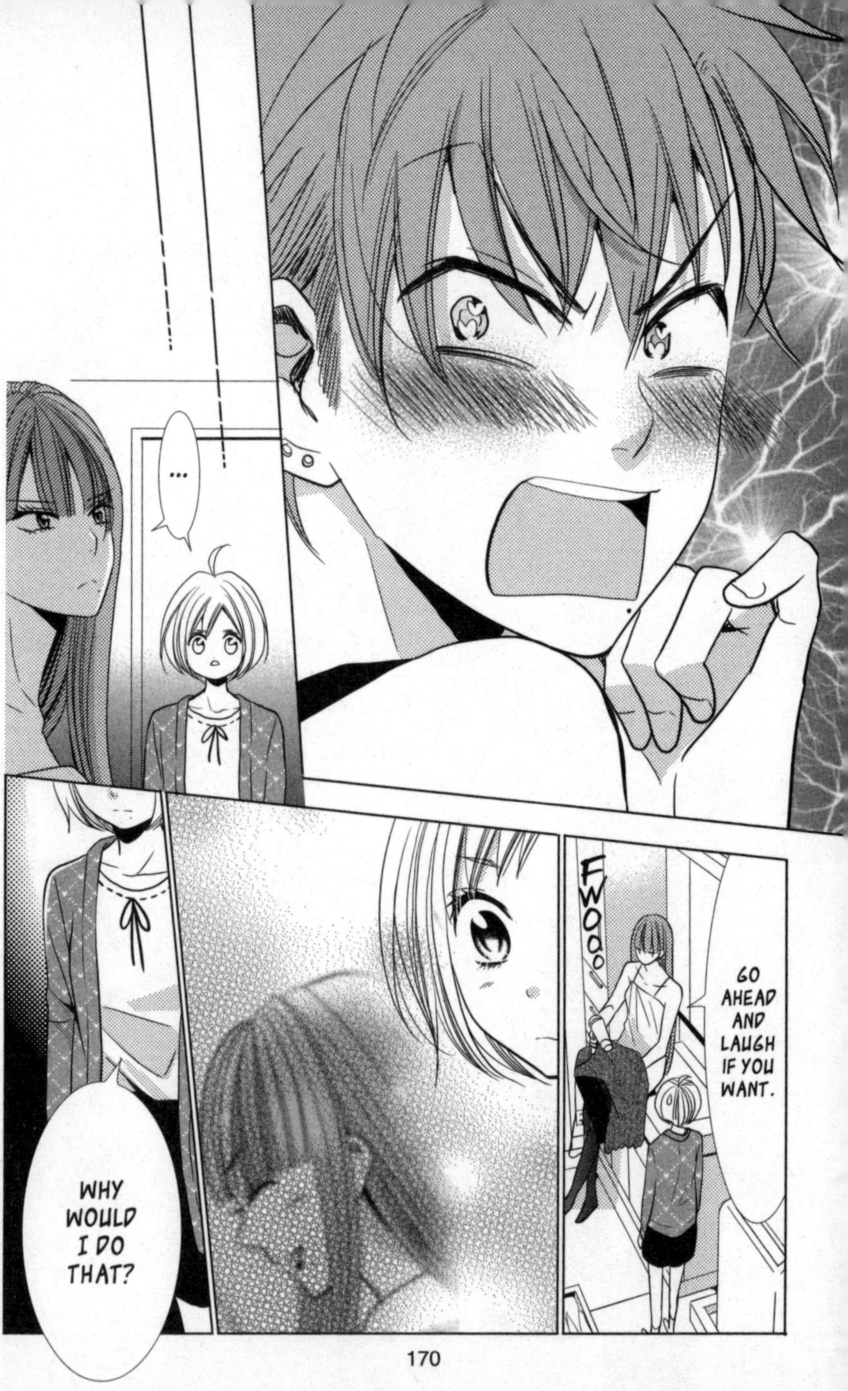
...
FWOOOO
GO AHEAD AND LAUGH IF YOU WANT.
WHY WOULD I DO THAT?

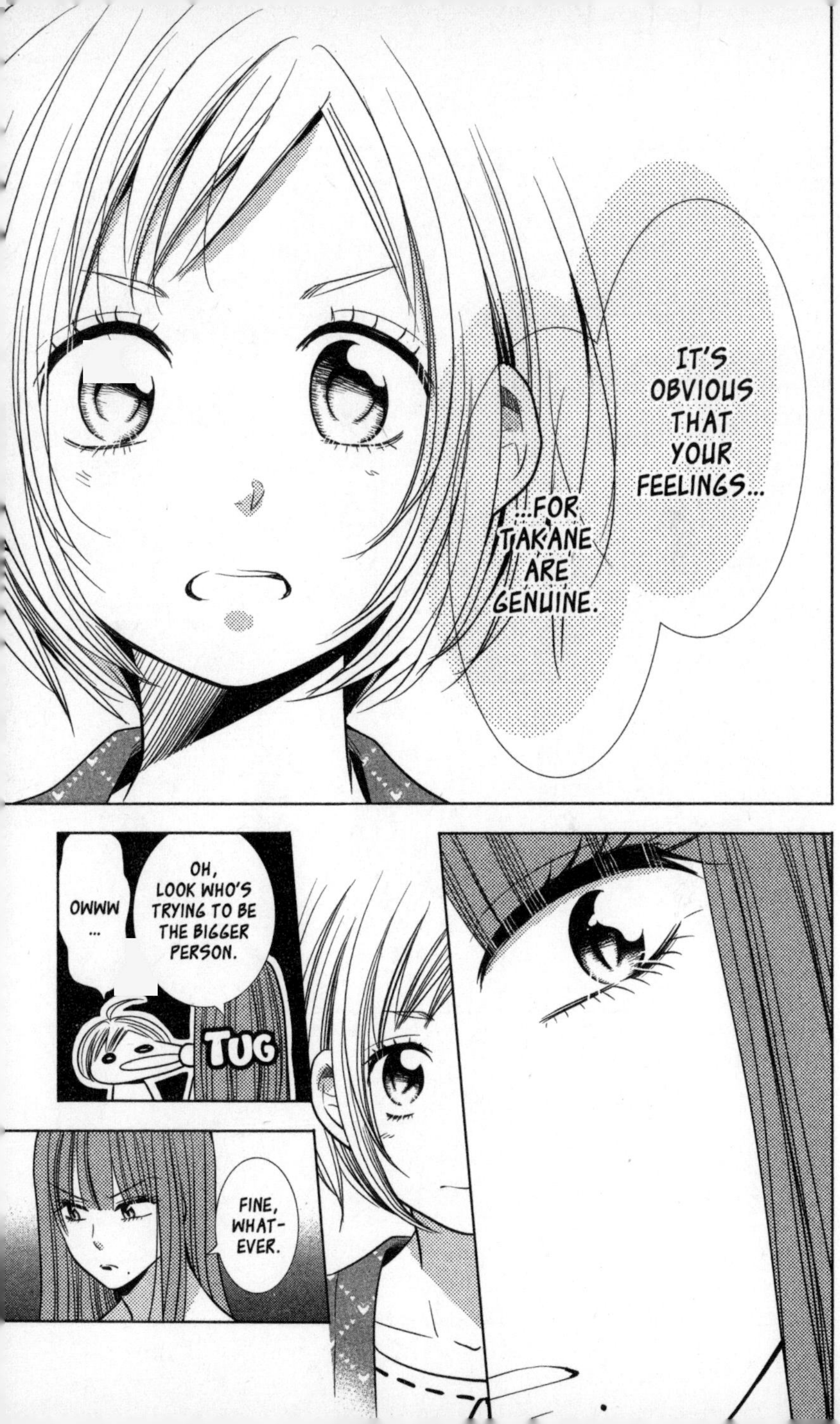
IT'S OBVIOUS THAT YOUR FEELINGS...
...FOR TAKANE ARE GENUINE.
OH, LOOK WHO'S TRYING TO BE THE BIGGER PERSON.
OWWW ...
TUG
FINE, WHAT-EVER.

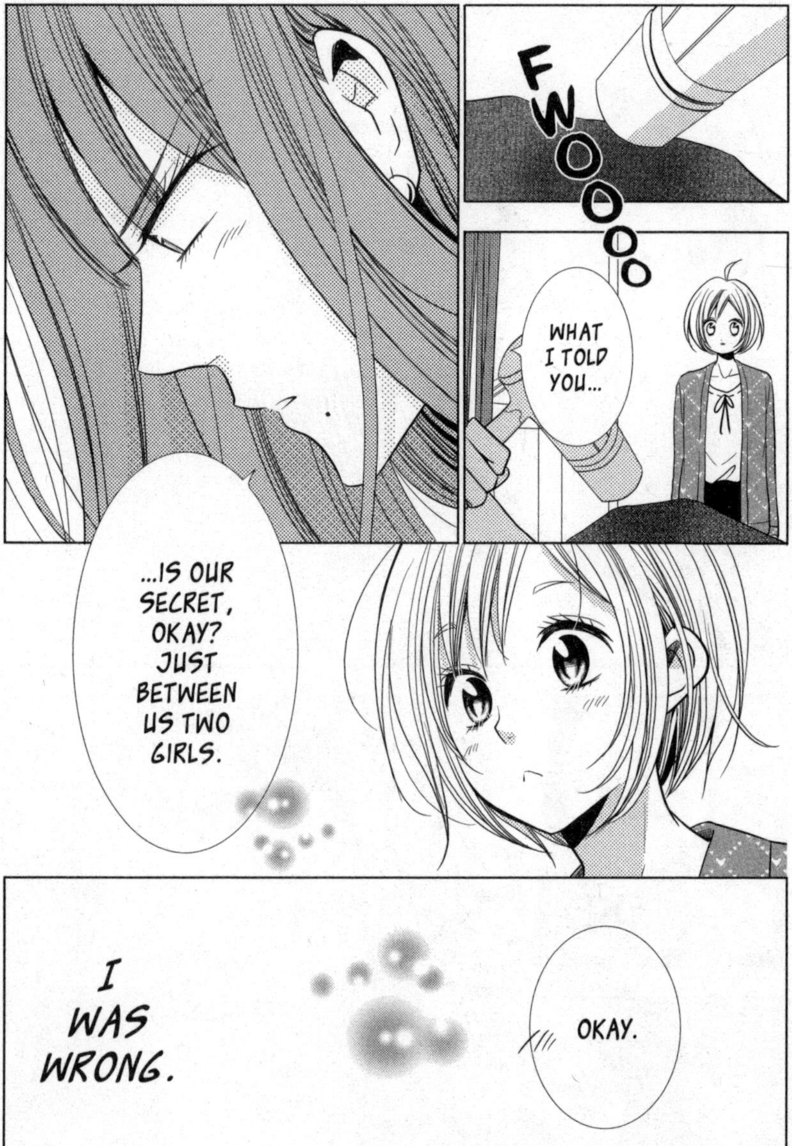
FWOOOO
WHAT I TOLD YOU...
...IS OUR SECRET, OKAY? JUST BETWEEN US TWO GIRLS.
OKAY.
I WAS WRONG.

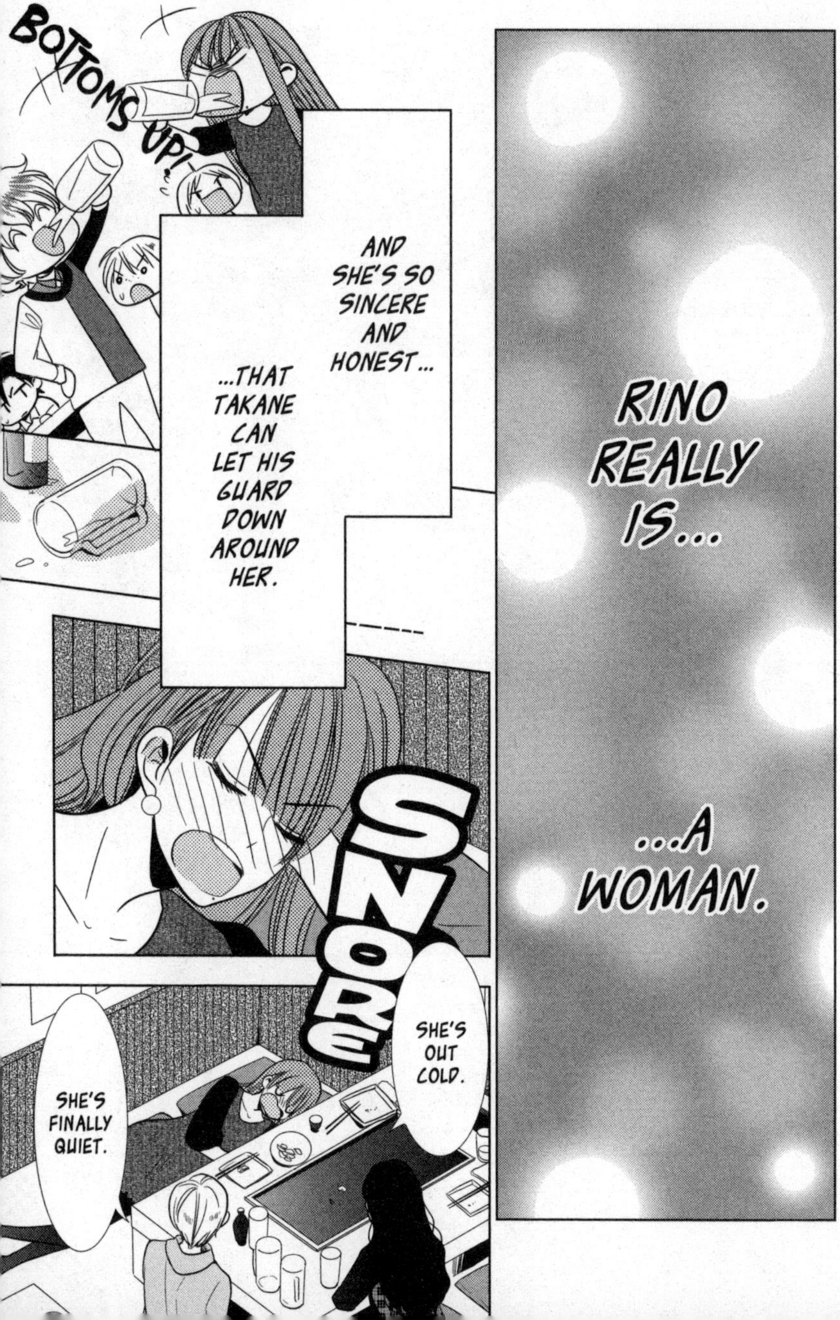
RINO REALLY IS...
...A WOMAN.
BOTTOMS UP!
AND SHE'S SO SINCERE AND HONEST...
...THAT TAKANE CAN LET HIS GUARD DOWN AROUND HER.
SNORE
SHE'S OUT COLD.
SHE'S FINALLY QUIET.

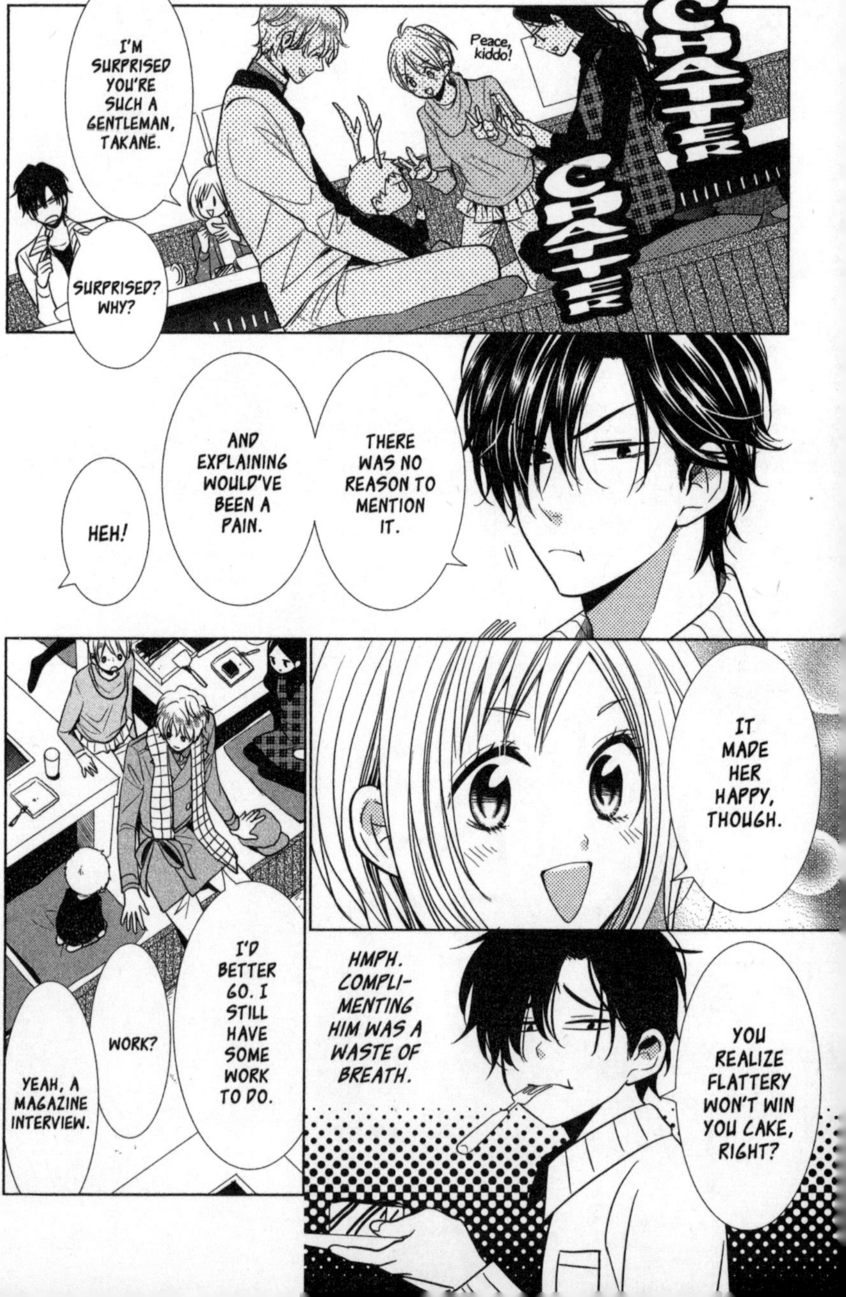
CHATTER CHATTER
Peace, kiddo!
I'M SURPRISED YOU'RE SUCH A GENTLEMAN, TAKANE.
SURPRISED? WHY?
THERE WAS NO REASON TO MENTION IT.
AND EXPLAINING WOULD'VE BEEN A PAIN.
HEH!
IT MADE HER HAPPY, THOUGH.
YOU REALIZE FLATTERY WON'T WIN YOU CAKE, RIGHT?
HMPH. COMPLI-MENTING HIM WAS A WASTE OF BREATH.
I'D BETTER GO. I STILL HAVE SOME WORK TO DO.
WORK?
YEAH, A MAGAZINE INTERVIEW.

YOU HAVE AN INTERVIEW? SHOULD YOU HAVE BEEN DRINKING?
HE ALWAYS ACTS HALF-DRUNK ANYWAY, SO IT DOESN'T MATTER.
THAT'S RIGHT.
YOU GIRLS ARE INTOXICATING.
Heh heh.
YOU HAVE THREE SECONDS TO GET OUT.
I'll come again, okay?
Come here.
MIZUKI.
NICOLA'S LEAVING. HURRY AND...
...GIVE HIM YOUR PRESENT.
W-WELL... I'M HAVING SECOND THOUGHTS...
Thank you for the food, beautiful lady!
Beautiful? Don't make me blush. Tee hee! ♥ Come again! ♥
OKAMON, WHAT IF I LEAVE IT WITH YOU AND YOU GIVE IT TO HIM NEXT TIME HE'S HERE...?
HUH?
NO WAY.
GO FOR IT.
GOOD LUCK!
DASH
SLIDE
HEY!
AAAAAAH!

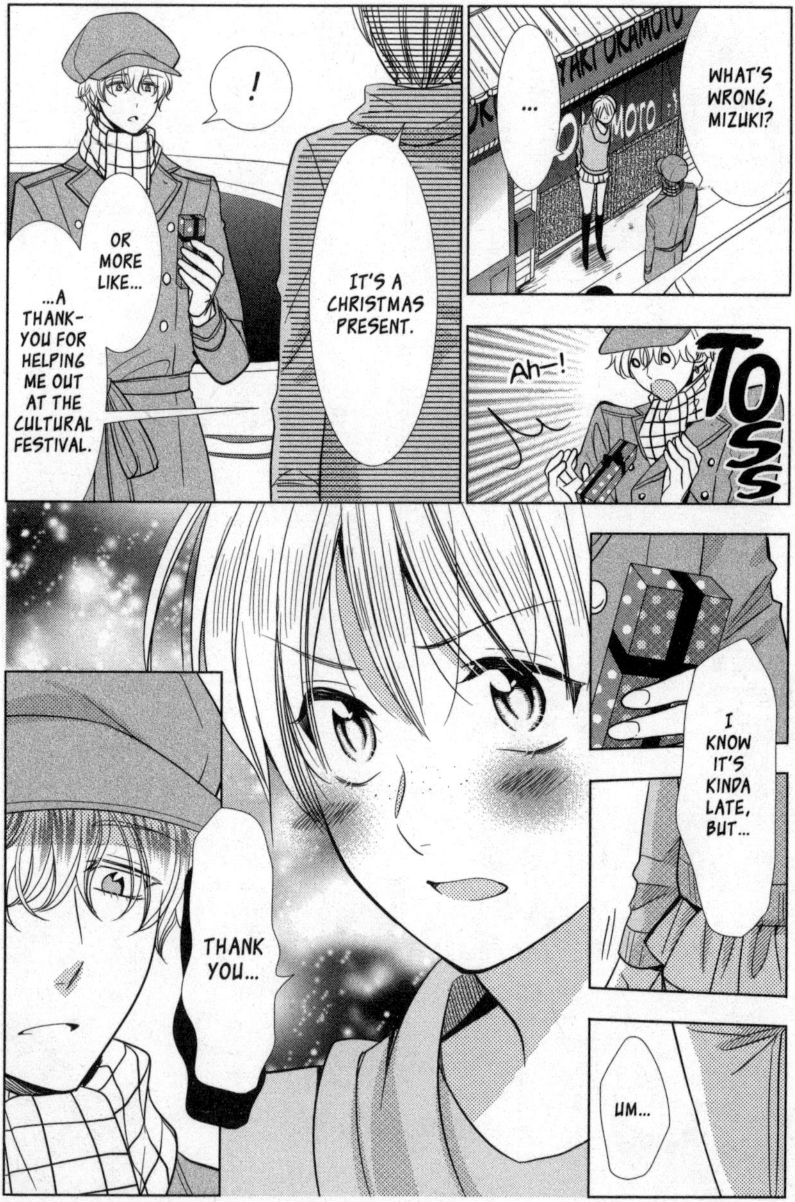
YAKI OKAMOTO
WHAT'S WRONG, MIZUKI?
...
TOSS
Ah—!
!
IT'S A CHRISTMAS PRESENT.
OR MORE LIKE...
...A THANK-YOU FOR HELPING ME OUT AT THE CULTURAL FESTIVAL.
I KNOW IT'S KINDA LATE, BUT...
UM...
THANK YOU...

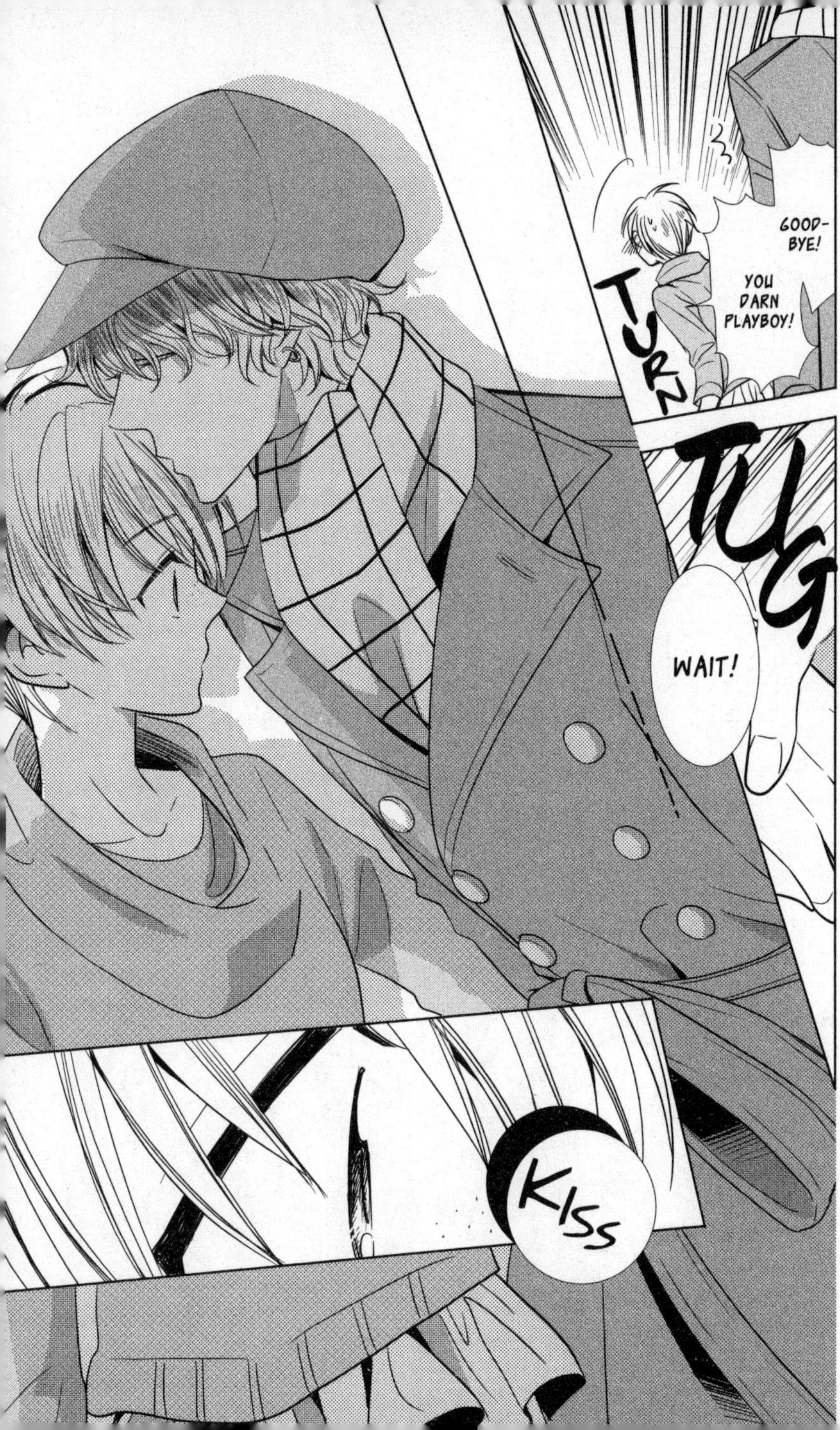
GOOD-BYE!
YOU DARN PLAYBOY!
TURN
TUG
WAIT!
KISS

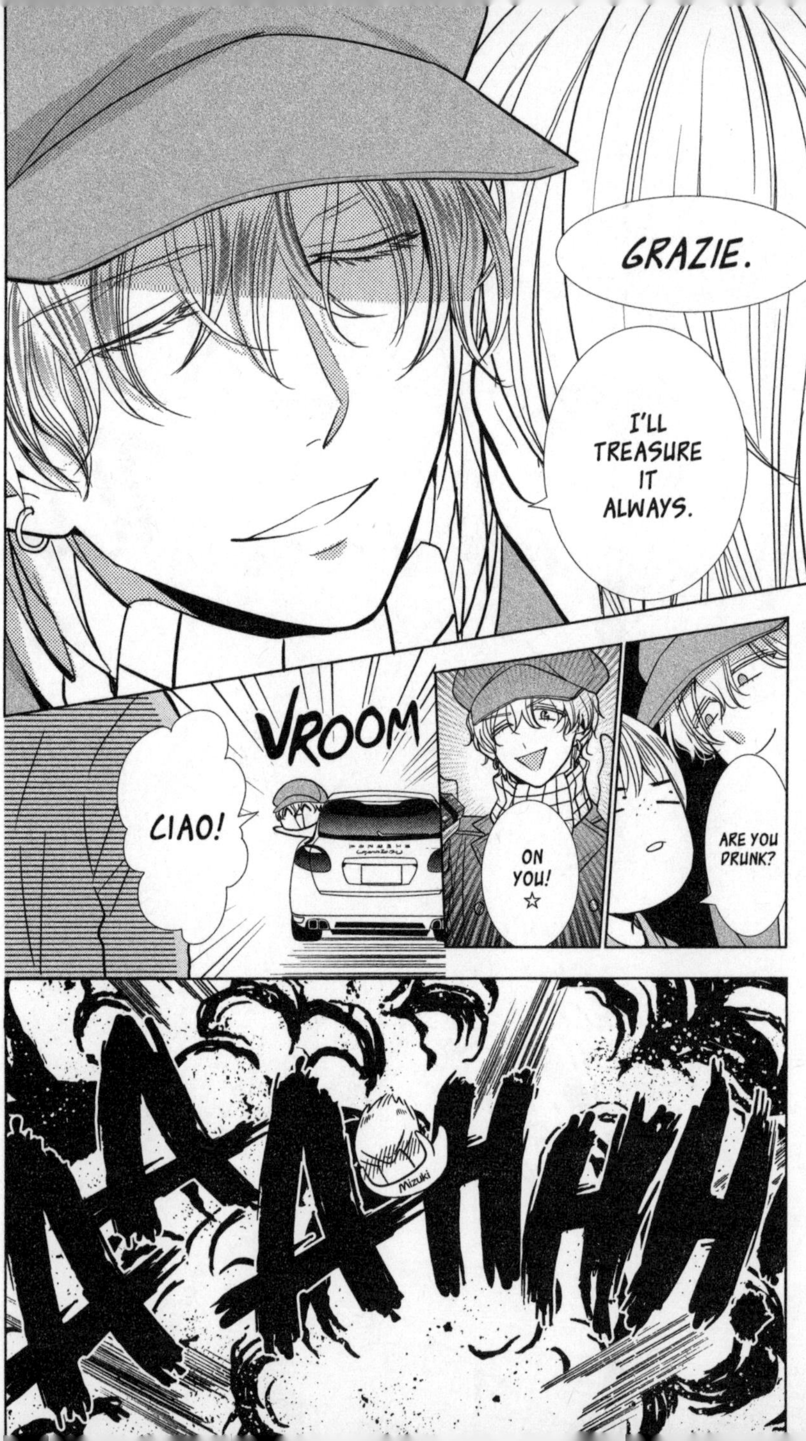
GRAZIE.
I'LL TREASURE IT ALWAYS.
ARE YOU DRUNK?
ON YOU! ☆
VROOM
CIAO!
Mizuki

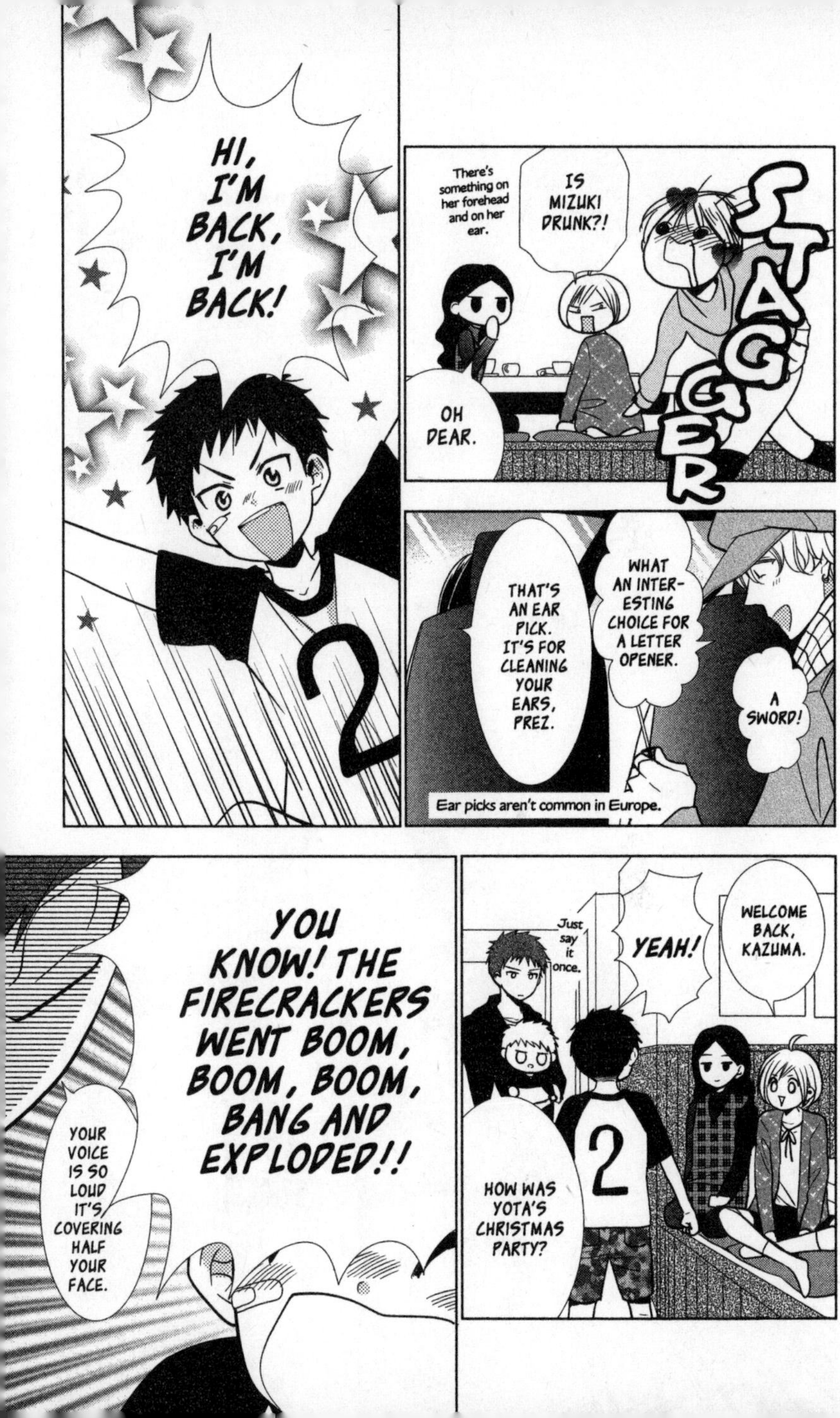
STAGGER
IS MIZUKI DRUNK?!
There's something on her forehead and on her ear.
OH DEAR.
WHAT AN INTERESTING CHOICE FOR A LETTER OPENER.
A SWORD!
THAT'S AN EAR PICK. IT'S FOR CLEANING YOUR EARS, PREZ.
Ear picks aren't common in Europe.
HI, I'M BACK, I'M BACK!
WELCOME BACK, KAZUMA.
YEAH!
Just say it once.
HOW WAS YOTA'S CHRISTMAS PARTY?
YOU KNOW! THE FIRECRACKERS WENT BOOM, BOOM, BOOM, BANG AND EXPLODED!!
YOUR VOICE IS SO LOUD IT'S COVERING HALF YOUR FACE.

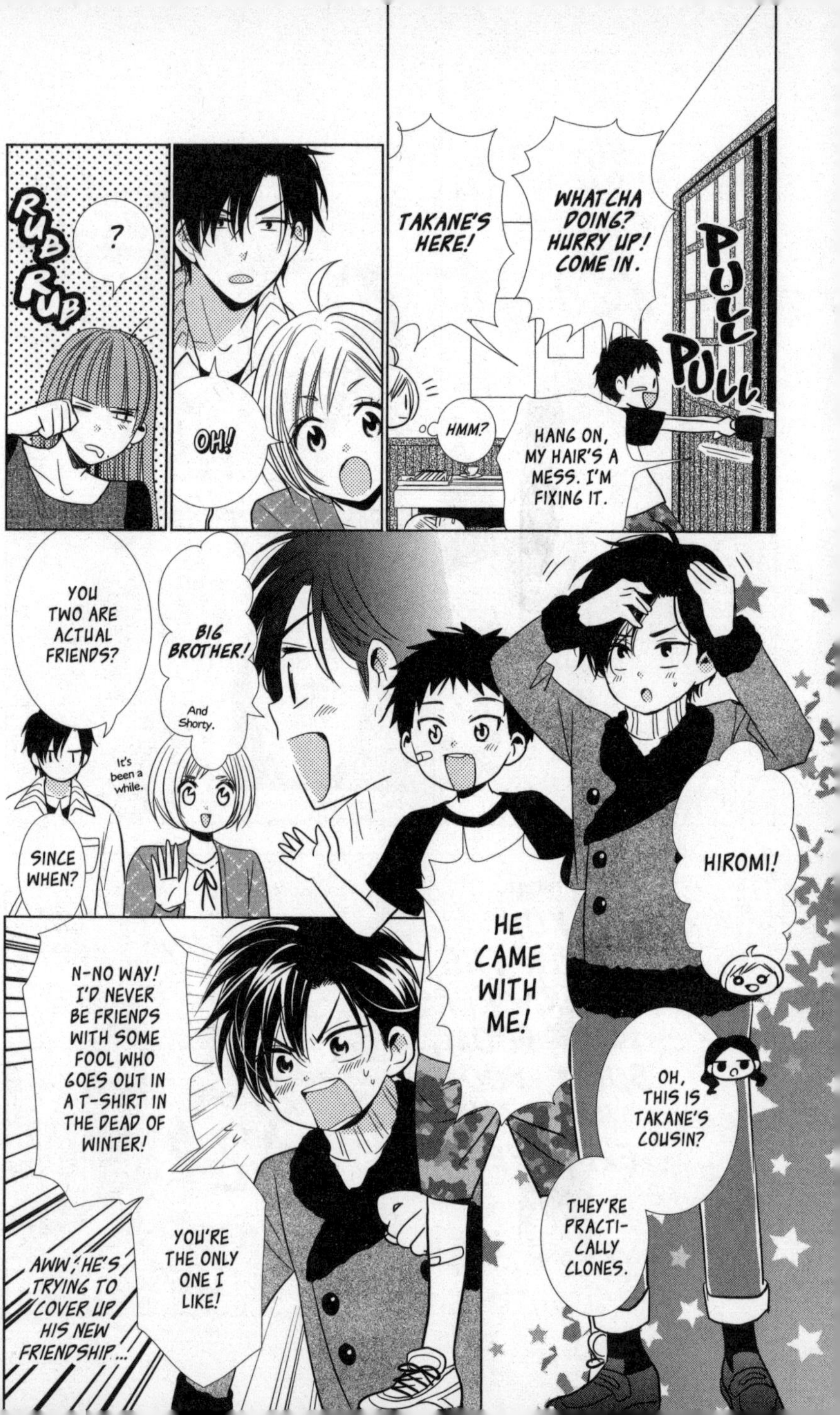
PULL PULL
WHATCHA DOING? HURRY UP! COME IN.
TAKANE'S HERE!
HANG ON, MY HAIR'S A MESS. I'M FIXING IT.
HMM?
OH!
RUB RUB
?
HIROMI!
BIG BROTHER!
And Shorty.
YOU TWO ARE ACTUAL FRIENDS?
It's been a while.
SINCE WHEN?
OH, THIS IS TAKANE'S COUSIN?
THEY'RE PRACTI-CALLY CLONES.
HE CAME WITH ME!
N-NO WAY! I'D NEVER BE FRIENDS WITH SOME FOOL WHO GOES OUT IN A T-SHIRT IN THE DEAD OF WINTER!
YOU'RE THE ONLY ONE I LIKE!
AWW, HE'S TRYING TO COVER UP HIS NEW FRIENDSHIP...

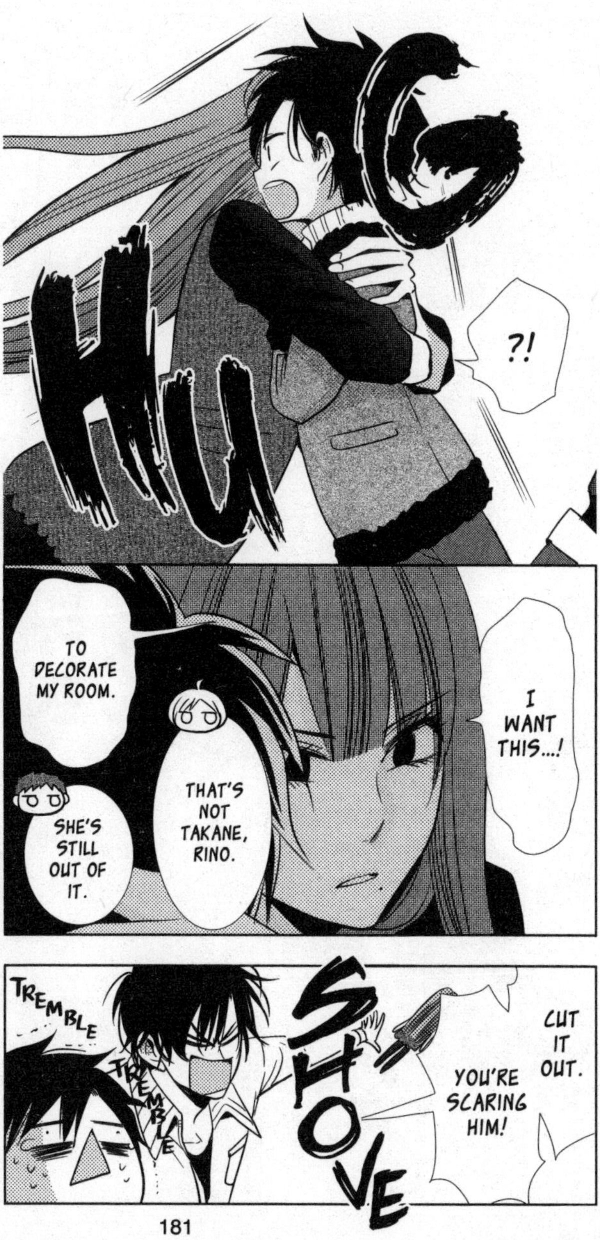
HUG
?!
I WANT THIS...!
TO DECORATE MY ROOM.
THAT'S NOT TAKANE, RINO.
SHE'S STILL OUT OF IT.
CUT IT OUT.
YOU'RE SCARING HIM!
SHOVE
TREMBLE
TREMBLE

• Rino Inokuma •

When she first appeared, some of you immediately suspected something. You guys are perceptive!

She's a sixth-year med student at a Kyoto university. When she's mad, sometimes she slips into Kansai dialect.

She loves Takane no matter how he treats her. She's loved him for years now, and sometimes her speech and mannerisms echo his.

I was careful to make her very different from Yukari, the other pretty female character who likes Takane. Yukari's calm and easygoing while Rino is sexier. (Sexiness is indicated by the beauty spot by her mouth. It's a simple little cue.)

She's skinny, but she's as strong as Takane. As you might expect since Takane's her type, she has zero interest in playboys.

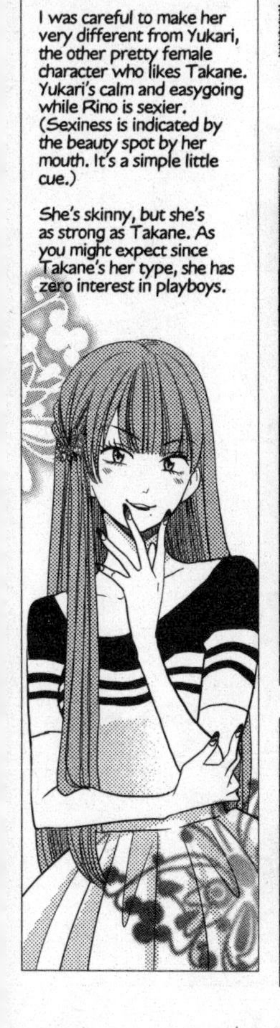

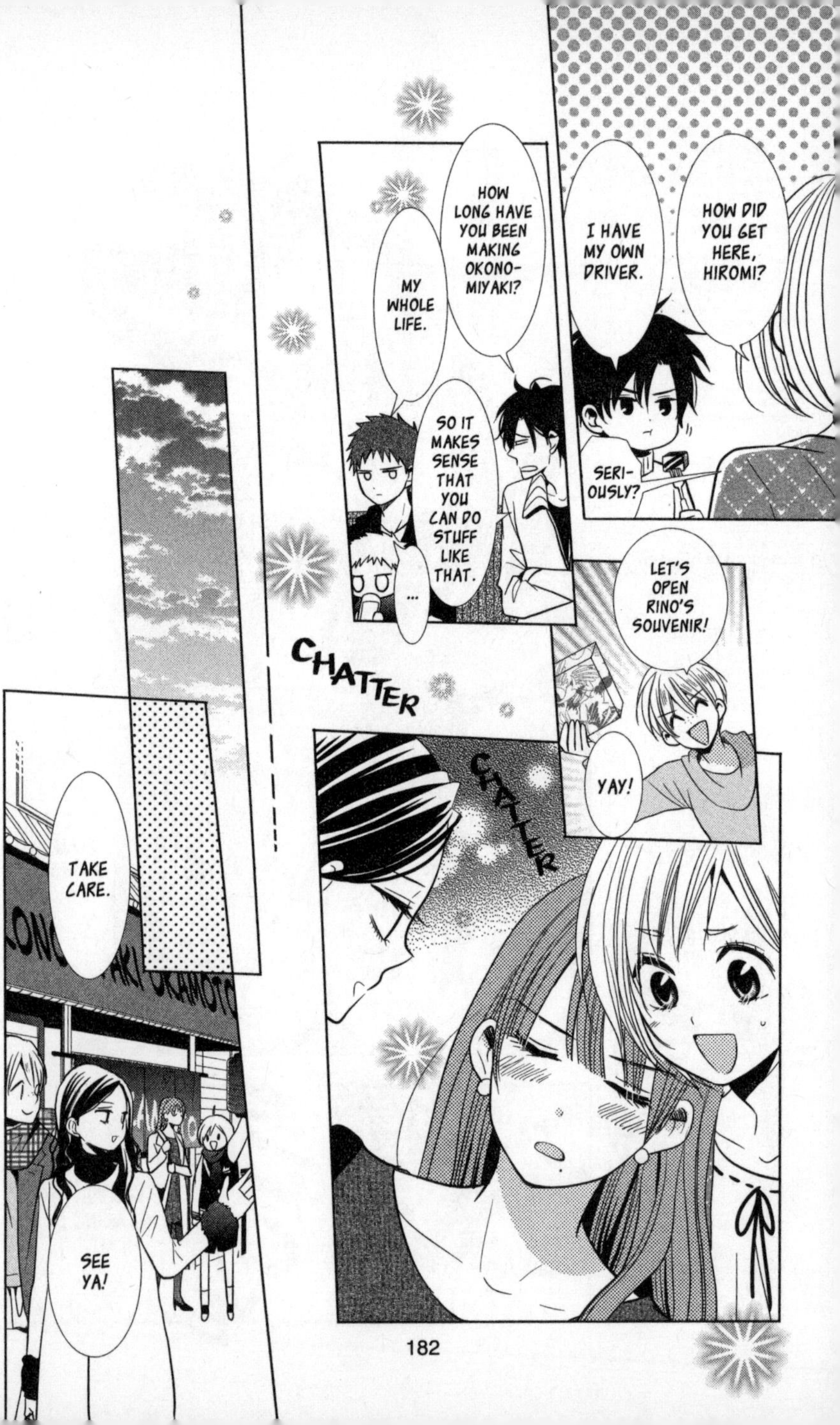
HOW DID YOU GET HERE, HIROMI?
I HAVE MY OWN DRIVER.
SERI-OUSLY?
HOW LONG HAVE YOU BEEN MAKING OKONO-MIYAKI?
MY WHOLE LIFE.
SO IT MAKES SENSE THAT YOU CAN DO STUFF LIKE THAT.
...
LET'S OPEN RINO'S SOUVENIR!
YAY!
CHATTER
CHATTER
TAKE CARE.
SEE YA!

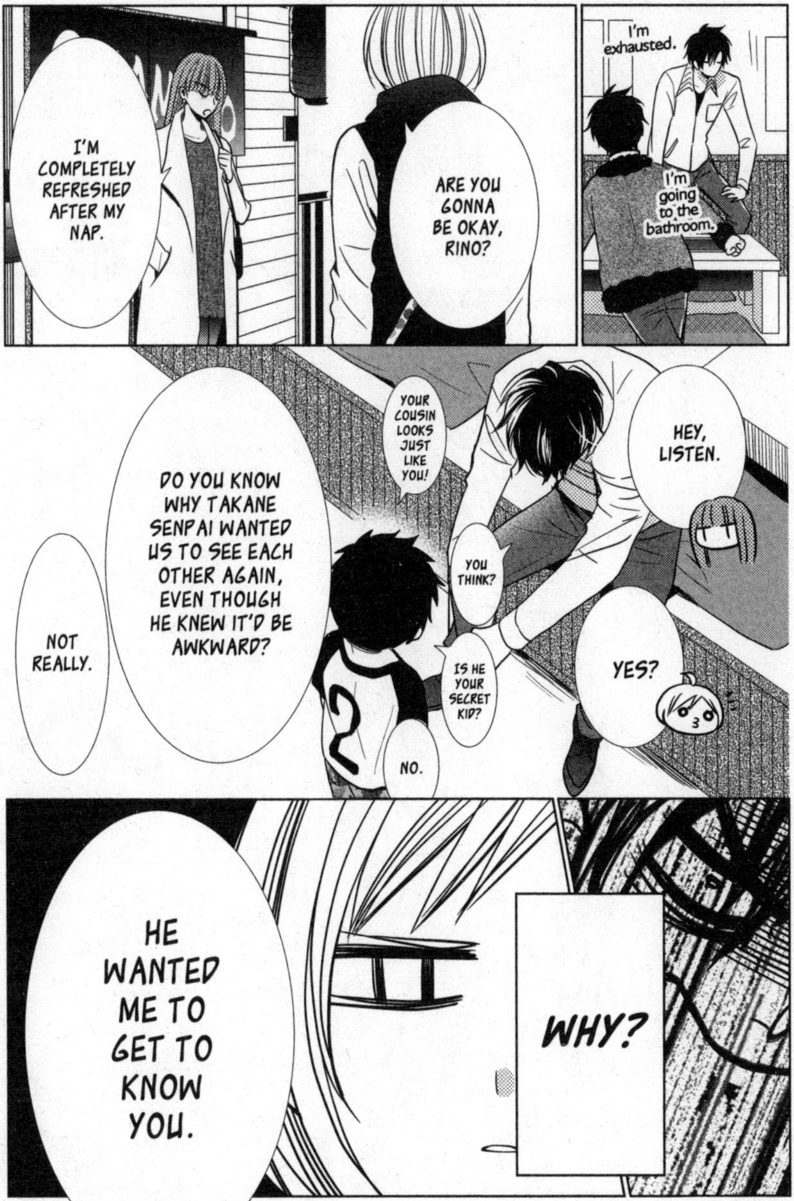
I'm exhausted.
I'm going to the bathroom.
ARE YOU GONNA BE OKAY, RINO?
I'M COMPLETELY REFRESHED AFTER MY NAP.
HEY, LISTEN.
YOUR COUSIN LOOKS JUST LIKE YOU!
YES?
YOU THINK?
IS HE YOUR SECRET KID?
NO.
DO YOU KNOW WHY TAKANE SENPAI WANTED US TO SEE EACH OTHER AGAIN, EVEN THOUGH HE KNEW IT'D BE AWKWARD?
NOT REALLY.
WHY?
HE WANTED ME TO GET TO KNOW YOU.

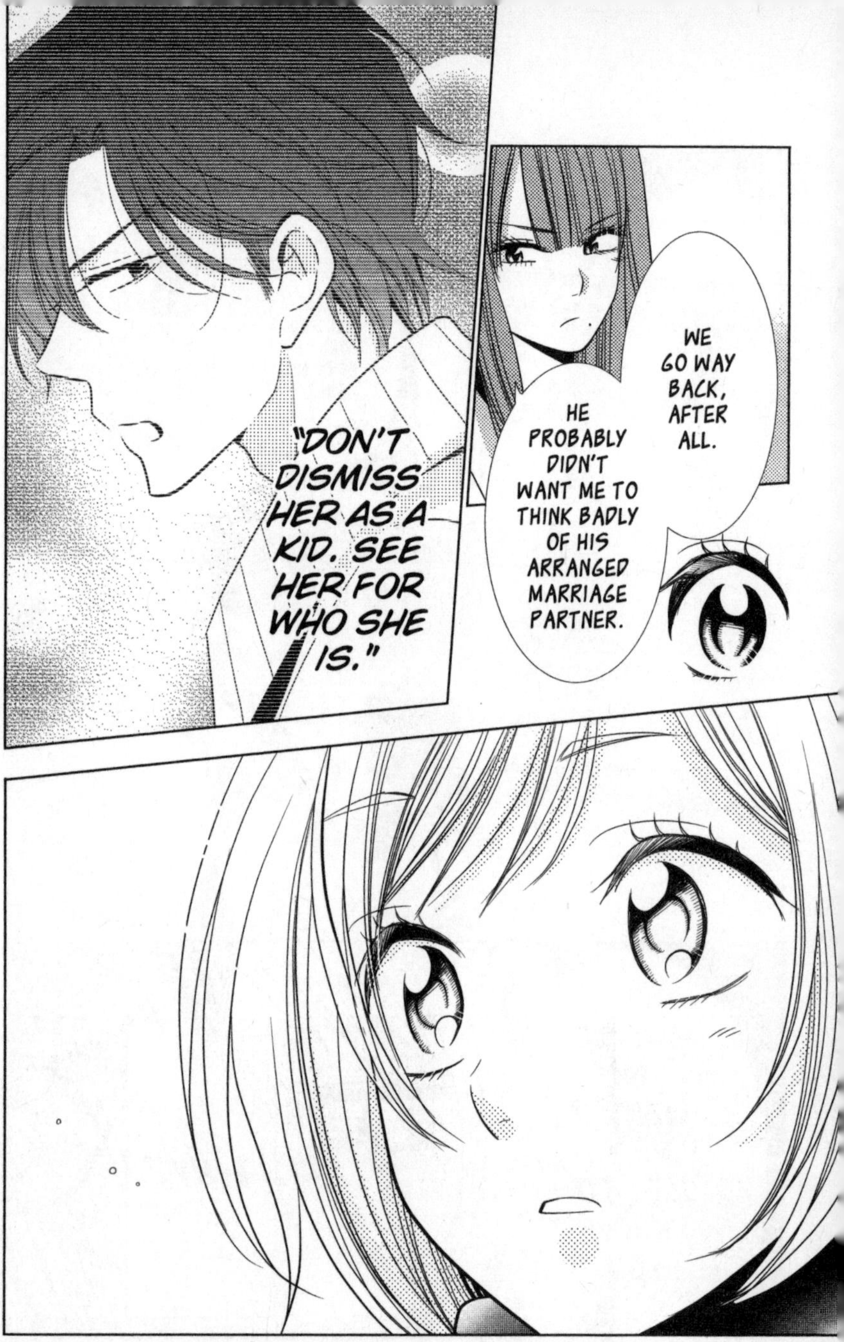
WE GO WAY BACK, AFTER ALL.
HE PROBABLY DIDN'T WANT ME TO THINK BADLY OF HIS ARRANGED MARRIAGE PARTNER.
"DON'T DISMISS HER AS A KID. SEE HER FOR WHO SHE IS."

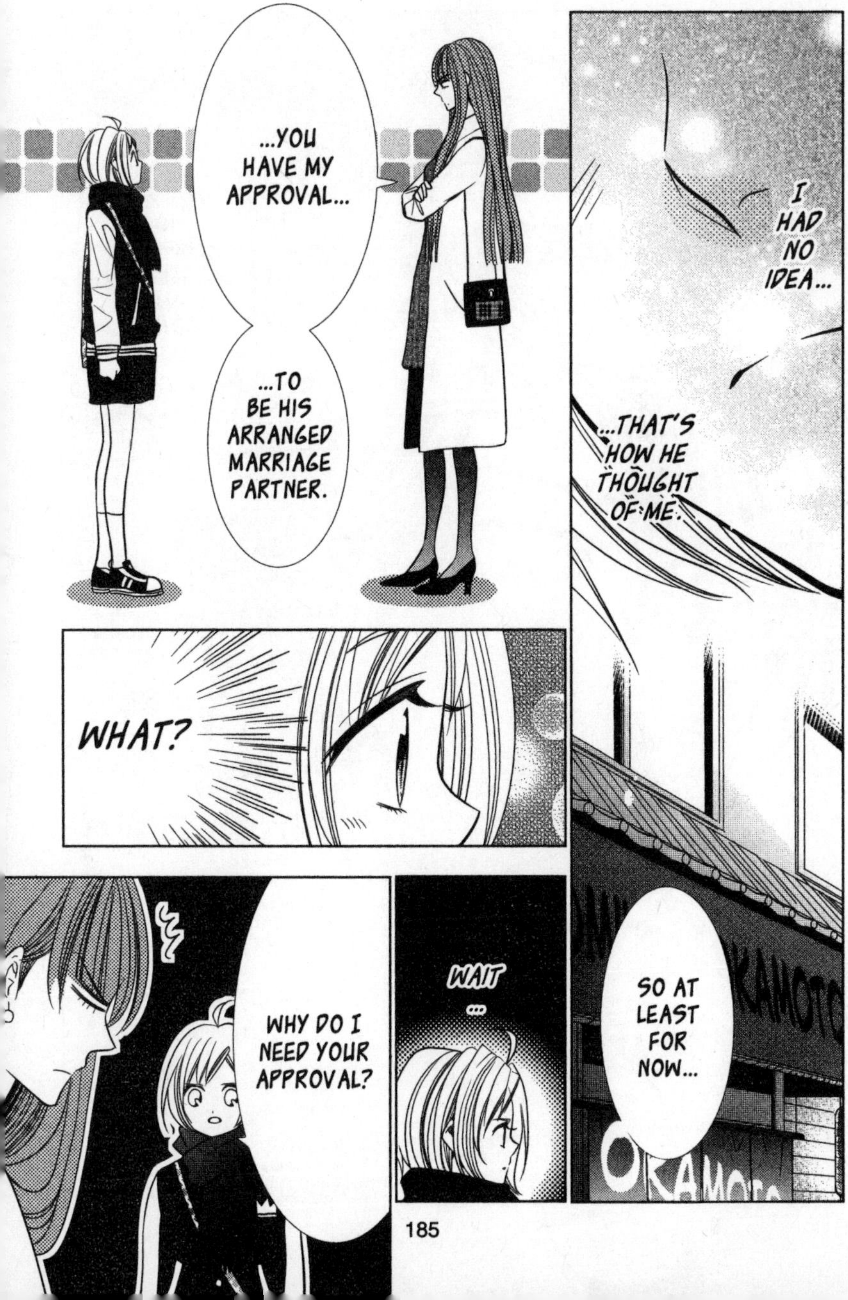
I HAD NO IDEA...
...THAT'S HOW HE THOUGHT OF ME.
SO AT LEAST FOR NOW...
...YOU HAVE MY APPROVAL...
...TO BE HIS ARRANGED MARRIAGE PARTNER.
WHAT?
WAIT...
WHY DO I NEED YOUR APPROVAL?

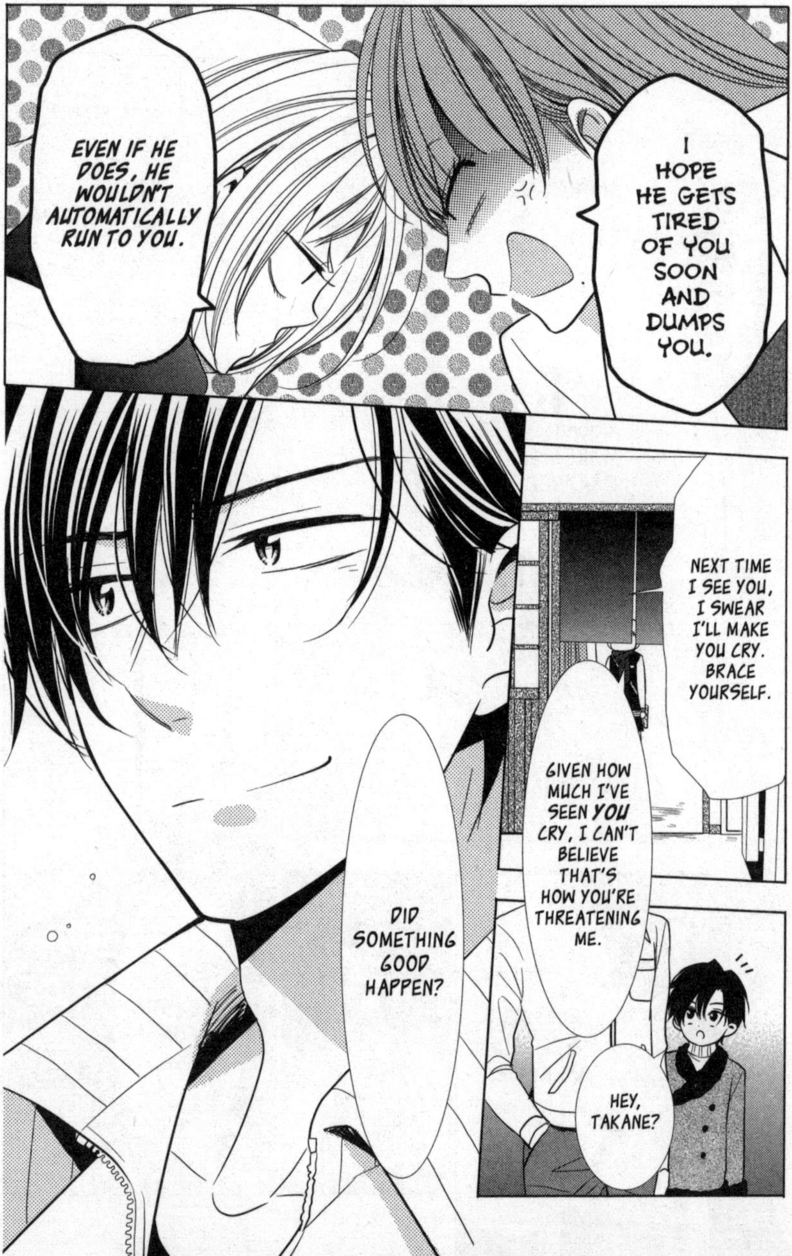
I HOPE HE GETS TIRED OF YOU SOON AND DUMPS YOU.
EVEN IF HE DOES, HE WOULDN'T AUTOMATICALLY RUN TO YOU.
NEXT TIME I SEE YOU, I SWEAR I'LL MAKE YOU CRY. BRACE YOURSELF.
GIVEN HOW MUCH I'VE SEEN *YOU* CRY, I CAN'T BELIEVE THAT'S HOW YOU'RE THREATENING ME.
HEY, TAKANE?
DID SOMETHING GOOD HAPPEN?

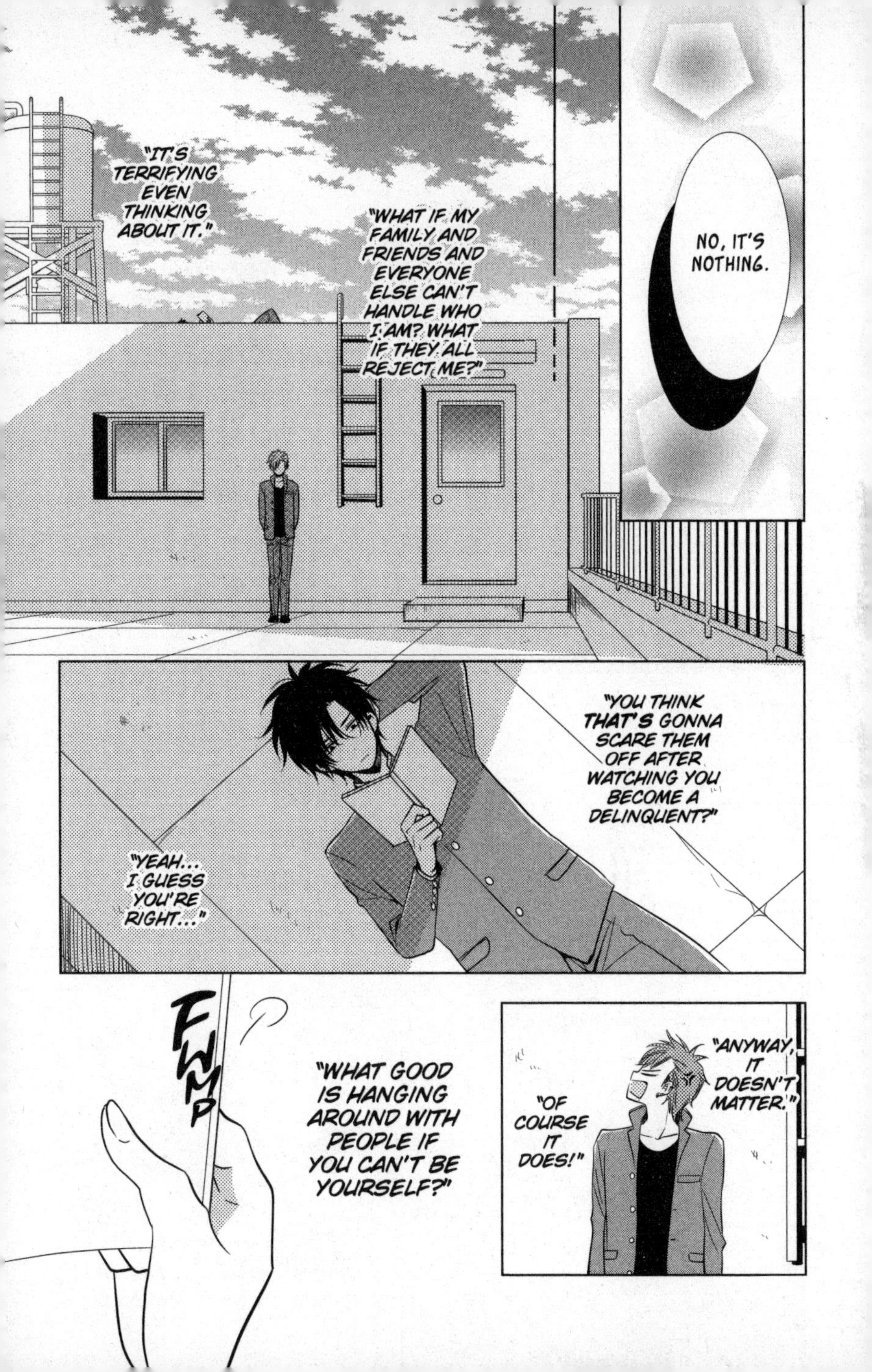
NO, IT'S NOTHING.
"WHAT IF MY FAMILY AND FRIENDS AND EVERYONE ELSE CAN'T HANDLE WHO I AM? WHAT IF THEY ALL REJECT ME?"
"IT'S TERRIFYING EVEN THINKING ABOUT IT."
"YOU THINK THAT'S GONNA SCARE THEM OFF AFTER WATCHING YOU BECOME A DELINQUENT?"
"YEAH... I GUESS YOU'RE RIGHT..."
"ANYWAY, IT DOESN'T MATTER."
"OF COURSE IT DOES!"
"WHAT GOOD IS HANGING AROUND WITH PEOPLE IF YOU CAN'T BE YOURSELF?"
FWMP

IF THE WORST HAPPENS, I'LL STILL BE HERE. SO DON'T SWEAT IT.

NAME: INOKUMA, TOSHIYUKI
ADDRESS: KYOTO CITY
ISSUED: XX/XX/XXXX
EXPIRATION DATE: XX/XX/XXXX

DRIVER'S LICENSE

CLASS

KYOTO
PUBLIC SAFETY
COMMSSION

HMM?

MM.

BRO, SHE FORGOT THIS.

Takane & Hana 5 / The End

A Child's Intuition

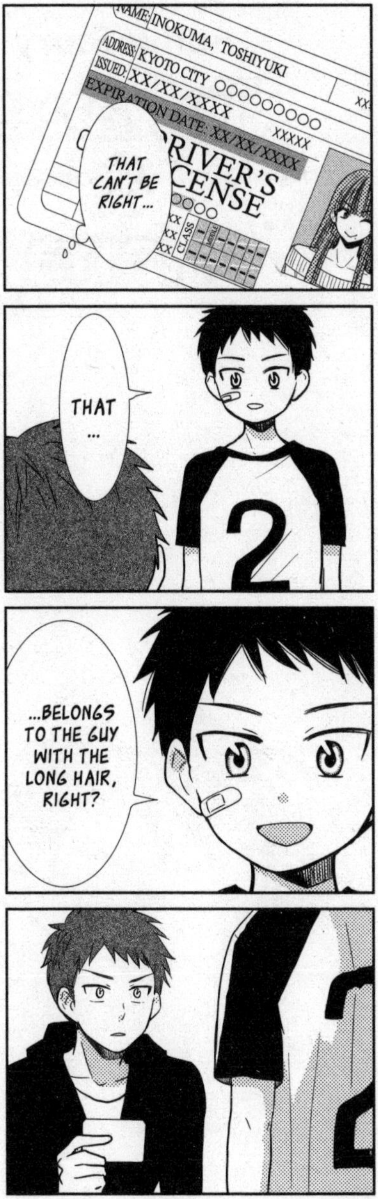
NAME: INOKUMA, TOSHIYUKI
ADDRESS: KYOTO CITY OOOOOOOOO
ISSUED: XX/XX/XXXX
EXPIRATION DATE: XX/XX/XXXX
THAT CAN'T BE RIGHT...
THAT ...
...BELONGS TO THE GUY WITH THE LONG HAIR, RIGHT?

Bonus Story Takane & Hana

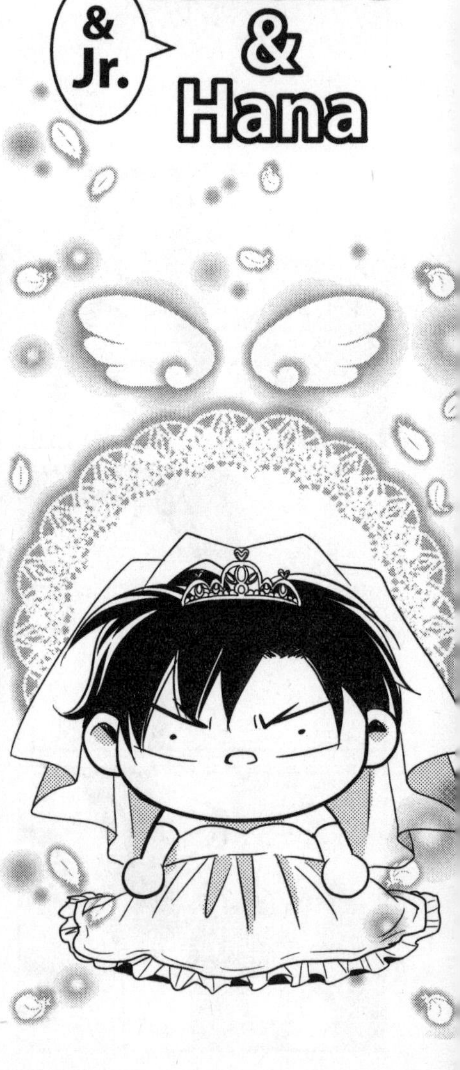
& Jr.

In Bloom

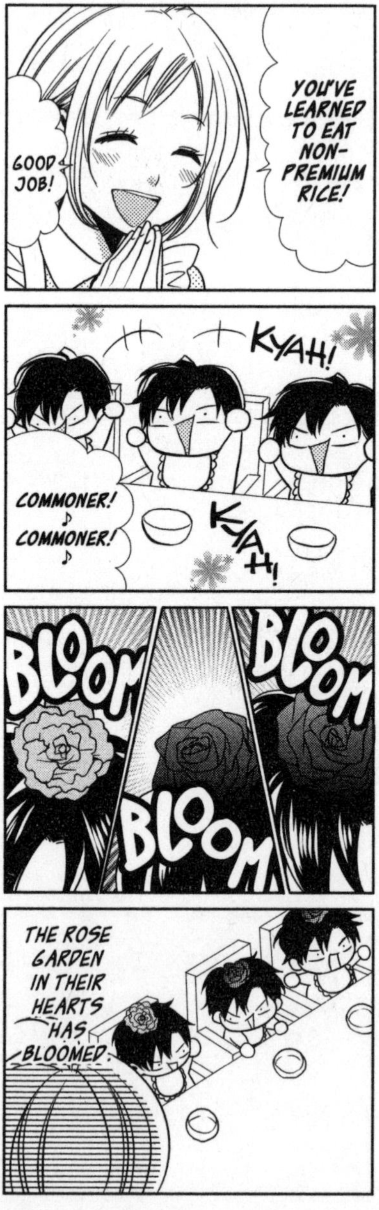
YOU'VE LEARNED TO EAT NON-PREMIUM RICE!
GOOD JOB!
KYAH!
KYAH!
COMMONER! ♪ COMMONER! ♪
BLOOM
BLOOM
BLOOM
THE ROSE GARDEN IN THEIR HEARTS HAS BLOOMED.

Brainwashed

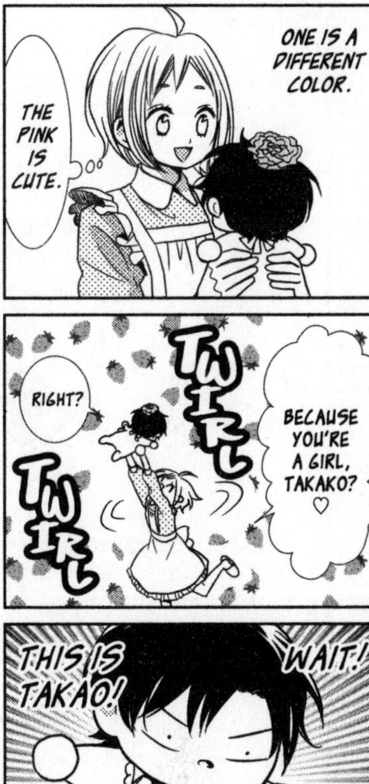
ONE IS A DIFFERENT COLOR.
THE PINK IS CUTE.
BECAUSE YOU'RE A GIRL, TAKAKO? ♡
TWIRL
RIGHT?
TWIRL
WAIT!
THIS IS TAKAO!
IT'S BECAUSE TAKANE ALWAYS GETS THEM MIXED UP!
Takako! ♥
Who's Daddy's little girl?

Strayed Off Course

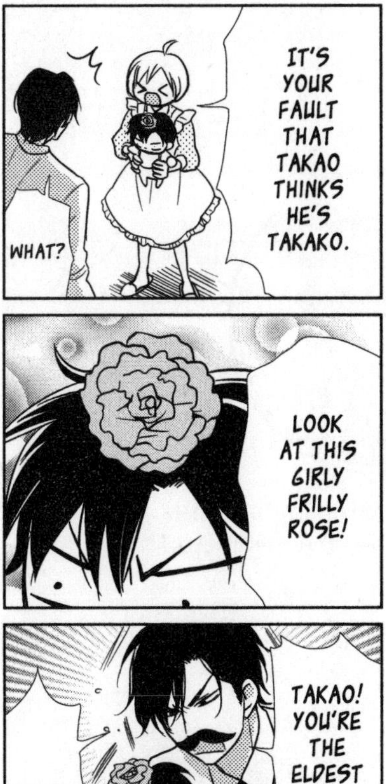
IT'S YOUR FAULT THAT TAKAO THINKS HE'S TAKAKO.
WHAT?
LOOK AT THIS GIRLY FRILLY ROSE!
TAKAO! YOU'RE THE ELDEST SON OF THE SAIBARA FAMILY!
YOU'RE A BOY!
BLOOM
SUDDENLY TAKAO'S FLOWER IS IRIDESCENT ...!
?!

Bonus Story: Takane & Hana & Jr. / The End

The cover theme is now "falling from the sky" rather than "bury the cover with stuff."

—YUKI SHIWASU

Born on March 7 in Fukuoka Prefecture, Japan, Yuki Shiwasu began her career as a manga artist after winning the top prize in the Hakusensha Athena Newcomers' Awards from *Hana to Yume* magazine. She is also the author of *Furou Kyoudai* (Immortal Siblings), which was published by Hakusensha in Japan.

Takane &Hana

VOLUME 5
SHOJO BEAT EDITION

STORY & ART BY **YUKI SHIWASU**

ENGLISH ADAPTATION **Ysabet Reinhardt MacFarlane**
TRANSLATION **JN Productions**
TOUCH-UP ART & LETTERING **Annaliese Christman**
DESIGN **Shawn Carrico**
EDITOR **Amy Yu**

Takane to Hana by Yuki Shiwasu
© Yuki Shiwasu 2016
All rights reserved.
First published in Japan in 2016 by HAKUSENSHA, Inc., Tokyo.
English language translation rights arranged with HAKUSENSHA, Inc., Tokyo.

Printed in the U.S.A.

Published by VIZ Media, LLC
P.O. Box 77010
San Francisco, CA 94107

10 9 8 7 6 5 4 3 2 1
First printing, October 2018

viz.com

shojobeat.com

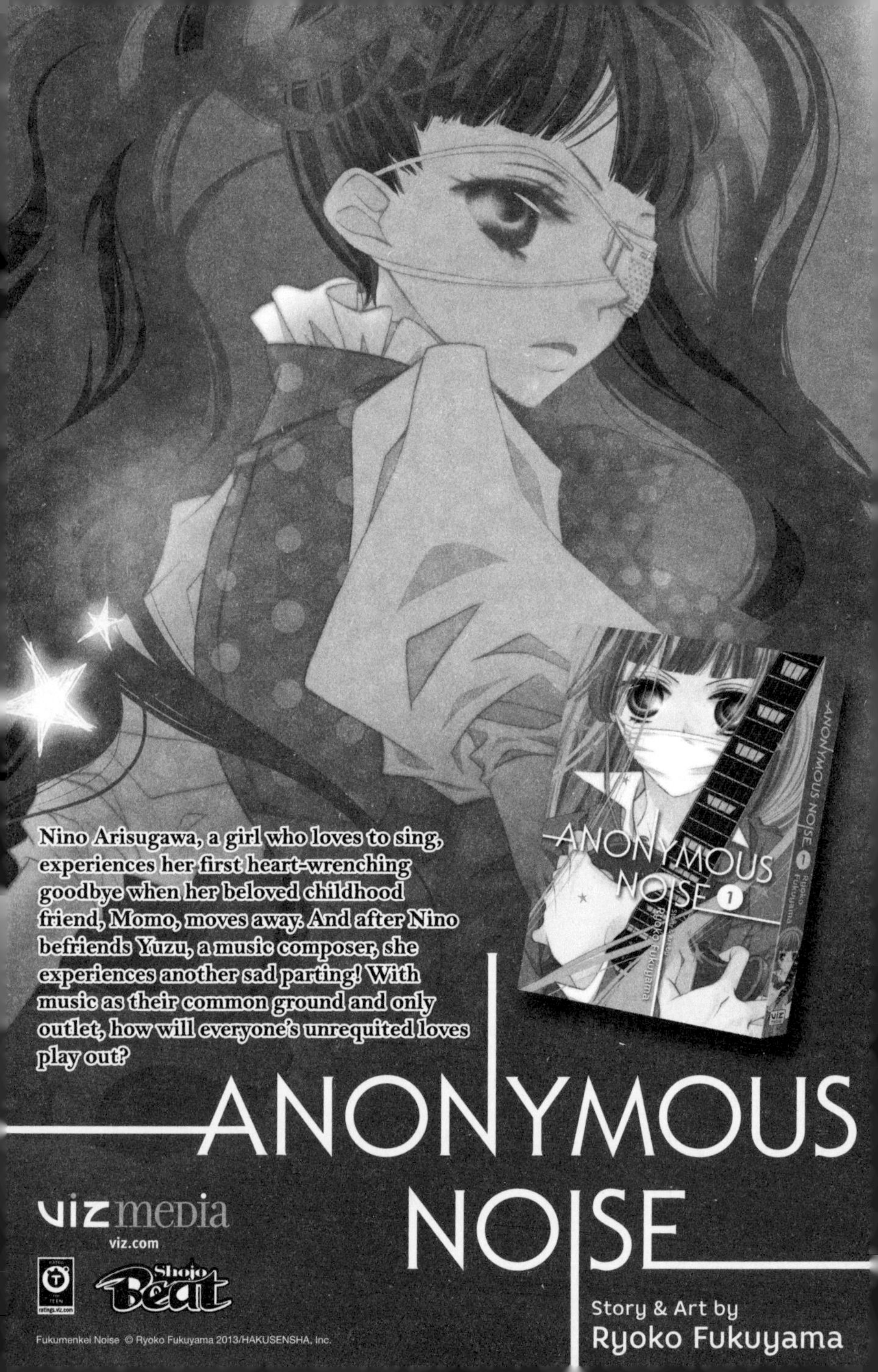

ANONYMOUS NOISE 1
Ryoko Fukuyama
Nino Arisugawa, a girl who loves to sing, experiences her first heart-wrenching goodbye when her beloved childhood friend, Momo, moves away. And after Nino befriends Yuzu, a music composer, she experiences another sad parting! With music as their common ground and only outlet, how will everyone's unrequited loves play out?
ANONYMOUS NOISE
viz media
viz.com
TEEN
ratings.viz.com
Shojo Beat
Story & Art by
Ryoko Fukuyama
Fukumenkei Noise © Ryoko Fukuyama 2013/HAKUSENSHA, Inc.

IDOL dreams

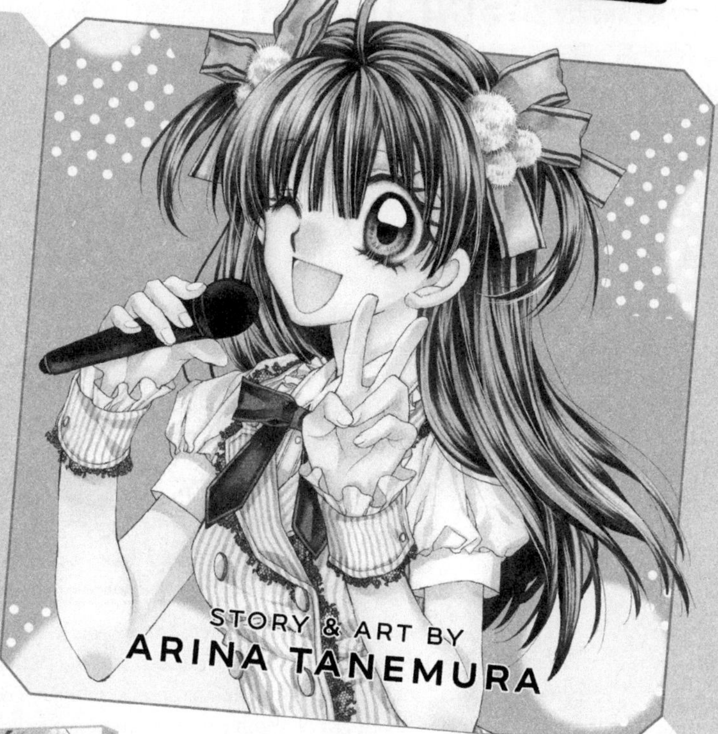
STORY & ART BY
ARINA TANEMURA

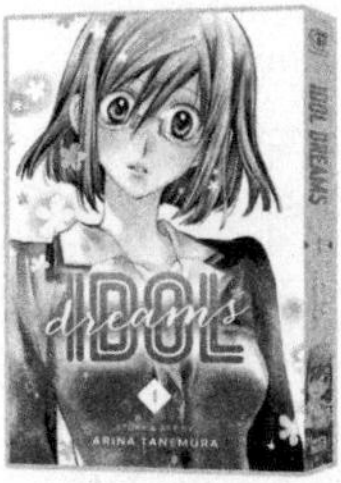

At age 31, office worker Chikage Deguchi feels she missed her chances at love and success. When word gets out that she's a virgin, Chikage is humiliated and wishes she could turn back time to when she was still young and popular. She takes an experimental drug that changes her appearance back to when she was 15. Now Chikage is determined to pursue everything she missed out on all those years ago—including becoming a star!

www.viz.com

ratings.viz.com

Behind the Scenes!!

STORY AND ART BY **BISCO HATORI**

From the creator of Ouran High School Host Club

Behind the Scenes!!
Behind the Scenes!!
01
01
BISCO HATORI
STORY AND ART BY
BISCO HATORI

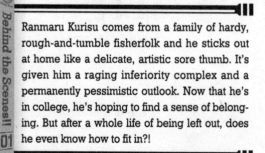

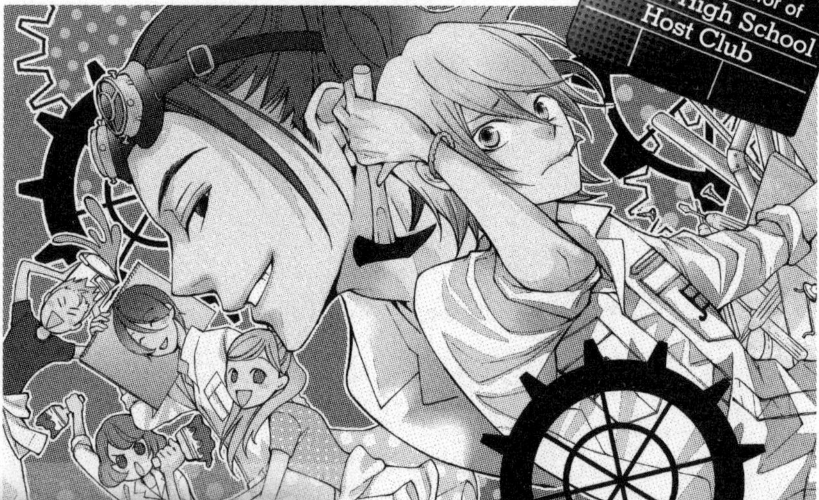

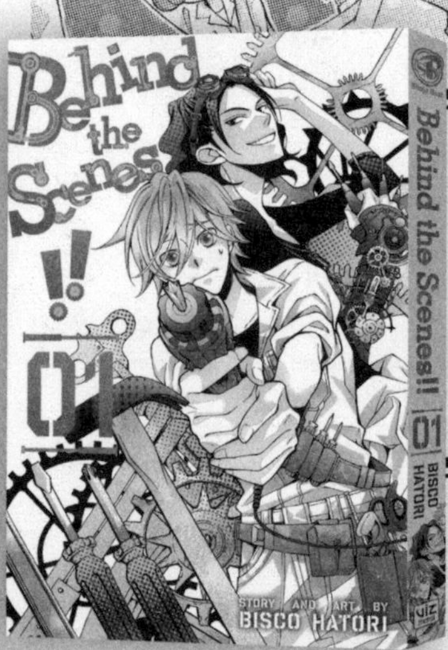

Ranmaru Kurisu comes from a family of hardy, rough-and-tumble fisherfolk and he sticks out at home like a delicate, artistic sore thumb. It's given him a raging inferiority complex and a permanently pessimistic outlook. Now that he's in college, he's hoping to find a sense of belonging. But after a whole life of being left out, does he even know how to fit in?!

RATED T FOR TEEN ratings.viz.com

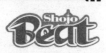

VIZ MEDIA
www.viz.com

Shojo Beat

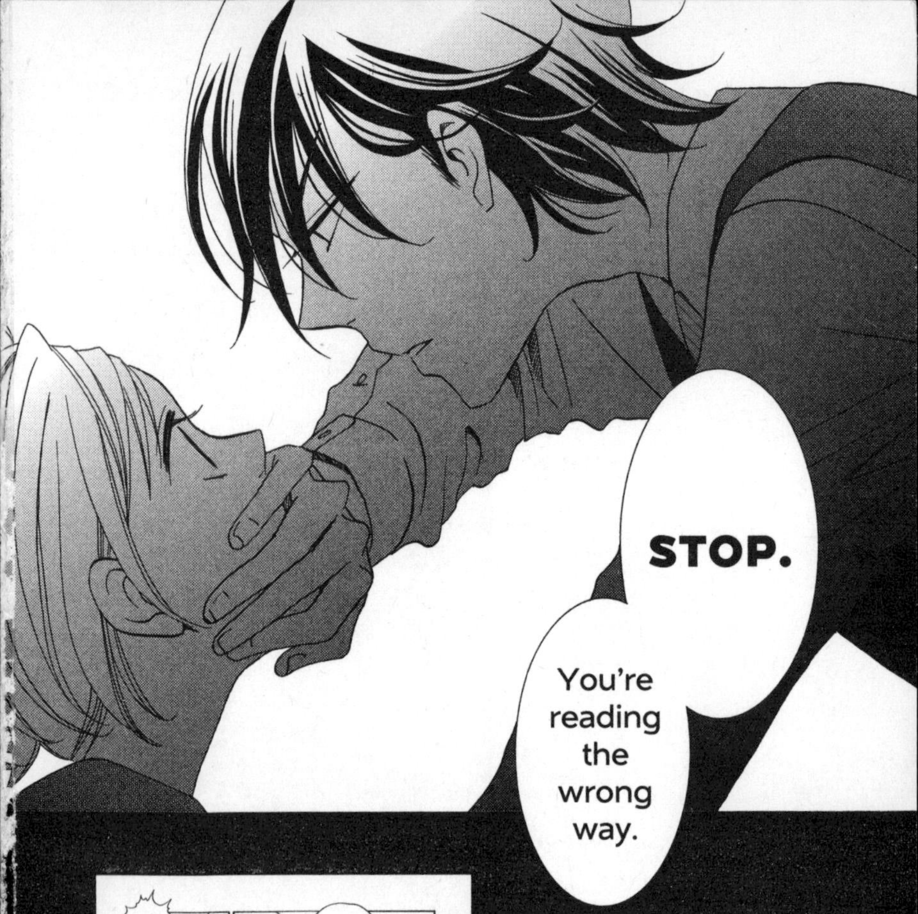
STOP.
You're reading the wrong way.

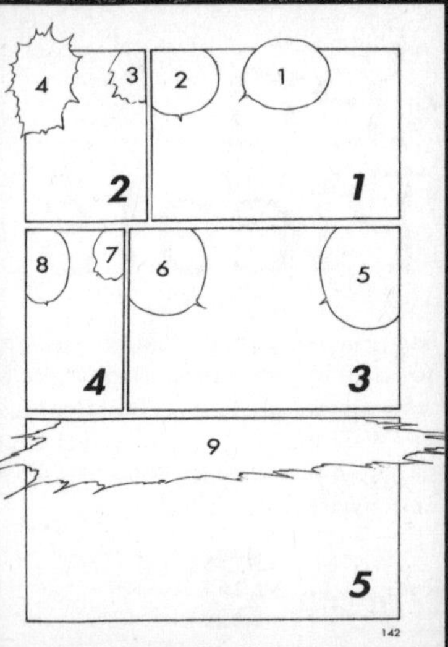
1
2
1
3
4
2
5
6
3
7
8
4
9
5
142

In keeping with the original Japanese comic format, this book reads from right to left—so action, sound effects and word balloons are completely reversed to preserve the orientation of the original artwork.

Check out the diagram shown here to get the hang of things, and then turn to the other side of the book to get started!